Henry Freeman

**Wonders of the World**

Places and Objects of Great Historic Interest

Henry Freeman

**Wonders of the World**
*Places and Objects of Great Historic Interest*

ISBN/EAN: 9783337247782

Printed in Europe, USA, Canada, Australia, Japan

Cover: Foto ©ninafisch / pixelio.de

More available books at **www.hansebooks.com**

# WONDERS OF THE WORLD.

## PLACES AND OBJECTS

OF

# Great Historic Interest,

*The Grandest Objects and Scenes in Nature,*

AND THOSE WORKS OF ART WHICH HAVE ACQUIRED A WORLD-WIDE FAME, ARE HERE DESCRIBED.

*WRITTEN AND COMPILED BY*

## HENRY FREEMAN, A. M.

FOR USE IN SCHOOLS AND FAMILIES, ILLUSTRATED BY

### STEREOSCOPIC VIEWS.

*PUBLISHED BY*
ALFRED MUDGE AND SON, BOSTON.
1873.

Entered, according to Act of Congress, in the year 1872, by
J. H. CLARK,
In the Office of the Librarian of Congress, at Washington.

# PREFACE.

THIS work has been compiled mostly from reference to books found in the Boston Public Library, where the compiler and his assistants have been permitted to sit and write day after day without interruption. The author's grateful acknowledgments are due to the kindness and courtesy of the Librarian and assistant librarians; to BENJAMIN DREW, Esq., author of "Pens and Types"; to CHARLES A. DREW, Esq., a graduate of Harvard University, and attorney-at-law, and to several other friends who have assisted him by kindly aid and suggestions.

It has been the compiler's intention to give due credit to the authors whose works he has consulted; if, in any case, this has been accidentally omitted, he sincerely regrets it. In many instances the principal facts have been collected and condensed from a great variety of sources, — gazetteers, encyclopedias, etc., — in which case, an enumeration of credits would occupy much space, and confer no benefit.

BOSTON PUBLIC LIBRARY, AUG. 23, 1872.

# TABLE OF CONTENTS.

INTRODUCTION.— PHOTOGRAPHY AND THE STEREOSCOPE.

CHAPTER I.— THE WHITE MOUNTAINS.
Lake Winnipiseogee. Plymouth. Eagle Cliff. Great Stone Face. Echo Lake. The Flume. Chocorua. The Story of Chocorua's Curse. North Conway. The Artist's Brook. The Nancy Tragedy. The Notch. The Willey House. Berlin Falls. The Mt. Washington Railroad. Lake Memphremagog . . . . . . . . . . page 13

CHAPTER II.— NIAGARA FALLS AND ST. LAWRENCE RIVER.
Niagara Falls from Prospect Point. Ferry House. Table Rock. Goat, or Iris Island. Terrapin Tower. The Three Sisters. Niagara in Winter. Suspension Bridge. The New Suspension Bridge. The Receding of the Falls. The Whirlpool. The Hermit of the Falls. Queenstown. Brock's Monument. River St. Lawrence. The Thousand Isles. The Rapids of the St. Lawrence. Montreal. Quebec. The Falls of Montmorenci. The Saguenay River . . . . . . . . . . . . . . . . . . 44

CHAPTER III.— PLYMOUTH, MASSACHUSETTS.
Burial Hill. Cole's Hill. Canopy over Rock. Pilgrim Hall. Leyden Street. Town Square. Duxbury. Captain's Hill. Extract from Webster's Oration . . . . . 68

CHAPTER IV.— PROVINCETOWN, MASSACHUSETTS.
Compact of Civil Government, signed by the Pilgrims on board the Mayflower, in Provincetown Harbor. Situation of Provincetown. Improvements since 1836 . . . 75

CHAPTER V.— BOSTON AND VICINITY.
Faneuil Hall. The State House. The Custom House. The Merchants Exchange. The New Post Office. Music Hall. Museum. The Public Library. Boston Common. Public Gardens. Bunker-Hill Monument. Harvard College. Mount Auburn. Eddystone and Minot Ledge Lighthouses . . . . . . . . . . . . 77

CHAPTER VI.— LOWELL, MASSACHUSETTS.
Merrimac River. The Site of the City. Pawtucket Falls. The Sixth Massachusetts Regiment. Monument to the First Martyrs of the Great American Rebellion . . . 96

CHAPTER VII.— NEW HAVEN, CT.
Situation. The Early Settlers. Blue Laws. City of refuge for the Regicides; Noble Elms. East and West Rocks. Yale College. Hillhouse Avenue. Housatonic River . . 98

CHAPTER VIII.— PHILADELPHIA, PENN.
How situated. The Original Plan of the City. Independence Hall. Carpenter's Hall. Independence Square. Washington Square. Girard College. Franklin's Grave and Epitaph. Philadelphia Library. United States Navy Yard. Laurel Hill. Fairmount Park . . . . . . . . . . . . . . . . . . . 105

CHAPTER IX.— BALTIMORE, MD.
How situated. General appearance. Washington Monument. Battle Monument. Druid Hill Park. Public Buildings . . . . . . . . . . . . 116

CHAPTER X.— DISTRICT OF COLUMBIA. WASHINGTON CITY.
The Capitol. President Fillmore. The Rotunda. Paintings. Statues. The New Dome. The New Senate Chamber. The Executive Mansion. Naval Observatory. Navy Yard. Patent Office. Smithsonian Institute. National Monument to Washington . . 119

CHAPTER XI.
NEW YORK OR THE ISLAND CITY. BROOKLYN. TICONDEROGA. LAKE GEORGE. SARATOGA SPRINGS . . . . . . . . . . . . . 125

CHAPTER XII.— WEST POINT AND THE CATSKILL MOUNTAINS.
Military Academy. Location. Most lovely of all lovely spots. Catskill Mountains. Village of Catskill. Mountain House; view from Clove of the Catterskill. Round Top and High Peak . . . . . . . . . . . . . . . . . 136

## CHAPTER XIII.—ITHACA AND VICINITY.

Cayuga Lake. Fall Creek. Cascadilla Creek. Cornell University. Enfield Falls. Taghanic Falls . . . . . . . . . . . . . . . page 138

## CHAPTER XIV.—BUFFALO, NEW YORK.

Situation. Founded by the Holland Land Company. Forest Lawn . . . . 139

## CHAPTER XV.—WATKINS GLEN, NEW YORK.

Town of Watkins. Entrance to Watkins Glen. Glen Cathedral. Glen of Pools. Glen Difficulty. Havana Glen . . . . . . . . . . . . 140

## CHAPTER XVI.—THE ADIRONDACK WILDERNESS.

Iron Deposits. The Great Indian Pass. The Saranac Lakes. The Au Sable Chasm. Table Rock . . . . . . . . . . . . . . . 144

## CHAPTER XVII.

NATURAL BRIDGE, VIRGINIA . . . . . . . . . . . . 151

## CHAPTER XVIII.—SCENERY OF NORTH CAROLINA.

The Mountain Region. The Black Mountains. Mount Mitchell. French Broad Stream. Chimney Rocks. Gingercake Rocks . . . . . . . . . . 154

## CHAPTER XIX.—TALLULAH FALLS, GEORGIA.

Lodore. Tempesta. Oceana. Horicon and Serpentine Falls . . . . . . 157

## CHAPTER XX.

ST. AUGUSTINE. NEW ORLEANS AND ST. LOUIS . . . . . . . . 159

## CHAPTER XXI.—CHICAGO.

The "Crib." The Chicago River. Parks. The Great Fire. Origin of the Fire. Course of the Fire. Relief for Chicago. "The Burning of Chicago" . . . . . 165

## CHAPTER XXII.

SPRINGFIELD AND ROCKFORD, ILLINOIS . . . . . . . . . . 189

## CHAPTER XXIII.—WISCONSIN.

The Dells of the Wisconsin and Devil's Lake. Milwaukee. Situation and Surroundings. 195

## CHAPTER XXIV.

CINCINNATI AND THE CINCINNATI FOUNTAIN . . . . . . . . 199

## CHAPTER XXV.—MAMMOTH CAVE, KENTUCKY.

Cave Hotel. Entrance to the Cave. The Cascade. Temperature. The Rotunda. The Church. The Giant's Coffin. The Maelstrom. End of Cave. Ownership . . 202

## CHAPTER XXVI.—CALIFORNIA.

California a Great State. Climate. One of the Wonders of this Great State. Agriculture the great interest of the State. The Fruits of California. The City of San Francisco. Improvement of Water Front. Fear of Earthquakes and its Effects. The novelties of the City. Seal Rocks. Farallone Islands. The Yosemite Valley. Its Wonders . 209

## CHAPTER XXVII.—NATIONAL PARK, NEAR THE HEAD WATERS OF THE YELLOWSTONE.

Act of Congress. Montana. Scenery of the Yellowstone. The Lower Cañon. The Devil's Slide. The Great Cañon. The Mud Volcano. The Giant Geyser. The Giantess Geyser. The Great Falls of the Missouri. Upper Waters of the Missouri. A Colorado Wonder. 227

## CHAPTER XXVIII.—SALT LAKE CITY.

Situation and General Description. Brigham Young's Vision. New Tabernacle. Temple. City Hall. The Saint's Theatre. Salt Lake . . . . . . . . . 238

## CHAPTER XXIX.—THE GREAT LAKES.

General Description of the Great Lakes. Lake Superior. Duluth. Apostle Islands. Keweenaw Point. Marquette. Iron Regions. Negaunee. Pictured Rocks. Straits of Mackinaw. Mackinaw Island. Lake Huron. St. Clair River. Lake St. Clair. Lake Erie . . . . . . . . . . . . . . . . 241

## CONTENTS.

### CHAPTER XXX.—ENGLAND.

England generally described. General view of London. House of Parliament from Poet's Corner. Buckingham Palace. The Crystal Palace. Windsor Castle. Peterborough Cathedral. Stonehenge. Ashburton. Lynton. Ilfracombe. Conway Suspension Bridge and Castle. Blenheim Palace and Park . . . . . . . . page 246

### CHAPTER XXXI.—SCOTLAND.

Abbotsford. Ben Nevis. Balmoral Castle. Drummond Castle. Ben Lomond. Glasgow. Edinburgh. Scott's Monument. Melrose Abbey . . . . . . . 257

### CHAPTER XXXII.—IRELAND.

Kilkenny Castle. Giant's Causeway. Pleaskin Head . . . . . . . 270

### CHAPTER XXXIII.—FRANCE.

General description. Paris. Fine Streets and Buildings. Elysian Fields. Triumphal Arch. Palaces. Universal Exposition, 1867 . . . . . . . . 276

### CHAPTER XXXIV.—SWITZERLAND.

Swiss Scenery. The Alps. Glaciers. Incidents in crossing Glaciers. Avalanches. Avalanche of the Rossberg . . . . . . . . . . . . 291

### CHAPTER XXXV.—SWITZERLAND CONTINUED.

Geneva. The Cascade of Arpenay. The Cascade of Chêde. Salanches. Servoz. The Village of Chamouni. The Valley of Chamouni. The Sea of Ice. The Glacier of the Bossons. Cavern in the Glacier. Hymn to Mont Blanc. Mont Blanc. Martigny. The Monastery of St. Bernard. The Gorge of the Trient. The Castle of Chillon . 306

### CHAPTER XXXVI.—SWITZERLAND CONTINUED.

Thun. Interlaken. Lauterbrunnen. The Jungfrau. The Eiger. The Wetterhorn. Grindelwald. The Glaciers. The Pass of St. Gothard. Altorf. Stanz. Lucerne. Rigi. The Valley of the Linth. Glarus. Appenzell. St. Gall. The Falls of the Rhine. Ragatz. Pfaffers . . . . . . . . . . . . . 324

### CHAPTER XXXVII.—NORTHERN ITALY.

The change from Swiss to Italian Scenery. Cormayeur. Aosta. Lake d'Orta. Mont Cenis. Genoa. Milan. Venice . . . . . . . . . . . 338

### CHAPTER XXXVIII.—SOUTHERN ITALY.

Rome. St. Peter's. The Vatican. The Gardens of the Vatican. The Church of St. Agnes. The Roman Forum. The Coliseum. Naples. Sicily. Palermo . . . . 347

### CHAPTER XXXIX.—HERCULANEUM AND POMPEII.

View of Naples and Mount Vesuvius. Pliny's Letters to Tacitus. Discovery of the Ancient Cities. House of Diomed. "The very Armor he had on." The Amphitheatre. Temple of Isis. The Forum . . . . . . . . . . . . . 363

### CHAPTER XL.—GIBRALTAR.

Bird's-eye view of the Town. Bay of Gibraltar. Rock of Gibraltar. The Fortress. 386

### CHAPTER XLI.—TURKEY AND GREECE.

Area of the Turkish Empire. Constantinople. Greece. Athens . . . . 388

### CHAPTER XLII.—SYRIA AND PALESTINE.

Syria and Palestine generally described. Jerusalem. Mount of Olives. Bethany. Mosque of Omar. Bethlehem. Baalbek. Damascus. Shiloh. Shechem. Nazareth. Mount Carmel. Dromedaries. Hebron. Mount of Transfiguration. Sinai. Cedars of Lebanon. 399

### CHAPTER XLIII.—EGYPT, OR THE LAND OF HAM.

What Egypt is called in the Bible. The Pyramids. Pompey's Pillar. Cleopatra's Needle. Cairo. Tombs of the Mamelukes. Mosque of Mohammed Ali. Tombs of the Caliphs. The Great Pyramid and Sphinx. Pyramid of Sakhara. Thebes . . . . 414

### CHAPTER XLIV.—THE BIG TREES OF CALIFORNIA.

Iscovery of the Trees. Botanical name. Calaveras Grove. Mariposa Grove . 425

# INTRODUCTION.

The seven wonders of the ancient world were, 1. The statue of the Sun at Rhodes, seventy cubits high, placed across the harbor, so that a large vessel could sail between its legs. 2. The Mausoleum, or sepulchre of Mausolus, king of Caria, built of marble, above four hundred feet in compass, surrounded with thirty-six beautiful columns. 3. The statue of Jupiter in Olympia, by Phidias. 4. The temple of Diana, at Ephesus, with one hundred twenty-seven pillars, sixty feet in height, with a splendid image of the goddess. 5. The walls of Babylon, built by Semiramis, fifty or eighty feet wide, and sixty miles in circuit. 6. The pyramids of Egypt. 7. The palace of Cyrus.

With the world's progress in discovery, science, and art, its wonders have multiplied more than a thousand-fold. They are not seven nor seventy times seven, but are as the stars of heaven for multitude. They are no longer confined to palaces and pyramids, to colossal statues and gorgeous mausoleums, to works of art, however imposing or grand ; but as God's works and ways are unfolded in ocean, earth, air, and the elements, we are forced at almost every step to exclaim, in the words of the prophet, re-echoed by Morse, "What hath God wrought!" or with Kepler, "O God, I think thy thoughts after thee!"

As the grandest productions of art, whether in the forms of painting, poetry, sculpture, or architecture, are but the methods which man employs to embody his thoughts ; so all that is beautiful, imposing, and grand in nature, are but the means which God employs to express His thoughts. The glorious sunsets and glowing landscapes are God's pictures and paintings. Niagara is one of God's poems, and the mountains have all been sculptured by His hand. The wonders of the Yosemite Valley, the Yellowstone, and the mighty Alps, are but some of the exhibitions of God's handiwork, a few striking expressions of God's thoughts.

Few can command the time, and fewer still the means, necessary to visit any considerable number of the objects of interest, beauty, and grandeur, which are scattered broadcast through all latitudes and over all lands. Is it not, then, a source of satisfaction and gratulation to be able, without incurring either the expense or the risks of travel, to gaze at leisure upon fac-similes of the choicest productions of art and the grandest scenery in nature? The art of photography, and the invention of the stereoscope, are wonders in themselves, and they can bring to our own homes and firesides all earth's wonders beside. A good stereoscope and a good selection of stereoscopic views constitute a valuable picture gallery, which should grace every home and every school-room. Their cost is a trifle compared with their value, for they make home and school attractive ; they cultivate in young and old a taste for whatever is beautiful in art or sublime in nature ; they stimulate an intelligent curiosity ; they create an interest in the study of geography and history, and tend to broaden the intellect and divert the attention of the young from the trashy and the frivolous, to such reading and amusements as are of real interest and value. It is hoped that this volume and the accompanying views may turn the attention of the young to interesting fact, and away from silly fiction. An indiscriminate use of the stereoscopic views should not be allowed, but the attention of the school should be confined to those connected with the lesson of the day. Let the teacher, for example, read from this book the interesting facts concerning Herculaneum and Pompeii, or any other places or objects, and when his scholars have got possession of the history or the facts read, let them, as they may have opportunity, look into the stereoscope, and see the reproductions of choice works of art and wonderful scenery in nature. In all cases the teacher should require scholars to learn all they can from this book and from all other sources of information to which they have access, in reference to places and objects, either immediately before or immediately after they are permitted to see them in the stereoscope, It is the remark of an English philosopher, that it is of little consequence whether a scholar first learns a word and then the object it represents, or whether he is first introduced to the object and then taught the word, provided he learns both very nearly at the same time. H. F.

BOSTON, Aug. 23, 1872.

### PHOTOGRAPHY AND THE STEREOSCOPE.

The art of photography rests upon the *sensitiveness* of certain substances, especially compounds of silver, to the action of light, by which their chemical or physical nature is changed. The term, therefore, includes all processes for "drawing by light," — even the use of indelible ink. The influence of light on animal life and vegetation was early noticed, and the darkening effect of light upon the chloride of silver was known to the alchemists. In the early part of this century, Wedgewood and Davy made the first experiments with a view to the adaptation of this peculiar sun-force to the performance of artistic drudgery. They moistened a sheet of paper with a solution of nitrate of silver, and projected the shadow of the object they wished to copy upon it. The portion upon which the light fell was darkened; that on which the shadow fell remained white. This process was only valuable for the promise that it held out, as it required hours to produce, at best, very poor silhouettes. It was abandoned for want of a means of *fixing* the pictures, that is, of preserving the white portion unchanged by the subsequent action of light to which it might be exposed. More subtle investigations by Herschell, Niepce, Daguerre, Talbot, and others, led to the discovery of many substances available for photographic purposes. These investigations culminated in the invention of Daguerre. Whilst employing a camera to assist him in his profession as a scene painter, in 1824, it occurred to him to search for some method for rendering permanent the beautiful pictures formed in the camera. The alchemists never had originated a more unpromising pursuit. So intense, though uniformly unsuccessful, were Daguerre's efforts, that his wife asked medical advice in regard to the symptoms of 'insanity in her husband. After years of toil in the most jealous secrecy, and attended only by continual disappointment, the following accident came to his assistance. It should not, however, detract from his merit, for he had been obliged to work his way across the path of such an accident, and to learn how to make it fruitful. In the course of his numerous experiments, he submitted polished silver tablets to the action of vapor of iodine, until the bright surface was converted into a creamy yellow one of iodide of silver. He then caused the image formed in the camera to fall upon the plates thus prepared, under varying conditions, with a faint hope that it might remain, but he was obliged to stow them away, one after another, in his rubbish-box, apparently unaffected, to be re-polished and re-used in pursuit of the same phantom. Upon taking one of these cast-away plates from the box to re-polish it, to his great astonishment he found upon it a perfect realization of his dream; as if some magician, in mockery of him, in the darkness of the closet, had drawn upon it the image to which it had been exposed in the camera.

He placed several iodized plates that had been exposed in the camera, in the box as before, each time, however, having first removed something from the box. Each time the *latent* invisible image formed by a short exposure in the camera was *developed* into a beautiful visible one in the box. At last, everything was removed but some mercury. The magician was detected. The mercury which had volatilized at ordinary temperature, had by reason of some change effected in the iodide of silver, only condensed upon the portions traced by light. By further experiments he succeeded in *fixing* the images, and in January, 1839, exhibited his first specimens. The French government, under lead of Arago and Gay Lussac, gave the process as "a gift to the world" by pensioning Daguerre and Niepce, his equally enthusiastic but less fortunate co-laborer.

Like many other great discoveries, this had ripened in several countries at the same time. In England, Talbot, on the 31st of January, read a paper on "A Method of Photogenic Drawing." His experiments had been directed chiefly to the production of natural objects, especially botanical specimens. His method was founded upon the darkening of chloride of silver. The production of "pictures of lace, leaves, and ferns, which," to quote his own language, "it would take the most skilful artist days or weeks of labor to trace or copy, is effected by the boundless powers of natural chemistry in a few seconds. He formed chloride of silver on a piece of paper, placed a leaf or engraving upon it, and exposed it to the sunlight. The light darkened the chloride beneath the transparent and white parts of the leaf or engraving, while the more opaque parts protected the chloride beneath them, and preserved it white. So also the bright sky of a picture formed in the camera would produce the darkest impression, and a dark object a very faint one. Such pictures with reversed light and shade are called *negatives*. It occurred to Talbot to place a negative upon chlorided paper, and thus to produce a negative of the negative, or a perfect copy of the original, called a *positive*. From a simple negative, in this way any number of positives can be made, and it thus becomes the photographic equivalent of an engraved plate. The calotype process was perfected by Talbot in 1841, and embodied Daguerre's discovery of a latent impression upon iodide of silver, which lessened the time required so much as to allow of the use of the camera, and the method of multiplication, suggested by himself, by the employment of paper, made transparent by waxing, to receive the image, instead of a silver plate.

Thus the *change of color* produced in chloride of silver by light, suggested the earliest form of photography. The formation, in a much shorter time, of an invisible or *latent*, but *developable* effect upon iodide of silver, gave rise to processes sufficiently sensitive for the camera, whilst the production of negatives upon transparent substances, such as waxed paper and glass, rendered possible a more extended application of photography, and the property which certain substances, as the hyposulphite of soda first suggested by Herschell, have, of dissolving unchanged portions of the silver compound, whilst they do not affect the portions acted on by light, afforded a simple means for *fixing* photographic pictures.

The process of Wedgewood and Davy required hours to catch the shadow of a stationary object. Now, ships scudding before the breeze, the breaking waves, the cannon ball at any instant of its flight, or even half-protruding from the muzzle, all leave their image on a film of matter more sensitive than the retina of the eye. Old methods of multiplication of photographic copies have been supplanted by more rapid and cheaper ones, and photo-lithography already begins to fulfil the promises it has long held out, by furnishing our atlases with the most accurate maps and our books with first-class illustrations. All arts and sciences have become more or less indebted to photography; and the numerous journals devoted solely to its interests, are continually filled with new processes and new applications. It is perfectly faithful in the minutest details; it commits no errors of observation; the smallest objects, the choicest revelations of the microscope, that demand much skill in the use of the instrument to be enjoyed by means of it, are placed before every one, enlarged by several thousand diameters "by the wonderful insight of heaven's broad and simple sunshine." In medical science, photographs of malformation and morbid structures are made to replace defective, though tediously executed, hand-drawings. The magnetic needle, as it obeys during the day the changes in the earth's magnetism, makes a continuous record of its variations on photographic paper; the mercury of the barometer records its fluctuations by the same means. The hourly phases of the sun and its eclipses, the bottom of the sea, the interior of the eye and of the pyramids, all are photographically mapped.

The stereoscope multiplies wonderfully the applications of photography. It affords an endless variety of objects from art and nature, from the statuary of the old world to the choicest fragments of the interior of the Mammoth Cave, in almost tangible form, for the fireside entertainment. It exhibits a new view of the moon, and reproduces perfectly geological, zoölogical, botanical, and mineralogical specimens, even to the lustre of the latter; and by a still further application of the stereoscopic principle in photosculpture, photography furnishes all the details necessary for a perfect statue.

Thus far, however, photography, though many-eyed, has been color-blind; but there are promises that in its future these monochromatic representations will be displaced by perfect reproductions of the pictures of the camera, in all their richness of color, just as they fascinated the visionary painter. The difficulties in the way seem to those most wise in these things to be almost insurmountable, but all are hopeful.

The earnest and unremitting experiments of Niepce de St. Victor, nephew of Niepce, Becquerel, and Poitevin, have advanced heliochromy to a point analogous to that at which Wedgewood and Davy left photography. Photographs in colors have been produced by Poitevin, but his process is *slow*, and his pictures, for *want of a perfect method of fixing*, are as evanescent as the shadows caught more than half a century ago. — *Leaf Prints.*

# WONDERS OF THE WORLD.

## CHAPTER I.

### THE WHITE MOUNTAINS.

"Thou who wouldst see the lovely and the wild
Mingled in harmony on Nature's face,
Ascend our rocky mountains. Let thy foot
Fail not with weariness; for on their tops
The beauty and the majesty of earth,
Spread wide beneath, shall make thee to forget
The steep and toilsome way."
*Bryant.*

OF the White Mountain region Edward Everett thus speaks: "I have been something of a traveller in our own country, and in Europe have seen all that is most attractive, from the Highlands of Scotland to the Golden Horn of Constantinople, but I have yet to behold a sublimer spectacle than that which is disclosed from Mount Washington, when, on some clear, cool summer's morning, at sunrise, the cloud curtain is drawn up from Nature's grand proscenium, and all that chaos of wilderness and beauty starts into life, the bare granitic tops of the surrounding heights, the precipitous gorges a thousand fathoms deep, which foot of man or ray of light never entered, — the sombre matted forest, the moss-clad rocky wall weeping with crystal springs — winding streams, gleaming lakes, and peaceful villages below; and, in the misty distance beyond the lower hills, faint glimpses of the sacred bosom of the eternal deep, ever heaving, as with the consciousness of its own immensity, all mingled in one indescribable panorama, by the hand of the Divine Artist."

The White Mountain range properly commences near the head waters of the Aroostook River, in Maine, and is regarded as one of the outliers of the Apalachian chain. South of the Androscoggin, in New Hampshire, it becomes a broad plateau of thirty miles in length and forty-five in breadth, extending nearly across the State, and southward to the Merrimac and Squam rivers, and to the lakes Winnipiseogee and Ossipee. From this plateau rise nearly twenty peaks, forming the picturesque White Mountains of the traveller, — the Alps of America.

So varied and magnificent is the scenery, so cool and bracing the atmosphere of this region, that it has long been a favorite summer resort. The worn merchant from the dusty city; the student wearied with his books; the gay belle and the man of fashion; the artist and the author, — all seek health and recreation in its cool retreats and shady glens.

The peaks form two groups: the Eastern, or White Mountains proper; and the Franconia group. These are between ten and twenty miles apart. The principal mounts of the Eastern group, commencing at the Notch on the south and passing around to Gorham at the northern extremity, were in 1820 christened as follows: Webster, Clinton, Pleasant, Franklin, Monroe, Washington, Clay, Jefferson, Madison, and Adams.

The highest of these, Mount Washington, the highest summit indeed of New England, is 6,288 feet above the level of the sea. Its bare and rugged top is even seen by the sailor coasting along the shore more than sixty miles distant. Other peaks have the following measurements: Adams, 5,759 feet; Jefferson, 5,657; Monroe, 5,349.

Geologically they are of metamorphic rock, the tops being

composed of huge masses of granite and gneiss. The accumulation of ages has given to the lower portions a hard and gravelly soil, capable of supporting only the hardiest plants.

The sides of the mountains are girt about with forests of birch, spruce, and fir, and still higher up with a zone of mosses, lichens, and hardy Alpine flowers. The highest summits are covered with snow nine months of the year.

Sudden and fierce mountain storms, loosening bowlders, and the scanty soil, render land-slides not unfrequent.

The Red-man looked with veneration upon these White Hills. The snow-capped peak of Mount Washington, Agiochook, was to him the abode of the Great Spirit, Manitou. They attracted early the attention of the settlers of New England, for in 1642 they were visited by Darby Field, and also by Thomas Gorges. The naturalist John Joselyn, who visited them between 1663 and 1671, published in 1672 the first description. Their baptismal title, Crystal Hills, was then changed to the name they now bear, — White Mountains seeming more nearly to express the meaning of their Indian name, Waumbek-Methna, which signifies "Mountains with snowy foreheads."

Settlers did not attempt to make this uninviting region their home until 1771. One can only wonder, when he considers the fertility and productiveness of other portions of our country compared with the granite barrenness of this, to say nothing of the long and severe winters on the stormy mountain-side, that those stalwart pioneers ever chose to wrest their livelihood from White Mountain soil.

Now, at length, have their children and children's children reaped the fruit of their toil, not as tillers of the soil, but in the rich harvest of boarders who annually seek their homes.

One can but shudder to read of the hardships of those earliest settlers. It often took them weeks, and sometimes months, to obtain food from the nearest settlements, and that too in times of want, when during those weary months of waiting, girding themselves with a leather strap to assuage the pangs of hunger, they lived on the roots of the forest. In the winter, wolves and bears devoured their cattle, and the snow buried their houses, while the necessities of life often could only be procured by long journeys on snow-shoes. Now, what a change! Not only have carriage roads and spacious hotels been built, but even the shrill whistle of the locomotive, proudly bearing the traveller up the steep side of Mount Washington, is heard re-echoing among deep gorges and overhanging cliffs.

The first inn in the White Mountain region was opened in 1803.

The chief visitors, until 1840, were scientific explorers. Then the Crawfords, the patriarchs of the hills, changed the foot-paths into bridle-paths, and from that time the tide of yearly visitors has increased, until now they have reached the present vast throng, which can be numbered only by thousands and tens of thousands.

The guardian spirits of the hills seem to have chosen for their prophet the late gifted Thomas Starr King, and to have given him, as by inspiration, a revelation of the beauty of their scenery. We have selected his words as the most fitting to give an adequate description of the views of the White Mountains.

Within the compass of the present work, of course, it will be only possible to mention a few of the more prominent points of beauty and interest.

*Lake Winnipiseogee.*—Forty miles south of Mount Washington, and nearly five hundred feet above the sea, lies Winnipiseogee. Thirty miles long, and varying from one to seven miles in breadth, shut in by hills and mountains in the very heart of a wilderness, there is not a lovelier lake in the world.

Does its name signify "The Smile of the Great Spirit," or "Pleasant Water in a High Place"? There has been a dispute, we believe, among the learned in Indian lore, as to the true rendering. Whatever the word means, the lake itself signifies both. Mr. Everett said, a few years since, that Switzerland has no more beautiful view for the tourist than the lake we are speaking of affords. And the Rev. Mr. Bartol, in his charming volume, "Pictures of Europe," tells us: "There may be lakes in Tyrol and Switzerland which, in particular respects, exceed the charms of any in the Western World. But in that wedding of the land with the water, in which one is perpetually approaching and retreating from the other, and each transforms itself into a thousand figures for an endless dance of grace and beauty, till a countless multitude of shapes are arranged into perfect ease and freedom, of almost musical motion, nothing can be beheld to surpass, if to match, our Winnipiseogee."

It is, of course, moving over the lake in a steamer or in a boat that this "musical motion" of the shores is caught.

We will abide the judgment of any tourist as to the extravagance of this quotation, if he becomes acquainted with the lake from the deck of a steamer, on an auspicious summer day. The sky is clear; there are just clouds enough to relieve the soft blue, and fleck the sentinel hills with shadow; and over the wide panorama of distant mountains, a warm, dreamy haze settles. Perhaps there is at first a faint breeze, just enough to fret the water and roughen or mezzotint the reflections of the shores. But as we shoot out into the breadth of the lake, and take in the wide scene, there is no ripple on its bosom. The little islands float over liquid silver, and glide by each other silently, as the movements of a dance, while our boat changes her heading. And all around, the mountains, swelling softly, or cutting the sky with jagged lines of steely blue, vie with the molten mirror at our feet for the privilege of holding the eye. The "sun-sparks" blaze thick as stars on the glassy wrinkles of the water.

Leaning over the side of the steamer, gazing at the exquisite curves of the water just outside the foamy splash of the wheels, watching the countless threads of silver that stream out from the shadow of the wheel-house, seeing the steady iris float with us to adorn our flying spray, and then looking up to the broken sides of the Ossipee mountains, that are rooted in the lake, over which huge shadows loiter; or back to the twin Belknap hills, with their verdured symmetry; or farther down, upon the charming succession of mounds that hem the shores near Wolfboro'; or northward, where distant Chocorua lifts his bleached head, so tenderly touched now with gray and gold, to defy the hottest sunlight, as he has defied for ages the lightning and storm; does it not seem as though the passage of the Psalms is fulfilled before our eyes,—"Out of the perfection of beauty God hath shined"?

The quiet of the water and the sleep of the hills seem to have the quality of still ecstasy. It is only inland water that can suggest and inspire such rest. The sea itself, though it can be clear, is never calm, in the sense that a mountain lake can be calm. The sea seems only to pause, the mountain lake to sleep and dream.

But there is one view especially exciting to one who has been a frequent visitor of the mountains. It is where Mount Washington is visible from a portion of the steamer's track for some fifteen or twenty minutes. Passing by the western declivity of the Ossipee ridge, looking across a low slope of the Sandwich range, and far back of them, a dazzling white spot perhaps — if it is very early in the summer — gleams on the northern horizon. Gradually it mounts and mounts, — a minute or two more, and the unmistakable majesty of Washington is revealed. *There* he rises, forty miles away, towering from a plateau built for his throne, dim green in the distance, except the dome, which is crowned with winter, and the strange figures that are scrawled around his waist in snow.

How appropriate the words of Whittier, —

> "Lake of the Northland! keep thy dower
> Of beauty still, and while above
> Thy solemn mountains speak of power,
> Be thou the mirror of God's love."

*Plymouth* is one of the villages to which a day or two, at least, should be devoted on the way to the mountains. Many visitors will be glad to learn that the old building remains here in which Daniel Webster made his first argument before a court. It is now used as a wheelwright's shop. The statesman wrote his name in large letters with red chalk, a short time before his death, upon the wall of the room which vibrated to his first legal efforts; but the autograph has since been covered by some ruthless hand with a daub from a paint-brush.

In scenery, Plymouth is remarkable for the beauty of its meadows, through which the Pemigewasset winds, and for the grace of its elm-trees. And Prospect Mountain, a hill within the village, commands a panorama so extensive and charming that an ascent of it should be accounted one of the great privileges of a trip to the mountains.

> "I felt the cool breath of the North,
> Between me and the sun;
> O'er deep still lake and ridgy earth,
> I saw the cloud-shades run.

> Before me, stretched for glistening miles,
>   Lay mountain-girdled Squam;
> Like green-winged birds, the leafy isles
>   Upon its bosom swam.
>
> "There towered Chocorua's peak; and west,
>   Moosehillock's woods were seen,
> With many a nameless slide-scarred crest
>   And pine-dark gorge between.
> Beyond them, like a sun-rimmed cloud,
>   The great Notch mountains shone,
> Watched over by the solemn-browed
>   And awful face of stone."

*Eagle Cliff.* — This is a sheer, precipitous wall of rock, fifteen hundred feet in height, on the eastern side of Franconia Notch. Except in some of the great ravines of the Mount Washington range, which it costs great toil to reach, there is no such exhibition of a perpendicular mountain wall to be found in the region.

It derives its name from the fact that a pair of the winged "Arabs of the air" have kept far up the cliff their "chamber near the sun."

There are those to whom the sight of this great crag, sharply set at the angle of a mountain wall, is one of the most enjoyable and memorable privileges of a tour among the hills.

*Great Stone Face.* — The most attractive advertisement of the Franconia Notch to the travelling public is the rumor of the "Great Stone Face," that hangs upon one of its highest cliffs. If its enclosing walls were less grand, and its water gems less lovely, travellers would be still as strongly attracted to the spot, that they might see a mountain which breaks into human expression, — a piece of sculpture older than the Sphynx, — an imitation of the human countenance that was pushed out from the coarse strata of New England thousands of years before Adam.

The marvel of this countenance, outlined so distinctly against the sky at an elevation of nearly fifteen hundred feet above the road, is greatly increased by the fact that it is composed of three masses of rock, which are not in perpendicular line with each other. On the brow of the mountain itself, standing on the visor of the helmet that covers the face, or directly underneath it on the shore of the little lake, there is no intimation of any human features in the lawless rock. Remove but a few rods either way from the spot where the profile is seen in clear outline, and the charm is dissolved. The best time to see this craggy countenance is about four in the afternoon of a summer day. It seems as if an enormous giant, or Titan, had sculptured his own likeness on the precipice. There is the broad arch of the forehead; the nose, with its long bridge; and the vast lips, which, if they could speak, would roll their thunder accents from one end of the valley to the other. The whole profile is about eighty feet in length. The expression is really noble, with a suggestion partly of fatigue and melancholy. He seems to be waiting for some visitor or message. On the front of the cliff there is a pretty plain picture of a man with a pack on his back, who seems to be endeavoring to go up the valley. Perhaps it is the arrival of this arrested messenger that the old stone visage has been expecting for ages. The upper portion of the mouth looks a little weak, as though the front teeth had decayed, and the granite lip consequently fallen in. Those who can see it with a thunder-cloud behind, and the slaty scud driving thin across it, will carry away the grandest impression which it ever makes on the beholder's mind; but when, after an August shower, late in the afternoon, the mists that rise from the forest below congregate around it, and, smitten with sunshine, break as they drift across its nervous outline, and hiding the mass of the mountain which it overhangs, isolate it with a thin halo, the countenance, awful but benignant, is "as if a mighty angel were sitting among the hills, and enrobing himself in a cloud vesture of gold and purple."

*Echo Lake.* — This is the only sheet of still water that nestles near any one of the higher White Mountains. It is rimmed by the undisturbed wilderness, and watched by the grizzled peak of Mount Lafayette; swept by the gentle edges of the summer breeze and burnished by the sunlight, it is a sweet and perennial symbol of purity and peace. Here the Pemigewasset takes its rise, its waters are borne down into the Merrimac, and contribute to the power that moves the wheels of Nashua and Lowell, and supplies a thousand operatives with bread.

What is a true definition of a mountain lake? It is a mirror, an interpreter of what infolds and oversweeps it. The climbing trees and the shadow of the steep shores make a large section of its borders dim with dusky green. The sky hues, blue or gray, brilliant or sober, dull or joyous, it clothes itself with. It answers to the temper of the wind, with smiling ripples, or slaty churlishness, or heaving petulance. It is glad in the colors of sunrise, and pensive as the flames of sunset cool in the west.

It is towards evening that visitors are usually drawn to the lake, to sail upon it, and hear the echoes from which it derives its name. The echoes are interesting, whether repeating from the mountain walls the notes of the voice, or

"Replying shrilly to the well-tuned horns,"

or rolling back on the shore the reports of the cannon that "tears the cave where Echo lies." These it returns in sevenfold reduplications of thunder, as wall behind wall of the mountain amphitheatre catches the sound on its crescent, and tosses it up towards old Lafayette.

*The Flume.* — Near the southern extremity of the Franconia Notch is a most romantic and picturesque ravine called the Flume. It is a remarkable fissure in the mountain, more than fifty feet high, and several hundred feet long, which contracts towards the upper end until it becomes only twelve feet in width. Through this narrow chasm breaks a dashing, roaring mountain torrent. A little bridge spans the narrowest part of the ravine. How wild the spot is! Which shall we admire most, the glee of the little stream that rushes beneath our feet, or the regularity and smoothness of the frowning walls through which it goes foaming out into the sunshine; or the splendor of the dripping emerald mosses that line them; or the huge bowlder, egg-shaped, that is lodged between the walls, just over the bridge where we stand, — as unpleasant to look at, if the nerves are irresolute, as the sword of Damocles, and yet held by a grasp out of which it will not slip for centuries?

If we could visit Franconia in winter we should, no doubt, find scenery more startling than any which the summer has to offer. Those of our readers will believe it who have seen stereoscopic views of the Flume when

"Those eagle-baffling mountains
Slept in their shrouds of snow; — beside the ways

"The waterfalls were voiceless — for their fountains
Were changed to mines of sunless crystal now,
Or by the curdling winds — like brazen wings

"Which clanged along the mountain's marble brow —
Warped into adamantine fretwork, hung
And filled with frozen light the chasm below."

*Chocorua.* — How rich and sonorous that word, Chocorua, is! Do not, O reader, commit the sin of which the Yankee inhabitants are guilty, and into which stage-drivers will tempt you, of flattening the rhythm and musical cadence of the word into "Corway." Lying south-southwest of Mount Washington, this peak is everything that a New Hampshire mountain should be. It bears the name of an Indian chief. It is invested with traditional and poetic interest. Its form is massive and symmetrical. The forests of its lower slopes are crowned with rock that is sculptured into a peak with lines full of haughty energy, in whose gorges huge shadows are entrapped, and whose cliffs blaze with morning gold. It is set in connection with lovely water scenery, with Squam and Winnipiseogee, and the little lake directly at its base. Nine miles from Conway lies this little Chocorua Lake, in which the rugged, lonely, and proud-peaked mountain reflects the ravage of its slopes, and the vigor of its lines. Many of the most competent artists, who have made faithful studies in New Hampshire, award superiority to Chocorua for picturesqueness over any view they have found of Mount Washington.

With the exception of Mount Adams, there is no peak so sharp as this mountain. Although it is but thirty-four hundred feet in height, the steepness of its ledges and the absence of any path make the scaling of it a greater feat than a walk to the top of Mount Washington by any of the bridle roads.

The mountain peak of Chocorua is crowned with an Indian legend, called

*The Story of Chocorua's Curse.* — A small colony of hardy pioneers had settled at the base of the mountain. Intelligent and independent men, yet there was one master-spirit among them capable of a higher destiny than he ever fulfilled. Cornelius Campbell had long been a zealous and active enemy of the Stuarts, and had political circumstances proved favorable, his talents and ambition would unquestionably have worked out a path to emolument and fame. The restoration of Charles II was the death-warrant of his hopes. Immediately flight became necessary, and America was his place of refuge. Being of a proud nature, he withdrew, with his family, to this remote settlement. From the Indians the settlers received neither insult nor injury, although they were their frequent visitors. Chocorua was a prophet among the Red-men, a dark, fierce savage, of giant size, and ungovernable passions. There was something fearful in the quiet haughtiness of his lips; it seemed so like slumbering power, — too proud to be lightly aroused, and too implacable to sleep again. In his small, black, fiery eye, expression lay coiled up like a beautiful snake. The white people knew his hatred would be terrible; but they never provoked it, and even the children became too much accustomed to him to fear him.

Chocorua had a son, nine or ten years old, to whom Caroline Campbell had occasionally made such gaudy presents as were likely to attract his savage fancy. This won the child's affections, so that he became a familiar visitant, almost an inmate of their dwelling; and, being unrestrained by the courtesies of civilized life, he would inspect everything, and taste of everything that came in his way. Some poison, prepared for a mischievous fox, was discovered and drunk by the Indian boy, and he went home to his father to sicken and die. From that moment jealousy and hatred took possession of Chocorua's soul.

The story of Indian animosity is always' the same. Cornelius Campbell left his hut for the fields early one bright, balmy morning in June. His last look was turned towards his wife, answering her parting smile; his last action, a kiss for each of his children. When he returned to dinner they were dead — all dead! and their disfigured bodies too cruelly showed that an Indian's hand had done the work.

In such a mind, grief, like all other emotions, was tempestuous. Then followed a calm a thousand times more terrible, — the creeping agony of despair, and afterward still, a wild, demoniac spirit of revenge. The death-groan of Chocorua would make him smile in his dreams; and when he waked, death seemed too pitiful a vengeance for the anguish that was eating into his very soul. Chocorua's brethren were absent on a hunting expedition, and the prophet often climbed a high precipice, looking out for indications of their return. Here Cornelius Campbell resolved to effect his deadly purpose. The morning sun had scarce cleared away the fogs, when Chocorua started at a loud voice from beneath the precipice, commanding him to throw himself into the deep abyss below. He knew the voice of his enemy; there was no way of escape. He replied, with an Indian's calmness, "The Great Spirit gave life to Chocorua, and Chocorua will not throw it away at the command of the white man." — "Then hear the Great Spirit speak in the white man's thunder!" exclaimed Cornelius Campbell, as he pointed his gun to the precipice. Chocorua, though fierce and fearless as a panther, had never overcome his dread of fire-arms. He placed his hands upon his ears to shut out the stunning report; the next moment the blood bubbled from his neck, and he reeled fearfully on the edge of the precipice. But he recovered himself; and, raising himself on his hand, he spoke in a loud voice, that grew more terrific as its huskiness increased: "A curse upon you, white men! May the Great Spirit curse you when he speaks in the clouds, and his words are fire! Chocorua had a son, and ye killed him while the sky looked bright! Lightning blast your crops! Winds and fire destroy your dwellings!

The Evil Spirit breathe death upon your cattle! Your graves lie in the war-path of the Indian! Panthers howl and wolves fatten upon your bones! Chocorua goes to the Great Spirit, — his curse stays with the white man!"

The prophet sank upon the ground; his bones were left to whiten in the sun. But his curse rested on the settlement. The tomahawk and scalping-knife were busy among them; the winds tore up trees, and hurled them at their dwellings; their crops were blasted, their cattle died, sickness came upon their strongest men. At last the remnant of them departed from the fatal spot to mingle with more prosperous and populous colonies. Cornelius Campbell became a hermit, seldom seeking or seeing his fellow-men; and two years after he was found dead in his hut.

*North Conway.* —

> "Full many a spot
> Of hidden beauty I have chanced to espy
> Among the mountains; never one like this;
> So lonesome, and so perfectly secure;
> In rugged arms how softly does it lie,
> How tenderly protected! Peace is here
> Or nowhere; days unruffled by the gale
> Of public news, or private; years that pass
> Forgetfully."
>
> *Wordsworth.*

Such is a fitting description of the little village which lies on the Saco River, about eighty miles northwest of Concord. It is on the direct route from Lake Winnipiseogee to the Notch and Mount Washington, and travellers to the mountains never fail to be charmed by the loveliness of its situation. Such a profuse and calm beauty sometimes reigns over the whole village, that it seems to be a little quotation from Arcadia, or a suburb of Paradise.

It is a short task to give the mountain framing of the

village. On the west the noble Mote Mountain guards it; on the east, the rough and bending Rattlesnake Ridge helps to wall it in; on the southwest, Chocorua manages to get a peep of its lovely meadows. Almost the whole line of the White Mountains proper, crowned in the centre by the dome of Mount Washington, closes the view on the northwest and north, — only some twelve or fifteen miles distant by the air. And nearer, on the northeast, swells the symmetrical Kearsarge, the queenly mountain of New Hampshire.

Situated in the valley of the Saco River, whose meadows extend for miles on either side, "a lovelier plain was never spread before a poet's feet to woo the willing thoughts abroad. In the north loom the White Mountains, blue and misty, yet boldly outlined. There is Mount Washington, rearing his broad, Jove-like throne amid his great brothers and supporters; these, with innumerable lesser mountains, gaze solemnly and serenely down the broad valley, and look new meanings in the ceaseless changes of the air and light."

In the village itself is —

*The Artist's Brook*, whose true celebration is found in artists' studies, for which it has furnished exquisite tangles of foliage and light; rough bowlders, around whose clinging mosses the water slips with a flash that can be painted, but a voice that cannot be entrapped. Does it not sing the song of Tennyson's brook?

> "I chatter, chatter, as I flow
>   To join the brimming river,
> For men may come, and men may go,
>   But I go on forever — ever."

Another stream in this vicinity is more honored by the sad story associated with it, than by the picturesqueness of the crags through which it hurries. It is called Nancy's Brook, and thus is told —

*The Nancy Tragedy.*—Late in the autumn of the year 1778, a poor but pretty girl, who lived with a family in Jefferson, was found frozen to death. She was engaged to be married to a young man of the same village. She had intrusted to him all her earnings, and the understanding was, that in a few days they should leave for Portsmouth, and be married there. During her temporary absence in Lancaster, nine miles from Jefferson, her betrothed started for Portsmouth, without leaving any explanation or message for her. She learned the fact of her desertion on the same day that her lover departed. At once she walked back to Jefferson, and, in spite of all warnings and entreaties, set out on foot to overtake the faithless fugitive. Snow had already fallen; it was nearly night; the distance to the first settlement near the Notch was thirty miles. There was no road through the wilderness but a hunter's path, marked by spotted trees. She pressed on through the night, against a snow-storm and a northwest wind, in the hope of overtaking her lover in the camp in the Notch, before he and the party he was with should start in the morning. She reached it soon after they had left, and found the ashes of the camp-fire yet warm.

She tried in vain to rekindle the fire in the lonely camp. But the fire in her heart did not falter, and still she moved on, wet, cold, and hungry, with resolution unconquered by the thirty miles tramp through the woods, on the bitter autumn night.

She climbed the wild pass of the Notch, which only one woman had scaled before, and followed the track of the Saco towards Conway. Several miles farther of the roughest part of the way she travelled, often fording the river. But her strength was spent, and she was found, near the little stream that bears her name, by the party in pursuit of her, chilled and stiff in the snow.

When the lover of the unhappy girl heard the story of

her faithfulness, her suffering, and her dreadful death, he became insane, and died not long afterwards a raving madman.

There are those who believe that often in still nights the valley walls echo the shrieks and groans of the restless ghost of Nancy's lover.

> "The leaves are falling, falling,
>     Solemnly and slow;
>  Caw! caw! the rooks are calling,
>     It is a sound of wo,
>         A sound of wo!
>
> "Through woods and mountain passes,
>     The winds, like anthems, roll!
>  They are chanting solemn masses,
>     Singing: 'Pray for this poor soul,
>         Pray — pray!'
>
> "And the hooded clouds, like friars,
>     Tell their beads in drops of rain,
>  And patter their doleful prayers; —
>     But their prayers are all in vain,
>         All in vain!"

*The Notch.* — The White Mountain Notch is a pass of great celebrity. Coming from the north or west, you enter it by an opening only twenty-three feet in width between two perpendicular rocks, one twenty and the other twelve feet high. The infant Saco trickles its way through this narrow opening, gradually expanding as it proceeds down the pass, and receiving other tributaries from the mountain-sides which form the walls of the gorge, and which tower to the height of about two thousand feet above the bed of the Saco.

When we reach these gloomy mountain walls, whose jaws, as we enter, seem ready to close together, we have an impression of mountain wrath and ravage that is seldom obtained elsewhere.

All description of the wildness and majesty of the scene are tame indeed to one who has passed into its tremendous depths. To know the Notch truly, one must drive to the top of Mount Willard, and look down into it. We are lifted twelve hundred feet over the gulf, on the brink of an almost perpendicular wall. The road below is a mere bird-track. The river looks like a slender keel from which spring up the ribs that form the hold of a tremendous line-of-battle-ship on the stocks. But a more exact and noble comparison is its resemblance to the trough of the sea in a storm. They are earth waves, these curving walls that front each other. They were flung up thus, it may be, in the passion of the boiling land, and stiffened before they could dash their liquid granite against each other, or subside by successive oscillations into a calm.

In this pass occurred, in 1826, the land-slide which destroyed the Willey family. The little Willey House still stands, an object of interest to tourists, and a monument of the great disaster which destroyed its occupants. The story is best told in the following ballad from the pen of Dr. T. W. Parsons: —

*The Willey House.* —

I.

Come, children, put your baskets down,
  And let the blushing berries be;
Sit here and wreathe a laurel crown,
  And if I win it, give it me.

'T is afternoon — it is July —
  The mountain shadows grow and grow;
Your time of rest and mine is nigh —
  The moon was rising long ago.

While yet on old Chocorua's top
  The lingering sunlight says farewell,
Your purple-fingered labor stop,
  And hear a tale I have to tell.

## II.

You see that cottage in the glen,
    Yon desolate, forsaken shed —
Whose mouldering threshold, now and then,
    Only a few stray travellers tread?

No smoke is curling from its roof,
    At eve no cattle gather round,
No neighbor now, with dint of hoof,
    Prints his glad visit on the ground.

A happy home it was of yore:
    At morn the flocks went nibbling by,
And Farmer Willey, at his door,
    Oft made their reckoning with his eye.

Where yon rank alder-trees have sprung,
    And birches cluster thick and tall,
Once the stout apple overhung,
    With his red gifts, the garden wall.

Right fond and pleasant, in their ways,
    The gentle Willey people were;
I knew them in those peaceful days,
    And Mary — every one knew her.

## III.

Two summers now had seared the hills,
    Two years of little rain or dew;
High up the courses of the rills
    The wild rose and the raspberry grew.

The mountain-sides were cracked and dry,
    And frequent fissures on the plain,
Like mouths, gaped open to the sky,
    As though the parched earth prayed for rain.

One sultry August afternoon,
    Old Willey, looking towards the West,
Said, "We shall hear the thunder soon;
    O! if it bring us rain, 't is blest."

And, even with his word, a smell
    Of sprinkled fields passed through the air,
And from a single cloud there fell
    A few large drops — the rain was there.

Ere set of sun a thunder-stroke
    Gave signal to the floods to rise;
Then the great seal of heaven was broke,
    Then burst the gates that barred the skies, —

While from the west the clouds rolled on,
    And from the nor'west gathered fast;
" We'll have enough of rain anon,"
    Said Willey — "if this deluge last."

For all these cliffs that stand sublime
    Around, like solemn priests appeared,
Gray Druids of the olden time,
    Each with his white and streaming beard,

Till in one sheet of seething foam
    The mingling torrents joined their might;
But in the Willeys' quiet home,
    Was naught but silence and " Good-night."

For soon they went to their repose,
    And in their bed, all safe and warm,
Saw not how fast the waters rose,
    Heard not the growing of the storm.

But just before the stroke of ten,
    Old Willey looked into the night,
And called upon his two hired men,
    And woke his wife, who struck a light;

Though her hand trembled, as she heard
    The horses whinnying in the stall,
And — "Children!" was the only word
    That woman from her lips let fall.

"Mother!" the frighted infants cried,
    "What is it? has a whirlwind come?"
Wildly the weeping mother eyed
    Each little darling, but was dumb.

A sound! as though a mighty gale
   Some forest from its hold had riven,
Mixed with a rattling noise like hail,
   God! art thou raining rocks from heaven?

A flash! O Christ! the lightning showed
   The mountain moving from his seat!
Out! out into the slippery road!
   Into the wet with naked feet!

No time for dress — for life! for life!
   No time for any word but this:
The father grasped his boys — his wife
   Snatched her young babes, but not to kiss.

And Mary with the younger girl,
   Barefoot, and shivering in their smocks,
Sped forth amid that angry whirl
   Of rushing waves and angry rocks.

For down the mountain's crumbling side,
   Full half the mountain from on high
Came sinking, like the snows that slide
   From the great Alps about July.

And with it went the lordly ash,
   And with it went the kingly pine;
Cedar and oak, amid the crash,
   Dropped down like clippings of the vine.

Two rivers rushed — the one that broke
   His wonted bounds and drowned the land,
And one that streamed with dust and smoke
   A flood of earth and stones and sand.

Then for a time the vale was dry,
   The soil had swallowed up the wave;
Till one star, looking from the sky,
   A signal to the tempest gave:

The clouds withdrew, the storm was o'er,
   Bright Aldebaran burned again;
The buried river rose once more,
   And foamed along his gravelly glen.

## IV.

At morn the men of Conway felt
   Some dreadful thing had chanced that night;
And some by Breton woods who dwelt
   Observed the mountain's altered height.

Old Crawford and the Fabyan lad
   Came down from Ammonoosuck then,
And passed the Notch — ah! strange and sad
   It was to see the ravaged glen.

But having toiled for miles in doubt,
   With many a risk of limb and neck,
They saw and hailed with joyful shout
   The Willey House amid the wreck.

The avalanche of stone and sand,
   Remembering mercy in its wrath,
Had parted, and on either hand
   Pursued the ruin of its path.

And there upon the pleasant slope,
   The cottage, like a sunny isle
That wakes the shipwrecked seaman's hope,
   Amid that horror seemed to smile.

And still upon the lawn before,
   The peaceful sheep were nibbling nigh;
But Farmer Willey at his door
   Stood not to count them with his eye.

And in the dwelling — O despair!
   The silent room! the vacant bed!
The children's little shoes were there —
   But whither were the children fled?

That day a woman's head, all gashed,
   Its long hair streaming in the flow,
Went o'er the dam, and then was dashed
   Among the whirlpools down below.

And further down, by Saco's side,
   They found the mangled forms of four,
Held in an eddy of the tide;
   But Mary, she was seen no more.

Yet never to this mournful vale
 Shall any maid in summer-time
Come, without thinking of the tale
 I now have told you in my rhyme.

And when the Willey House is gone,
 And its last rafter is decayed,
Its history may yet live on
 In this your ballad I have made.

*Berlin Falls.* — North and east of Mount Washington, these Falls are on the Androscoggin River, and descend over two hundred feet in the course of a mile. We do not think that in New England there is any passage of river passion that will compare with them.

The ride to Berlin Falls is charming. The road is on the western bank of the Androscoggin all the way. The river moves now and then in such sweeping curves, and is overhung for most of the distance by a mountain foliage so massive and varied, and the gradual descent of the riverbed gives the current, during a great portion of the way, so much briskness, while the mountain views behind are so majestic, that the six miles' ride, if we drive in an open wagon, do not seem long enough, however eager we may be to see the cataract. The Falls are close by the road. It is a winding granite gorge through which the river rushes, over the narrowest part of which a stout bridge is thrown.

Visitors should alight at the lowest part of the cataract, and go out through a little thicket of trees upon a mossy ledge, about fifteen feet above the current, where they can face the sweeping torrent. How madly it hurls the deep transparent amber down the pass, and over the bowlders, — flying and roaring like a drove of young lions, crowding each other in furious rush after prey in sight! On the bridge, we look down and see the current shooting swifter than the "arrowy Rhone," and overlapped on either side by the hissing foam thrown back from each of the rock walls. Above the bridge we can walk on the ledge of the right-hand bank, and sit down where we can touch the water and see the most powerful plunge of all, where half the river leaps in a smooth cataract, and around a large rock, which, though sunken, seems to divide the motion of the flood; a narrow and tremendous current of foam shoots into the pass, and mingles its fury with the burden of the heavier fall.

Other falls of note are: the Silver Cascade, a beautiful thread of water descending from far up the side of Mount Webster; Ripley's Falls, on a tributary of the Saco; the falls of the Ammonoosuck, which in the course of thirty miles descends over five thousand feet; and the Crystal Cascade and Glen Ellis Fall, near the Glen House, on a tributary of the Androscoggin.

*The Mount Washington Railroad.* — One of the attractions of the mountains is the railroad up the Washington mount. A Chicago man, Mr. Marsh, was the originator of this scheme. The application for a charter to the New Hampshire legislature, was seconded, and the mover desired to add a substitute, that it *be extended to the moon.* But this derisive remark only made the success of the experiment more marked. After finishing a quarter of a mile, Mr. Marsh invited the superintendents of some ten railroads in New England to test his plan.

About four hundred and fifty spectators from the various hotels came to witness the experiment. After ascending and descending, these railroad officers unanimously voted it a triumphant success. I need not add that capitalists vied in their haste to secure the stock. It is a wonderful affair, since by a road three miles in length you rise to a perpendicular height of 3,624 feet, equal to one foot in a yard. Should it rise according to the steepest grade over the Alleghanies, it would require sixty-five miles to reach the height.

One of our party, a Chicago man, examined the machinery and the seven different kinds of brakes with great care. Then turning to the conductor, Mr. Dodge, he said, "Captain, after looking at your train, I feel quite unwilling to trust myself to ascend in it." — "What defect, stranger, do you discover? We aim to make it as perfect as human skill can devise." — "Don't you see that *the engine is without a cowcatcher?*" As the train ascends backward, the Chicago wit brought down the house. All entered the cars conscious that they had not Elijah's chariot or the angel band to bear us in safety.

Timid ladies cry and sometimes scream, but the crowd only laugh them out of their fears. It does appear decidedly perilous, and men of iron nerve, descending at times, grow very pale. It is simply an ordinary elevator, without the chain. Accidents have occurred in our wholesale stores and hotels, and may again. But thus far, none have taken place here. — *Interior*.

*The Summit of Mount Washington.* — The effect of standing on the summit of Mount Washington is a bewildering of the senses at the extent and lawlessness of the spectacle. It is as though we were looking upon chaos. Around you in every direction are confused masses of mountains, bearing the appearance of a sea of molten lava suddenly cooled, whilst its ponderous waves were yet in commotion. In a few moments we become accustomed to this, and begin to feel the joy of turning round, and sweeping a horizon that is drawn, in part, outside of New England. Northward we look beyond the Canada line. On the southeast gleams a rim of silver light, — it is the Atlantic Ocean, sixty-five miles distant, laving the shores of Maine. Lakes of all sizes, from Lake Winnipiseogee to mere mountain ponds, — and "mountains, beneath you, gleam misty and *wide.*" Far to the northeast is Mount Katahdin looming out of the wilderness of Maine. The nearer range of the Green Mountains are clearly visible. To the south and southwest are Mounts Monadnock and Kearsarge, while the space between is filled with every variety of landscape, — mountain and hill, plain and valley, lake and river. The line of the Connecticut we can follow, from its birth, near Canada, to the point where it is hidden by the great Franconia wall. Two large curves of the Androscoggin we can see. Broken portions of the Saco lie below us like lumps of light. The sources of the Merrimac are on the farther slope of a mountain that seems to be not more than the distance of a rifle-shot.

The story is told of Daniel Webster, who ascended the mountain on foot, with only the assistance of a guide. When he arrived at the summit, he is said to have given utterance to the following words: "Mount Washington, I have come a long distance, and have toiled hard to arrive at your summit, and now you have given me a cold reception. I am extremely sorry that I shall not have time enough to view this grand prospect which lies before me, and nothing prevents but the uncomfortable atmosphere in which you reside." The rostrum was the grandest, and the audience the smallest, which was ever honored by a formal speech by the great orator.

The following is a description of a night-scene from Mount Washington.

After a time the heavens are swept clean of clouds, and the moon moved patiently up among the constellations, looking serenely upon the gulfs and pits, and blasted peaks of the mountains. But what are all the grandeurs of these pimple-hills, to that calm, cold splendor that looks through the fresh sweeping air, — that tremendous circuit of stars, from the nearest of which our globe is invisible and unsuspected, whose light, unshaken by our blustering winds, converges on this lonely peak, — that awful dome which floats in immensity on the pulses of palpable force! I did not expect to get a sense of the height of Mount Washington by looking up from its roof rather than by looking down. But it was so. I never before gained such a feeling of its loftiness and loneliness, as looking up, when the valleys were veiled, to the Dipper and the Zenith. Half a minute at a time was all my brain could bear. To be fastened one night on Mount Washington, alone, compelled to face the firmament, I am sure would almost crush my reason.

The wind swept all night over us in an unabating gale; and as I lay under the blankets of the Summit House, that view of the sky haunted me, and drove away sleep. I seemed to have a sensation of the earth's motion, — that we were lying on that little foretop of New England, while our planet ship was scudding twelve hundred miles a minute, over star-islanded immensity.

*Lake Memphremagog.* (*H. L. Burt.*) — In the great basin that lies between the White and Green Mountains, and on the borders of Vermont and Canada, is Lake Memphremagog, one of the loveliest inland lakes within the limits of New England. Its name is of Indian origin, and signifies Beautiful Water. Though differing in many particulars, in general appearance it more nearly resembles the far-famed Lake George than any other body of water that has come under our observation, and is so regarded by old travellers who are familiar with both. There are no marshes along its borders, and its shores are rock-bound, while the water is cold and clear as crystal. Here and there are beautiful islands, covered with spruce and other forest trees, adding variety to the scene. On the west shore are high mountains, overlooking the lake and the country around it, while on the east is a long range of hills, sloping down in places to the water's edge. The scenery, which is so varied, is quite unlike any found elsewhere in New England, and there is a charm about it that is fascinating to all lovers of the picturesque and beautiful in nature. It matters not whether one is silently studying the myriad forms of beauty that are spread before him in so great profusion, or is gazing upon the distant mountain peaks that seem to touch the blue sky above, or is watching the golden shadows that flit across the placid lake, there is something that is so suggestive and so beautiful that the eye never wearies, and the mind is refreshed with this communion with nature. As the steamer ploughs the lake close up to the lofty mountain, going within its very shadows, and the eye takes in the scenery that is so unlike anything that it is accustomed to, the traveller catches some of that inspiration that must have animated those dusky sons of the forest, and led them to exclaim, when they first looked down from the wood-crowned heights above upon the long and narrow lake, stretching away to the north, "Memphremagog!" Beautiful Water!

There is something, too, in this northern air, that exhilarates and increases one's love of nature. The heavy, murky atmosphere, that is so oppressive in midsummer, in the overheated cities, is unknown here on the banks of Memphremagog. The currents of air that flow over and are cooled on the high mountain elevations, or come up the lake, seem to give one new life, infusing greater animation. The sunsets, too, are peculiarly beautiful. The blue sky seems almost transparent, while the golden tinge that is shed over land and water, gives the face of nature a charm and coloring that sets the painter's art at defiance. It touches and quickens the inner nature of man, and he longs for a closer intimacy with that Spirit which seems to pervade everything, and create so much that is wonderful and beautiful.

The lake is from one to two miles wide on an average, and is thirty miles long, reaching from the village of Newport, in Vermont, on the south, to Magog, a Canadian hamlet, on the north. Full two thirds of the lake is in Canada, and the boundary line is easily distinguished, — south of it there being more thrift and enterprise than is seen just north over the line in Canada. The water in most places is very deep and cold, and is just the place for the lake trout which are caught each year in great abundance.

*Balance Rock and Skinner's Cave.* — Two of the principal objects of interest in the lake are Balance Rock and Skinner's Cave. They are situated on islands about twelve miles north of the southern end of the lake. Balance Rock is on Long Island, and will be noticed at the southern end as the steamer goes north. It is a great granite bowlder poised upon a single point, and must have been brought down from the north in the great flow of ice that is supposed to have taken place in remote ages, and here lodged.

Skinner's Cave is at the north end of Skinner's Island. There is a legend connected with this cave, that is handsomely told in verse, and can be found in Burt's Connecticut Valley and White Mountain Guide, and all lovers of the mysterious will be interested in reading it. The island was named after Captain Uriah Skinner, the bold smuggler of Magog, and the legend has reference to this remarkable character, who flourished along this lake many years ago.

*Owl's Head.* — A range of mountains extends nearly the whole length of the western shore of Memphremagog, the most prominent of which is Owl's Head. The base of this mountain is twelve miles from the southern end of the lake. I rises quite abruptly from the shore of the lake, and, as seen from one point, looks like a great hay-stack, the top of which seems to come to a sharp point. The summit is nearly 3,000 feet above the lake, and is one mass of jagged rock, looking as though it had been broken up by some volcanic agency. In one of the rock chambers on the summit, the Golden Rule Lodge of Freemasons, of Stanstead, Canada, hold a lodge once a year, on the 24th of June. Masonic emblems and inscriptions are found painted on the rock where the lodge is held.

The view from the summit is remarkably beautiful, as well as extensive. From it one can get a better idea of the wildness of the scenery of northern Vermont and Canada than from any other point. North, the great Canadian forest seems to stretch away to the River St. Lawrence. In a clear day, with the aid of a glass, the tall, bright spires of Montreal are visible. West, is the Green Mountain range, Jay Peak standing prominently in the foreground. Southeast are the White Mountains, Mount Washington reaching above its lofty neighbors. The more immediate view is also equally interesting, and includes the lakes and villages that help to add variety to the scene.

## CHAPTER II.

NIAGARA FALLS AND ST. LAWRENCE RIVER.

FLOW on forever, in thy glorious robe,
   Of terror and of beauty. Yea, flow on,
Unfathom'd and resistless. God hath set
His rainbow on thy forehead, and the cloud
Mantled around thy feet. And He doth give

Thy voice of thunder power to speak of Him
Eternally — bidding the lip of man
Keep silence, and upon thine altar pour
Incense of awe-struck praise.

    Earth fears to lift
The insect trump that tells her trifling joys
Or fleeting triumphs, 'mid the peal sublime
Of thy tremendous hymn. Proud ocean shrinks
Back from thy brotherhood, and all his waves
Retire abashed. For he hath need to sleep,
Sometimes like a spent laborer, calling home
His boisterous billows, from their vexing play
To a long dreary calm: but thy strong tide
Faints not, nor e'er with failing heart forgets
Its everlasting lesson, night nor day.
The morning stars that hailed creation's birth,
Heard thy hoarse anthem mixing with their song,
Jehovah's name; and the dissolving fires,
That wait the mandate of the day of doom,
To wreck the earth, shall find it deep inscribed
Upon thy rocky scroll.

    Lo! yon birds,
How bold! they venture near, dipping their wing
In all thy mist and foam. Perchance 't is meet
For them to touch thy garments' hem, or stir
Thy diamond wreath, who sport upon the cloud
Unblamed, or warble at the gate of heaven
Without reproof. But as for us, it seems
Scarce lawful with our erring lips to talk
Familiarly of thee. Methinks, to trace
Thine awful features with our pencil's point
Were but to press on Sinai.

    Thou dost speak
Alone of God, who poured thee as a drop
From His right hand — bidding the soul that looks
Upon thy fearful majesty be still,
Be humbly wrapped in its own nothingness,
And lose itself in Him.

          — *Sigourney.*

The Falls of Niagara may justly be classed among the Wonders of the World. They are the pride of America, unequalled in grandeur, magnitude, and magnificence by any other known cataract, and have, since they were discovered, exerted an attractive influence over millions of the human race, who have flocked thither, year after year, to gaze upon the tumultuous crash of water, with feelings of the deepest solemnity. The power and majesty of the Almighty are perhaps more awfully exhibited and more fully realized in this stupendous waterfall than in any other scene on earth.

The great lakes of North America — Superior, Michigan, Huron, and Erie — pour the flood of their accumulated waters into Lake Ontario through a channel of about thirty-six miles in length. This channel is named the Niagara River, and is part of the boundary between Canada and the State of New York. Twenty-two miles below its commencement at Lake Erie, occur the famous Falls of Niagara. These Falls are divided into two, by Iris or Goat Island. The American Falls are nine hundred feet wide, by one hundred and sixty-three feet high. The Horse-Shoe or Canadian Fall is two thousand feet wide, and one hundred and fifty-four feet high. The origin of the name is uncertain, but is supposed to signify "Thunder of Waters." The roar of the Falls is sometimes heard at a great distance, though, of course, it is constantly modified by the direction and strength of the wind. Often it cannot be heard three miles distant, and again it rolls over the land to the shores of Lake Ontario, and across its waters even to Toronto, forty-six miles away. Over this magnificent precipice the irresistible tide rushes at the rate of one hundred million tons of water every hour! The rapids extend for a mile above the Falls, the waters rolling in great swells as they rush swiftly down among the rocks, and are carried with immense velocity over the edge of the precipice, and form a grand curve as they fall clear of the rocky wall into the boiling pool at the base. The space between this sheet of water and the wall widens at the bottom, the strata being there of a loose shaly character, and consequently hollowed out by the continued action of the spray. A cave is thus formed behind the Fall, into which, on the Canadian side, persons can enter, and pass by a rough and slippery path towards Goat Island. The river above the Falls is studded with islands of all sizes, amounting to thirty-seven in number. The width of the stream varies from several hundred yards to three miles. At the Falls it is about three quarters of a mile wide.

The village of the Falls lies on the east side of the river, in the immediate vicinity of the grand cataract. The hotels here, and on the opposite shore, are excellent. The chief of them are the Cataract House and the International Hotel on the American side, and the Clifton on the Canadian shore.

*Suspension Bridge above the Rapids.* — Here the first perceptions of power and grandeur begin to awaken in our minds. The noble river is seen hurrying on towards its final leap; and as we stand upon the bridge, we look down upon the gushing flood of water, that seems as if it would sweep away our frail standing-ground, and hurl us over the dread precipice whose rounded edge is but a few yards farther down. This is the finest point of view from which to observe the *rapids above the Falls*. The fall of the river, from the head of the rapids to the edge of the precipice, is nearly sixty feet; and the tumultuous madness of the waters, hurling and foaming in wayward billows and breakers down this descent, as if fretting with impatience, is a fine contrast to the uniform magnificent sweep with which at length they gush into the thundering flood below.

This bridge spans the torrent between the shore and Bath Island; a second suspension bridge connects Bath Island with Goat Island; and beyond Goat Island there are a few scattered rocks, which are connected with it by means of a third bridge. These rocks lie on the very brink of the precipice between the American Falls and the Horse-Shoe Fall, and on them stands a tower named the Terrapin Tower, which commands a magnificent view of Niagara.

*Niagara Falls from Prospect Point.* — The eastern bank of the river, just above the Falls, is called Prospect Point. Here at one wide sweep we behold Niagara, stretching from the American to the Canadian side in magnificent perspective. Just at our feet the smooth, deep masses of the American Falls undulate convulsively as they hurl over the precipice, and dash, in a never-ending succession of what we may term passionate bursts, upon the rugged rocks beneath. Beyond, and a little to the left, is Goat Island, richly clothed with trees, its drooping end seeming as if it, too, were plunging, like the mighty river, into the seething abyss. Just off the Point is seen the Terrapin Tower, and right in front of us is the great Horse-Shoe Fall, uttering its deep, deafening roar of endless melody, as it plunges majestically into that curdling sea, and from which the white cloud of mist spouts high in air, and partially conceals the background of Canada from view. Far down in the river below, the ferry-boats are seen dancing on the angry waters. It is a solemnizing prospect, and we should suppose that few could gaze upon it without feeling that they had attained to a higher conception of the awful power and might of the Eternal. This point was the last residence of Francis Abbot, the Hermit of Niagara. Within a short distance is the —

*Ferry House.* — Here there is a curious inclined plane, down which we descend in cars, and which are worked by means of a water-wheel and a rope; there is also a stair connected with this, at the foot of which the ferry-boat waits to convey passengers over to the Canadian side. The view of the American Fall from below is grand beyond description. Dangerous as the river appears here, it is often crossed by small boats, and the little steamboat, called the "Maid of the Mist," navigates this portion of the river, taking persons up nearly to the foot of the Falls.

One of the finest views of Niagara is had from Table Rock, on the Canadian side.

*Table Rock.* — The impression of the view from this point is best told in the words of Charles Dickens.

"When we were seated in the little ferry-boat, and were crossing the swollen river immediately before both cataracts, I began to feel what it was; but I was in a manner stunned, and unable to comprehend the vastness of the scene. It was not until I came on Table Rock, and looked — Great Heaven, on what a fall of bright green water! — that it came upon me with its full might and majesty.

"Then when I felt how near to my Creator I was standing, the first effect and the enduring one, instant and lasting, of the tremendous spectacle, was Peace. Peace of mind, tranquillity, calm recollections of the dead, great thoughts of eternal rest and happiness: nothing of gloom or terror. Niagara was at once stamped upon my heart, an image of beauty, to remain there, changeless and indelible, until its pulses cease to beat forever.

"O, how the strife and trouble of daily life receded from my view, and lessened in the distance, during the ten memorable days we passed on that Enchanted Ground! What voices spoke from out the thundering water; what faces, faded from the earth, looked out upon me from its gleaming depths; what Heavenly promise glistened in those angel tears, the drops of many hues that showered around, and twined themselves about the gorgeous arches which the changing rainbows made!

"To wander to and fro all day, to see the cataract from all points of view, to stand upon the edge of the Great Horse-Shoe Fall, marking the hurried water gathering strength as it approached the verge, yet seeming, too, to pause before it shot into the gulf below; to gaze from the river's level up at the torrent as it came streaming down; to climb the neighboring heights and watch it through the trees; to see the wreathing water in the rapids hurrying on to take its fearful plunge; to linger in the shadow of the solemn rocks three miles below, watching the river as stirred by no visible cause it heaved and eddied and awoke the echoes, being troubled yet far down beneath the surface, by its giant leap; to have Niagara before me, lighted by the sun and by the moon, red in the day's decline, and gray as evening slowly fell upon it; to look upon it every day, and wake up in the night and hear its ceaseless voice: this was enough.

"I think of it in every quiet season now; still do those waters roll and leap, roar and tumble, all day long; still are the rainbows spanning them a hundred feet below; still, when the sun is on them, do they shine and glow like molten gold; still, when the day is gloomy, do they fall like snow or seem to crumble away like the front of a great chalk cliff, or roll down the rock like dense, white smoke. But always does the mighty stream appear to die as it comes down, and always from its unfathomable grave arises that tremendous ghost of spray and mist which is never laid; which has haunted this place with the same dread solemnity since darkness brooded on the deep, and that first flood before the deluge — light — came rushing on creation at the word of God."

Table Rock is no longer the extensive platform that it once was, large portions of it having fallen from time to time. It overhangs the terrible caldron close to the Horse-Shoe Fall, and the view from it, as already described, is most sublime. In 1818, a mass one hundred and sixty feet long broke off and fell into the boiling flood; in 1828, three immense masses fell. In 1829, another fragment fell, and in 1850, a portion of about two hundred feet in length and one hundred feet thick. On one of these occasions some forty or fifty persons had been standing on the rock a few minutes before it fell! The work of demolition still goes on, and soon Table Rock will exist only in memory.

A short distance from Table Rock there is a stair by which we can descend under the overhanging cliff, and if we desire it, don the waterproof habiliments provided for us and go —

*Under the Horse-Shoe Fall.* — The view here is awfully grand. As we gaze upwards at the frowning cliff that seems tottering to its fall, and pass under the thick curtain of water, so near that it seems as if we could touch it, and hear the hissing spray, and are stunned by the deafening roar that issues from the misty vortex at our feet, an indescribable feeling of awe steals over us, and we are more than ever impressed with the tremendous magnificence of Niagara. In alluding to this view a graphic writer says: "After scrambling among piles of huge rocks that obstruct his way, the traveller gains the bottom of the Falls, where the soul can be susceptible of but one emotion, namely, that of uncontrollable terror. It was not until I had, by frequent excursions to the Falls, in a measure familiarized my mind with the sublimities, that I ventured to explore the penetralia of the cataract. The precipice over which it rolls is very much arched underneath; while the impetus which the water receives in its descent projects it far beyond the cliff, and thus an immense gothic arch is formed by the rock and the torrent.

"Twice I entered this cavern, and twice I was obliged to retrace my steps, lest I should be suffocated by the blasts of dense spray that whirled around me; however, the third time I succeeded in advancing about twenty-five yards. Here darkness began to encircle me; on one side the black cliff stretched itself into a gigantic arch far above my head, and on the other the dense hissing torrent formed an impenetrable sheet of foam with which I was drenched in a moment. The rocks were so slippery that I could hardly keep my feet; while the horrid din made me think the precipice above was tumbling down in colossal fragments upon my head.

"It is not easy to determine how far an individual might advance between the sheet of water and the rock; but were it even possible to explore the recess to its utmost extremity, scarcely any one, I believe, would have courage to attempt an expedition of the kind.

*Goat, or Iris Island.* — This island is half a mile long by a quarter broad, and contains about seventy acres, and is heavily wooded. In 1770, a man placed some goats here to pasture; hence its name. Its other name, Iris, is derived from a number of beautiful rainbows that are so frequently seen near it. It is impossible to paint the ever-rising column of spray that spires upward from the foaming gulf below, or the prismatic glory that crowns it, for there indeed has God forever "set His bow" in the cloud.

*Terrapin Tower.* — This tower occupies a singular and awful position. A few scattered masses of rock lie on the very brink of the great fall, seeming as if unable to maintain their position against the tremendous rush of water. Upon these rocks the tower is built. It is approached from Goat Island by a wooden foot-bridge, which is usually wet with spray, so that one must be careful in crossing. In 1852 a gentleman fell from this bridge, and was carried to the edge of the Fall. Fortunately he stuck between two rocks, and was rescued by having lines thrown to him, which he fastened around his body, and was thus drawn ashore.

The tower was erected in 1833, by Judge Porter; and

from its summit we obtain the most magnificent view that can be conceived, — the rapids above rolling tumultuously towards you, the green water of the mighty Falls at your feet, below you the hissing caldron of spray, and the river with its steep banks beyond, — in fact, the whole range of the Falls themselves, and the world of raging waters around them, are seen from this commanding point of view.

The perpendicular precipice at the lower end of Goat Island may be descended by a stairway called

*Biddle's Stairs.* — These stairs are firmly secured to the cliff, and said to be quite safe. They are eighty feet high. The total descent from the top of the bank to the bottom is one hundred and eighty-five feet. Between this point and the centre fall is the spot where the celebrated Sam Patch made his famous leaps. Sam made two leaps in 1829. A long ladder was placed at the foot of the rock, and fastened with ropes in such a manner that the top projected over the water. A platform was then laid from the top of the ladder to the edge of the bank above. Hundreds of thousands of spectators crowded every point within sight of the place on both shores, eager to behold the extraordinary spectacle of a man "jumping over the Falls." Sam walked along the giddy platform, made his bow, and went down, feet first, ninety-seven feet into the river.

Not content with this achievement, Sam Patch afterwards made a higher leap at the Genesee Falls. Again at the same place he made another jump, from the height of one hundred and twenty-five feet! This was his last. The poor fellow never rose again, and his body has never been found.

*The Three Sisters.* — These are three small islands lying side by side near the head of Goat Island. Three costly and substantial bridges span the channels which separate the Three Sisters from each other and from Goat Island. The rapids here are very fine, surpassing in volume the rapids under Goat Island bridge, and much more beautiful in appearance.

From one of the Sisters a gentleman named Allan was rescued by the gallant Mr. J. R. Robinson, in the summer of 1841. Mr. Allan had started alone in his boat for the village of Chippewa, and in the middle of the river broke one of his oars. Being unable to gain the shore, he endeavored with the remaining oar to steer for the head of Goat Island, but the rapid current swept him past this point. As he approached the outer island of the Three Sisters, he steered with the cool energy of despair towards it; and leaped ashore, while his boat sprang like a lightning-flash down the rapid and over the Horse-Shoe Fall. For two days Mr. Allan remained on the island, and then fortunately succeeded in making a fire with some matches he happened to have in his pocket. Crowds of people assembled to assist in and witness the rescue, which was accomplished by Robinson, who, having managed to pass a rope from island to island, reached him with a skiff.

Another narrow escape was made here by a father and son in the year 1850. The son, a boy ten years of age, was paddling his father — who was drunk at the time — over to their home on Grand Island. The father was unable to guide the frail canoe, which was carried into the rapids, and descended with fearful rapidity towards the Falls. The wretched father could do nothing to save himself, but the gallant boy struggled with the energy of a hero, and succeeded in forcing the canoe between Goat Island and the Three Sisters. Here they were in imminent danger of passing over the little cascade between these islands, but, providentially, as they neared it a wave upset the canoe, and left them struggling in the water. The place was shallow, the boy gained a footing, and seizing his father by the collar, dragged him to the shore, where hundreds of anxious spectators received them with shouts of joy.

Gull Island is a small island just above the Horse-Shoe Fall. It has never been trodden by man. About two miles higher up the river is the —

*Burning Spring.* — This curious spring is very interesting. The water, being charged with sulphuretted hydrogen gas, takes fire when a light is applied to it, and burns with a pale, bluish flame.

The Battle of Chippewa was fought in this neighborhood on the 5th of July, 1814.

*Cave of the Winds.* — It is situated at the foot of the rock between Goat and Luna Islands, and is considered by some to be one of the finest and most wonderful sights on the American side. The cave has been formed by the action of the water on the soft substratum of the precipice which has been washed away, and the limestone rock left arching over head. In front, the transparent Falls form a beautiful curtain. In consequence of the tremendous pressure on the atmosphere, this cave is filled with perpetual storms, and the war of conflicting elements is quite chaotic. A beautiful rainbow, quite circular in form, quivers amid the driving spray when the sun shines. Along the floor of this remarkable cavern the spray is hurled with considerable violence, so that it strikes the walls and curls upwards along the ceiling, thus causing the rough turmoil which has procured for this place its title of the Cave of the Winds.

*Niagara in Winter.* — In all its phases this wonderful cataract is sublime, but in winter, when its dark green waters contrast with the pure white snow, and its frosty vapor spouts up into the chill atmosphere from a perfect chaos of ice and foam, there is a perfection of savage grandeur about it which cannot be realized in the green months of summer.

In this season, ice is the ruling genius of the spot. The spray that bursts from the thundering cataract encrusts every object in a coat of purest, dazzling white. The trees bend gracefully under its weight, as if in silent homage to the Spirit of the Falls.

Every twig is covered, every bough is laden; and those parts of the rocks and trees on which the delicate frost-work will not lie, stand out in bold contrast. At the foot of the Falls, block rises on block in wild confusion, and the cold, dismal-looking water hurries its green floods over the brink, and roars hoarsely as it rushes into the vortex of dazzling white below. The trees on Goat Island seem partially buried; the bushes around have almost disappeared; the houses seem to sink under their ponderous coverings of white; every rail is edged with it; every point and pinnacle is capped with it; and the dark form of the Terrapin Tower stands like a lone sentinel guarding this scene of magnificent desolation.

When the sun shines, all becomes radiant with glittering gems, and the mind is almost overwhelmed with the combined effects of excessive brilliancy and excessive grandeur. But such a scene cannot be described.

"From age to age — in winter's frost, or summer's sultry beam,
By day, by night, without a pause — thy waves with loud acclaim,
In ceaseless sounds, have still proclaimed the Great Eternal Name."

*Niagara Suspension Bridge.* — This noble and stupendous structure spans the river about two miles below the Falls. It is the work of Mr. John A. Roebling, of Trenton, New Jersey, and was begun in 1852. The bridge is of enormous strength. Over it pass the carriages of the Great Western and New York Central Railroads, and cars of every description run without the slightest vibration. The cost of its construction was $500,000; and cars first crossed it in the spring of 1855. The road for carriages is suspended twenty feet below the railway line.

The following statistics of this enormous bridge will be interesting. The height of the towers on the American side is eighty-eight feet; those on the Canada side are seventy-eight feet high. Length of the bridge is eight hundred feet, width twenty-four feet, height above the river two hundred and fifty feet. There are four enormous wire cables of about ten inches in diameter, which contain about four thousand miles of wire; and the ultimate capacity of the four cables is about twelve thousand tons. The total weight of the bridge is eight hundred tons, and it combines, in an eminent degree, strength with elegance of structure.

*The New Suspension Bridge.* — This bridge was commenced in 1867, and opened to the public January 1st, 1869. The cost of the bridge was $120,000. It is located 1,800 feet below the American Falls on the American side, landing on the Canada side only eight or ten rods below the Clifton House. The towers on the Canadian side are one hundred and twenty feet high, and on the American side one hundred and six feet high. The span is one thousand two hundred and thirty feet from tower to tower. The height from the water to the floor of the bridge is two hundred and fifty-six feet. There is a single track for carriages, and a space on one side for foot passengers. The bridge has at each side a strong railing five feet high; the estimated strength of the structure is over one hundred and fifty tons, and as ten or fifteen tons is all that could well be placed on the bridge at any one time by its ordinary traffic, the greatest confidence prevails as to its stability. As it has passed through several winters with its load of ice and frozen spray, it is no longer an experiment but a fixed fact, and full confidence has been established. The bridge stands as a lasting monument to J. F. Bush, who conceived the project and carried it to a successful termination.

The erection of this bridge brings Goat Island and Table Rock within easy walking distance. The view from the centre of it is exceedingly fine; suspended in mid-air, in full view of both the American and the Horse-Shoe Falls, the river above and below, with its beautiful banks, presents a view never before enjoyed by visitors to this wonderful and beautiful resort.

*The Receding of the Falls.* — It has been ascertained beyond all doubt that the Falls do recede, but the rate of this retrograde movement is very uncertain, and we have reason to believe it must have been, in time past, *irregular.* It has long been supposed that the Falls originally plunged over the cliff at Queenston, and that they have gradually eaten their way back, a distance of seven miles, to their present position. It is further conjectured that they will continue to cut their way back in the course of ages to Lake Erie, and that an extensive inundation will be caused by the waters of the lake thus set free. Recent geological research has shown that this result is quite improbable, and it seems likely that in the course of ten thousand years they will have diminished to half their present height, and will be retarded in their retrograde progress by the fall of large masses of rock from the cliff above. Should they still recede, they will be so diminished in height as to be almost lost before reaching Lake Erie.

It has been calculated that Niagara has been going back at the rate of a yard annually; but one foot per annum is considered, by Sir Charles Lyell, a much more probable conjecture. And, as stated, this rate of recession has, in all likelihood, not been uniform, but in many parts of its course Niagara has remained almost stationary for ages.

*Lundy's Lane Battle-Ground.* — This is about a mile and a half from the Falls near the Clifton House. This great battle between the Americans and the British was fought on the 25th of July, 1814. The number of killed and wounded on both sides was about equal, and both parties claim the victory.

*The Whirlpool.* — About three miles below the Falls the river takes an abrupt turn, and shoots with great violence against the cliff on the Canada side, forming what is called the Whirlpool. This is the place where the "Maid of the Mist" was overwhelmed, and lost her smoke-stack. This little boat left her moorings, about a quarter of a mile above the old suspension bridge, June 15, 1861, and swung boldly out into the river, to try one of the most perilous voyages ever made. She shot forward like an arrow of light, bowed gracefully to the multitude on the bridge, and with the velocity of lightning passed on to meet her doom. Many beheld this hazardous, daring adventure, expecting every instant she would be dashed to pieces, and disappear forever. Amazement thrilled every heart, and it appeared as if no power short of *Omnipotence* could save her. "There! there!" was the suppressed exclamation that escaped the lips of all. "She careens over! she is lost! she is *lost!*" But guided by an eye that dimmed not, and a hand that never trembled, she was piloted through those maddened waters by the intrepid Robinson, in perfect safety. The boat lost her smoke-stack, but otherwise received no injury, being very strongly built.

This whirlpool is also associated with the sad and tragic fate of

*Francis Abbot, The Hermit of the Falls.* — His history and melancholy end are of great interest, — this is the story.

In the year 1829, a young stranger of pleasing countenance and person made his appearance at Niagara. He brought with him a large portfolio, and several books and musical instruments. For a few weeks he paid daily and nightly visits to the most interesting points of Niagara, and at length became so fascinated with the sublimity of the scene, that he resolved to take up his abode there altogether. No one knew whence the young stranger came. He applied for permission to build for himself a cottage on one of the Three Sisters, but being prevented, he took up his residence in an old cottage on Goat Island. Here the young hermit spent his days and nights in silent contemplation of the great cataract; and when winter came, the dwellers on the mainland saw the twinkle of his wood fire, and listened wonderingly to the sweet tones of music that floated over the troubled waters, and mingled with the thunder of the Falls.

This wonderful recluse seemed never to rest. At all hours of day and night he might be seen wandering around the object of his adoration. There was at this time a single beam of timber carried out ten feet over the fathomless abyss. Along this beam he often passed and repassed in the darkness of the night. . He even took pleasure in grasping it with his hands, and thus suspending himself over the awful gulf. Not content with gazing on the rapids, he regularly bathed in the turbulent waters. One day in June, 1831, he went to bathe in the river below the Falls. Not long afterwards his clothes were found still lying on the bank, but Francis Abbot was gone,—the poor hermit had taken his last bath. Still 'the body was not found, the depth and force of the current below being exceedingly great. Those searching for it passed on to the Whirlpool. There, amid those boiling eddies, was the body, making fearful and rapid gyrations upon the face of the black waters. It would plunge and disappear, and again emerging it was fearful to see it leap half its length above the flood, then float motionless as if exhausted, and anon spring upward, and seem to struggle like a maniac battling with a mortal foe. For days and nights this terrible scene was prolonged. After ten days of effort they were able to recover the body, and bear it to his desolate cottage. There they found his faithful dog guarding the door. Heavily had the long period worn away while he watched for his only friend. He scrutinized the approaching group suspiciously, and would not willingly give them admittance. A stifled wail at length showed his intuitive knowledge of his master, whom the work of death had effectually disguised from the eyes of men. On the pillow was his pet kitten, and in different parts of the room were his guitar, flute, violin, portfolio, and books scattered, the books open as if recently used. It was a touching sight: the hermit mourned by his humble retainers, the poor animals that loved him, and ready to be laid by strange hands in a foreign grave. He was buried near the Falls he loved so well, and his early history, and the reasons which led him to Niagara, have ever remained a mystery.

*Queenston.* — Leaving Niagara and its immediate vicinity, passing down the river, we come to Queenston, a small, picturesque town on the Canada side, worthy of notice chiefly on account of the memorable battle that took place on the neighboring heights, on the 13th of October, 1812. A monument was erected in commemoration of the British general who fell in this battle. This elegant monument, called—

*Brock's Monument,* is nearly two hundred feet in height, surmounted by a Corinthian capital, on which is wrought, in relief, a statue of the Goddess of War. On this capital is the dome, nine feet high, which is reached, by two hundred and fifty steps, from the base on the inside. On the top of the dome is placed a colossal statue of General Brock.

The view from this monument is most gorgeous. In the far distance on either side stretches the richly-wooded landscape, in the midst of which flows the now tranquil Niagara River; and, beyond, the magnificent sheet of Lake Ontario stretches away like a flood of light to the horizon.

Passing down Lake Ontario, we come to its outlet, the *River St. Lawrence.* The basin of this river is famous for the grandeur and beauty of its natural scenery. The Thousand Isles, and Rapids of the St. Lawrence, the Falls of Montmorenci, and the grand scenery of the Saguenay River, are the admiration of thousands of tourists.

*The Thousand Isles.* — They are situated at the emergence of the St. Lawrence from the lake, and stretch themselves down the centre of the river for a distance of forty miles. There are in fact no less than one thousand eight hundred of these "emerald gems in the ring of the wave," of all sizes, from the islet a few yards square, to miles in length. These islands have been the scene of most exciting romance. From their great number, and the labyrinth-like channels among them, they afforded an admirable retreat for the insurgents in the last Canadian insurrection, and for American sympathizers with them, who, under the name of "Fenians," sought to embarrass the British government. Among these was one man, who, from his daring and ability, became an object of anxious pursuit to the Canadian authorities; and he found a safe asylum in these watery intricacies, through the devotedness and courage of his daughter, whose inimitable management of her canoe was such, that against hosts of pursuers she baffled their efforts at capture, while she supplied him with provisions in these solitary retreats, rowing him from one place of concealment to another, under shadow of night.

*The Rapids of the St. Lawrence.* — These are three in number: the Long Sault, the Coteau Rapids, and the Lachine. The Long Sault is nine miles in length, and a raft will drift through in forty minutes. The scenery is beautiful, and at the same time terrible. When the vessel enters, the steam is shut off, and she is carried forward by the force of the stream alone. The surging waters present all the angry appearance of the ocean in a storm; the noble boat strains and labors; but unlike the ordinary pitching and tossing at sea, this going downhill by water produces a highly novel sensation, and is, in fact, a service of some danger, the imminence of which is enhanced to the imagination by the tremendous roar of the headlong, boiling current. Great strength, courage, and dexterity are required in the pilot; for if the head of the steamer were not kept straight with the course of the rapid, she would be immediately submerged, and rolled over and over.

Some idea of the peril of descending a rapid may be entertained, when it requires four men at the wheel, and two at the tiller, to ensure safety. Although several boats have been struck and destroyed, there have never been, we believe, any lives lost.

*Montreal.* — This is the largest, the most populous city, and the commercial metropolis of British North America. It is situated on an island, and at the base of Mount Royal. Its population is about 150,000. The city, as seen from its approach by steamboat, with Mount Royal for a background, covered with beautiful villas, interspersed here and there with tall spires, is majestic, and for beauty almost unrivalled. Among objects of interest in the city or vicinity, stands pre-eminent the Victoria Bridge. This is one of the wonders of the world. It is a tubular structure, the railway trains passing through the tube, while there is a balcony on the outside with a foot-path for passengers. The bridge rests upon twenty-four piers, and is a mile and a quarter long. At the centre it is sixty feet above the summer level of the St. Lawrence. Each pier is furnished with an ice-breaker, which forms a portion of the pier itself. This is necessary, as it is calculated that each buttress will have to bear the pressure of 70,000 tons of ice, when the winter breaks up, and the large ice-fields come sweeping down the St. Lawrence, which have destroyed former bridges. The entire cost was nearly $7,000,000.

*Quebec.* — The city of Quebec has a remarkably picturesque situation between the two rivers, St. Lawrence and St. Charles. It is divided into Upper and Lower Towns. The Upper Town is well fortified, and includes within its limits the Citadel of Cape Diamond, the most formidable fortress in America. The Lower Town is chiefly devoted to business connected with shipping, and occupies a narrow strip which has been reclaimed from the river. The site is mainly supported on piles of timber which have been driven into the channel, ballasted with stone, and covered with a roadway of earth. Quebec, for an American city, is certainly a very peculiar place, — a military town, surrounded by walls and gates, defended by numerous heavy cannon, garrisoned by troops, it is, in its leading features, a city of the seventeenth century, — a quaint, curious, drowsy, but healthy location for human beings, abounding in grim-looking old guns, sentries, pyramids of shot and shell. Such, high up in the skies, is the airy locality called the Upper Town.

*The Falls of Montmorenci.* — These falls are over the northern bank of the St. Lawrence, eight miles from Quebec, where the Montmorenci joins that river. The fall is unbroken, its height two hundred and fifty feet, and width fifty feet. This place is a celebrated scene of winter amusements. During the frost the spray from the falls accumulates so as to form a cone some eighty feet in height. There is also another cone of inferior altitude, of which visitors make the most use. They carry " toboggins," — long, thin pieces of wood, — and having arrived at the summit, place themselves on these, and slide down with immense velocity. It requires much skill to avoid accidents, and sometimes people do tumble head over heels to the bottom. Ladies and gentlemen both enter with equal spirit into this amusement. Visitors generally drive to this spot in sleighs, taking their provisions with them, and, upon the pure white cloth nature has spread for them, partake of their repast, and enjoy a most agreeable picnic. One does not feel in the least cold, as the exercise so thoroughly warms and invigorates the system.

*The Ice Cone at the Falls of Montmorenci.* — This account of the sport of sliding down the Ice Cone at the Falls of Montmorenci is taken from a description written by an English traveller. A picnic party is made up at Quebec, and they drive out in sleighs to the Falls. The rest of the account we give in the writer's own words: —

"But here we are at the foot of the Falls of Montmorenci, and the Ice Cone is before us. 'What is this Ice Cone?' some one may ask. It is simply the frozen spray from the Falls, which, accumulating, becomes in a short time a solid mass of ice, and, before the winter months are over, reaches the height of seventy or eighty feet; in shape something like an inverted wine-glass without the stem. It is ascended by a series of rough steps cut in the side. At its base several chambers have been hewn out. One serves as a retiring-room for the ladies; another is devoted to the use of the men; and here, from a speculative Canadian, may be procured brandy and divers 'drinks' by all who choose to buy. Snug enough rooms they are, too, though the walls are of ice and the floors the same. Near the large cone is another, formed by the same agency, but smaller, through being more remote from the Fall, down which the ladies disport themselves. Few try the large one, albeit we have seen one or two who were bold enough to do so.

"But now for the ascent; and then — O, horror! — the descent. Several are already climbing the rough steps, and we join the toiling throng. In a few minutes we are at the summit, and arrived there we take a glance around. Far away the eye ranges over a snowy desert to the distant bank of the St. Lawrence and the gray hills of Maine, while nearer the white roofs of Quebec glisten in the cold rays of the wintry sun. Before us, in the middle distance, lies the Island of Orleans, its woody summits leafless, gaunt, and grim. Immediately beneath us traineaus are darting in all directions, or are being dragged back for another slide. Behind us is the cataract; its spray is falling in hard little pellets on our coats. Have a care! go not too near the Falls side of the Cone, lest you chance to slip over; if so, heaven rest your soul! for earth will never see you more; you would drop into the deep water at the foot of the Falls, and be carried under the ice, no man knows whither. Some half dozen unfortunates have in fact thus slipped, and so disappeared forever.

"And now to business. The man in front of us is just off; he slips over the side, and in an instant is out of sight. A few moments more and he reappears, shooting across the plain at a tremendous rate; in about half a mile his course is finished, and he and his guide (two little black specks in the distance) are seen returning for another trip. It is our turn next, and, before it comes, just a few words as to the emotions of a novice on making his first journey down the Cone. Its shape prevents a glance down the sides; except the limited area of its summit, no standing-room is visible within a circuit of perhaps three hundred yards. You are not in the habit of amusing yourself by sliding down the roof of a house, and you feel that you are on the eve of going through an exaggerated performance of that nature. Did not honor forbid, you might prefer returning by the ignominious but safer route you have just mounted by; but that is out of the question. In another minute, quitting your scanty foothold, you will be launched into space; there is no help for it — you must make the best of the inevitable! There is no time for hesitation, more sliders are arriving, and we must make room for others. 'Now, sare! all ready, sare?' inquired my red-capped guide. He is already seated on the front part of the traineau, his legs projected on each side, his heels dug into the ice to prevent an untimely start. I seat myself behind him, curl my legs round his waist, and place my feet between his knees; take a firm hold of the stern end of the traineau, and commend myself to the care of Providence and my Canadian friend. He lifts his heels — a slight push is given us behind, and — we are off!

"Ha, ha! The traineau starts and bounds clear into the air. I involuntary tighten my hold. We fall some ten feet, and, again touching the slippery surface, bound off again. Another drop, and we are on the more sloping side of the Cone; we fly down it breathless. In another instant we have reached the bottom; sharp icy splinters, ploughed up by the iron runners, hit us in the face, and sting as shot would; nothing stops us; we skim over the level at railway speed for some quarter of a mile or more, when, the acquired velocity exhausted, we roll off our quaint conveyance, shake the snow from our coats, and prepare to return.

"Reader, did you ever dream you had slipped over a cliff, and were helplessly falling — falling — falling — until, with a violent bump, you awake, as it were, at the bottom, more frightened than hurt? If so, you have experienced a very similar sensation to that of the first slide down the Ice Cone. The sport, as I have said before, is not entirely without danger; one man was killed and another had his leg broken during one winter I passed in Quebec, by the collision with the iron runners of the traineau. Still, accidents do not often happen, and after the disagreeable novelty of the first attempt is over, the bound into the air and lightning-rush become wonderfully exciting, and the Cone is a favorite resort all through the winter.

" With us, in this instance, the game grows fast and furious. The Cone is alive with an ascending and descending string of sliders; traineaus are darting in all directions over the plain, and tumbles in the snow are numerous. The ladies, too, on their lower eminence, are as busy as we, and are attended by the less adventurous or the more gallant of the men. Two Canadian gentlemen of our party astonish us. Not content with the excitement of the Cone, they climb the precipitous cliff, which, rising to the height of between two and three hundred feet, bounds the left bank of the Montmorenci River, below the Falls. About half-way up the rock they launch their traineaus. Good heavens! they will be dashed to pieces! Not at all. Rushing down with frightful speed, the impetus they have acquired carries them over the lesser and nearly to the summit of the principal Cone, when, turning, they slip down the side and glide like birds far away over the plain. This is a feat we are unable to emulate; but to Canadians, who are as handy with a traineau as a Madras Indian is with his catamaran, it is a trifle." — *Illustrated Family Almanac*, 1871.

*The Saguenay River.* — The Saguenay is the largest tributary to the great St. Lawrence, and unquestionably one of the most remarkable rivers on the continent. That portion of the river which extends from Ha-ha! Bay to the St. Lawrence, a distance of nearly sixty miles, is noted for the grandeur of its wonderful scenery. The river forces its way through dark, frowning, perpendicular cliffs of granite and sienite; one of them, Cape Trinity, towering up one thousand five hundred feet above the river, another near it, called Point d'Eternité, still more lofty. The depth of the river is remarkable. At one point it is, by measurement, one mile and a fourth in depth, at another a mile and a half. The shores are continuous bluffs, many of them towering perpendicularly into the air, seeming ready to totter and fall at any moment. It appears awful, in steaming up the Saguenay, to raise the eyes and behold hanging directly overhead a mass of granite weighing perhaps a million tons. Here, as at Niagara, we feel the insignificance of man, as we gaze upon the Almighty's handiworks.

## CHAPTER III.

### PLYMOUTH, MASSACHUSETTS.

THE fame of the founders of Plymouth has extended not only to the limits of Christendom, but even in the outlying lands of missionary effort has the story of their self-denial, their sufferings and sacrifices, their unfaltering trust, and their exuberant success, served to illustrate the principles they professed, and to recommend for universal adoption the gospel, their rule of faith and practice, which taught them, what all like them should learn, — that the severest trials man can endure are, "light affliction, which is but for a moment, and worketh for us a far more exceeding and eternal weight of glory."

The rock on which the Pilgrims landed has become sacred, and fragments of it are sought as emblems of the cross they voluntarily took up in furtherance of the great principles of political and religious freedom.

Plymouth presents a very picturesque appearance, being built on slopes and hill-sides, while several of its principal streets are terraced by lofty stone-walls.

The street first laid out by the Pilgrims, and on which their first houses — seven in number — were erected, is now known as "Leyden Street." The site was chosen with an eye to defence from the savages by whom they were surrounded. It extended westerly from the waters of the harbor, and terminated at a lofty hill (now called Burial Hill), where they erected a fort, the embanked outlines of which are still plainly marked. On the south side of the street the houses were placed; the rear being protected by the precipitous banks of "Town Brook."

From the top of Burial Hill is a fine view of the town, with its many objects of interest: the wide perspective of hills on the south, west, and north, and of the harbor on the east. Clark's Island, where the forefathers passed the Sunday prior to their final landing, is visible at a distance of about three miles. In a northeasterly direction is Duxbury, including the lofty landmark of Captain's Hill, once the residence of Miles Standish.

The first house of worship was erected in Town Square, but the precise spot is not indicated; it was near the churches now standing that the first assembly of the Puritans of New England gathered for the worship of God, and where church and congregation first called and settled a minister.

In the Town Square are five magnificent elms which were transplanted in 1784.

On the south side of Leyden Street, the dwelling well known as the residence of Mr. Samuel D. Holmes stands on the site of the first house erected in the colony.

Cole's Hill, easterly of the Burial Hill, and at a much less elevation, gives a near view of the harbor and of the immortal rock. It is supposed that the many who fell before the unaccustomed climate during the earlier years of the settlement, were buried on Cole's Hill; but, like that of the more ancient pilgrim, Moses, the place of their sepulture "knoweth no man unto this day." Surrounded as they were by savage tribes, it was a wise policy to conceal the extent of their losses.

> " The weary Pilgrim slumbers —
>     His resting place unknown —
> His eyes were closed, his hands were crossed,
>     The dust was o'er him thrown;
> The drifting soil, the mouldering leaf,
>     Along the sod were blown;
> His name has melted into earth;
>     His memory lives alone.
>
> " So let it live unfading,
>     The memory of the dead,
> Long as the pale anemone
>     Springs where their tears were shed;
> Or raining in the summer wind,
>     In flakes of burning red,
> The wild rose scatters with its leaves
>     The turf on which they bled.
>
> " Yes, till the frowning bulwarks
>     That guard this holy strand,
> Shall sink beneath the trampling surge,
>     In beds of sparkling sand, —
> While in the waste of ocean,
>     One hoary rock shall stand,
> Be this its latest legend, —
>     'Here was the Pilgrims' land!'"

In the office of the Registry of Deeds are carefully preserved many early documents, to which are affixed the autographs of several of those who came in the "Mayflower." The ink, better than more modern inks, yet retains its primitive blackness, and the writing is very legible.

While the war for independence was being waged, an effort was made by the towns-people to raise the venerated rock from its bed, with a view to removing it to Town

Square. During their efforts to dislodge it, a portion was broken off. The people hailed this accident as a favorable omen of the separation of the colonies from the mother country. The rock was suffered to remain in its original bed; the detached portion was removed to the southeastern quarter of the Town Square, near the great elm, where it remained until the building of Pilgrim Hall. It now reposes within the enclosed space in front of the hall, protected by an elliptical iron fence, on the panels of which are cast in raised letters the names of the Forefathers.

Pilgrim Hall contains the collected relics — the remaining household gods, as it were — of the Pilgrim Fathers: the chairs of Governors Carver and Bradford; various articles of furniture; the sword of Standish, — strength; and the silken sampler of Lorea, — beauty. One of the most touching exhibitions in the hall is that of the simple household goods and arms of the courteous, wise, but unfortunate sachem, Iyanough. In 1861, a ploughman near Hyannis (*Etym*. Iyanough's land, Iyanough's, Hyannis) struck an ancient brass kettle. About it were stone tools and utensils, and beneath it the bones of a man who had been buried in a sitting posture. A deed of land from Iyanough, for which the consideration was a brass kettle, served to identify the remains. On the walls of the hall are portraits of some eminent men of Plymouth, including Deacon Spooner, the noted wit, and Dr. James Thacher, whose "Annals of the Revolution" are well known.

A search among the many inscriptions on Burial Hill reveals but few names of the passengers in the "Mayflower." The vagueness of information with respect to the resting-places of the majority of the Pilgrims spreads a sanctity over the ancient town; and as we walk its streets, we are especially reminded of the line of Young, —

"Where is the dust that has not been alive?"

The following is an extract from a Discourse delivered at Plymouth, December 22d, 1820, in Commemoration of the First Settlement of New England, by Daniel Webster: —

"There is a local feeling, connected with this occasion, too strong to be resisted; a sort of *genius of the place*, which inspires and awes us. We feel that we are on the spot where the first scene of our history was laid; where the hearths and altars of New England were first placed where Christianity and civilization and letters made their first lodgment, in a vast extent of country, covered with a wilderness, and peopled with roving barbarians. We are here at the season of the year at which the event took place. The imagination irresistibly and rapidly draws around us the principal features and the leading characters in the original scene. We cast our eyes abroad on the ocean, and we see where the little barque, with the interesting group upon its deck, made its slow progress to the shore. We look around us, and behold the hills and promontories where the anxious eyes of our fathers first saw the places of habitation and of rest. We feel the cold which benumbed, and listen to the winds which pierced them. Beneath us is the Rock, on which New England received the feet of the Pilgrims. We seem even to behold them as they struggle with the elements, and, with toilsome efforts, gain the shore. We listen to the chiefs in council; we see the unexampled exhibition of female fortitude and resignation; we hear the whisperings of youthful impatience, and we see, what a painter of our own has also represented by his pencil, chilled and shivering childhood, houseless, but for a mother's arms, couchless, but for a mother's breast, till our own blood almost freezes. The mild dignity of Carver and of Bradford; the decisive and soldier-like air and manner of Standish; the devout Brewster; the enterprising Allerton; the general firmness and thoughtfulness of the whole band; their conscious joy for dangers escaped; their deep solicitude about dangers to come; their trust in heaven; their high religious faith, full of confidence and anticipation, — all these seem to belong to this place, and to be present on this occasion, to fill us with reverence and admiration.

"'If we conquer,' said the Athenian commander on the morning of the decisive day of Marathon, — 'If we conquer, we shall make Athens the greatest city of Greece.' A prophecy, how well fulfilled! 'If God prosper us,' might have been the more appropriate language of our Fathers, when they landed upon this Rock,— ' If God prosper us, we shall here begin a work which shall last for ages ; we shall plant here a new society, in the principles of the fullest liberty and the purest religion ; we shall subdue this wilderness which is before us; we shall fill this region of the great continent, which stretches almost from pole to pole, with civilization and Christianity; the temples of the true God shall rise, where now ascends the smoke of idolatrous sacrifice; fields and gardens, the flowers of summer and the waving and golden harvests of autumn, shall extend over a thousand hills, and stretch along a thousand valleys, never yet, since the creation, reclaimed to the use of civilized man. We shall whiten this coast with the canvas of a prosperous commerce; we shall stud the long and winding shore with an hundred cities. That which we sow in weakness shall be raised in strength. From our sincere but houseless worship there shall spring splendid temples to record God's goodness; from the simplicity of our social union, there shall arise wise and politic constitutions of government, full of the liberty which we ourselves bring and breathe; from our zeal for learning, institutions shall spring, which shall scatter the light of knowledge throughout the land, and, in time, paying back where they have borrowed, shall contribute their part to the great aggregate of human knowledge; and our descendants through all generations, shall look back to this spot, and to this hour, with unabated affection and regard. . . . .

"The hours of this day are rapidly flying, and this occasion will soon be passed. Neither we nor our children can expect to behold its return. They are in the distant regions of futurity, they exist only in the all-creating power of God, who shall stand here, a hundred years hence, to trace, through us, their descent from the pilgrims, and to survey, as we have now surveyed, the progress of their country during the lapse of a century. We would anticipate their concurrence with us in our sentiments of deep regard for our common ancestors. We would anticipate and partake the pleasure with which they will then recount the steps of New England's advancement. On the morning of that day, although it will not disturb us in our repose, the voice of acclamation and gratitude, commencing on the Rock of Plymouth, shall be transmitted through millions of the sons of the Pilgrims, till it lose itself in the murmurs of the Pacific seas.

"We would leave for the consideration of those who shall then occupy our places, some proof that we hold the blessings transmitted from our fathers in just estimation; some proof of our attachment to the cause of good government, and of civil and religious liberty; some proof of a sincere and ardent desire to promote everything which may enlarge the understanding and improve the hearts of men. And when, from the long distance of an hundred years, they shall look back upon us, they shall know, at least, that we possessed affections which, running backward, and warming with gratitude for what our ancestors have done for our happiness, run forward also to our posterity, and meet them with cordial salutation, ere yet they have arrived on the shore of Being.

"Advance, then, ye future generations! We would hail

you, as you rise in your long succession, to fill the places which we now fill, and to taste the blessings of existence, where we are passing, and soon shall have passed our own human duration. We bid you welcome to this pleasant land of the fathers. We bid you welcome to the healthful skies and the verdant fields of New England. We greet your accession to the great inheritance which we have enjoyed. We welcome you to the blessings of good government and religious liberty. We welcome you to the treasures of science and the delights of learning. We welcome you to the transcendent sweets of domestic life, to the happiness of kindred and parents and children. We welcome you to the immeasurable blessings of rational existence, the immortal hope of Christianity, and the light of everlasting truth!"

## CHAPTER IV.

### PROVINCETOWN, MASS.

BANCROFT asserts that Cape Cod was the "first spot in New England ever trod by *Englishmen*." On the 15th May, 1602, Gosnold found himself "embayed with a mighty headland." He anchored in fifteen fathoms, and his crew caught great plenty of codfish, from which circumstance he named the land *Cape Cod*. The captain went to land, and found the shore bold, and the sand very deep. A young indian, with plates of copper hanging in his ears, and a bow and arrow in his hand, came to him, and in a friendly manner offered his services.

It was on board the "Mayflower," in the harbor of this place, on Nov. 11, 1620, that the famous COMPACT was made by which the Pilgrim Fathers of New England instituted Constitutional Republican government in this country. The document is so important that we give it entire, save the signatures, — forty-one in number.

"In the name of God, amen. We whose names are under written, the loyal subjects of our dread sovereign lord, King James, by the grace of God, of Great Britain, France and Ireland, King, Defender of the Faith, &c. Having undertaken for the glory of God, and advancement of the christian faith, and the honour of our King and country, a voyage to plant the first colony in the northern parts of Virginia; do by these presents solemnly and mutually, in the presence of God and one another, covenant and combine ourselves together into a civil body politick, for our better ordering and preservation, and furtherance of the ends aforesaid: and by virtue hereof, do enact, constitute and frame such just and equal laws, ordinances, acts, constitutions and officers, from time to time, as shall be thought most meet and convenient for the general good of the colony; into which we promise all due submission and obedience. In witness whereof, we have hereunto subscribed our names, at Cape Cod, the eleventh of November, in the reign of our Sovereign Lord, King James, of England, France and Ireland, the eighteenth, and of Scotland the fifty-fourth, Anno. Dom. 1620."

Provincetown is unique. Situated as it is on the inner shore of the Cape, with sand-hills between it and the outer shore, it of necessity occupies, for the most part, a single street, which is about two miles in length. Forty or fifty years since, a person on entering the harbor first noticed a long row of boats anchored near the shore. Behind these, just above the reach of the tide, was a long row of wind-mills, by means of which sea-water was pumped up into shallow vats, for the making of salt by solar evaporation. Among and beyond the salt-vats were flakes for curing fish; then came the long street of clean, deep, white beach sand, along which — some supported on skids to avoid the drifting sand — were the houses and shops of the inhabitants. Cultivation was unknown, — there was no soil to cultivate.

Among the sand-hills was an extensive tract of pond and swamp intermingled, known as "Shank-painter Pond." About 1836 a Mr. Thomas Lothrop took possession of this tract, and commenced the cultivation of cranberries, — having prepared the ground by shovelling sand into the pond. Prior to his time there was but one horse kept in the town, and but two or three cows. Mr. Lothrop created fresh meadow. Others did the same. Loam was brought in, in vessels. Gardens were commenced. The fish cast up on the shore, or caught in seines, furnished a good "superphosphate." When the surplus revenue was divided, Provincetown, with its dividend, built a plank sidewalk the whole length of their main street. The place is wealthy from the product of its fisheries, and there is no limit to its public spirit. A railroad from Boston already extends beyond Orleans, on the Cape, and, at this time, it is rapidly pushing to Provincetown.

A fine structure, which serves for a town-house and a high school, stands on the top of "High Pole Hill," — a very conspicuous landmark, "known to every sailor, and visited by every wind that blows."

## CHAPTER V.

### BOSTON AND VICINITY.

BOSTON was originally "by the Indians called Shawmut"; but the colonists of 1630 named it Trimountaine. Charlestown, which was occupied by them in July, 1630, was abandoned because there was found no good spring of water; and the peninsula close by, having been bought, the settlement was transferred thither on the seventh of September. On the same day, the court ordered, that Trimountaine should be called Boston, in memory of Boston in Old England, from which many of the colonists had emigrated.

The name Trimountaine, which has been transformed into Tremont, was peculiarly appropriate. As seen from Charlestown, the peninsula seemed to consist of three high hills, and the highest of the three was itself a tri-mountain, having three sharp little peaks.

To the early history of Boston we are indebted for some of the most quaint and interesting pictures of early New-England life.

"The General Court" combined in itself all the prerogatives which are now distributed among various branches of civil and ecclesiastical government: it made laws, and interpreted them; it arraigned criminals, tried and sentenced them. The *range* of its functions was marvellous. It decided questions of church polity, settled points of theological discussion; it regulated domestic economy, told men what they should eat, and how much they might drink; it was the arbiter of fashion, prescribed the width of sleeves, the size of wigs, the fineness of lace; it watched over the private, as well as the public, talk of men and women, and took vigorous measures to restrain the garrulity of the latter; it called to its bar those who lived idly, as well as those who lived viciously. Perhaps the most unique performance it ever took in hand was the summoning of a body of Indians to be catechised as to their willingness to keep the Ten Commandments. The replies of these old heathen evince not a little shrewdness. When inquired of as to the worship of God, they answered: "We desire to reverence the God of the English, because we see he doth better to the English than other Gods do to others." A promise being exacted of them not to do any work on the Sabbath day, they replied:

"That is easy for us who have not much work to do on any day, and we will take this care on that day."

The first meeting-house erected in Boston was a humble structure, of which nothing is known, except the walls were covered with mud and the roof was covered with thatch. In 1676, we find the following singular enactment: "Ordered, that hereafter no pew shall be built *with a door into the street.*" Considering the infirmities of human nature, it is not very strange that the less godly among the people should have caused these private doors to be cut in the side of the meeting-house, and occasionally escape thereby from the long services inflicted upon them. For, when it came to prayers and sermons stretching through a whole day, and never ceasing until the going down of the sun, — *relays* of ministers being on hand to take up the doctrine as one after another gave out, — and when we consider still further, that all able-bodied persons were obliged to be present at public worship, under severe penalties for unnecessary absence, it is difficult to avoid having some little sympathy with those feeble folk who "built their pews with doors in the street."

Boston was from the first a commercial town. At the close of the seventeenth century it was the largest and wealthiest town in America, and now it ranks next to New York in commercial importance. The influence of Harvard College, in Cambridge, has ever been strong upon Boston; but a public school was voted by the town in 1635, three years before Harvard was founded. Here the first newspaper published on the continent, the "Boston News Letter," appeared in 1704.

All are familiar with the most honorable record of events in Boston, preceding and during the Revolutionary War: the resistance of the Stamp Act; the Boston Massacre; the destruction of tea in Boston Harbor; the sufferings and heroism of the people while the town was occupied by the

British; their joy when their deliverance was effected and the place was taken by Washington, and their unbounded patriotism throughout the war.

During the war of 1812, Massachusetts furnished more men than any other State. Again, in the war of the Rebellion, Boston alone sent to the army and navy 26,119 men, of whom 685 were commissioned officers.

Boston, at the present time the second commercial city in the United States, has a population of over 250,000. Hardly a vestige of the Boston in its first century remains. The face of the country has been completely transformed. The hills have been cut down, and the flats surrounding the peninsula have been filled, so that it is a peninsula no longer. The streets which were formerly so narrow and crooked as to give point to the joke that they were laid out on the paths made by the cows in going to pasture, have been widened, graded, and straightened. South and East Boston, Roxbury and Dorchester have been added to the original limits of Boston, so that now the present area of the city is ten thousand one hundred and seventy acres, — nearly fifteen times as great as the original area.

Of the few relics that remain of the olden time, the most conspicuous and the most famous is

*Faneuil Hall*, — so often, and so appropriately called, the "Cradle of Liberty." The building was a gift to the town by Peter Faneuil in 1742. Its object was a public market and a town hall. In 1761 it was destroyed by fire, but immediately rebuilt by the town. In the stirring events which preceded the Revolution, it was put to frequent use. The spirited speeches and resolutions uttered and adopted within it were a most potent agency in exciting the patriotism of all the American colonists. In every succeeding great crisis in our country's history, thousands of citizens have assembled beneath this roof to listen to the patriotic eloquence of their leaders and counsellors. The great Hall is peculiarly fitted for popular assemblies. It is seventy-six feet square, and twenty-eight feet high. The floor is entirely destitute of seats, by which means the capacity of the hall, if not the comfort of the audiences, is greatly increased. Numerous large and valuable portraits adorn the walls, — an original full-length painting of Washington, by Stuart; another of the donor of the building, by Col. Henry Sargent; Healy's great picture of Webster replying to Hayne; excellent portraits of Samuel Adams, and the second President Adams; of General Warren, Edward Everett, Abraham Lincoln, and others prominent in the history of Massachusetts and the Union. The Hall is never let for money, but is at the disposal of the people whenever a sufficient number of persons, complying with certain regulations, ask to have it opened.

*The State House.*—Among the public buildings of the city, this, from its position, is most conspicuous. It stands on the summit of Beacon Hill, fronting the Common. It was erected in 1798, on ground termed in the grant, "Governor Hancock's pasture." The edifice is surmounted by a dome fifty feet in diameter and thirty feet high, the summit of which is one hundred and twenty feet from the ground. Within the rotunda hours may be spent by the stranger in examining the objects that deserve attention. Here is the fine statue of Washington, by Chantrey; here the battle-flags borne by Massachusetts soldiers in the war against Rebellion. Also, relics of the olden time, and busts of distinguished men. From the ceiling of the Hall of Representatives we find suspended the ancient codfish, emblem of the direction taken by Massachusetts industry in the early times. The view from the cupola is unsurpassed by anything in the United States, if not in the world. Every portion of the city is before the eye of the beholder. The harbor is spread out towards the east, embosoming a multitude of islands, and whitened with a thousand sails. On the other hand is an illimitable expanse of country adorned with fruitful fields, and everywhere dotted over with elegant villas and flourishing villages, while to the north towers Bunker-Hill Monument, marking the place where the first great battle of the Revolution was fought.

*The City Hall.* — This elegant building was completed in 1865, at the cost of more than half a million. The material of the exterior is of the finest Concord granite. The interior is equally as perfect in its arrangement as is the exterior in beauty and richness. The Louvre dome, which is surmounted by an American eagle and a flagstaff, is occupied within by some of the most important offices of the city. Here is the central point of the fire-alarm telegraphs. An alarm from the most distant part of the city is communicated instantaneously to the watchful operator, who is on duty day and night, and at once the bells in all parts of the city are tolling out the number of the district in which the fire has been discovered, and the engines are proceeding at full speed towards it. All the officers of the city have commodious and comfortable quarters within the building.

*The Custom House.* — Situated on State Street, and near the head of Long Wharf. It was begun in 1837, and was twelve years in building. The walls, columns, and even the entire roof are of granite. It is built in the form of a cross, and surmounted by a dome. The foundations rest on three thousand piles. Massive columns entirely surround the building, and are thirty-two in number, — each a single stone, costing about five thousand dollars. The entire cost of the building was upwards of a million of dollars.

*The Merchants Exchange.* — This is a magnificent fire-proof building, situated on the south side of State Street. The front is composed of Quincy granite, with five pilasters, each a single stone forty-five feet high. The roof is wrought iron. The great central hall is occupied by the Sub-Treasury of the United States. In the basement is the city Post-office, soon to be removed to

*The New Post-Office*, which when completed will be the finest public building in New England. It has a front of over two hundred feet on Devonshire Street, and occupies a whole square. When the corner-stone was laid, Oct. 16, 1871, the President of the United States, and several members of his cabinet, were present to add interest to the occasion.

*Boston Music Hall.* — Of the many places of amusement and entertainment with which Boston abounds, we have space to mention only three, — the Music Hall, Boston Museum, and Boston Theatre.

Standing on Tremont Street at the head of Hamilton Place, and looking down the place, one may see a plain and lofty brick wall without ornament or architectural pretension. This building is the Boston Music Hall, one of the noblest public halls in the world, and the pride of every music lover of Boston. The hall was first opened to the public in 1852. It would require more space than can be devoted to the subject to give even a list of the great singers and famous lecturers whose voices have been heard within its walls. It is safe to say that in no other single hall in the country have so many and so choice programmes of music been performed, and no other hall has furnished a platform for so many distinguished orators during the past twenty years. It is one hundred and thirty feet in length, seventy-eight in breadth, and sixty-five in height. No one who has been inside the hall needs to be told of its architectural beauty, its spaciousness, or the brilliant and beautiful light shed down from the hundreds of gas jets which encircle the wall far above the upper balcony. The fine statue of Apollo, the admirable casts presented by Miss Cushman, and, above all, the magnificent statue of Beethoven by Crawford, deserve the attention of every visitor. But all these works are speedily forgotten in the presence of the glorious instrument, — the "Great Organ," the chief ornament and attraction of the Music Hall. It was built in Ludwigslust, in Germany, and cost over $60,000. It has eighty-nine stops, and nearly six thousand pipes. Its entire height is sixty feet, breadth forty-eight feet, and depth twenty-four feet. Its architecture is exceedingly rich and appropriate, it is in all its parts most perfect, and on the whole the largest organ in the country.

*Boston Museum.* — It is situated on Tremont Street, and is one of the oldest places of amusement in Boston. The museum proper is very large and interesting, filled with curiosities and works of art. The theatre is large, and the "star" system is wholly discarded. This theatre is a very great favorite, and has long been known as the "Orthodox Theatre."

*Boston Theatre.* — This is the largest regular place of amusement in New England, and one of the finest. This is the house usually engaged for the representation of Italian, German, and English Operas. Most of the great American actors, and many distinguished foreigners, have appeared on this stage. Among a host of others, we mention only the names of Jefferson and Owens, Booth and Forrest, Ristori and Janauschek, Nilsson and Parepa Rosa, Kellogg and Phillips.

*The Public Library.* — Situated on Boylston Street, and facing the Common, is the elegant building which contains the largest library, save one, in the country. This immense library, which has been collected in the short space of twenty years, is valuable, not only from the variety, excellence, and number of the volumes it contains, but from its accessibility. It is absolutely open to all, and no assessment is made upon those who make use of its privileges. It is conducted on most liberal principles. If a purchasable book, not in the library, is asked for, it is ordered at once; and the inquirer for it, is notified when it is received. The total number of volumes at the date of the last report was 192,958, and of pamphlets, 100,383. The circulation, during the previous year, amounted to 380,343 separate issues. The Boston Public Library is thus the first on the continent in the number of issues, although it is exceeded in the number of volumes by the Library of Congress.

We have spoken of a few of the more prominent of the public buildings of Boston. It would be impossible even to mention all that are of great interest to the visitor. Thoroughfares are lined with elegant and substantial structures, spacious avenues with costly dwellings, each several building of which were worthy a description.

Boston contains a great number of literary, educational, and scientific institutions, — the Boston Athenæum, rapidly becoming one of the most richly endowed and splendid literary institutions in the world; the Massachusetts Historical Society; the American Academy of Arts and Sciences; the Medical College connected with Harvard University; the Lowell Institute, and many other similar societies.

Boston is a city of churches. It has nearly one hundred and fifty church edifices of various denominations. The oldest of these is Christ Church (Episcopal), built in 1723. Next in age is the Old South Church, erected in 1730. This is perhaps the most noted church building in the United States. It is internally very quaint and interesting. Its sounding-board over the pulpit, its high, square box-pews, its double tier of galleries, in fact its whole appearance, attract the visitor's attention. The Old South is frequently mentioned in histories of Boston, before and during the Revolution. Here were held the series of meetings that culminated in the destruction of the detested tea, on which the colonists would pay no tax. In 1775, the British soldiers occupied this building as a place for cavalry drill. They established a grog-shop in the lower gallery. They covered the floor with about two feet of dirt. In 1782 the building was thoroughly repaired. This meeting-house was chosen, in 1712, as the place in which to have the annual election sermon preached before the Governor and General Court, and the ancient custom is still observed.

A chapter could well be written on the number, elegance, and magnificent proportions of Boston Hotels. We can only name a few of the most prominent: the American House, the largest Hotel in New England; the Revere House, which has entertained more distinguished men than any other in Boston, — the Prince of Wales, President Grant, and the Grand Duke Alexis have been its guests; the Parker House, said to be by Charles Dickens the best hotel he had known in America; the Tremont House; Continental Hotel; Hotel Boylston; and St. James.

*Boston Common.* — There is nothing in Boston of which Bostonians are more truly proud than of the Common. Other cities have more pretentious public grounds, but none of them can boast of a park of greater natural beauty, or better suited to the purposes to which it is put. There are no magnificent drives, for teams are not admitted within the sacred precincts. Everything is of the plainest and homeliest character. A part of the Common is left to itself, and is as barren as the feet of ten thousand youthful ball-players can make it. There is the Frog Pond, with its fountain, where boys may sail their miniature ships at their own sweet will. There is the deer-park, a popular resort for the youngest of the visitors. All the malls and paths are shaded by fine old trees. On summer evenings the throng of promenaders is very great, and thus testifies to the value placed by all classes upon this opportunity to get a breath of fresh air in the heart of the city. The Old Elm is perhaps the chief object of interest. This great tree is certainly the oldest known tree in New England. It was large enough to find a place on the map engraved in 1722, and on the great branch broken off by the gale of 1860 could be easily counted nearly two hundred rings, carrying the age of that branch back to 1670. Various other gales have greatly mutilated it, and limbs have been restored to their former places at great cost, and a number are now secured by iron bands and bars.

*Public Gardens.* — A large part of what is now the beautiful and attractive Public Gardens was once covered by the tides, and the rest was known as "the marsh at the foot of the Common." For many years it was used for a ropewalk, and not until 1859 did it become the inalienable property of the city. Since that time much has been done to adorn and beautify it, and it is now a favorite resort. The area is about twenty-one acres. The pond in the centre is laboriously irregular in shape, and wholly artificial. There are several interesting works of art in the Public Garden. There is a small but very beautiful statue of Venus rising from the sea; a statue in bronze of the late Edward Everett; but the most conspicuous of all is the great equestrian statue of Washington, regarded by many as the finest piece of the kind in America.

*Old Granary Burying-Ground.* — In one of the busiest parts of Boston lies this ancient landmark; it is bounded by

Beacon, Tremont, and Park Streets. It is the most interesting of old Boston grave-yards. Within the little enclosure lie the remains of some of the most eminent men in the history of the country. Nine Governors of the colony and State; two of the signers of the Declaration of Independence; Paul Revere; Peter Faneuil; and many others familiar to students of American history. On the front of one of the tombs is a small white marble slab with the inscription, "No. 16. Tomb of Hancock," which is all that marks the resting-place of the first signer of the Declaration of Independence. In another part is the grave of the great Revolutionary patriot, Samuel Adams.

*Bunker-Hill Monument.* — No other city in the country can boast of such suburbs as Boston. Pre-eminent in importance among the objects of notice outside of the city is the grand monument in Charlestown, erected to commemorate the battle of Bunker Hill. It stands on Breed's Hill, usually called Bunker Hill, near the spot where the brave Warren fell. The corner-stone was laid by Marquis La Fayette, on the fiftieth anniversary of the battle. Eighteen years afterwards it was completed, and the oration at its dedication was delivered by Daniel Webster. It consists of a plain granite shaft, two hundred and twenty feet high. Within is a winding stairway, by which it is ascended to a chamber immediately under the apex, containing four windows, which afford a magnificent panoramic view of the surrounding country. In this chamber are two of the four cannon which constituted the whole train of field artillery possessed by the Americans at the commencement of the Revolutionary War.

The following is an extract from an Address delivered at the laying of the Corner-Stone of the Bunker-Hill Monument, by Daniel Webster: —

"We know, indeed, that the record of illustrious actions is most safely deposited in the universal remembrance of mankind. We know, that if we could cause this structure to ascend, not only till it reached the skies, but till it pierced them, its broad surfaces could still contain but part of that which, in an age of knowledge, hath already been spread over the earth, and which history charges itself with making known to all future times. We know, that no inscription on entablatures less broad than the earth itself, can carry information of the events we commemorate, where it has not already gone ; and that no structure, which shall not outlive the duration of letters and knowledge among men, can prolong the memorial. But our object is, by this edifice, to show our own deep sense of the value and importance of the achievements of our ancestors; and, by presenting this work of gratitude to the eye, to keep alive similar sentiments, and to foster a constant regard for the principles of the Revolution. Human beings are composed, not of reason only, but of imagination also, and sentiment; and that is neither wasted nor misapplied which is appropriated to the purpose of giving right direction to sentiments, and opening proper springs of feeling in the heart. Let it not be supposed that our object is to perpetuate national hostility, or even to cherish a mere military spirit. It is higher, purer, nobler. We consecrate our work to the spirit of national independence, and we wish that the light of peace may rest upon it forever. We rear a memorial of our conviction of that unmeasured benefit which has been conferred on our own land, and of the happy influences which have been produced, by the same events, on the general interests of mankind. We come, as Americans, to mark a spot which must forever be dear to us and our posterity. We wish, that whosoever, in all coming time, shall turn his eye hither, may behold that the place is not undistinguished where the first great battle of the Revolution was fought. We wish, that this structure may proclaim the magnitude and importance of that event, to every class and every age. We wish, that infancy may learn the purpose of its erection from maternal lips, and that weary and withered age may behold it, and be solaced by the recollections which it suggests. We wish, that labor may look up here, and be proud in the midst of its toil. We wish, that, in those days of disaster, which, as they come on all nations, must be expected to come on us also, desponding patriotism may turn its eyes hitherward, and be assured that the foundations of our national power still stand strong. We wish, that this column, rising towards heaven among the pointed spires of so many temples dedicated to God, may contribute also to produce, in all minds, a pious feeling of dependence and gratitude. We wish, finally, that the last object on the sight of him who leaves his native shore, and the first to gladden his who revisits it, may be something which shall remind him of the liberty and the glory of his country. Let it rise, till it meet the sun in his coming; let the earliest light of the morning gild it, and parting day linger and play on its summit. . . .

" We have the happiness to rejoice here in the presence of a most worthy representation of the survivors of the whole Revolutionary army.

" Veterans! you are the remnant of many a well-fought field. You bring with you marks of honor from Trenton and Monmouth, from Yorktown, Camden, Bennington, and Saratoga. Veterans of half a century! when, in your youthful days, you put everything at hazard in your country's cause, good as that cause was, and sanguine as youth is, still your fondest hopes did not stretch onward to an hour like this! At a period to which you could not reasonably have expected to arrive; at a moment of national prosperity such as you could never have foreseen, you are now met here to enjoy the fellowship of old soldiers, and to receive the overflowings of an universal gratitude.

"But your agitated countenances and your heaving breasts inform me that even this is not an unmixed joy. I perceive that a tumult of contending feeling rushes upon you. The images of the dead, as well as the persons of the living, throng to your embraces. The scene overwhelms you, and I turn from it. May the Father of all mercies smile upon your declining years, and bless them! And when you shall here have exchanged your embraces; when you shall once more have pressed the hands which have been so often extended to give succor in adversity, or grasped in the exultation of victory, then look abroad into this lovely land, which your young valor defended, and mark the happiness with which it is filled; yea, look abroad into the whole earth, and see what a name you have contributed to give to your country, and what a praise you have added to freedom, and then rejoice in the sympathy and gratitude which beams upon your last days, from the improved condition of mankind."

*Harvard College.* — Cambridge is the site of the most famous, as well as the most ancient university in the country. It was but six years after the settlement of Boston, that the General Court appropriated four hundred pounds for the establishment of a college at Newton, as Cambridge was then called. Two years after, the institution received the liberal bequest of eight hundred pounds from the estate of Rev. John Harvard, of Charlestown. The College was named after its generous benefactor, and the name of the town was changed to Cambridge, Mr. Harvard having been educated at Cambridge in Old England.

The College was thus placed on a firm foundation, and by good management, and the almost lavish generosity of alumni and other friends, it has assumed and steadily maintained the leading position among the colleges of the country, its only rival being Yale. The college long ago became a university. Schools of law, medicine, dentistry, theology, science, mining, and agriculture have been established in connection with it. The widest liberty prevails here in the matter of religious belief, and every student has the right to attend whatever church he or his parents may choose, provided he attend "stated worship" *somewhere.*

The college yard contains a little more than twenty-two acres, and nearly the whole available space is occupied by the numerous buildings required by an institution of such magnitude.

The number of students in all branches of the university, by the latest catalogue, was 1,214. There are nine libraries connected with the institution, containing in all 192,000 volumes.

Besides the distinguished men of science whom the college summons to her halls, Cambridge is the home of three of the foremost of American poets, — Longfellow, Lowell, and Holmes, — and they all are or have been professors in the university.

*Mount Auburn.* — This renowned and beautiful cemetery is situated about a mile west of Harvard University. It comprises an area of about one hundred and twenty-five acres. The surface is remarkably diversified, giving unusual opportunities to the landscape gardener to improve the natural beauty of the scenery. There are several sheets of water, and high hills and deep vales in abundance. A natural growth of forest-trees covers a large portion of the grounds, adding a simple, majestic, and most appropriate ornament to this hallowed spot, over which are scattered tombs and monuments, most costly and elegant, and of the most various and exquisite workmanship. The entrance of the cemetery is a massive gateway in the Egyptian style, and near by is a very beautiful chapel, in which are performed the funeral services. — *Boston Illustrated.*

*Eddystone and Minot's Ledge Lighthouses.* — The Eddystone Lighthouse is the most distinguished in the world, both on account of the difficulties attending its construction, and the fact that it is the type of all structures of the kind which have since been erected. Several lighthouses had been erected on the Eddystone rocks, in the English channel, about fourteen miles S. S. W. from the port of Plymouth, and each in turn had been swept away in terrible storms, and not a remnant of the lighthouses nor a trace of the inmates was ever seen afterward.

In 1756 Smeaton was selected to rebuild the Eddystone. He determined to use stone for the material, and the shape of the trunk of a large tree as his model. The stones were joined by dovetailing, and the different courses were connected by stone dowels. The work was finished 1759. It has stood for more than a hundred years, a monument of the skill of the designer and builder, and an example to all engineers.

Minot's Ledge Lighthouse is erected on the outer rock of a ledge lying off the town of Cohasset. It is situated about eight miles E. S. E. of Boston Light, and is a projecting point very dangerous to vessels coming into Boston from seaward. The difficulties of erecting a lighthouse on this rock cannot be exaggerated. The attention of commercial men and mariners was drawn to the dangers of this point many years ago, and in 1847 an appropriation was made by Congress for the construction of a lighthouse on the rock. It was determined to erect an iron pile structure, at the top of which was to be the keeper's dwelling, and this was to be surmounted by the lantern enclosing the illuminat'ng apparatus. The plan of the work was an octagon, the side of which at the base was nine and a half feet, the diameter of the circumscribing circle, twenty-five feet. Iron piles, ten inches in diameter where they leave the rock, were inserted five feet into it, at each angle of the octagon and at its centre. These were firmly braced and tied together by wrought-iron braces. At a height of fifty-five feet above the highest point of the rock, the heads of the piles were firmly secured to a heavy casting. Above this casting the floor of the dwelling was placed. The structure was finished in the autumn of 1849, and stood until April 15th, 1851, when it was carried away by one of the most terrific storms that had ever occurred on the Atlantic coast. All of the iron piles were twisted off at short distances above their feet. At the time of its destruction, the spray in the bay, and the consequent impossibility of seeing any object from the land, prevented the time of its demolition from being noticed, and the only two who witnessed its destruction have carried their knowledge with them to a watery grave.

In 1852, Congress appropriated money for rebuilding the lighthouse, and a design was originated by the Lighthouse Board and approved by the Secretary of the Treasury early in 1855. The design was for a granite tower in the shape of the frustum of a cone. The base is thirty feet in diameter, and the whole height of the stone-work is eighty-eight feet. The lower forty feet are solid. The stones of the courses are dovetailed in the securest manner. The work was commenced early in the season of 1855, and an idea of the difficulties to be overcome may be formed from the fact, that although every moment in which it was possible to work upon the rock was taken advantage of, it was not until the last part of the season of 1857 that any stones were laid, the whole of the intervening time having been taken up in levelling the foundation bed. In the season of 1857 four stones were laid, in 1858 six entire courses were laid, and in 1859 the whole of the solid portion of the structure and half of the remainder, making a total height of sixty feet, were placed. It was first lighted in the fall of 1859.

*Minot's Ledge.*

  Like spectral hounds across the sky
   The white clouds scud before the storm,
  And naked in the howling night
   The red-eyed lighthouse lifts its form.
  The waves with slippery fingers clutch
   The massive tower, and climb and fall,
  And, muttering, growl with baffled rage
   Their curses on the sturdy wall.

  Up in the lonely tower he sits,
   The keeper of the crimson light;
  Silent and awe-struck does he hear
   The imprecations of the night.
  The white spray beats against the panes
   Like some wet ghost that down the air
  Is hunted by a troop of fiends,
   And seeks a shelter anywhere.

  He prays aloud — the lonely man
   For every soul that night at sea,
  But more than all for that brave boy
   Who used to gayly climb his knee, —
  Young Charley, with the chestnut hair
   And hazel eyes and laughing lip;
  "May heaven look down," the old man cries,
   "Upon my son, and on his ship!"

  While thus with pious heart he prays,
   Far in the distance sounds a boom —
  He pauses, and again there rings
   That sullen thunder through the room.
  A ship upon the shoal to-night,
   She cannot hold for one half hour —
  But clear the ropes and grappling-hooks,
   And trust in the Almighty power!

On the drenched gallery he stands,
  Striving to pierce the solid night;
Across the sea the red eye throws
  A steady crimson wake of light.
And where it falls upon the waves
  He sees a human head float by,
With long, drenched curls of chestnut hair,
  And wild but fearless hazel eye.

Out with the hooks! one mighty fling!
  Adown the wind the long rope curls.
O! will it catch? Ah! dread suspense,
  While the wild ocean wilder whirls.
A steady pull, — it tautens now!
  O, his old heart will burst with joy,
As on the slippery rocks he pulls
  The breathing body of his boy!

Still sweep the spectres through the sky,
  Still scud the clouds before the storm,
Still naked in the howling night
  The red-eyed lighthouse lifts its form.
Without, the world is wild with rage,
  Unkennelled demons are abroad;
But with the father and the son
  Within, there is the peace of God.
                    — *Fitz James O'Brien.*

---

## CHAPTER VI.

### LOWELL.

OF Massachusetts cities, Lowell ranks next to Boston in population and importance. It is the principal cotton-manufacturing town of New England, and is situated on the Merrimac River, near the mouth of the Concord, twenty-five miles northwest from Boston. The almost unrivalled advantages which Lowell enjoys for manufacturing are derived from a descent of about thirty-three feet in the Merrimac

River, known as Pawtucket Falls, which, by the aid of several canals, furnishes about twelve thousand horse-power. The first canal was an enterprise of Newburyport merchants and ship-builders to raft lumber around the falls, a distance of one and a half miles. In 1821 the water-power attracted the attention of some Boston capitalists, who bought up the neighboring farms and the interest in the old canal, which they enlarged and reconstructed. They also laid out town-lots and mill-sites, which were sold as rapidly as the growth of the town required. It was named for Francis C. Lowell, of Boston, who first interested himself in the enterprise of introducing cotton manufacturing into the United States in 1811–14. In 1864 there were thirteen manufacturing corporations in Lowell, owning fifty-four mills, and employing an aggregate capital of $13,850,000. The number of yards of cloth produced per week were, 2,394,000 of cotton, 44,000 of wool, and 25,000 of carpeting. All the mills are heated by steam and lighted by gas.

Besides manufactories for cotton and woollen goods, there are other extensive manufacturing establishments, most prominent of which are: the Lowell Machine Shop, with a capital of $600,000; Lowell Bleaching Corporation, capital $300,000; and the Medical Laboratory of J. C. Ayer & Co., one of the most extensive in the United States. The cost of drugs, sugar, and spirit used yearly in this laboratory amounts to $647,180; also, the proprietors spend $60,000 annually in advertising, besides circulating about 5,000,000 almanacs.

The site of the city has many inequalities, but the streets are regularly laid out, and contain many elegant houses.

The Sixth Massachusetts Regiment, principally from Lowell, was the first to enter the field in response to the call of President Lincoln (April 15th, 1861) for 75,000 volunteers. The regiment left Lowell on the 16th; on the 19th was attacked by a mob in Baltimore, and two of its members,

Ladd and Whitney, both of Lowell, were killed. A monument to the memory of these first martyrs of the great American Rebellion has been erected in a public square in the heart of the city.

## CHAPTER VII.

### NEW HAVEN.

NEW HAVEN, one of the capitals of Connecticut, is situated on New Haven Bay, four miles from Long Island Sound. It is the twenty-fifth city of the Union, with a population of 50,000. In 1637, several influential and wealthy Englishmen came to New England, seeking a place to found a colony. They chose the beautiful plain on the Quinnipiac, the present site of New Haven. The settlers were stern, uncompromising Puritans, who visited the slightest offences with the severest punishments. They were the authors of the celebrated and curious "Blue Laws," a few of which we give: —

"No one shall run on the Sabbath day, or walk in his garden, or elsewhere, except reverently to and from meeting.

"No one shall travel, cook victuals, make beds, sweep house, cut hair, or shave on the Sabbath day.

"No woman shall kiss her children on Sabbath or fasting day.

"The Sabbath shall begin at sunset on Saturday.

"To pick an ear of corn growing in a neighbor's garden shall be deemed theft.

"Whosoever wears clothes trimmed with gold, silver, or bone lace, above 1s. per yard, shall be presented by the grand jurors, and the selectmen shall tax the offender £300 estate.

" Whosoever brings cards or dice into this dominion shall pay a fine of £5.

" No one shall read common prayer books, keep Christmas or set days, eat mince pies, dance, play cards, or play on any instrument of music except the drum, trumpet and Jew's harp.

" The selectmen on finding children ignorant may take them away from their parents, and put them in better hands at the expense of their parents.

" A wife shall be deemed good evidence against her husband.

"No man shall court a maid in person or by letter, without first obtaining consent of her parents; £5 penalty for the first offence; £10 for the second; and for the third, imprisonment during the pleasure of the court."

New Haven was "a city of refuge" for Generals Goffe and Whalley and Colonel Dixwell, three of the English regicides. They were kindly received by the people, but could not appear in public for fear of capture. For some time they were concealed in a cave on West Rock, and often narrowly escaped being taken; once they were under the bridge over which their pursuers passed. A marble monument in the rear of Centre Church marks the resting-place of Colonel Dixwell. Generals Whalley and Goffe at last found shelter in Rev. John Russell's house in Hadley, in which town, it is certain, Whalley died about 1676. Goffe died probably in 1680. Benedict Arnold was a resident of New Haven and the captain of the Governor's Guards, with whom he started for Lexington, immediately after the news of the battle. New Haven suffered equally with its sister towns of the seaboard during the Revolution. In the summer of 1779 it was invaded by General Tryon, who, after being stubbornly and bravely resisted by the militia, took possession of the place, and sacked it.

The pride and glory of New Haven are its noble elms. No city in the world can exhibit such grand old shade-trees. Well does it bear the graceful title, "The City of Elms." The people are indebted for these to the efforts of Hon. James Hillhouse, who planted them, near the close of the eighteenth century. The rows on each side of Temple Street interlock their branches, forming a complete arch, which reminds one, viewing the intricate tracery of the rugged limbs against the background of dark foliage, of the vaulted roof of some old cathedral, with the massive trunks for pillars. New Haven might also be called the city of parks, for they are many and attractive. The "Green," where several churches and the state-house stand, is the largest. The general feature of the country — a plain intersected with low ranges of hills — gives a pleasing variety to the landscape, and furnishes handsome drives around the city.

East and West Rocks are two bold and rugged cliffs, which stand as sentinels on each side of the city. One thus speaks of a visit to the former: —

> "'The morning dawn'd with tokens of a storm —
> A muddy cloud athwart the eastern sky
> Glow'd with omens of a tempest near;'

Yet I ventured to stroll out to East Rock, two miles east-northeast of the city. Crossing the bridge at the factory owned by the late Eli Whitney, inventor of the cotton gin, I toiled up the steep slope through the woods to the summit of the rock, nearly four hundred feet above the plain below. This rock is the southern extremity of the Mount Tom range of hills. It lies contiguous to a similar amorphous mass called West Rock, and both are composed principally of hornblende and feldspar, interspersed with quartz and iron. The oxyd of iron, by the action of the rain, covers their bare and almost perpendicular fronts, and gives them their red appearance, which caused the Dutch anciently to designate the site of New Haven by the name of Red Rock. The fronts of these rocks are composed of assemblages of vast irregular columns similar in appearance to the Palisades of the Hudson, and, like them, having great beds of debris at their bases. A view from either will repay the traveller for his labor in searching the summit. That from East Rock is particularly attractive, for it embraces the harbor, city, plain, and almost every point of historical interest connected with New Haven, or Quinnipiack, as the Indians called it.

> 'I stood upon the cliff's extremest edge,
> And downward far beneath me could I see
> Complaining brooks that played with meadow sedge,
> That brightly wandered on their journey free.'

Winding through the plain were Mill River and the Quinnipiack, spanned by noble bridges near the city, that lay stretched along the beautiful bay ; and — .

> 'Beyond
> The distant temple spires that lift their points
> In harmony above the leaf-clad town —
> Beyond the calm bay and the restless sound,
> Was the blue Island stretching like a cloud,
> Where the sky stoops to earth: the rock was smooth,
> And there upon the table-stone sad youths
> Had carved unheeded names, to weave for them
> That insect immortality that lies
> In stone, for ages, on a showman's shelf.'"

But the chief attraction of New Haven is Yale College. It was founded in 1700, and after being temporarily located in different towns of the colony, was permanently established in 1717 at New Haven, and was called Yale after its principal donor, Elihu Yale, of London, governor of the East India Company, a native of New Haven.

The following brief survey of the college is condensed from "Appleton's Journal" : —

"There is nothing in the appearance of 'Old Yale,' as the stranger looks upon the long and dingy row of plain brick buildings, to correspond with the national reputation of the college, or with the culture which is popularly supposed to come from a four years' residence within the academic walls. Even the best and newest buildings are placed almost out of sight, so that they seem to be peeping through the intervals, as Ik Marvel once expressed it, as glimpses of better things to come. Plain as the buildings are, they have two merits, — they are historic, and they are true to the poverty of the olden time and the unpretentious character of the early builders. If the walls of these old buildings could speak, what tales they could tell of hard thought and study; of youthful enthusiasm and ambition; of deep reflections on the grave questions of the soul; of poetical fancies; of lifelong friendships here begun; of thanksgiving frolics and songs and jokes; of unexpected interruptions from tutors, of sickness, and welcome visitors from home, with now and then a call from some fair Beatrice; of alarm from British invaders in 1779; of sieges in the war of 'Town versus Gown'; of illuminations in honor of a new accession to the presidency; of hopes and fears; of solid purposes and foundations; of kind instructions and enduring counsel. Stories of Kent and Calhoun and Jeremiah Mason, of Roger Sherman and James Hillhouse, of Professors Silliman and Kingsley, of the poets Percival and N. P. Willis, are afloat in the rooms which they frequented while students here; and the old chapel, now named the Athenæum, where freshmen recite, might echo a telling sermon of eloquent Dr. Dwight, or an academic harangue of polyglot Dr. Stiles.

"Walking from the New Haven Hotel to the north end of the square in front of the long line of seven buildings — four dormitories, two recitation buildings, and the chapel — which face the public green, we soon come to signs of reconstruction in Yale College. At the corner of Elm and College Streets, 'Farnam Hall,' a large and handsome structure, has been erected, — a modern lodging-hall for students. The building is the first of a new line of dormitories standing between the old buildings and the street. On the northern side of the square, parallel with Elm Street, is Durfee, a still newer hall. It is also a dormitory, built of uncut New Jersey limestone, and is the largest if not the handsomest building on the square. To the west of the brick row of buildings are two stuccoed halls, one of which was built as a monumental gallery to receive the well-known historical paintings of Colonel John Trumbull, 'friend and aide of Washington,' and the other is still used as a repository of the college cabinet of minerals, fossils, shells, and other specimens, which await a more secure and spacious home in the 'Peabody Museum,' founded by the great philanthropist of our day. Still farther to the west are three stone buildings, comparatively new, the Library, Graduates' Hall, and the Art School. The latter is the most costly and substantial structure yet built for the college, and was built under the personal oversight of the donor, Mr. A. R. Street, of New Haven, a short time before his death, in 1866.

"Outside of the College square are several other buildings which belong to the university. Among the most important of these is the Sheffield Scientific School, a large and convenient hall, where a college of science is established.

"The Yale Divinity School occupy a new and costly edifice, situated directly north of the College Green. The style of the building may be generally described as modern French Gothic, adapted to academic use. Its material is red brick, variegated and ornamented with Nova-Scotia stone and black brick trimmings. The brick is laid in black mortar. The college societies also possess small but unique halls, the most elegant of which is that belonging to 'Scroll and Key.' The university of Yale is now in a most flourishing condition, having over eight hundred students."

The finest public buildings of the city are the Court House and the Custom House. Hoadley's marble building on Church Street, and the new Insurance building on Chapel Street, are also worthy of mention. The State House is a stuccoed building, modelled after the Parthenon. Hillhouse Avenue is a very beautiful street, being lined on each side by the mansions of wealthy citizens, whose grounds are laid out with the greatest care. The city cemetery will repay a passing visit. There are placed the old tombstones of the seventeenth and eighteenth centuries, with their quaint inscriptions. New Haven carries on large manufactories, chiefly those of carriages and clocks. The shipping business is not as extensive as formerly, the harbor gradually filling up. Long Wharf, extending into the harbor, is over half a mile in length, the longest wharf in the United States. Fort Hale, situated on the bay, is an interesting monument of the Revolution.

In connection with New Haven, it may be well to speak of the

*Housatonic River*, — which at Derby, eight miles distant, is crossed by the largest dam in our country. The scenery along the banks of the stream is very picturesque. The falls at New Canaan, Connecticut, will especially delight the lover of the beautiful in nature. The source of the river is in Berkshire County, Massachusetts, and it empties into Long Island Sound, about a dozen miles from New Haven.

## CHAPTER VIII.

#### PHILADELPHIA.

PHILADELPHIA, the second city in the Union in point of population, is situated between the Delaware and Schuylkill Rivers, about six miles above their junction, and, following the river and the bay, ninety-six miles from the ocean. It was planned and settled by William Penn, accompanied by a colony of English Friends, or Quakers, in 1682, after a regular purchase from the Indians, ratified by a treaty in due form. The name Philadelphia, Brotherly Love, was selected by Penn more because of its intrinsic significance than from historical regard to the city of that name in Asia Minor; and the policy of Penn and his associates was consistently and practically peaceful to a degree entitling him to claim its recognition in the name of the city which he founded. The Indian name of the place was Coaquenaque, or Coaquanock.

The original plan of the city contained nine streets running from the Delaware to the Schuylkill, crossed by twenty-one running north and south. In the centre was a square of ten acres, and in each quarter of the city one of eight acres. The city was confined to these narrow limits until 1854, when the Legislature, commiserating its overcrowded condition, wedged in as it was among its lusty children, Kensington, Germantown, Northern Liberties, West Philadelphia, Southwark, and the rest, took them all in at one grasp, and incorporated the whole county of Philadelphia, — a territory twenty-three miles long, and averaging five and a half broad, having an area of one hundred and twenty square miles.

The disposition to give her citizens comfortable homes is

Philadelphia's greatest pride and glory. With a population less than that of New York, she has more houses. The poorest of all the poor are scarcely compelled to live in quarters too small for them, and every mechanic can have a house for himself on payment of a moderate rental.

St. Albans' Place is an instance of what can be done for providing cheap yet tasteful homes for people. Two rows of houses, moderate in size, but built with an eye to substantial comfort, face each other across a wide street. They are built for people who do not use carriages, and the street corresponds with them. All down the middle of it stretches a miniature park, where flowers bloom and fountains sparkle, and on either side of it there is ample room for children to play and adults to pass. The families move in and the marketing is sent home through alleys at the back of the houses, leaving the street in front to serve as a common garden for the dwellers on its borders.

Philadelphia might with propriety be termed the —

*Historical City* of the Union, as it contains more souvenirs of our early history than any other. Most famous and most dear to the heart of every American is Independence Hall.

> "Here rose the anthem which all nations, hearing,
> In loud response the echoes backward hurled;
> Reverberating still the ceaseless cheering
> Our continent repeats it to the world."

> "This is the hallowed spot, where first unfurling,
> Fair Freedom spread her blazing scroll of light;
> Here, from oppression's throne the tyrant hurling,
> She stood supreme, in majesty and might."

Little need be said of Independence Hall, for it is known wherever America herself is known, and its history is familiar to every school-boy. It is a plain brick building, erected between 1729 and 1734, of small architectural pretensions, but of venerable aspect. In the east room of the main building, Independence Hall proper, the second Continental Congress met, and there, on the fourth of July, 1776, the Declaration of Independence was adopted, and from the steps leading into the Independence Square, then the State House yard, it was read to the multitude assembled by the joyful pealing of the bell overhead, — the same bell which now, cracked and useless, but with its grand prophetic motto — "Proclaim liberty throughout all the land, unto all the inhabitants thereof " — still intact, stands on a pedestal in the memorial-room. And in the room over that (Congress Hall) Washington delivered his farewell address. Independence Hall is preserved as befits the glorious deed that was done in it. The furniture is the same as that used by Congress; portraits of our country's heroes crowd the walls, and relics of our early history are everywhere.

Not far from Independence Hall is a building which deserves more than any other the proud title of the Cradle of American Independence. It is Carpenter's Hall, the place where, as an inscription on the walls proudly testifies, "Henry, Hancock, and Adams inspired the delegates of the colonies with nerve and sinew for the toils of war"; the place where the first Continental Congress met, and where the famous " first prayer in Congress " was delivered by Parson Duché on the morning after the news of the bombardment of Boston had been received, and men knew indeed that war was " inevitable." The old man's prayer brought tears to the eyes of even the grave and passionless Quakers who were present, and the voices which had opposed the proposition to open the sessions of Congress with prayer, were never raised for that purpose again.

Close beside Independence Square is Washington Square, once a "Potter's field." Many soldiers, victims of the small-pox and camp fever, were buried here during the Revolution. The ground under the waving trees and spring grass, where the birds sing and children play, is literally "full of dead men's bones," but the grass is no less green and the sunshine is no less bright on that account, and the dead sleep none the less peacefully for the life above them.

> "The good knights are dust,
> And their swords are rust;
> Their souls are with the saints, we trust."

The oldest of the relics of antiquity, or what passes for antiquity in this New World, is the old Swedes' church in Southwark, the ancient Wicaco. This venerable edifice was built in 1700, to take the place of a log structure which was erected in 1677, and served equally well for a church or fort, as the exigencies of those somewhat uncertain times might demand. The present church is of brick, and is still regularly used.

Another relic is Penn's cottage in Letitia Street, — a little two-story brick house built for his use, probably before his arrival in the settlement. It has curiously enough withstood the march of improvement which has swept away many more pretentious structures.

A few steps from this is a small brick house of unique appearance, now used as a tobacco store; but a hundred years ago it was the celebrated "London Coffee-House," where all the dignitaries of the city were accustomed to meet and — O, primeval simplicity! — fill the exhilarating cup, and pledge each other in — piping hot coffee. No stronger drink was sold there.

On Second Street, north of Market, stands Christ Church, on the site of the first church used by the followers of Penn. Tradition says, that the frame building built by them in 1695 was used as a place of worship until the walls of the new building enclosed it and were roofed over, when the old church was taken down and carried out piecemeal. The present edifice was begun in 1727, and finished by raising the steeple in 1753-4. The bells in this high tower are said to be the oldest on this side of the Atlantic, — certainly the oldest chime. The massive timbers which uphold these bells are as sound as when put in a century ago, and look as if they were good for another century at least.

The view from the outlook of the steeple, one hundred and fifty feet from the ground, is beautiful enough to repay visitors for all the risk they run of cracked crowns and broken necks in ascending the dark and tortuous stairs. The Delaware, with its puffing steamers and white-sailed ships, lies almost at the feet of the spectator, and is spread like a panorama for miles and miles. Away to the south a gleaming line indicates the junction of the two rivers, at League Island. Nearer the eye, the masts of Uncle Sam's big ships at the navy yard are displayed; ferry-boats steam steadily across the river; and restless tugs ply up and down, convoying vessels a dozen times their size, or dashing about in search of a tow; all the wharves are crowded with vessels of all sizes, from the great ocean steamer to the diminutive "tub," and all the river is white with arriving and departing sails. Smith's and Windmill Islands lie in mid-stream almost opposite, and Petty's Island lies a short distance above. Near it a cloud of dust and a forest of masts mark the great coal-shipping port of the Reading Railroad, at Richmond; and, beyond, the river ripples and sparkles until lost in the hazy distance. Across the river are Camden and Gloucester, and behind them the level sands of New Jersey stretch away, so flat and unbroken by anything that would obstruct the vision, that it requires no great stretch of the imagination to believe that with a glass of moderate power one might see the waves of the Atlantic, sixty miles away as the crow flies.

Inland the eye ranges over the entire city, from League Island on the south, far beyond Germantown on the north, and from the Delaware to points far west of the Schuylkill. Second Street, the longest built-up street in the city, runs straight as an arrow northward, until its course is lost among the trees in the suburbs. Dozens of church spires rise into the air, the tall white stand-pipe of the Kensington Water Works standing conspicuous among them on the Delaware side of the river, matched by that of the Twenty-fourth Ward Works on the west side of the Schuylkill. To the northwest, Girard College stands boldly out; the Moorish dome of the Broad-street Jewish synagogue rises south of it; and almost due west of the spectator the massive bulk of the Masonic Temple, and the graceful spires, brown and white, of the churches at Broad and Arch, mark the spots which are destined to contain, in the near future, a collection of architectural triumphs unrivalled in the city. Bits of green, set here and there among the crowding houses, indicate the public squares; and, beyond all, the eye rests delighted on the leafy richness of Fairmount Park and of the open country in the suburbs.

Within the grave-yard, on Fifth and Arch Streets, of Christ Church, rests the dust of many of the early and renowned citizens of Philadelphia, the most distinguished of whom was Dr. Benjamin Franklin. His grave is beside that of his wife, marked according to his wishes, with a plain marble stone with this inscription: —

> Benjamin
> and } Franklin.
> Deborah
>
> 1790

At the age of twenty-two Franklin wrote the following epitaph for himself: —

> The Body
> of
> BENJAMIN FRANKLIN,
> Printer,
> Like the cover of an old Book,
> Its contents torn out
> (And stripped of its lettering and gilding),
> Lies here, food for worms.
> But the work shall not be lost,
> For it will (as he believed) appear once more
> In a new and more elegant edition,
> Revised and corrected
> by
> *The Author.*

A historical monument of great interest is the "Treaty Monument," marking the place of the great elm-tree under which William Penn made his famous treaty with the Indians, — "the only treaty ever ratified without an oath; and the only one never broken." The tree was blown down in 1810, when it was ascertained to be two hundred and eighty-three years old.

"Hultsheimer's New House," a plain, brick, three-story building, once Jefferson's boarding-house, and the place where he wrote the immortal Declaration of Independence, is another cherished memento of our national birth still standing.

It will be impossible within our limits to give more than a passing glance at a few of the many noble buildings of Philadelphia. The finest specimen of Grecian architecture in America is —

*Girard College,* — for which Philadelphia is indebted, as for so many other benefits, to Stephen Girard. The building is in the Corinthian style, the cella or main body of the building being one hundred and sixty-nine feet in length by one hundred and eleven in breath, surrounded by a magnificent colonnade of thirty-four columns fifty-five feet high and six feet in diameter. This colonnade extends the length of the building to two hundred and eighteen feet, and a breadth of one hundred and sixty feet. The height is ninety-seven feet.

Stephen Girard came to Philadelphia a poor, penniless French boy, but by perseverance, integrity, and unceasing industry, he amassed a large fortune, so that at the time of his death, in 1831, his property amounted to about $9,000,000. Two millions of this he bequeathed for the erection and support of Girard College, a school for orphans. As many poor white male orphans as the endowment can support are admitted between the ages of six and ten years, fed, clothed, and educated, and between the ages of fourteen and eighteen are bound out to mechanical, agricultural, or commercial occupations. The present number of pupils is about five hundred and fifty.

Besides this bequest, Mr. Girard left nearly all the remainder of his property for founding charitable institutions and for the improvement of the city.

The stranger visiting Philadelphia will naturally consider

*Chestnut Street*, as the representative of the city. Its noble buildings, its handsome stores, and especially the crowds which at all times throng its sidewalks, induce one to associate the idea of Philadelphia with this single street; and it is this which presents itself to his mind's eye whenever the city is afterwards named in his hearing. We cannot, of course, mention but a few of the many noble buildings on Chestnut Street or in its immediate vicinity.

The Custom House, having one of its two fronts on this street, is in imitation of the Parthenon at Athens, and is one of the purest specimens of Doric architecture in the country. The building was completed in 1824, at the cost of $500,000.

On Fifth Street, a few steps from Chestnut Street, is the

Philadelphia Library, one of the staidly solemn things which seem to preserve still the spirit of the city's Quaker founders. It was founded in 1731, — mainly through the influence of Dr. Franklin, whose statue in marble is placed over the entrance, — and took possession of its present buildings in 1790. It observes the rules which were made for its government in 1781. The Loganian Library is in the same building. Both libraries united contain about 95,000 volumes.

On the southwest corner of Sixth and Chestnut stands the imposing brown-stone pile of the "Ledger" building, one of the lions of the city.

The extensive and elegant front of the Masonic Temple, a very beautiful building, next attracts attention. It was once considered the largest of its kind in the United States; but it has become too small, and a new one is in process of erection by the brethren of the mystic tie. Not far from this is the far-famed Continental, the largest hotel in the city. It is six stories high, and is built of Albert and Pictou sandstone, and very fine pressed brick.

At 1122 Chestnut Street, the building of the American Sunday School Union finds itself in the very centre of business now, but when erected, in 1854, it was quite "out of town." This is the head-quarters and central office of the Union; but its branches ramify all over the world, and its missionaries are continually extending its sphere of usefulness.

We next pass the splendid building containing Bailey & Company's jewelry store, and also the building of the Young Men's Christian Association.

The next building which we notice is the United States Mint, a structure of Ionic order, copied from a temple at Athens. It is of brick, faced with marble ashlar.

. The new building of the Presbyterian Board of Publication

stands nearly opposite the mint. It is a handsome four-story edifice, with a front of white granite, trimmed with Aberdeen stone.

The southern terminus of —

*Broad Street*, is at League Island, where the United States Navy Yard is situated. The report of the Secretary of the Navy thus tersely sums up its advantages : —

"A navy yard so ample in its proportions, in the midst of our great coal and iron district, easy of access to our own ships, but readily made inaccessible to a hostile fleet, with fresh water for the preservation of the iron vessels so rapidly growing into favor, surrounded by the skilled labor of one of our chief manufacturing centres, will be invaluable to our country."

One in passing along Broad Street will pass by many large and handsome churches, and other buildings, which it will be impossible to mention or describe; among these, however, are the Horticultural Hall, American Academy of Music, the building of the Union League, and the new Masonic Temple.

*Laurel Hill*, is confessedly the leading cemetery of Philadelphia in size, location, and beauty of adornment. It is situated on a sloping hill-side bordering on the Schuylkill; the extensive grounds are skilfully laid out; and the monuments and other decorations are as elaborate as affection could suggest or munificence bestow.

A number of smaller cemeteries are situated in the vicinity of Laurel Hill, and some important ones are located in parts of the city which have still a rural aspect. Monument Cemetery is situated on Broad and Berks Streets, and is remarkable for a fine granite monument to the joint memories of Washington and Lafayette, which stands in the centre, and gives name to the cemetery.

*Fairmount Park.* — Fairmount Park, new though it is, has already attained a reputation second only to that of Central Park, New York, and only second because Fairmount is not yet old enough to be as widely known. Fairmount needs no eulogist. It speaks for itself. Situated on both sides of the beautiful Schuylkill, extending, on the cityward side, from old Fairmount, in a northeasterly direction, as far as the Wissahickon, and stretching, on the western side, from a point nearly opposite Fairmount to the falls of the river at Manayunk, it is more than three times as large as Central Park.

The great and distinctive features of the Fairmount Park, are its perfect natural adaptation to the purpose to which it is put, its thorough rurality, and the breadth and variety of its landscape and perspective. It would perhaps be difficult to point out anywhere a spot concentrating in the same space so many elements of the beautiful and picturesque. The ruggedness of the native rock; the view of the adjacent river and falls; the four reservoirs, resembling so many silver lakes; the flowers and the rich verdure of the level plat and of the hill-sides, added to the sparkling play of numerous fountains, — all combine to form a landscape of exquisite and almost unequalled beauty.

The Park has been peculiarly fortunate in having obtained within its limits several private country-seats whose former occupants had in some instances adorned them with all that art and money could furnish. Within the Park are situated the Fairmount Water Works; the mansion of Robert Morris, the great financier of the revolution; the Belmont mansion, the home of Richard Peters — poet, punster, patriot, and jurist — during the whole of his long life; the ancient house built by John Penn, a grandson of William Penn; and also a small frame building known as Grant's Cottage, which was brought here from City Point, where it had been used by that general as his head-quarters.

The finest road in the park is the "Vista Drive." This drive is remarkable for the varied and romantic beauty of its views. It winds for seven miles through the entire length of the park, along the sides of the western hills overlooking the river, and presents a series of natural vistas of land and water scenery, which break like sudden glimpses of fairy-land upon the gaze of the delighted pilgrim from the hot and dusty city.

A net-work of such drives and foot-paths deftly lead over hill and through glade, from changing sunshine to shadow, from river margin to woodland deep, with ever recurring vistas of rare beauty and variety. These, and the skilful dotting of flower-beds and fragrant shrubberies here and there, are all that is needed to transform the spot into one of the loveliest and most delightful parks in this country, if not in the world. — *Phila. Illustrated.*

## CHAPTER IX.

### BALTIMORE.

BALTIMORE is the sixth city of the country in point of population. It is situated on an arm of the Patapsco River, fourteen miles from its entrance into the Chesapeake. It has a harbor sufficiently capacious to accommodate two thousand vessels, and its outer bay has depth enough for the largest merchant ships.

The general appearance of Baltimore is striking and picturesque, and the city appears to advantage from nearly every point of view. It is regularly laid out, yet with sufficient diversity to avoid tameness; its surface undulating; its streets of good width; aided by its fine climate, it is one of the healthiest cities in the American Union, or, indeed, in the world. An aspect of cheerful elegance pervades the city, which is peculiarly attractive to strangers; the larger mansions are generally in good taste, and not being densely crowded together as in some of the more northern cities, but having in many cases handsome side-yards attached, they give an impression of space and comfort. In smaller dwellings, especially those for the workers in trades, neatness and thrift are displayed. From her several monuments, Baltimore is frequently designated as the "Monumental City." In 1809 the Legislature granted permission to erect a monument to General Washington. This was erected at the intersection of Charles and Monument Streets, on a lot of ground given for the purpose by Colonel John Eager Howard. . It is a Doric column of white marble rising from a base fifty feet square and thirty-five feet high. The shaft of the column is one hundred and sixty feet high, and is surmounted by a colossal statue of Washington fifteen feet high, making the entire height one hundred and seventy-five feet. The Battle Monument is in the centre of Monument Square, formed by the intersection of Calvert and Fayette Streets. This is also of white marble, and is fifty-three feet high. It was erected to the memory of the citizens who fell in defence of Baltimore, September 12 and 14, 1814. It consists of a square base, with a pedestal, ornamented at four corners with a sculptured griffin. A fascial column rises from the base with bands, upon which are inscribed the names of those who perished. A statue representing the genius of Baltimore surmounts the column. Two smaller monuments in other parts of the city commemorate the attack on Baltimore. One of these to the memory of two young mechanics who shot the British commander, General Ross, and were themselves instantly killed; the other is erected to Colonel George Armistead, the defender of Fort McHenry in 1814. On this occasion, during the bombardment of the fort, the famous song of the "Star Spangled Banner" was composed by Francis S. Key.

Baltimore contains many large and handsome public buildings. Many of the churches are also very fine. The Roman Catholic Cathedral, the most imposing, is in the form of a cross, and surmounted by a lofty dome, and two bell-towers. It contains two beautiful paintings, one, "The Descent from the Cross," presented by Louis XVI of France; the other, "St. Louis burying his officers and soldiers before Tunis," presented by Charles X. Baltimore is the see of the Roman Catholic primate of the United States. Of the several parks of the city, the largest and most attractive is Druid Hill Park, containing five hundred and forty-eight acres. Its surface is gently undulating for the most part, but occasionally rises into bold eminences, from which fine views of the city or the surrounding country may be had. Excellent drives and walks and bridle-paths have been laid out through the woods and grassy interspaces, and some ornamental shrubs and evergreens have been planted to give greater variety to the lawn-like grounds. But the chief attraction of the park is its natural beauty. It is charmingly sylvan, rustic, home-like; and although there is much to be done in the way of improvement, no touch of the landscape gardener could add a grace to the fresh negligence of its glades and dells, and little trickling springs and cool secluded nooks.

## CHAPTER X.

### DISTRICT OF COLUMBIA.

District of Columbia created by Congress, July 16, 1790.
Corner-stone of the District laid, April 15, 1791.
Corner-stone of the Capitol laid, by George Washington, Sept. 18, 1793.
U. S. Government removed from Philadelphia to Washington, June, 1800.
Congress first convened in the new Capitol, third Monday of November, 1800.

THE District of Columbia was, until February 21, 1871, neither a State nor territory, but was governed directly by the Congress of the United States, its inhabitants having no representation, and no voice in the Federal election. At the date above named, a territorial government was, by act of Congress, provided with a governor, and council of eleven members, appointed by the president for a term of four years, and a House of Delegates elected by the people, consisting of twenty-two members. The same act repealed the charters of the cities of Washington and Georgetown, on and after June 1.

Originally this district included one hundred square miles; but the city of Alexandria was, in 1846, retroceded to the State from which it had been taken. Maryland lies upon all sides, except the southwest, where it is separated from Virginia by the Potomac River.

*Washington City*, the political Capital of the United States, is in the District of Columbia, on the banks of the Potomac River. It is forty miles from Baltimore, one hundred and thirty-six from Philadelphia, and two hundred and twenty-six from New York, with which cities, as well as with all the chief towns of the Union, it is connected by railway. When the original plan of Washington shall be realized in its full growth to the proportions it was designed to reach, it will be in its own right, and without the aid of its official position, one of the great cities of the Union. It would be difficult to invent a more magnificent scheme than that of the founder of Washington, or to find a location more eligible for its successful execution. Its easy access from the sea gives it every facility for commercial greatness, and its varied topography almost compels picturesque effect and beauty. The site was chosen by Washington himself.

The scene from the lofty position of the dome of the Capitol, or from the high terrace upon which this magnificent edifice stands, is one of unrivalled beauty, and it gives the visitor at once and thoroughly a clear idea of the natural advantages of the region, and of the character, extent, and possibilities of the city. Looking eastward, for the space of a mile or more, over a plain yet scarcely occupied, the eye falls upon the broad and beautiful waters of the Potomac, leading by Alexandria and the groves of Mount Vernon to the sea. Turning westward, it overlooks the city as it at present exists, upon the great highway of Pennsylvania Avenue, to the edifices of the State and Treasury Departments and the President's house, the avenue dropping towards its centre as a hammock might swing between the two elevated points. Around, on other rising grounds, the various public edifices are seen with fine effect; and turning again to the left, the eye takes in the broad acres of the new national Park, in which are the many unique towers of the Smithsonian Institution, and the soaring shaft of the Washington Monument; off in the distance, across Rocky Creek, are the ancient-looking walls and roofs of Georgetown.

*The Capitol*, in its magnitude and in its magnificence of marble and domes, and upon its bold terrace height, will have attracted the visitor's curious wonder miles distant, whichever way he may have approached. The corner-stone of this imposing structure was laid by Washington himself, with great masonic array, Sept. 18, 1793. In 1814 it was burned by the British, together with the library of Congress, the President's house, and other public works. It is built of freestone, and painted white. In 1818 it was entirely repaired, and in 1851 (July 4) President Fillmore laid the corner-stone of the new wings, on which occasion the Hon. Daniel Webster delivered a brilliant oration. Its whole length is seven hundred and fifty-one feet, and the area covered is four and one third acres. The surrounding grounds, which are beautifully cultivated, and embellished by fountains and statuary, embrace thirty acres. The Senate Chamber and the Hall of the Representatives of the Congress of the United States, are in the wings of the Capitol, on either side of the centre building.

The next grand feature of the Capitol is the *Rotunda;* its diameter is ninety-six feet, and height two hundred and twenty. On the first floor it is divided into eight panels; in these are paintings representing respectively, Embarkation of Pilgrims for America, by Weir; Landing of Columbus, by Vanderlyn; Baptism of Pocahontas, by Chapman; Discovery of the Mississippi River by De Soto, by Powell; Declaration of Independence; Surrender of General Burgoyne; Surrender of Cornwallis and the British Army at Yorktown, by Col. John Trumbull. Between the panels, in *basso relievo,* are four historical subjects, representing the Preservation of Capt. John Smith, by Pocahontas; Landing of the Pilgrims on Plymouth Rock; Penn's treaty with the Indians; Conflict between Daniel Boone and the Indians. There are also specimens of sculpture of the heads of Columbus, La Salle, Sir Walter Raleigh, and Cabot, by Causici and Capelleno. On the outside of the east door are also statues of Columbus,

The Indian Woman, and two of colossal size, representing Peace and War, by Persico. In the Park is Greenough's colossal statue of Washington, his right hand pointing towards heaven, and in the left holding a Roman sword.

*The New Dome* resembles the modern rather than the antique structures of this character; it is two hundred and twenty feet from floor to ceiling, and from the western grounds is about four hundred feet high. A spiral staircase winds around between the interior and exterior, from the floor to the summit, and at various heights are colonnades, from which the visitor will have magnificent views.

The dome is decorated with pilasters, rich cornices, and entablatures, springing up towards the sky; and crowning the pinnacle of this beautiful and grand piece of art is a bronze statue of Freedom, twenty feet high, commenced by Crawford, and since his death completed by Clark Mills.

*The New Senate Chamber* is in the north wing of the Capitol, is one hundred thirteen feet, three inches long, eighty feet, seven inches wide, and thirty-six feet high. The ceiling is of cast iron, with large skylights, having in the centre of each, in color, the arms of a State or territory. The walls and ceiling are richly colored. There are panels and niches yet to be filled with paintings and statuary. The galleries seat about 1,200 persons.

*The Hall of Representatives* is in the south wing, is one hundred thirty-nine feet long, ninety-three feet wide, and thirty-six high. It is built on about the same general plan as the Senate Chamber. The decorations are rich, but of darker color than the Senate. It is also to be adorned with paintings and statuary. Galleries seat 1,000 persons.

*The Executive Mansion.* — The President's mansion, or White House, as it is familiarly called, is on Pennsylvania

Avenue, between Fifteenth and Seventeenth Streets, and fronting Lafayette Square. It was erected in 1792, rebuilt after the war of 1812. It is built of freestone, and painted white. The lawns around, containing some twenty acres, drop gradually towards the Potomac River. This elegant but not imposing edifice is two stories high, one hundred seventy feet long, and eighty-six feet deep. On the north front, upon Pennsylvania Avenue, the building has a portico, with four Ionic columns, under which carriages pass. A circular colonnade of six Doric pillars adorns the Potomac front. In the centre of the lawn, across the avenue, on the north, is Clark Mills' bronze equestrian statue of General Jackson, erected in January, 1853. The artist has the honor of being the first to succeed in erecting a statue representing a steed poised upon its hind feet, with no other support. It is cast of cannon taken by Jackson, and cost $50,000. Near the President's mansion on the one side are the very plain buildings of the navy and the war departments, and on the other side the Treasury Department.

*U. S. Naval Observatory*, situated on E north, corner Twenty-fourth west, on the banks of the Potomac towards Georgetown. The site is a beautiful one, having a commanding view of the surrounding country. It occupies a high rank among the observatories of the world, there being but one — that in Russia — superior to it. By it is regulated the time of the city and government, and from it is calculated the latitude and longitude of the Western Hemisphere.

*The Navy Yard*, on the Eastern Branch, about three fourths of a mile southeast of the Capitol, has an area of twenty-seven acres, enclosed by a substantial brick wall. Within this enclosure, besides houses for the officers, are shops and warehouses, two large ship-houses, and an armory, which, like the rest of the establishment, is kept in the finest order. Open for visitors from morning until sunset.

*The Patent Office* is within the square occupied by the Interior Department, and bounded by Seventh and Ninth and F and G Streets. The halls, containing an almost endless variety of models of inventions, are open from 9 A. M. to 3 P. M.

*The Smithsonian Institution* is within the area of the New Park, west of the Capitol, and south of Pennsylvania Avenue. This noble institution was endowed by James Smithson, Esq., of England, "for the increase and diffusion of knowledge among men." The edifice is constructed of red sandstone, in the Norman or Romanesque style. Its length is four hundred fifty feet; its breadth one hundred forty; and it has nine towers from seventy-five to one hundred fifty feet high. It contains a lecture-room capacious enough to hold 2,000 auditors; a museum of natural history, two hundred feet in length; a superb laboratory; a gallery for pictures and statuary. The immense library, formerly in this institution, has been transferred to the Congressional Library.

*The National Monument to Washington* is in the hall. The base is to be a circular temple, two hundred fifty feet in diameter, and one hundred feet high, upon which there is to be a shaft of seventy feet base, and five hundred feet high; the total elevation of the monument being six hundred feet. The temple is to contain statues of Revolutionary heroes and relics of Washington. It is to be surrounded by a colonnade of thirty Doric pillars, with suitable entablature and balustrade. Each State contributes a block of native stone or other material, which is to be placed within the interior walls. The work on the monument stopped some years ago, and there is nothing to be seen as yet but a plain shaft about one hundred fifty feet high. Many of the blocks furnished by States can be seen on application to the keeper, who is ever ready to show visitors about.

## CHAPTER XI.

NEW YORK, OR THE ISLAND CITY; BROOKLYN, TICONDEROGA, LAKE GEORGE, SARATOGA SPRINGS.

"AS the eye of the visitor first takes in the island city of New York from some lofty eminence, — say Brooklyn Heights, which probably affords the most comprehensive view, — a hundred questions arise in his mind, as to its dimensions, its gigantic commerce, its ships and docks and stately edifices, with numerous other statistical queries upon which he may desire to be informed.

"The city is situated at the mouth of the Hudson River, eighteen miles from the Atlantic Ocean, in latitude about 41°, longitude 74°. The city and county are identical in limits, and occupy the entire surface of Manhattan Island; Randall's, Ward's, and Blackwell's Islands in the East River; and Bedloe's, Ellis's, and Governor's Islands in the bay, — the last three being occupied by the United States government.

"*Manhattan Island*, on which the city proper stands, is thirteen and a half miles in length, with an average breadth of one and three fifths miles, forming an area of nearly twenty-two square miles, or fourteen thousand acres. The islands in East River and the bay make four hundred additional acres.

"The surface of the island was originally very rough. A rocky ridge ran from the southern point northward, sending out several jagged spurs, which, after branching irregularly for about five miles, culminated in Washington Heights (two hundred and thirty-eight feet above tide-water), and in a sharp, precipitous promontory, one hundred and thirty feet high, at the northern extremity of the island. Most of the rock is too coarse for building purposes, and the entire stratum is evidently the production of some violent upheaval. Most of the lower portion of the island is composed of alluvial sand-beds; and there were also many swamps in different quarters, though the few remaining marshes are rapidly disappearing, and being filled in for new streets. The principal swamp was the deep valley which crossed the island at Canal Street. It long ago shared this fate, and now forms the business centre of the city.

"Manhattan Island is by survey divided into 141,486 lots, of which about 60,000 are built upon; so that, at a rough estimate, and making allowance for the number absorbed by Central Park, there is still room for as many more houses, and over double the present population.

"The city proper extends from the southern extremity (Battery Point), and is compactly built for a distance of about six miles, and irregularly on the east side to Harlem, four miles farther.

"On the west side it is almost solidly built to about Fifty-ninth Street, and thence irregularly to above Bloomingdale (Seventy-eighth Street), whence occur the refreshing greenness, and long lines of country-seats and elegant suburban residences of Manhattanville and Washington Heights.

"*The Harbor of New York* is one of the finest and most beautiful in the world.

"At the extreme lower part of the island is *The Battery*, one of the most striking monuments of respectability and beauty run to wretchedness and squalor, that can be found in any but the oldest countries. The Battery exists to-day an example of the changes a few years will bring. Without going back to the old time, when it was a great grass-grown field, sprinkled with windmills, and made homely with flocks and herds of pasturing sheep and cattle, men still in their prime can recollect it as the favorite promenade of the wealthiest and most fashionable class of the city. Hither came, on pleasant summer evenings, the fathers and mothers of the generation of to-day, for health, the fresh sea-breeze, flirtation, and enjoyment generally. They, in their unexpanded thought, had more faith in it than their sons and daughters have in Central Park.

"*Central Park.* — There are many public enterprises intended for the benefit of the city, which mistaken calculations or official corruption have made complete or comparative failures. One, at least, can be presented, which has more than fulfilled the most sanguine expectations that were ever entertained of it. This notable exception is the Central Park. We call it 'Central' Park now; had we done so fifteen years ago, we should have been looked upon as lunatics. Allowing something for the foresight of the projectors who named it, there is likelihood that, in less than a quarter of a century, those who called it 'Central' will be regarded as — speaking mildly — short-sighted speculators. But, regarding it as it is now, it is unquestionably the most beautiful park of its age in the world, and, even leaving the matter of age out of the question, it is doubtful if any park can be found to surpass it in features of natural and artificial beauty. The admission must be made that its features of natural beauties were few. They were mainly bowlders and swamps. But engineering science came into the field, and the results have been those that the story of Aladdin suggested to us, or that might have occurred in the twinkling of a brilliant dream. It may truthfully be said there is no more beautiful or attractive spot on earth. The Park has outgrown its faults of juvenescence. Its trees may not be as noble in the grandeur of age, as those which line the avenues that lead up to the ancestral castles plentiful in Europe; the country is not old enough for that; but what wonders a few years can accomplish have been accomplished in and by the Central Park. It has trees that need not be ashamed to show what they can do in the *sub tegmine fagi* line of business. The shrubberies are as luxuriant as any at Sydenham or Chatsworth. The lakes are more artistically laid out and bordered than in any rival place of the kind. The architectural decorations are beyond comparison, while the practical accommodations for the public have never been approached. In summer, verdant with every shade of green, it is glorious, and in winter it has attractions which only those who have enjoyed them know. Nothing could possibly be so delightful as a moonlight night's skating on its frozen sheets of water, unless it were a summer evening's music-festival upon its emerald swards.

"To come down to mechanical details about the Park's dimensions is more than ought to be expected. Suppose it does commence at Fifty-ninth Street and extend to One-hundred-and-tenth, is that to be allowed to interfere with the little touch of romance one feels about it? Why should one's illusions of its illimitable vastness be circumscribed by being told it is thirteen thousand five hundred and seven feet, nine and four tenths inches in length, and twenty-seven hundred and eighteen feet, six and nine tenths inches in breadth, making a superficial area of eight hundred and forty-three acres? Why speak by name of its numerous gates, when everybody knows by this time how to get to it and into it? Why speak more fully of its grottos and caverns and eyries? Are they not known to the multitude of the people? And the menagerie? Well, it is not complete yet. There may be lions of Africa, and Bengal tigers and elephants to come along after a while; but in the mean time we have to be content with numerous waterfowl and such other additions as foreign and domestic donors may supply. It is good as it is, and future enterprise will make it better. In a very few years there will be a first-class zoölogical collection in the Central Park.

"The scene presented by the numerous fine drives of the Park during the afternoons of a good season, is a brilliant, ever-changing pageant, quite as varied as that presented by Rotten Row in London, and far more extensive. The finest teams and most extensive vehicles of our wealthy classes are mingled with cheap hackney-coaches, — not cheap in price, however, — bearing pleasure parties of smaller means, but equally independent, and strangers from the hotels, with now and then a rusty old barouche, or rockaway, in which some old farmer of Westchester or Jersey has driven into the city, in order to show his daughters the Park of which they have heard and read so much.

"Excepting the signs of heraldry, — and even these are seen at times, — the turn-outs of our commercial princes and wealthy sporting men will vie in completeness and splendor with those of the nobility of Europe.

" n fine weather the elegant turn-out of Commodore Vanderbilt is often a striking feature on the road. Dexter, or some other king of the trotting turf, with Bonner holding the ribbons, may be seen spurning the smooth way, and defiant of opposition. Fellows's incomparable four-in-hand, for which Louis Napoleon, when Emperor, is said to have offered a great sum, also frequently graces the drive. And there are others too numerous to particularize. One cannot see the Park to advantage from a carriage window, as the most picturesque places are accessible only to the pedestrian.

If the visitor drives through the Park, let him leave his carriage at the mall, and see the superb terrace that leads down to the Lake; at the Ramble, and wander through its leafy shades, visiting the *Cave* — the most picturesque bit in the Park — and the *Belvedere*, now building at the upper end of the Ramble, where he may obtain a wide view of this splendid pleasure-ground.

"*The Tour* or *Drive* is a spacious macadamized road for vehicles, with a wide foot-path on either side. It makes the entire circuit of the grounds. In its serpentine course it embraces all the great architectural and scenic features of the Park. In its course it crosses many fine bridges and archways, now over and now under the foot-paths and bridle-roads. It presents a brilliant and inspiriting spectacle, as seen upon sunny afternoons, when alive with the whirl of a thousand gay and gorgeous carriages, bearing the *elite* and fashion of the city through their daily airing.

"*The Bridle Road* follows the great carriage-way with many capricious *detours* through all the long circuit of the Park. It is entirely shut out, however, from the carriage route, which it never crosses except upon archways above or below. It is intended exclusively for horsemen, and is nowhere accessible to vehicles, though equestrians may enter the carriage-roads when they please. The total length of the Bridle Road is between five and six miles.

"*The Ramble* is a charmingly wooded labyrinth of thirty-two acres, lying upon the broad hill-slope which drops down from the lower end of the old reservoir at Seventy-ninth Street to the margin of the Central Lake. It is a wonderfully secluded and quiet spot, quite undisturbed in all its generous extent by any road except the intricate foot-paths, through rich shrubbery of ever-changing form and tint, leading the willing wanderer amidst their inexplicable mazes, now into the grateful shade of some Arcadian bower, and anon to the crest of some rocky cliff, overlooking the sunlit landscape far and near. It is the spot of all spots in the great Park for dreams and revery, and will naturally become sacred to sentiment and love.

" *The Central Lake* is an exquisite reach of bright waters, covering an area of twenty acres, and bounded by a shore of infinite variety and beauty. Upon the upper side are the wooded slopes of the Ramble, stealing down with gentle, grassy step, or jutting out in bold, rocky promontory. At the southeast is the grand marble esplanade of the Terrace, with its gorgeous arches, fountains, steps, and statues. At its narrow base beyond — where it is almost cut in two like a modern belle — it is spanned by a noble wrought-iron foot-bridge, with a single arch of eighty-seven and a half feet. This structure is called the Bow Bridge, from its general likeness in form to a long bow; and sometimes the Flower-Bridge, in consideration of the heavy vases of trailing plants which surmount its abutments. Another beautiful bridge carries a carriage-road and walk over the channel connecting the main and western portion of the lake, and yet another, near by, — most picturesquely constructed of wood, — conducts a foot-path across the little bayou which approaches the western cape of the Ramble. Pretty boats dot the surface of the lake, bearing visitors, for a moderate fee, hither and thither. . . . Whole fleets of snow-white swans, too, are ever gliding in stately progress through the winding waters. . . . When the ice is in suitable condition, the fact is announced by the elevation of a red ball upon the Tower Hill above. The welcome news is repeated. . . . Every one tells his neighbor that the "Ball is up!" whereupon, no matter how cold it may be, all the world, young and old, rich and poor, men and maidens, rush pell-mell to the Park, forthwith put on skates, and hold high saturnalia there from earliest morn to latest night.

"*The Mall* is a beautiful lawn in the southwest, between Sixty-fifth and Seventy-second Streets. Here is a grand promenade thirty-five feet broad, and twelve hundred and twelve feet long, flanked on either side by rustic seats and by a double row of overarching elms. One of the southern approaches to the Mall is under the elegant marble archway called the alcove, and thence by broad steps ascending on either hand. Northward, the spacious walk terminates in a scene of unwonted beauty upon the upper esplanade of that imposing structure known as the Water Terrace. At this happy point, seats are arranged for the cosy enjoyment of the orchestral strains which fill the grateful air at appointed days and hours.

"*The Flower Garden* occupies the area upon the Fifth Avenue between Seventy-third and Seventy-fifth Streets.

"Four thoroughfares cross the Park, from east to west, so constructed by means of tunnels and other contrivances, as not to interrupt the landscape, or practically effect any division of the park. — The sum of the foot-paths, all told, will make a comfortable walk of twenty-one and three quarter miles; and in all this great stretch, the wanderer will meet neither horse nor vehicle to disturb the quiet tenor of his way. — Very much of the southwest quarter of the Lower Park is occupied by large open lawns, which are to be used as play-grounds for children, for cricket, and other sports of bat and ball, and for occasional military parades and reviews. The largest of these beautiful commons contains fifteen acres. The numerous bridges and archways of the Park form one of its pleasantest and most unique features. These structures were required for the crossing of the traffic roads, the passage of the brooks and lakes, and for the carrying of the carriage, bridle, and foot paths over or under each other. The whole number of ornamental bridges designed for the grounds is about thirty.

" *The Cave* is a bold and romantic rock chamber which opens northward at the western slope of the Ramble, and southward upon a little arm of the lake. It was discovered by chance, but not in its present spacious and accessible form, for it owes all its availability to the judicious assistance of art.

" *Tower Hill* above the Ramble is one of the highest points in the Park. Its topography naturally suggested the use which has been made of it as a general observatory. . . .

" One hundred and thirty-six acres of the central area of the park are occupied by the Croton reservoirs. . . .

" The Park is not for the present day alone, but for all the generations yet to come; and if the generous people of New York shall be remembered and blessed by their posterity for any good deed, above all others it will be for this inestimable gift." — *T. Addison Richards, in Harper's Mag.*

"*Brooklyn*, while incorporated as a distinct city, is practically identical with New York. Brooklyn is reached by numerous ferries; in time, the East River will be spanned by a bridge, now begun, which promises to be the most remarkable piece of engineering in the country. In Brooklyn is Greenwood Cemetery, reached by numerous lines of cars, starting from the ferries. Greenwood is the handsomest cemetery in the country, both as regards the beauty of its surface, and the elegance of its monuments.

" *Prospect Park*, Brooklyn, is a noble park, and well worth visiting. It may be reached by cars starting from the ferries. It contains over five hundred acres; is beautifully wooded;

has artificial lakes, fine drives, and is very attractive. Clinton Avenue, Brooklyn, is lined with embowered villas, and very beautiful. A view of New York from Brooklyn Heights — reached best by Wall-street ferry—is superb; the heights are crowded with splendid residences. The Navy Yard is also in Brooklyn (reached by ferry to Bridge Street); the Atlantic docks (Hamilton ferry, foot of Broadway) should be visited." — *American.*

*Ticonderoga.* — A post-town of Essex County, New York, on the west side of the south end of Lake Champlain, and at the north end of Lake George; twelve miles south of Crown Point; ninety-five north of Albany. There is a valuable iron-mine in this township. Ticonderoga fort, famous in the history of the American wars, is situated on an eminence on the west side of Lake Champlain, just north of the entrance of the outlet from Lake George into Lake Champlain, fifteen miles south of Crown Point, twenty-four north of Whitehall. It is now in ruins. Considerable remains of the fortifications are still to be seen. The stone walls of the fort, which are now standing, are, in some places, thirty feet high. Mount Defiance lies about a mile south of the fort, and Mount Independence is about half a mile distant, in Orwell, Vt.

*Lake George.* — This lake is thirty-three miles long and two miles wide, principally in the counties of Washington and Warren, N. Y. It discharges itself into Lake Champlain at Ticonderoga. This lake is surrounded by high mountains, and is surpassed in the romantic by no lake scenery in the world. The waters are deep and clear, abounding in the finest of fish. In consequence of the extraordinary purity of the water, the French formerly procured it for sacramental purposes; for which reason, it was by them termed Lake Sacrament. Rogers' Rock is on the west side of the Lake, two miles from its outlet. It rises from the water at an angle of 45° to a height of three hundred or four hundred feet. It received its name from Major Rogers, who, to evade his Indian pursuers, ascended the rock on the land side with snow-shoes ; and throwing his pack down the precipice on the water side, turned his feet about on his snow-shoes and travelled back with them heel foremost ; thus leading the Indians to suppose that two persons had ascended the rock, and precipitated themselves into the lake. This lake was conspicuous during the French and Revolutionary wars, forming the most convenient connection between Canada and the Hudson. Hence the establishment of the forts at the head of the lake, and also in part of fort Ticonderoga.

*Saratoga Springs* is the name applied to a township and watering-place in the State of New York, thirty-six miles by rail north of Albany. The village is in the north part of the township, and is situated on a sandy plain, partly surrounded by fine groves, and watered by Ellis creek, and other branches of Kayaderoseras creek. The springs — of which there are ten or twelve, with various properties, but all saline and chalybeate — issue from a limestone formation, which underlies the whole surface of sandy soil, upon which the town is built; and most of them come to the surface near the margin of a small stream, which runs through the town on the east of the principal street. There are numerous large, elegant hotels here ; the springs being annually resorted to by from 30,000 to 40,000 persons, during the summer season. The principal springs are known as the Congress, the Putnam, the Iodine, the Pavilion, the Union, etc. Many invalids have received permanent benefit from the use of these medicated waters.

## CHAPTER XII.

#### WEST POINT AND CATSKILL MOUNTAINS.

NIAGARA has its majestic grandeur, Lake George its picturesque beauty; but the Hudson has West Point and the Highlands.

Around West Point cluster a thousand sacred memories and traditions; memories of the Revolution, and the band of heroes who fought the good fight which gave us our freedom. West Point has sent forth an army of gentlemen, of scholars, and of warriors. It has also sent forth a band of engineers, to whose unremitted labors the mariners owe an unending debt of gratitude, — engineers who have laboriously mapped the coast, and indicated the dangerous reefs and shoals.

Space will not enable us to enter fully into a description of the course of instruction pursued here; suffice it to say, that the fact of a young man having passed through the course is a clear proof of his being an officer and a gentleman in the broadest sense. An author in a recent publication says : " West Point has ever tended to ennoble all who have enjoyed its advantages, and profited by them. It has stamped an unmistakable seal on each of its children. Let all Americans be proud of their Military Academy; let them be proud of its professors, and proud of its location."

In regard to location, it is the most lovely of all lovely spots on the river; series of mountains, hills, and cliffs arise above and around it; below, the lordly Hudson rolls in ceaseless flow, dotted with a thousand sails, and teeming with life as the splendid steamers; well called floating palaces, pass and repass.

Still farther up the river, the next point of great attraction for the traveller is the —

*Catskill Mountains.* — From the river, one is struck with their quiet grandeur and imposing appearance. If one is so fortunate as to view them from the Highlands, a few miles east of the river, when the sun is descending behind their summits, and gilding them with its parting rays, he may witness most beautiful displays of color, and purple tints reflected into the atmosphere from the mountain-sides, such as, before seen only on canvas, he regarded as exaggerations of the painter.

From the village of Catskill, a road of twelve miles leads to the Mountain House, perched upon a mountain terrace, two thousand five hundred feet above the level of the river. The view from this spot is of a most extensive character, and embraces a region of ten thousand square miles in extent, portions even of Vermont, Massachusetts, and Connecticut being in a fine day plainly visible; whilst at least sixty miles of the Hudson River can be seen shining like a broad belt at our feet. Sunrise, as seen from the windows of the hotel, presents a spectacle of great magnificence. The twin lakes, nestled beside each other in their mountain bed, are soon reached, and their outlet conducts to what are perhaps the most striking features of the Catskills, the cascades of the mountain streams, and the deep gorges, or "cloves," through which these find their way to the lower lands. The *Clove of the Catterskill* is a remarkable ravine five miles in length. It is wild and savage and romantic enough for the most ardent lover of rough scenery. The falls of the little stream within are very beautiful; the water leaps down a perpendicular rock in two falls, one four hundred and eighty feet in height, and another of eighty feet, emptying through the Clove into the plain below. In the winter season, the upper fall becomes encased in a hollow column of blue ice, which reflects in the rays of the sun the brilliant colors of the prism. Other gorges and cloves are in this immediate vicinity, all noted for their picturesqueness, and tempting to the pencil of the artist.

The highest summits are Round Top and High Peak, each somewhat more than three thousand feet above the level of the sea.

## CHAPTER XIII.

### ITHACA AND VICINITY.

AT the head of Cayuga Lake lies Ithaca, politically a village, but rapidly assuming the proportions and dignity of a city. It extends all the way across the valley and far up on either hill-side, and is closely built for nearly two miles east and west.

Perhaps the most remarkable feature of the scenery at the head of the lake is the number of gorges and ravines, which have been worn into the surrounding hills by the streams which pour down the lakeward slopes.

Fall Creek, the most northerly of the streams which pass through the city, rivals Trenton in every essential feature of gorge scenery. Within a mile of distance there are eight falls, the highest of which, the Ithaca Fall, is a hundred and fifty feet. Of the others, Forest Fall, Foaming Fall, Rocky Fall, and Trip-hammer Fall, the heights range from sixty to thirty feet of perpendicular fall.

About half a mile south of Fall Creek is Cascadilla Creek, smaller and possessing more delicate varieties of scenery. Its cascades are accessible, however, only by the more hardy explorers. Between these two ravines, Cornell University is located, so that the roar of Fall Creek and the dashing waters of Cascadilla mingle their ceaseless bass with the music of university chimes.

Six miles from the city in a southwesterly direction is Enfield Falls, a spot of much interest on account of the great depth which a stream of moderate dimensions has furrowed into the earth. The water reaches the main fall through a narrow cañon a hundred feet deep, and then tumbles down, almost perpendicularly, a hundred and eighty feet, into a chasm whose walls rise three hundred feet on either side. The most noted and perhaps the most impressive of all the waterfalls about the head of Cayuga Lake, is Taghanic, situated some ten miles northwest of the city, and about one mile up from the west shore. The interesting features of this spot are the very deep ravine, the great height of the cataract, its sharply defined outlines, and the magnificent view of the lake and country which is presented here. The water breaks over a clean-cut "table rock," and falls perpendicularly two hundred and fifteen feet. Except in floodtime the veil of water breaks up, and reaches the bottom in mist and sheets of spray. From the bottom of the gorge the walls of rock rise nearly four hundred feet, as cleanly cut as though laid by the hand of a mason.

We have mentioned only the most prominent of the gorges and waterfalls. Within a radius of ten miles from Ithaca are said to be no less than two hundred and fifty cascades and cataracts. — *Appleton's Monthly.*

## CHAPTER XIV.

### BUFFALO, N. Y.

BUFFALO, the county seat of Erie County, New York, is situated at the eastern extremity of Lake Erie and at the head of Niagara River. It was founded by the Holland Land Company in 1801, and during the war between England and the United States in 1814 it was burned by a force of Indians and British, for which loss an appropriation of eighty thousand dollars was granted by Congress. The city has a water-front of about five miles on the lake and river. A portion of the river-front is a bold bluff sixty feet above the river and Erie Canal which passes near it. The more elevated portion of the site affords fine views of the city, Niagara River, Canada shore, the lake and bay, and the hilly country to the southeast. Buffalo is, in the main, handsomely built. Its streets are broad and straight, and for the most part intersect each other at right angles. Main, Niagara, and Delaware Streets are particularly worthy of mention. The streets in the more elevated portions are bordered with a profusion of shade-trees, and the more important avenues have many fine residences. Among the principal public buildings are the Court House, City Hall, Custom House, State Arsenal, and the Young Men's Association building. Of the churches, St. Paul's and St. John's (Episcopal), St. Joseph's Cathedral (Catholic), the North, Central, and Delaware street churches (Presbyterian), and the new Universalist church, are especially deserving of mention. Forest Lawn, a handsome cemetery, is situated in the suburbs of the city.

## CHAPTER XV.

### WATKINS GLEN, N. Y.

IT has been comparatively a few years since the scenery of interior New York has attracted outside attention, or been appreciated by those living among it. Of all the lakes that form the cluster from Oneida to Keuka, Cayuga and Seneca are by far the largest and the most important. At the head of the former is Ithaca, a name brought prominently before the American public as the seat of Cornell University. At the head of the latter is Watkins, noted for its glen.

The town of Watkins nestles in a narrow valley, amid a profusion of shrubbery, and within the shadow of Buck Mountain. Passing up the main street, parallel with the mountain slope, a walk of a quarter of a mile brings one to a shallow stream which has cut its way through the lower slope of the mountain range, and formed for itself a short pass which terminates abruptly, at a short distance, in a lofty wall. The wall is not, however, continuous on the same line, but falls back in the centre, and forms a cavernous recess, from one angle of which the stream issues. Behind this solemn gateway of natural masonry, broken and abraded by time and the action of the elements, lies the glen.

The entrance to Watkins Glen is a rude stairway braced firmly into the rock. This brings one into Glen Alpha, as it has been somewhat fantastically styled, where a narrow but secure bridge crosses the chasm; and from this bridge a fine view is had of the first cascade, as it pours swirling through a rift in the rocks, and falls, roaring and foaming, into a deep basin scooped out of the solid rock-bed by the constant chafe and fret and turmoil of the waters. One then follows a narrow winding foot-path cut out of the face of the cliff, until all farther progress is barred by a transverse wall, over which the waters of Long Cascade fall from a great height into the dark pool below. At this point the rugged and lofty walls of the gorge draw closer together. Where the foot-path ends, a long staircase, wet with the mist and spray of the cascade, is flung at an angle of ninety degrees across the chasm, and at its upper end connects with another foot-path, which leads to a series of cascades, dropping from one low ledge to another, deep pools and broad shallows intervening.

Going farther on, the aspect of the place grows weird and ghastly. The rocks take on more grotesque forms. The air is cold and moist. The path, a mere ledge in the face of the rocks, overhangs a deep chasm, at the bottom of which the waters chafe and struggle and broil. Overhead the gray walls rise tier upon tier, inclining gradually towards each other, until finally, far upward, only a narrow strip of sky can be seen with the light struggling dimly through a fringe of hemlocks.

Beyond this gloomy pass a succession of stairways and another path, where the glen is more open, lead to a stairway reaching a shelf on the north side of the ravine, where the Mountain House, built somewhat after the style of a Swiss chalet, stands. Leaving the Mountain House, the path dips steadily downwards, almost to the bed of the stream; and, after passing a series of small cascades and rapids one crosses a bridge to the opposite side of the gorge, where the cliffs, rent and torn into every conceivable shape, first contract and then expand into an enormous amphitheatre, to which has been given the name of Glen Cathedral. The area is vast. The immense walls, nearly circular in form, rise to a great height, and, where they terminate skyward, are crowned with the green pendulous foliage of the hemlock. The floor of this amphitheatre is almost as level as if it had been paved by human hands, and over the great slabs of rock, laid regularly and close-jointed, the stream spreads out but an inch or two in depth, flowing easily and quietly, with scarcely a ripple to break the smoothness of its surface.

Passing through a break in the great circular wall, the tall cliffs recede upward from their base; then suddenly close again, and in the remote distance another cascade is seen flowing whitely over its rocky ledge, and pouring its waters into the gorge. Nearing this fine cascade, another stairway thrown across the gorge gives access to what is called the Glen of Pools, from the variety and extent of its water-worn basins. Standing on the bridge and looking up the gorge, the eye falls on a series of cascades and rapids, low and broad but very beautiful. Beyond these, again, cascades of greater breadth drop from one rocky ledge to another, foaming and seething; while over the southern wall, and the pathway that leads to it, a thin stream, falling from a great height, spreads itself out like a thin veil of silver mist, and mingles its waters with those in the rock-bound channel far below. This is called the Rainbow Fall.

Passing still along a narrow tortuous patch, a mere cleft in the rock, and up other stairways, one dimly sees a slender cascade of considerable height. Again crossing a bridge and following a fresh path for some distance, steps cut out of a projecting angle of the wall lead to a higher level, where the rocks curve inward, and the passage is made by stooping and the exercise of great caution. In this way the end of Glen Difficulty is reached,— a dark, solemn abysm shrouded in gloom, and whose walls are clammy and cold with the continual drip and ooze of water.

By the pathway, striking along the long, slender cascade to which we have already alluded, one enters the most picturesque portion of the gorge. It is more open, more airy, is full of light and shade from occasional bursts of sunshine breaking through, and has the additional advantage of compact masses of foliage. At the head of this gorge is a singularly fine cascade, falling in one unbroken column, from the height of some twenty feet, into the deep pool, which it has scooped out for itself by constant attrition. Flowing over the pool, the water forms a new succession of cascades and rapids, dips into little irregular basins as it passes onward down into the Glen of Difficulty, and thence again onward and downward over rocky ledges, through deep, water-worn channels, by tortuous ways, walled in by great cliffs towering upward, now contracting until the sky is almost shut out, now expanding into broad areas, until the gateway of the valley is reached, two miles distant from the remotest point described, and eight hundred feet below it.

Three miles south of Watkins is Havana Glen. It is very picturesque, more airy, and quite easy of access, but wanting in those elements of gloom and vastness and solemn grandeur which are the peculiar characteristics of Watkins Glen. Nevertheless there is a class of tourists who admire Havana Glen even more than its great and singularly strange rival.

It is well worth stopping at Watkins, not only for the purpose of exploring the glens, but also to visit the fine waterfalls that break in broad sheets of silver over the sides of the hills, and, uniting their tributary streams in the valleys, flow thence into the lake. A pleasant excursion may likewise be made on the lake itself, which presents along its shores many points of attraction and beauty. Fed, it is thought, by internal springs, the lake has never been known, even in the coldest weather, to be frozen over. The depth of its dark green waters is yet unknown. No soundings yet made have touched the bottom in certain places, although the line has gone down seven hundred feet. The bodies even of the drowned, when they once sink, never afterward rise to the surface. — *Appleton's Monthly.*

## CHAPTER XVI.

### THE ADIRONDACK WILDERNESS.

THE Adirondack Wilderness, or the "North Woods," as it is sometimes called, lies between the Lakes George and Champlain on the east, and the River St. Lawrence on the north and west. It reaches northward as far as the Canada line, and southward to Booneville. Its area is about that of the State of Connecticut. The southern part is known as the Brown Tract Region, with which the whole wilderness, by some, is confused, but with no more accuracy than any one county might be said to comprise an entire State. Indeed, "Brown's Tract" is the least interesting portion of the Adirondack region. It lacks the lofty mountain scenery, the intricate mesh-work of lakes, and the grandeur of the country to the north. It is the lowland district, comparatively tame and uninviting. Not until you reach the Racquette do you get a glimpse of the magnificent scenery which makes this wilderness to rival Switzerland. There, on the very ridge-board of the vast water-shed which slopes northward to the St. Lawrence, eastward to the Hudson, and southward to the Mohawk, you can enter upon a voyage the like of which, it is safe to say, the world does not anywhere else furnish. For hundreds of miles I have boated up and down that wilderness, going ashore only to "carry" around a fall, or across some narrow ridge dividing the otherwise connected lakes. For weeks I have paddled my cedar shell in all directions, swinging northerly into the St. Regis chain, westward nearly to Potsdam, southerly to the Black River country, and from thence penetrated to that almost unvisited region, the "South Branch," without seeing a face but my guide's, and the entire circuit, it must be remembered, was through a wilderness yet to echo to the lumberman's axe. It is estimated that a thousand lakes may, yet unvisited, lie embedded in this vast forest of pine and hemlock. From the summit of a mountain, two years ago, I counted, as seen by my naked eye, forty-four lakes gleaming amid the depths of the wilderness like gems or purest ray amid the folds of emerald-colored velvet. Last summer I met a gentleman on the Racquette who had just received a letter from a brother in Switzerland, an artist by profession, in which he said, that, having travelled over all Switzerland, and the Rhine and Rhone region, he had not met with scenery which, judged from a purely artistic point of view, combined so many beauties in connection with such grandeur as the lakes, mountains, and forests of the Adirondack region presented to the gazer's eye. And yet thousands are in Europe to-day as tourists, who never gave a passing thought to this marvellous country, lying, as it were, at their very doors.

I know nothing which carries the mind so far back towards the creative period as to stand on the shore of such a sheet of water, as is often met with in this wild region, shut in on all sides by mountains, mirrored from base to summit in its placid bosom, bordered here with fresh green grass and there with reaches of golden sand, knowing that, as you behold it, so has it been for ages. The water which laves your feet is the same as that which flowed when the springs which feed it were first uncapped. No rude axe has smitten the forests which grow upon the mountains; even the grass at your side is as the parent spire, which He who ordereth all commands to bring forth seed after its kind. All around you is as it was in the beginning.

Who that has ever visited the Adirondacks does not grow enthusiastic as he recalls the beauty and solemn splendor of the night, as he has beheld it while being paddled across some one of its many hundred lakes? The current of air which I had noted at the camp, cool and refreshing after the hot summer's day, was too steady and slight to stir a ripple on the glassy water. The sky was in its bluest tint, sobered by darkness. In the southern heavens, and even up to the zenith, the stars were mellow and hazy, shorn of half their beams by the moist atmosphere through which they shone. A few, away to the south, lying back of a stratum of air saturated almost to the density of vapor, beamed like so many patches of illuminated mist. But far to the north and west, whence at intervals a thin gleam of lightning shone, reflected from some far-off, nether region, the low growl of thunder was occasionally heard. Above, in the clear, cool blue, the star which never moves, the Dipper, and countless other orbs, differing in glory, revealed in sharp, clear outlines their stellary formations. The waveless water was to these heavens a perfect mirror; and over that seamless surface, over planets and worlds shining beneath us, over systems and constellations the minutest star of which was visible, we softly glided. With bowed head I gazed into that illuminated sea. I thought of that other sea, which is "of glass like unto crystal" before the throne, and the glory which must forever be reflected from its depths. "Is this the same world of cities and cursing in which I lived a week ago?" I said to myself, "or have I been translated to some other and happier sphere? Around me on all sides, as I gazed, night dusky and dim sat on the mountains and brooded over the starry sea, and the all-enveloping silence of the wilderness rested solemnly over all. As I sat and mused, — yea, and worshipped, — memory stirred within me; the words of the Psalmist came to my lips, and I murmured, "This is night which showeth wisdom, and the melody of which has gone out through all the world." — *Murray*.

"In all this rugged portion of New York, iron deposits are to be found, and the abundance and richness of the ores through the Adirondack Hills, especially so called, led long ago to the establishment of very extensive 'works' in their midst.

"On the banks of many of the lakes are catacombs of huge skeleton trees which have been killed by the overflow of the water; and weird and wild are the desolate scenes, down among the forest dead men. . . . Two or three miles from Lake Sanford is a clearing called Newcombe Farm, which commands a wide and noble view of the chief summits of the Adirondack group. Among the rocks in Lake Sanford there is an old formation called Napoleon's Cap, from its striking likeness to the immortal chapeau of that famous hero. The cap seems to have dropped overboard, and to be floating quietly on the water.

" *The Great Indian Pass* is one of the most famous scenes in all the Adirondack region. It is a wild gorge, precipitously walled at one point by the colossal cliffs which so frequently dignify the landscape around. By and by, when the engineer shall have tamed its rough nature by path and road, it will be a ready route eastward to Lake Champlain.

" *The Saranac Lakes* proper are three in number. The lower waters are some six miles in length, and occasionally of great depth. They are full of picturesque islands, of curious headlands, of inviting bays, with shores of striking interest crowned in the distance by many a fantastic mountain-top.

" *The Upper Saranac, St. Regis and Tupper's Lakes*, as indeed do all the waters of this region, abound in trout and other excellent fish; and deer and other game are numerous among their densely-wooded embankments. The vegetation of this region is luxuriant in tree and shrub, in grass and flower and weed; gigantic pines of many varieties, soaring balsams and spruce, trailing hemlocks, the vermilion-berried mountain-ash, with all the families of maple, beech, and birch. Rank grasses and many-hued plants deck the banks, and the fresh footprints of the deer are everywhere thick upon the shore, which they visit to feed on the lilies with which the lakes are covered."

*The Au Sable Chasm.* — Within two and a half miles of

Port Kent, on the way to Keesville and the Adirondacks, is the most wonderful chasm or gorge that is to be found in North America. Such freaks or works of nature are not unknown in Scotland and Switzerland, but I do not know of anything like this in our country. My friend, Mr. Watson, and his son, W. C. Watson, Jr., Esq., of Keesville, a young lawyer, carried me to this chasm, and I shall give you an account of it in the very words of my host and guide: —

"The passage of the Au Sable River along its lofty and perpendicular banks, and through the Chasm at the high bridge, is more familiar to the public mind than most of the striking and picturesque features of that romantic stream. The continued and gradual force of the current, aided perhaps by some vast effort of nature, has formed a passage of the river through the deep layers of sandstone rock, which are boldly developed above the village of Keesville, and form the embankment of the river, until it reaches the quiet basin below the high bridge. In the vicinity of Keesville, the passage of the stream is between a wall on either side of fifty feet in height; leaving these the river glides gently along a low valley, until suddenly hurled over a precipice, that creates a fall of singular beauty. Foaming and surging from this point over a rocky bed until it reaches the village of Birmingham, it there abruptly bursts into a dark, deep chasm of sixty feet.

"A bridge, with one abutment upon a rock that divides the stream, crosses the river at the head of this fall. This bridge is perpetually enveloped in a thick cloud of spray and mist. In winter the frost-work encrusts the rocks and trees with the most gorgeous fabrics; myriads of columns and arches and icy diamonds and stalactites glitter in the sunbeams. In the sunshine, a brilliant rainbow spreads its arc over this deep abyss. All these elements, rare in their combination, shed upon this scene an effect inexpressibly wild, picturesque, and beautiful. The river plunges from the latter precipice amid the embrasures of the vast gulf, in which for nearly a mile it is quite hidden to observation from above. It pours in a wild torrent, now along a natural canal, formed in the rocks in almost perfect and exact courses, and now darts madly down a precipice. The wall rises on a vertical face upon each side, from seventy-five to one hundred and fifty feet, whilst the width of the chasm rarely exceeds thirty feet, and at several points the stupendous masonry of the opposite wall approaches within eight or ten feet. Lateral fissures, deep and narrow, project from the main ravine at nearly right angles. The abyss is reached through one of these crevices by a stairway descending to the water by two hundred and twelve steps. The entire mass of these walls is formed of laminæ of sandstone rock, laid in regular and precise structures, almost rivalling the most accurate artificial work. The pines and cedars starting from the apertures of the wall spread a dark canopy over the gulf. The instrumentality which has produced this wonderful work is a problem that presents a wide scope for interesting, but unsatisfactory speculation.

"At the foot of the stairway is a platform, separated by a narrow, deep chasm, from what is called the Table Rock. Through this passage, the river, compressed into a deep and limited channel, rushes with the impetuosity of a mill-race. The Table Rock was formerly reached by walking upon a log over the chasm, and was a favorite but somewhat dangerous resort of picnic parties, until a tragic event arrested the habit. A Mr. Dyer, an Episcopal minister, was, some years ago, in the act of leading a lady across this log, when suddenly losing his balance he fell into the rushing torrent, and never rose to the surface, nor was his body seen by the horror-stricken spectators until days afterwards, when it was found far below upon a shallow in the river." — *New York Observer.*

## CHAPTER XVII.

#### THE NATURAL BRIDGE, VIRGINIA.

THE Natural Bridge, situated in Rockbridge County, in the western part of Virginia, has been from about the middle of the eighteenth century an object of curiosity and admiration in Europe as well as in America. Whatever traveller came to the western world to compare its natural grandeur with the grandeur of art and architecture in the countries he had left, went first in the north to the Falls of Niagara, and in the south to the world-famous bridge. Among these may be mentioned the courtly and distinguished Marquis de Chastellux, major-general in the French army, who visited the place, and from whose rare volumes we quote a few paragraphs of interest : —

"Having thus travelled for two hours," writes the Marquis, "we descended a steep declivity, and then mounted another. . . . At last my guide said to me, 'You desire to see the Natural Bridge, don't you, sir? You are now upon it; alight, and go twenty steps either to the right or left, and you will see this prodigy.' I had perceived that there was on each side a considerably deep hollow, but the trees had prevented me from forming any judgment or paying much attention to it. Approaching the precipice I saw two great masses or chains of rocks which formed the bottom of a ravine or rather of an immense abyss. But placing myself, not without precaution, upon the brink of the precipice, I saw that these two buttresses were joined under my feet, forming a vault of which I could yet form no idea but of its height. After enjoying this magnificently tremendous spectacle, which many persons could not bear to look at, I went to the western side, the aspect of which was not less imposing, but more picturesque. This Thebais, these ancient pines, these enormous masses of rocks so much the more astonishing as they appear to possess a wild symmetry, and rudely concur as it were in forming a certain design,— all this apparatus or rude and shapeless nature, which art attempts in vain, attracts at once the senses and the thoughts, and excites a gloomy and melancholy admiration.

"But it is at the foot of these rocks, on the edge of a little stream which flows under this immense arch, that we must judge of its astounding structure. There we discover its immense spurs, its back bendings, and those profiles which architecture might have given it. The arch is not complete, the eastern part of it not being so large as the western, because the mountain is more elevated on this than on the opposite side. It is very remarkable that at the stream there appear no considerable ruins, no trace of any violent laceration which could have destroyed the kernel of the rock and have left the upper part alone subsisting; for that is the only hypothesis which can account for such a prodigy. We can have no possible recourse either to a volcano or a deluge, no trace of a sudden conflagration, or of a slow and tedious undermining by the water."

The most striking view of the arch is from below. An Englishman wrote of it: "Then, there is the arch, distinct from everything and above everything! Massive as it is, it is light and beautiful by its height, and the pine-trees on its summit seem now only like a garland of evergreens; and elevated as it is, its apparent elevation is wonderfully increased by the narrowness of its piers, and by its outline being drawn on the blue sky. O, it is sublime! So strong and so elegant! Springing from earth and bathing itself in heaven! I sat and gazed in wonder and astonishment. I had quickly, too quickly, to leave the spot forever; but the music of those waters, the luxury of those shades, the form and color of those rocks, and that arch — that arch rising over all, and seeming to offer a passage to the skies — O, they will never leave me!"

From the summit to the surface of the stream below is two hundred and fifteen feet; and thus the Natural Bridge is fifty-five feet higher than Niagara. There are many traditions of the daring of some of the numerous visitors to this interesting locality, in climbing or venturing to the brink of the precipice. Perhaps the most thrilling is that of the unshrinking nerve displayed by Miss Randolph, a young Virginian, a great belle of her time, which was the early portion of the present century. The young lady had ridden with a gay party of youthful maidens and gallant cavaliers to the bridge, and reached it on a beautiful evening of summer. Miss Randolph is said to have been a young lady of surpassing loveliness, — tall, slender, with sparkling eyes, cheeks all roses, and noted for her gayety and mirthful abandon. Reaching the summit of the bridge, the party dismounted, cautiously approached the brink fringed with trees growing among the rocks, and gazed into the gulf beneath. Of the terrible character of the spectacle, President Jefferson's words will give some idea. "Though the sides of the bridge are provided in some parts with a parapet of rocks," he says, "yet few men have resolution to walk to them and look over into the abyss. You involuntarily fall on your hands and feet, creep to the parapet and look over it. Looking down from this height about a minute gave me a violent headache; the view is fearful and intolerable."

Reaching this dizzy brink, the party of young ladies and gentlemen gazed below, when one of the gallants, pointing to a broken stump of a huge cedar which had once towered aloft upon a jagged abutment separated by an intervening cleft from the main structure, expressed his conviction that no human being lived sufficiently daring to stand erect upon it. A gay laugh echoed the words, a silken scarf brushed by him, and the whole party uttered a cry of terror. Miss Randolph at one bound had reached and now stood erect upon the dizzy pinnacle. Her companions looked at her white and speechless as so many corpses. Her death seemed certain. A wild spirit of bravado had given her courage for this terrible proceeding; but perched thus on her slight footing above the frightful abyss she must lose her nerve, grow dizzy, and be hurled upon the rocks beneath, — the beautiful being of a moment since, — a mass of mangled and unrecognizable flesh and bones. For an instant the daring young lady stood erect, riding-whip in hand, her scarf floating, her eyes sparkling with triumph; then at a single bound she regained her former position, and, with a gay laugh, asked if any gentleman could do as much.

Tradition says, that despite their gallantry the youthful cavaliers exhibited their good judgment by declining. Miss Randolph's stump remained in its place many years, and the incident gave the young lady a species of celebrity throughout Virginia. — *Appleton's Monthly.*

## CHAPTER XVIII.

#### SCENERY OF NORTH CAROLINA.

THE mountain region of North Carolina furnishes views equal to those of the White Mountains. Its distance from large and populous cities, and its situation in the south, will prevent it from soon becoming a national summer resort like our northern hills. Although the mountains abound in cool springs of water, they are without lakes. Game is found in abundance, so that there are equal attractions for the hunter and the tourist. One will also here be free from the annoyance felt by many in the fashionableness of northern retreats, for both nature and the people are found almost in their pristine simplicity. The old stage-coach still rattles along the turnpike, and the shrill horn of the postman reechoes among the hills. The ferry-boat, manned by a negro and propelled by a pole, or drawn along a rope, still conveys the traveller across the numerous creeks. But in a few years, when the railroads have penetrated the mountains, these relics of the good olden time will, I fear, be no more.

The Black Mountains, the culminating group of the Appalachian system, named from the dark growth of evergreens which cover their summits, are the most attractive and picturesque mountains of North Carolina. They are situated in Yancey and Buncombe Counties, and are the highest peaks west of the Rocky Mountains, — twelve of them surpassing Mount Washington. Standing, however, on a plateau two thousand feet in height, they do not appear as lofty.

Mount Mitchell, one of this group, is interesting not only for its scenery, but also since it stands as the monument and sepulchre of the late Dr. Mitchell, of the university of North Carolina. He was the first who ascertained that these mountains were the highest east of the Rocky Mountains. While paying them a second visit to settle some disputed points, having lost his way in the night, he fell from a precipice into a pool, where his lifeless body was found. His remains were interred on the highest point of the mountain, which bears his name, 6,576 feet above the level of the sea.

Among the mountain streams that have their source among these towering hills is the famous French Broad, whose wild and romantic course abounds in the most picturesque and beautiful scenery. It cuts its way through mountain gorges of fearful height, runs dimpling among green hills, winds itself around mountain islands, whose heavy and tangled undergrowth, with their clinging vines and glowing flowers, are of tropical luxuriance, sleeps sullen and dark between huge cliffs, rushes down rocky declivities with a deafening roar, ever changeful in its wild beauty. A fine highway follows the banks of the river, often trespassing on its waters. The adjacent hill-sides are exceedingly steep, and their soil astonishingly rich. A low-country man on his way through the valley, once asked a hill-side farmer: —

"I say, squire — you don't grow corn up there?"

"Well, I reckon I do."

"How much do you get to the acre?"

"Twenty-five bushels of shelled corn or thereabouts."

"Just one more question, squire,— How do you ever plant it?"

"Well, we just load up our old shot-guns with corn, and stand down here and shoot it into the ground. It don't need any cultivating, and if it did, we are all too lazy to give it any."

On the borders of the French Broad are the celebrated Chimney Rocks,— a series of lofty cliffs broken at their summits into detached piles of rock, which have the likeness of colossal chimneys. These rocks rise abruptly to the height of nearly three hundred feet. A little beyond these cliffs a turn in the road brings the traveller to the famous Painted Rocks, another series of stupendous cliffs rising to an altitude of two hundred and sixty-three feet, direct from the river's edge, and having a reddish-brown color, from which their name is probably derived, though some accounts attribute their designation to the Indian pictures said still to be seen on them.

*Gingercake Rocks.* This remarkable pile of rocks gives its name to the mountain summit upon the top of which it is seen. They are situated in the mountainous part of Burke

County, amidst wild and romantic scenery. The pile consists of two rocks of different form and character, so poised as to stand firmly on an exceedingly small base. The first or lower section, composed of a brittle slate stone, is in the form of the half of an inverted pyramid. Its truncated top, which, by its inverted position becomes the base, upon which the whole is supported, is only four feet in diameter. The centre of gravity to this part of the pile would fall much without the base upon which it rests, were it not most accurately balanced in its position by the second or superincumbent rock, which is a table of mountain granite, thirty-two feet in length, eighteen in breadth, and two feet thick, resting horizontally upon the other, with a sufficient excess of its projection and weight, opposite to the preponderance of the inverted pyramid beneath, to produce a perfect counterpoise. The form and outline of this upper rock is as remarkable as that of the other, being as true in the proportions above given as if it had come from the hand of an artist. The lower section is about twenty-nine feet high, which, being increased by the thickness of the upper section, makes the whole altitude thirty-one feet.

## CHAPTER XIX.

### TALLULAH FALLS, GEORGIA.

"THE Cherokee word 'Tallulah' means the terrible, and was originally applied to the river of that name, on account of its fearful falls. This stream rises among the Alleghany Mountains, and is a tributary of the Savannah in Northern Georgia. It runs through a mountain land, narrow, deep, clear, and cold, and subject to every variety of mood. During the first half of its career, it winds among the hills in uneasy joy, and then for several miles it wears a placid appearance, and you can scarcely hear the murmur of its waters. Soon tiring of this peaceful course, however, it narrows itself for an approaching contest, and runs through a chasm whose walls, about two miles in length, are for the most part perpendicular; and, after making five distinct leaps, as the chasm deepens, it settles into a turbulent and angry mood, and so continues until it leaves the gorge, and regains its wonted character. The total fall of water within the two miles has been estimated at four hundred feet, and the several falls have been named Lodore, Tempesta, Oceana, Horicon, and Serpentine. What they have done that they should have been so wretchedly christened, has always been a mystery. At this point the stream is exceedingly winding, and the granite cliffs on either side vary in height from six hundred to nine hundred feet, while the mountains which back the cliffs reach an elevation of fifteen hundred feet. Many of the pools are large and deep, and the rocks are everywhere covered with the most luxuriant mosses. The vegetation of the whole chasm is particularly rich and varied, for you find here not only the pine, but specimens of every variety of the more tender trees, together with lichens and vines and flowers which would keep a botanist employed for half a century. Only four paths have been discovered leading to the margin of the water, and to make either one of these descents requires much of the nerve and courage of the samphire gatherer. Through this immense gorge a strong wind is ever blowing, and the sunlight never falls upon the cataracts without forming beautiful rainbows which contrast strangely with the surrounding gloom and horror; and the roar of the waterfall perpetually ascending to the sky comes to the beholder with a voice that bids him to wonder and admire. As a natural curiosity the Falls of Tallulah are on a par with the River Saguenay and the Falls of Niagara. Other striking features of this chasm are the Devil's Pulpit, Devil's Dwelling, the Eagle's Nest, the Deer Leap, Hawthorne's Pool, and Hawk's Sliding Place, whose several names convey an idea of their characteristics or associations. After emerging from its magnificent chasm, the Tallulah River runs quietly through a beautiful vale, which is so completely hemmed in by hills as to be inaccessible to a vehicle of any description.

Such a place could hardly fail to have an Indian legend associated with it. Many generations ago, according to the Cherokees, it so happened that several famous hunters, who had wandered from the west towards the Savannah River, never returned. The curiosity and fears of the nation were excited, and they sent a delegation of medicine men to go and find the lost hunters. They visited the east, and when they returned they reported that they had discovered a dreadful chasm in a strange part of the country. They said it was a very wild place, and inhabited by a race of little people, who dwelt among the rocks and under the waterfalls; that they were the enemies of the Cherokee nation; and they knew that these little people had decoyed these missing hunters to death in the waters of Tallulah. In view of this legend, it is worthy of remark, that the Cherokees, before departing for the far west, always avoided the Falls of Tallulah, and were never found hunting or fishing anywhere in the vicinity."

## CHAPTER XX.

### ST. AUGUSTINE, NEW ORLEANS, AND ST. LOUIS.

ST. AUGUSTINE, the oldest town in the United States, founded in 1565, stands on a flat, sandy level, encompassed for miles and miles by what is called "scrub," a mixture of low palmettoes and bushes of various descriptions. Its history carries one back almost to the Middle Ages. For instance, Menendez, who figured as commandant in its early day, was afterward appointed to command the Spanish Armada, away back in the times of Queen Elizabeth; but, owing to the state of his health, he did not accept the position.

In the year 1586, Elizabeth then being at war with Spain, her Admiral, Sir Francis Drake, bombarded St. Augustine and took it, helping himself, among other things, to seven brass cannon, 2,000 pounds in money, and other booty. In 1665, it was taken and plundered by the buccaneers; in 1702, besieged by the people of the Carolinas; in 1740, besieged again by General Oglethorpe of Georgia.

The aspect of St. Augustine is quaint and strange, in harmony with its romantic history. It has no pretensions to architectural richness or beauty, and yet it is impressive for its unlikeness to anything else in America. It is as if some little, old, dead-and-alive Spanish town, with its fort and gateway and Moorish bell towers, had broken loose and floated over here, and got stranded on a sand-bank. Here you see the black gowns and shovel hats of priests, the convent with gliding figures of nuns, and in the narrow, crooked streets meet dark-browed people with great Spanish eyes and coal-black hair. The current of life here has the indolent, dreamy stillness that characterizes life in old Spain. In Spain, when you ask a man to do anything, instead of answering, as we do, "In a minute," the invariable reply is, "In an hour,"—and the growth and progress of St. Augustine has been according.

There it stands, alone, isolated, connected by no good roads or navigation with the busy living world. Before 1835, St. Augustine was a bower of orange-trees. Almost every house looked forth from these encircling shades. The frost came and withered all, and in very few cases did it seem to come into the heads of the inhabitants to try again. The orange-groves are now the exception and not the rule; and yet for thirty years it has been quite possible to have them. — *Mrs. Stowe, in the Christian Union.*

*New Orleans.* — New Orleans is situated on the left bank of the Mississippi River, about one hundred miles from its mouth. It was settled by the French in 1718; in 1763, with the colony of Louisiana, it was transferred to Spain, and in 1803 to the United States. New Orleans is called the Crescent City, from its situation on the bend of the river. It is protected from the overflowing of the river by a levee, which, from the yearly alluvial deposits, it has been necessary for shipping purposes continually to widen. The levee is the liveliest and most interesting part of the city. There are congregated hundreds of splendid steamers, and thousands of nondescript boats, thickly interspersed with ships of the largest size, and flying the signals of every civilized people. Its length and breadth are covered with bales of fleecy cotton, great piles of corn in sacks, hogsheads of sugar and molasses, great stacks of bacon, bales of hemp, barrels, boxes, crates, machines, and mules. Stalwart negroes with herculean muscles hurry to and fro, bearing great burdens, now on their heads, now on their shoulders, or now on trucks, amid a babel of oaths and cries. Every nationality seems to be represented; and French and German one hears almost as frequently as English. Over each pile of merchandise is a little flag with a quaint device, to designate the owner. Jackson Square, a short distance from the levee, is a well-kept park of small size, containing an equestrian statue of General Jackson. The Old French Market is a very interesting place, since there may be seen French, Germans, Spaniards, Chinese, Indians, Creoles, Negroes, and representatives of almost every nationality. The Custom House, not yet completed, is a magnificent building, the largest public building in America except the Capitol at Washington. New Orleans has also several large and fine hotels, churches, and warehouses. It is the greatest cotton mart in the world, and has the largest river trade in the United States.

*St. Louis.* — St. Louis was transferred to the United States by the Spanish in 1803. In 1830 its population was less than 7,000, but now it is the fourth city of the Union, being only surpassed by New York, Brooklyn, and Philadelphia. It is situated on the Mississippi, twenty miles below the mouth of the Missouri, on two limestone plateaus, one twenty, the other sixty feet above the floods of the Mississippi. The ascent to the first plateau is somewhat abrupt; the second rises more gradually, and spreads out into an extensive plain, affording fine views of the city and river. The city is well laid out with streets of ample width, which, with a few exceptions, intersect each other at right angles. Front Street, extending along the levee, is upwards of a hundred feet wide, and built up, on the side facing the river, with a range of massive stone warehouses, which make an imposing appearance as the city is approached by water. The city is remarkably well built, most of its warehouses and a large proportion of its public edifices and dwellings being of brick or stone. The city extends some eight miles along the river, and four miles back from the river. The levee along the river affords facilities for steamboats to discharge their cargoes, superior to those of any other city on the Mississippi.

It may be doubted whether any city of the Union has improved more rapidly than St. Louis in the style of its public buildings. Among these are the Court House, occupying a whole square, the architecture of which resembles that of the

Capitol at Washington; the Centre Market; the Custom House, costing $350,000; the City Hall; the Cathedral, and many other churches; the Southern Hotel, the Planters House, and other hotels.

The literary and educational institutions of St. Louis have, considering their recent origin, attained a high degree of excellence. The University of St. Louis, organized in 1832, under the direction of the Catholics, is a well-ordered, well-sustained, and a most efficient institution. The medical college connected with it is also very flourishing. The Washington University, incorporated in 1853, is an institution intended to embrace the whole range of university studies except the theological, and afford opportunity for complete preparation for every sphere of practical and scientific life. In connection with the public schools of St. Louis there is a library containing 20,000 volumes, which is an important accessory to the educational advantages of the schools. This library also contains many works of art, besides Indian curiosities, which will repay a visit.

The statue of Thomas Benton in Franklin Square is an object of interest. With the right hand pointing to the west, and the well-known prophecy engraved, " The Way to the East," the effect of the silent speaker is impressive, and the more so as that prophecy is now fulfilled.

At the breaking out of the Rebellion, in no place did the passions of sectional strife burn with an intenser flame than in St. Louis, it being both a northern and a southern city in its character. Then, so bitter was the feeling, the most intimate families were separated, never to speak to each other again, although they might live in the same block. The bullet-holes may still be seen in houses, where they fought in the streets. The removal of the United States arms by stealth into Illinois, the capture of Fort Jackson, where walls of earth are still visible, the prompt action of General

Lyon, and the rule of General Fremont, are incidents that will not be soon forgotten.

One object of especial attraction in the vicinity of St. Louis is the celebrated garden of Mr. Gray, which has now been presented to the city.

The citizens of this city, for a few years past, have been greatly interested in the hope of one day having the national capital removed within their limits. Even without it, they expect their city to be the largest in the interior off the seaboard, if not in the whole country.

*The St. Louis Bridge.* — One of the wonders of the West, if not of the world, is the bridge in process of construction over the Mississippi River at St. Louis. This marvel of engineering skill is under the direction of Chief Engineer James B. Eads, well known for his various inventions in naval and military defences. No river in the world presents such obstacles for erecting piers as the Mississippi does in the ever-shifting sands of its treacherous bottom, and yet the Father of Waters has been defied and conquered, and monuments of masonry rising from its dark waters bear witness of its subjection to the will of man. The bridge will have three spans, each formed with four ribbed arches of cast steel. The centre span will be five hundred and fifteen feet, and the side ones four hundred and ninety-seven feet each, in the clear. There will be two roadways: the upper one will be for carriages, horse-cars, and foot passengers; the lower one for railway trains. The width of the bridge and its height above high water will be each fifty feet. The estimated cost of the bridge is $5,000,000.

## CHAPTER XXI.

### CHICAGO.

CHICAGO, the fourth city of the Union in point of population, and the third in commercial importance, is too well known to require a description, and is too much altered and disfigured by the great fire, and too rapidly undergoing changes in its reconstruction, for any present description to do it justice, or to represent what it really is, or will be in a few years. To give any adequate conception of its past growth, grandeur, and prosperity, in which respects it has exceeded the expectations of its most sanguine friends, is, to say the least, a difficult task.

An Englishman speaks thus of his impressions of Chicago in 1870 : —

"By the residents, Chicago is often styled the 'Garden City.' Both its citizens and its admirers sometimes claim for it the still more dignified title of the 'Queen City of the West,' or the 'Queen City of the Lakes.' The pride they take in it is extreme, and the language in which they express their feelings is high-flown. This appears quite natural to the traveller who has journeyed from England to the United States, in order to witness the marvels which human industry and energy have wrought on the surface of the vast American Continent. Books and newspapers may have prepared him for an extraordinary spectacle, yet neither tables nor statistics nor any printed statements can enable him to realize the grandeur of an impression produced by a stay, however short, in the modern city of Chicago. With a sensation of incredulity hardly to be repressed, he listens to the stories which tell of the city's foundation and history. Forty years have not yet elapsed since the site of palatial dwellings was distinguished from the surrounding wilderness by a log fort, in which two companies of soldiers were stationed for the protection of a few traders, who collected furs from the Indians in exchange for trinkets. In those days civilized men regarded a visit to the shores of Lake Michigan much in the same light as many persons now regard a visit to the sources of the Nile. Those who made the journey had to brave the attacks of ferocious animals; had to face the perils incident to an inhospitable and uncultivated region; had to live in constant dread of an attack from Indians, more deliberately cruel than any beast, and more crafty than any other enemy in human shape. The wild men and wild animals have both disappeared. The land which once yielded a precarious subsistence to the hunter, now repays the skilful farmer an hundred-fold. Where weeds formerly throve in rank profusion, peach-trees are now heavy with precious fruit. A city of palaces has taken the place of a few miserable hovels. Similar transformations have occurred in other parts of the globe. Venice and Holland do not fall short of Chicago as evidences of what man can achieve in his struggle with rugged nature and hostile elements. Yet the growth of either was the work of many years, as well as of much toil; whereas Chicago has waxed great and famous within the memory of men still living, and not yet old. If another Queen Scheherezade were compelled to rehearse a tale of enchantment for the gratification of an exacting husband, she might find in the authentic story of the rise of Chicago materials which would produce a result as striking as that caused by a recital of the fabulous doings of Aladdin."

But to recur to the history of the city. The site of Chicago was first visited by Marquette, a Jesuit missionary, in 1673; but there was no regular occupancy of the place until 1804, when the United States government established a military post at the mouth of the Chicago River, called Fort Dearborn. At the close of the Black Hawk war in 1832, the country was thrown open to settlement, and Chicago began to excite general attention throughout the United States as a desirable point for residence and investment. In 1840 Chicago contained a population of 4,470; in 1860, 109,263; and, at the time of the fire, scarcely less than 300,000 souls.

Nothing could be more uninviting than the original site of the city. Ridges of shifting sand bordered the lake shore; while inland, and stretching beyond the range of vision, was a morass supporting a rank growth of blue-joint grass, with here and there a clump of jack oaks. Through this morass wound the sluggish river, only flushed by the spring and fall freshets.

In 1833 a post-office was established, and the mail was brought weekly on horseback from Niles, Michigan. In 1837, Chicago became incorporated as a city, and William B. Ogden was chosen its first mayor. From that time to the present, the history of the growth of the city becomes too complex to be traced, except in a comprehensive form. A series of public improvements was devised, which made Chicago one of the pleasantest and healthiest cities in the Union. A system of underground drainage was established, which required the original surface in many places to be raised eight feet. This change of grade involved the necessity of raising many of the largest structures in those streets adjacent to the river. Such immense buildings as the Tremont and Briggs Houses, the Marine Bank, and, in fact, entire blocks, were lifted up with little or no interruption of business.

To supply the city with pure water, Lake Michigan was resorted to as an unfailing reservoir. A "crib" forty feet in height, and nearly one hundred feet in diameter, was floated to a site in the Lake, two miles from shore, and there sunk. From this a tunnel was built to the shore. By means of enormous pumps the water is forced up a tower, one hundred and thirty feet high, whence its own pressure distributes it to different parts of the city.

The intercourse between the three divisions of the city, up to a recent time, had been effected only by swing bridges, which were a serious impediment to navigation, and equally so, by their continuous turning, to vehicles and pedestrians. To obviate this, two tunnels were constructed under the river, — one at La Salle Street, and one on Washington Street.

The Chicago River, advantageous as it is to navigation and the commercial interests of the city, was, nevertheless, until a short time since, a sore plague-spot in its midst. It was a sluggish, vile stream, with scarcely a perceptible current. To purify its waters the canal connecting it with the Illinois River was deepened, which turned the current backward, and caused the cool, clear waters of the lake to flow through it towards the Mississippi.

Nor can we omit a mention of the parks of Chicago. Already blessed with large and beautiful parks, she was not content, but her enterprising citizens projected and carried into effect a Boulevard system of magnificent proportions. The whole city, with the exception of the lake side, will soon be environed by these elegant drives and continuous pleasure-grounds.

We will not occupy our space by describing the palatial buildings of Chicago that were, — the Pacific Hotel, the Court House, McVickar's Theatre, Crosby's Opera House, the Palmer House, the Michigan Southern Depot, Field and Leiter's Dry Goods House, and the many other wonderful and magnificent structures which gave way before the all-devouring flame. These soon will be thought of no more, for their places will be occupied by edifices if possible still more costly and elegant.

*The Great Fire.*—A fire unrivalled for extent and destruction of property, in the annals of history, visited the city of Chicago, October 8th, 1871. The fire consumed nearly 3,200 acres, or nearly five square miles. The great fires of London, Moscow, and Constantinople, all combined, will scarcely equal the Chicago fire in the amount of space burned over. They also swept away districts but imperfectly built, which subsequent enterprise beautified and adorned; but this fire wiped out the most substantially built and beautifully adorned portions of the city. Nearly twenty-five thousand buildings of all descriptions were levelled with the ground, and the number of human beings rendered homeless was, at the very lowest calculation, 111,000. The loss of property and damage to business was from three to four hundred millions of dollars.

For two days the city was a rolling ocean of flame, and presented an aspect whose awful grandeur might rival the spectacle of a seething, roaring volcano. No buildings of iron, stone, or brick were able to withstand the terrific force of the fire, fanned by a driving hurricane from the southwest, but all like wax were melted. To understand this appalling fact it must be remembered that the very finest and most solidly built portion of the city was surrounded and sprinkled with a vast number of frame buildings, and was thus, as it were, encircled by fuel of the driest and most inflammable description. Once the wood, tar, and shingles were well lighted, the more lightly built portion of the city was a terrific furnace, and the buildings of iron and marble were as nothing to withstand the fearful flames.

Moreover, there had been a baking of earth, trees, and dwellings in the dry air of a rainless autumn, until everything had been cooked to a crisp igniting point. For nearly fifteen weeks there had not fallen enough rain to penetrate the earth one full inch. The fire department also was wearied out, having worked unceasingly for twelve hours the night before, in subduing a conflagration which had been thrown out as a skirmish line for the mighty hosts of flame that were to follow. And, worse than all, a driving gale of wind was surging up from the southwest, — a gale so violent as to threaten disastrous hurricane, and to whip the waters of the lake into the white frenzy of a storm.

*Origin of the Fire.* — The origin of the fire is not known, or rather no investigation has yet been able to ascertain by what agency the first building was ignited. The story about the old woman who went into her stable to milk her cow by the light of a kerosene lamp, which lamp said cow kicked over, is a pure fabrication. The fire first broke out in a small stable to the rear of a frame building on the north side of DeKoven Street, almost half-way between Jefferson and Clinton Streets. Whether it originated from a spark blown from a chimney on that windy night, or was set afire by human agency, it is impossible to determine. There is no proof that any persons had been in the barn after nightfall that evening. The fire was first discovered by a drayman, about twenty-five minutes past nine on Sunday night, and, owing to the distance from the nearest engine-houses, ten minutes elapsed before water could be thrown, and then the fire had such headway among the wooden buildings, that, although the whole fire department was called out, on account of the severe gale it was found impossible to control it.

*The Course of the Fire.* — From its starting-point the fire spread east, west, and north with incredible swiftness, and as it extended it gained in strength and fierceness, travelling faster and faster. The furious wind now commenced to catch up burning shingles, showers of charcoal, sparks, and fire-brands of all kinds, carrying them towards the northeast with terrible effect. From Clinton Street to the south branch of Chicago River, the whole space was covered with lumber-yards, wooden buildings, quantities of coal, and, in short, everything that would make a good fire. With the exception of a few buildings at the corner of DeKoven and Canal Streets and a few on Canal itself, everything was burned to ashes, the very streets being scorched and blackened. But the remainder of the west side was saved. The fire had reached the portion devastated by the flames in the conflagration of Saturday night. North of Harrison and Van Buren Streets was the blank space upon which the fire of the previous evening had spent itself, and the skeleton walls and scorched brick afforded nothing for it to feed upon. Were it not for this fact, the south side would have been as completely destroyed as the north had been. As it was, the fire ate up more than fifty squares of the west division, also devouring four or five bridges to the south side. Beyond the open space of the old burnt area was the river, and beyond that were the proud edifices of the business heart of Chicago. Here, all thought, the fire-wraith would bow to circumstances too powerful for its fury.

But this was not to be. Hardly pausing to take breath, the allied terrors of tempest and flame leaped in fell carnival over into the South Division. From this time onward there was but one sad story of destruction. All the grand blocks of stone and marble crumbled away into dust at the breath of the destroyer. Palaces of trade, hotels, halls, theatres, and churches alike swelled the volume of flame that seemed to reach the sky. Following in its track, or rather giving way to its encroachments, the first great pang of sorrow came to the despairing spectators when the flames stormed up to the Pacific Hotel. This superb edifice occupied the whole block in which it was situated, and had just been erected at an immense cost. The building, by its imposing dimensions and fine architecture, was one of the chief ornaments of the doomed city, and was one of the largest hotels in the world. Far north of Van Buren Street the fire licked up gigantic squares of marble palaces, and approached the Court House. This splendid building occupied the centre of a square, and owing to its isolated situation, it being surrounded by fire-proof buildings, it was considered free from danger. But even before the sea of flames surrounded it, the ruthless wind hurled flaming brands and sparks upon the great dome, and the edifice was soon a mass of flames. The watchman started the machinery that tolled the ponderous bell, and fled from the building. The bell boomed forth the news of the terrible catastrophe, until the vast dome tottered, reeled, and fell, crashing into the interior with all the weight of several million pounds. The awful shock shook the burning city, and then the Chief of the Fire Department threw up his arms in despair; for he felt that all hope was gone.

The prisoners were liberated when it became evident that the Court House was doomed, and all escaped with the exception of five murderers, who were securely handcuffed and marched off by the police.

The interior of the Post-Office was completely eaten out by the devouring fire. Near it were many of the finest buildings Chicago could boast of, including the elegant hotels between Madison and Lake Streets; the splendid office of the "Chicago Tribune," McVickar's Theatre, and the Palmer House, all stood within a few squares of the glowing walls of the Post-Office. Soon the flame, advancing eastwardly, seized upon the Palmer House, wrapping it from roof to basement in a shroud of yellow fire; the flames, bursting from the roof, leaped astonishing distances to yet intact edifices. In a very short space of time, all the surrounding buildings were fiercely blazing.

It was about four o'clock in the morning when the announcement was made that the flames had crossed into the North Division. Then the terrible tidings were whispered that the water-works were in ruins, and that the only friend man had found among the elements was taken from him in this his hour of necessity.

The people dwelling in the North Division — which indeed was mostly composed of dwelling-houses — soon found themselves compelled to flee to the lake shore. The fire now advanced without an enemy to oppose it, and swept on towards the cemetery which bounded Lincoln Park on the south. One remarkably handsome wooden residence, together with a fine conservatory, were, however, spared by the hungry element, which left no other building standing in its destroying path.

By night-fall of that fearful Monday a great number of refugees had collected in the cemetery at the end of Lincoln Park, and many had endeavored to dispose themselves as comfortably as possible until the light of another morning should enable them to make their final escape. But the fire-wraith hesitated not at the pollution of the quiet homes of the dead, and was soon curling the leaves and snapping the brush at the cemetery's entrance. Another stampede was all that was left to the heart-sick multitude of living ones, who vainly sought to catch a few hours of fitful rest upon the graves of the sleepers below, whom even this tyrant of conflagration could not disturb. Out from the cemetery swarmed the stricken ones, and into the Park, from which they were again routed by the untiring pursuit of the wind and the flames. The only rest was upon the chilly margin of the lake, and the bleak wilderness of the open prairie. The edge of the lake was lined with its dreary quota of those who, twenty-four hours before, had gone to rest in happy homes, at the close of a Sabbath, differing to them from no other Sabbath which had preceded it, but which was the dividing line between prosperity and utter ruin.

The fire, after ploughing away every vestige of the North Division, ceased not in its work of ruin until Fullerton Avenue, the extreme northern limit of the city, was attained. Here, with nothing further upon which it could riot, it at last died away in the second night of its carouse; and just as the long-prayed-for rain came pattering coolly down, the Chicago Fire passed into history.

*Incidents of the Fire.* — We take the liberty to insert the following thrilling description, written immediately after the fire, by the pen of a graphic writer: —

"The air was filled with flying cinders, which, hurled aloft by the fierce intensity of the breeze, eddied and floated in the firmament, and fell again to the earth three and four blocks distant. These cinders drifted about the corners of streets and alleys like snow under the effects of a winter's breeze. They ignited whole rows of buildings at once. It was impossible to protect the city from their advances: Terrified at the rapidity with which the flames spread, the people hastily threw out into the streets what household goods they could, and with valuables in their hands stood gazing as if stupefied at the destruction of their homes. At about the hour of ten, it being then seen that the flames, despite the efforts of the firemen, could not be checked, every bell in the city, fire-bell, church-bell, school-house and engine bell, began ringing. The object was to arouse the sleeping populace, that they might bring, as best they could, their goods to a place of safety. Drays and express wagons hastened through the streets, laden with all imaginable sorts of goods, and drove hurriedly towards the lake side near the park. Sick and decrepit persons were unceremoniously thrown upon the tops of beds, and almost battered to pieces by the hurling of bandboxes, china-ware, portmanteaus, clocks, looking-glasses, doll-babies, poodle dogs, umbrellas, bird-cages, musical instruments, silverware, smoothing-irons, and all sorts of household truck. Fainting women, half-clad women, screaming women, hysterical women, and even laughing and dancing women lined the walks. Shouts and yells for expressmen to transport these helpless women and children, mingled with the indescribable noise from the roaring of the flames; the whistling of the engines, the howling of the wind, clangor of bells, trumpet sounds of the firemen, and the hurly-burly in the streets — were the noises that added to the confusion of the scene. By midnight the flames had spread in a direct line forward over three miles of houses. Nothing can be said that would describe adequately the unparalleled intensity of the fire. A building seemingly fire-proof would catch fire, and in ten minutes' time the roof, with a fearful crash, would fall in, sending up a thickening storm of sparks and cinders, that, alighting on fresh territory, would soon give notice of their rapidly germinating seeds of immense volumes of flame. The firmament glowed with them. The leaping flames, as they licked up some more than usually inflammable substance in drug and liquor stores, would arise to steeple heights in the heavens, and shed a lurid glare upon the doomed city. The clouds of smoke rolled away to the northward, and all around the sphere of fire the intense darkness of the sky added by contrast to the terrors of the scene. On Clark Street a new pavement of cedar blocks and tar had just been put down, and the street was only partially open for public traffic, although the pavement was completed. It caught fire, and instantaneously, from one end of the street to the other, fierce flames broke out, — it was a perfect channel of fire.

"Some of the more fortunate pedestrians upon that street

made their escape into alleys and cross streets, some of them having the clothes burned off their backs, so sudden and spontaneously fierce were the flames. It is known that some persons in this street were unable to escape, and, asphyxiated and rendered senseless, fell unexpected victims to the flames. In the tall buildings on either side many clerks had their lodgings. Some of these made their escape half clad. Others, who had during the day indulged in dissipation, and had retired to bed stupefied by excesses, did not awaken in time, and perished before assistance could be rendered. Two young men, it is said, appealed from a fourth-story window to the impotent by-standers, for rescue from the furnace of fierce heat that wrapped the building. No relief was possible. In another moment the roof fell upon them, the walls tottered in, and they found their death and burial-place amid the heaps of ashes. Just how many persons met their fate in this manner, it is impossible to say. The wildest rumors were current, but amid the unparalleled excitement everywhere surrounding the scene, but little heed was given to these stories, and no effort made to ascertain their truth. The uproar increased ; the flames spread ; the firemen became despairing ; the shouts and clamors of the women and children and the roar of the flames filled the air. Two fire-engines of the south division became surrounded by the flames and were left to their fate, the jaded firemen being unable to bring them out. As the danger became imminent, and hopes of saving the business part of the city lying between the river, the south branch, and the lake were abandoned, the proprietors of hotels aroused their guests, and warned them that the only prospect of escaping with their lives lay in immediate flight.

"This was between the hours of twelve and one.

"Now, to add fresh terrors to the scene, were heard repeated explosions, sounding like a continual cannonade. Drug and liquor stores, and places where oil was stored, burned and burst, and fear of powder — happily but a fear — took possession of the multitude. At the Tremont House the elevator became useless, and the sleeping guests, a large number being babies, hurried down-stairs. The clatter of the removal of trunks and the hurrying of domestics impeded the passage-ways. Several persons in their eagerness jumped down the stairs, and limped away. Others in their haste left beneath their pillows watches and money, only discovering their losses when they had reached the Michigan Central depot, — then supposed to be a perfectly safe place. A crowd of persons hastened thither, some carrying beds, some sewing-machines, and one lady had six canary-birds in a cage in one hand, and an immense family Bible in the other. She said, 'I was determined to bring these off, if I lost all the rest.' Another young woman was seen carrying two large paintings, evidently those of her father and mother. She was but partially clad, and amongst all her household wealth sought to preserve these filial mementos as being to her most precious.

"The tug-boats were busy towing vessels out into the lake, where they anchored off the burning city. Many persons sought refuge on these vessels, and the little pleasure-boats kept about the newly-made park between the Michigan Central Railroad track and the original lake shore, where many of them were employed in transporting persons and goods to the vessels anchored without. One large bark, being towed out, was caught by some flying cinders and went down the river, her mast and cordage enveloped in flames. She was drawn out into the lake, and there, it is supposed, scuttled, as in a short time no vestige of her was seen. The shower of cinders increased as the wind grew in power after midnight, and cinders as large as apples were hurled for a distance of half a mile before striking the earth. The air had the appearance of being full of fiery rockets and shooting flames.

"The fire at this time had acquired a circumference of over two miles. It writhed in and out in sinuosities like a serpent. If the crowd of safety-seeking wretches had been large before, it now appeared to be doubled. Women appealed to passengers upon the walks for assistance to remove their goods, and numerous hacks and express wagons carrying fainting women and sick persons hurriedly drove by. The horses were wild with affright, and leaped and pranced and shied as if conscious of the misery and devastation that the elements were heaping on the city. The fire worked towards the lake down Michigan Avenue, and from thence to the north side of the river. At 2 o'clock all the bridges were consumed. The showers of partially consumed sparks and dust and ashes fell upon the multitudes, until not a face but was blackened to an Ethiop's hue.

"The Crosby Opera House, the Tremont, the Sherman, Wood's Museum, Hooley's Opera House, and everything, nearly, on the north side of Lake Street, was completely licked up or gutted by the flames. The Court House, having an iron roof, was thought to be fire-proof. Between sixty and seventy prisoners were confined in the cells in the basement. At this time it was known that the water supply had failed, the water-works being gone. The firemen had ceased their labors, and apathy and despair had taken possession of the citizens. The proprietor of a large jewelry store on Lake Street, crazed at the prospect of his inevitable losses, unlocked the doors of his building, and called on the crowd to help him carry into the street his stock. The rushing throng hastened into the store, and carried out rich silver-ware, costly clocks, and trays of various kinds of jewels. These were deposited in the centre of the street; but there is too much ground for belief that the coveted loot was more the purpose of the crowd than any desire to save the jeweller's stock.

"The night wore slowly away. It seemed as if morning would never dawn. As more and more a sense of the terrible calamity became apparent, as the wind continued unabated, and as the lurid flames spread in an impregnable line of miles in length forward, many persons threw themselves on their knees in the streets, and prayed vehemently for heavenly succor. A half-mad enthusiast mounted a pile of furniture in Dearborn Street, and began a rambling discourse, in which he prophesied that the day of judgment was at hand, and called on all to make their peace with God.

"At 4 o'clock the gas-works blew up, and every house was left in darkness. The explosion shook the whole city, and aroused new terror. Down at the various depots, all night long, the locomotives were busy drawing out rolling stock and freight. Most of the freight stored in the Michigan Central depot was brought to a place of safety, and all of their rolling stock brought beyond the reach of the flames. No breakfast could be had in the entire city, as the means of cooking had been destroyed with the hotels, and private families gave no thought to what they should eat, being bent only on saving their effects.

"Ten thousand people, with immense piles of household goods, were congregated on the lake shore as the morning dawned. These people had saved but little provisions, and the cries of the children arose in one long lamenting wail. The flames still roaring and advancing, the air still full of cinders, the explosions still constant, the water supply exhausted, the firemen worn out, the fire-engines idle, the throng of fleeing citizens increasing, the wind still blowing fiercely, the smoke drifting still to the northward, the roar of the flames still heard above all, the cries and complaints of the populace still resounding, and naught silenced but the bells. Wherefore should they add their clamor?"

*Sufferings of Women.* — The great whirlwind of fire was no respecter of persons, and did not accommodate its course to any of the desires or movements of our people. The sick, the dying, and the dead were all in its path, and consumed by its torrid breath. Many women, in pains of childbirth, driven from shelter by the flames, were found away out on the prairies, or on the shores of the lake, the bleak winds chilling them and extinguishing the new life just ushered into the world. In scores of instances, both mother and child were dead, without attendance, and unrecognized. With no sympathizing friends, no helping hand, no eye save God's to witness their agony and despair, they passed to "a land of darkness as darkness itself, and of the shadow of death; without any order, and where light is darkness." It is trebly hard under such conditions, —

"To feel the hand of death arrest our steps,
Throw a chill blight o'er all one's budding hopes,
And hurl one's soul untimely to the shades,
Lost in the gaping gulf of black oblivion."

A daughter of an eminent clergyman gave birth to a child, during the rush and panic of the wild flight of women and children along the lake shore, and in some inexplicable way was separated from her friends, and neither mother nor child have been found.

A lady was carried out of the Sherman House in the arms of her husband, a new-born babe clasped to her breast, and both mother and child died before reaching a place of safety. The father was last seen marching along the shore of the lake, with the dead woman and child in his arms, shouting, laughing, and blaspheming, in all the delirium of grief. He was unquestionably burned or drowned.

Among women of the baser sort, who had their dens and haunts in Wells, Clark, and other streets in the burned district, there were tragedies innumerable, and probably more horrible deaths than among persons occupying ten times the space in other parts of the city. As the flames attacked their squalid tenements, they were seen issuing forth scantily clad, some almost nude, many in a maudlin stage of intoxication, others rubbing their eyes in drowsy stupidity, — dismayed, weeping, laughing, cursing, and singing. One, somewhat intoxicated, carried a young child which she abandoned before walking a single square; and it would have been consumed had not a patrolman rescued it. Another carried a bottle, from which she quaffed frequent and copious draughts, and, despite the urging of her companions, finally lagged behind, and was left to her fate. A young girl in tawdry attire, after emerging from a low Wells-street hovel that had just ignited, swore that she would sooner lose her life than her gay new hat, and went back in quest of it. She did not return.

*A Heart-Rending Mistake.* — A family was just rushing from their smoking residence, that the fire had only that moment attacked, when the wife said to her husband: —

"You have the baby, Charles?"

"No; I thought you took him."

"Mary has him, then?"

"O no, mem; I brought the silver."

The babe is still in the house, and the father rushes back to save him. The half-distracted mother, supported by the faithful servant, awaits his return in an agony of fear. The roof is on fire, and flames are just bursting from the upper windows, when he appears with the precious bundle.

"I wrapt him closely, so he would not inhale the smoke."

"Is he asleep?"

"Yes; very soundly."

"Let's hurry along to a safer place and unwrap his face, or he will smother."

When a little remote from the raging flames and blinding smoke, they undid the carefully guarded parcel, and found within — nothing but a large pillow. The child had been left to the flames. The mother understood her great bereavement in an instant, then her mind darkened, and she is hopelessly a maniac.

*A Strange Error.* — The great uncertainty regarding the fate of friends, for several days succeeding the fire, and the absence of any thoroughly organized effort to trace those who were missing, occasioned untold anxiety, and in several instances resulted in the most terrible misapprehensions. A young man telegraphed to relatives in Syracuse, as follows :

"I am safe, but father cannot be found. He was probably asleep, and burned to death.
"FRED."

In less than two hours after the receipt of the above, the parties in Syracuse were astounded by this despatch from the father : —

"Everything burned, and Fred is missing. Have n't seen him since the general alarm, and fear the worst.
"R. J. F."

Father and son were at once informed of the safety of each other by return messages, and were soon reunited.

*A Happy Occasion.* — There never was a happier reunion of people who had been given up as lost by their friends, than that which occurred at one of the relief "head-quarters" on Thursday succeeding the calamity. A well-known gentleman was relating to sympathizing friends that, in his desire to save his cash-box, which contained bonds and money for a large sum, he had been neglectful, for the moment, of the safety of his wife and children, that he lost sight of them in the great rush of flying and panic-stricken citizens, and that they were either burned or trampled to death. Pausing a moment in the narration, he overheard the sound of a familiar voice in the adjoining room, and springing to his feet, he rushed through the door: —

"My dear wife!"

"O, my husband!"

were the ejaculations that reached the ears of those within hearing. The wife was there, accompanied by the children, and was relating to some acquaintances the circumstances attending the loss of her husband and all their property. She was about to apply for relief of absolute necessities in the way of food and raiment, when she was interrupted by the arrival of her companion alive and well. They were at once clasped in each other's arms, and stood there silent, overcome, in an eloquence of joy that could find no expression in words. The children — there were three — laughed, cried, and shouted, and at last the oldest, a fine boy of twelve, gave vent to his feelings in words that have since become historic: "Bully for father! the fire couldn't burn *him!*" An expression at once so vigorous and original broke the spell, and everybody returned to the realities of the occasion. The family were all there; they had saved enough to ensure comfort; and the benevolent German who gave refuge to the wife and children in his poor cottage during the hour of peril, and divided with them his frugal loaf, now rejoices in the addition of a thousand-dollar government bond to his worldly possessions.

*Horrors.* — Several persons were severely injured and some killed outright, during their flight, by bricks, stones, cornices, etc., from the falling buildings. One man carrying a child in his arms, and leading another by the hand, was struck on the head by a stone, scattering his brains over the little ones. The horrified mother uttered a heart-rending shriek, gave one look of unutterable anguish at her dead companion, then seized the children and hurried away.

A newspaper reporter writes that he saw a woman kneeling in the street with a crucifix held up before her, and the skirt of her dress burning while she prayed. She appeared absorbed in her devotions and regardless of danger. While the reporter was looking at her, a runaway team attached to a truck dashed her to the ground, and she was left mangled and torn.

On the battlements of one of the high blocks in Randolph Street, a man was seen standing and wildly gesticulating, with the terrible flames raging and roaring through all the apartments beneath, and escape entirely cut off. All who saw him knew that he was doomed to a terrible death, for rescue was out of the question. Still he gesticulated, pointing in various directions, and was evidently trying to make the people understand some plan of relief which he thought feasible, but all in vain, for his voice was drowned in the tremendous roar of wind and flame. At length the great walls became unsteady, swerved for a moment in mid-air, and then came down with a crash and weight that shook the very ground, and the life of him who stood there a moment before, imploring help, was crushed out in the glowing furnace of destruction.

*Relief for Chicago.* — On the morning of the 9th of October, 1871, the telegraphic wires flashed to every part of this nation, and to nearly every portion of the civilized world, the shocking intelligence that Chicago was in flames, hundreds of lives had been destroyed, and ten thousand families were homeless, shelterless, scantily clad, and suffering intensely with cold, hunger, fatigue, and fright. The whole world was appalled. It was difficult to realize the great calamity. It seemed an exaggeration, and all hoped at first that it would prove such. But later despatches more than confirmed the previous intelligence; and ere midday Mayor Mason, of the doomed city, had telegraphed to the mayors of the principal cities in the country, the fact of the utter destitution of the people, and appealing for food, clothing, and the other necessaries of life.

His touching appeal roused the nation. The great heart of humanity throbbed with emotion. A sublime human sympathy, limited to no section, nation, or race, to no party, creed, or social condition, instantly was displayed, and money and supplies flowed in upon the stricken city without stint or measure. Cities and towns all over the country made haste to vie with each other, both in the amount of their contributions and the speed with which they should forward them. No city can honestly claim the credit of having been the first in the work, for action was *simultaneous* throughout the land, and in a few hours after receipt of the news, great trains of supplies were on their way from New York, Boston, Philadelphia, Pittsburg, Cincinnati, St. Louis, Louisville, and all the cities of importance.

All honor to the relief committees, the noble, self-sacrificing band of men and women who freely and unceasingly gave their time and strength, night and day, in caring for the wants of the destitute and needy! The record of their noble efforts is recorded in God's Book of Remembrance, and in the ages of the great Hereafter they shall reap their reward. — *Lakeside Monthly, and Chicago as It was and as It is, and other sources.*

## The Burning of Chicago.

### BY WILL M. CARLTON.

*From Our Fireside Friend (Chicago).*

'T was night in the beautiful city,
The famous and wonderful city,
The proud and magnificent city,
The queen of the North and the West.
The riches of nations were gathered in wondrous and plentiful store;
The swift-speeding bearers of commerce were waiting on river and shore;
The great staring walls towered skyward, with visage undaunted and bold,
And said, " We are ready, O Winter! come on with your hunger and cold!
Sweep down with your storms from the Northward! come out from your ice-guarded lair!
Our larders have food for a nation! our wardrobes have clothing to spare!
Far off from the corn-bladed prairies, and out from the valleys and hills,
The farmer has swept us his harvests, the miller has emptied his mills;
And here in the lap of our city the treasures of Autumn shall rest,
In golden-crowned, glorious Chicago, the Queen of the North and the West! "

II.

'T was night in the church-guarded city,
The templed and altar-decked city,
The sacred and spire-adorned city,
The Queen of the North and the West.
And out from the beautiful temples that wealth in its fulness has made,
And out from the haunts that were humble, where Poverty peacefully prayed,
Where praises and thanks had been offered to Him where they rightly belonged,
In peacefulness quietly homeward the worshipping multitude thronged.
The Pharisee, laden with riches, and jewelry, costly and rare,
Who proudly deigned thanks to Jehovah he was not as other men are,
The outcast who yearningly waited to hear the glad bidding, " Come in,"
The penitent saddened and humble, imploring forgiveness of sin;
And thus went they quietly homeward, with sin and omissions confessed,
In spire-adorned, templed Chicago, the Queen of the North and the West.

III.

'T was night in the sin-burdened city,
The turbulent, vice-laden city,
The sin-compassed, rogue-haunted city,
Tho' Queen of the North and the West.

And low in their caves of pollution great beasts of humanity growled;
And over his money-strewn table the gambler bent fiercely, and scowled;
And men with no seeming of manhood, with countenance flaming and fell,
Drank deep from the fire-laden fountains that spring from the rivers of hell;
And men of no seeming of manhood, who dreaded the coming of day,
Prowled, cat like, for blood-purchased plunder from men who were better than they;
And men with no seeming of manhood, whose dearest-craved glory was shame,
Whose joys were the sorrows of others, whose harvests were acres of flame,
Slunk, whispering and low, in their corners, with bowie and pistol tight-pressed,
In rogue-haunted, sin-cursed Chicago, though Queen of the North and the West.

### IV.

'T was night in the elegant city,
The rich and voluptuous city;
The beauty-thronged, mansion-decked city,
Gay Queen of the North and the West.

And childhood was placidly resting in slumber untroubled and deep;
And softly the mother was fondling her innocent baby to sleep;
And maidens were dreaming of pleasures and triumphs the future should show;
And scanning the brightness and glory of joys they were never to know;
And firesides were cheerful and happy, and comfort smiled sweetly around;
But grim Desolation and Ruin looked into the window and frowned,
And pitying angels looked downward, and gazed on the lovely below,
And longed to reach forth a deliverance, and yearned to beat backward the foe;
But Pleasure and Comfort were reigning, nor danger was spoken or guessed,
In beautiful, golden Chicago, gay Queen of the North and the West.

### V.

Then up in the street of the city,
The careless and negligent city,
The soon-to-be-sacrificed city,
Doomed Queen of the North and the West.

Crept, softly and slyly, so tiny it hardly was worthy the name,
Crept, slowly and soft through the rubbish, a radiant serpent of flame,

The South wind and West wind came shrieking, "Rouse up in your
 strength and your ire!
For many a year they have chained you, and crushed you, O demon of fire!
For many a year they have bound, and made you their servant and slave!
Now, rouse you, and dig for this city a fiery and desolate grave!
Freight heavy with grief and with wailing her world-scattered pride and
 renown!
Charge straight on her mansions of splendor, and battle her battlements
 down!
And we, the strong South-wind and West-wind with double fury possessed,
Will sweep with you over this city, this Queen of the North and the
 West!"

### VI.

'T was morn in this desolate city,
The ragged and ruin-heaped city,
The homeless and hot-smoking city,
The grief of the North and the West.

But down from the West came the bidding, "Queen, lift in courage thy
 head!
Thy friends and thy neighbors awaken, and hasten, with raiment and
 bread!"
And up from the South came the bidding, "Cheer up, fairest Queen of
 the Lakes!
For comfort and aid shall be coming from out our savannas and brakes!"
And down from the North came the bidding, "O City, be hopeful of
 cheer!
We've somewhat to spare for thy sufferers, for all of our suffering here!"
And up from the East came the bidding, "O City, be dauntless and bold!
Look hither for food and for raiment — look hither for credit and gold!"
And all through the world went the bidding, "Bring hither your choicest
 and best,
For weary and hungry Chicago — sad Queen of the North and the West!"

### VII.

O crushed, but invincible city!
O broken, but fast-rising city,
O glorious, but unconquered city,
Still Queen of the North and the West!

The long, golden years of the future, with treasures increasing and rare,
Shall glisten upon thy rich garments — shall twine in the fold of thy hair!
From out the black heaps of thy ruins new columns of beauty shall rise,
And glittering domes shall fling grandly our nation's proud flag to the
 skies!

From off the wide prairies of splendor the treasures of Autumn shall pour,
The breezes shall sweep from the northward, and hurry the ships to thy shore!
For Heaven will look downward in mercy on those who 've passed under the rod,
And hap'ly again they will prosper, and bask in the blessings of God.
Once more thou shalt stand mid the cities, by prosperous breezes caressed,
O, grand and unconquered Chicago, still Queen of the North and the West!

## CHAPTER XXII.

### SPRINGFIELD AND ROCKFORD, ILLINOIS.

SPRINGFIELD, the capital of Illinois, is situated on a beautiful prairie, four miles from the Sangamon River. Its streets are broad, intersect each other at right angles, and are tastefully adorned with shade-trees. From the beauty of the place and the surroundings, it is termed the "Flower City."

Springfield was laid out in 1822, and has always exhibited a spirit of enterprise remarkable even for a western city. Among its early residents there was an unusual number of men of more than ordinary talents, many of whom afterwards acquired national distinction. Among these may be mentioned Abraham Lincoln, Stephen A. Douglas, E. D. Baker, and many others who are yet living. In 1837, with a population of only eleven hundred, the city pledged itself to the amount of $50,000, to secure the State capital, — an undertaking of considerable magnitude, when we consider the smallness of the town, struggling with all the disadvantages of a new country, the privations of which cannot be realized by those living in these days of railroads.

Springfield was the first city in the State outside of Chicago to build water-works, a street railroad, and adopt an extensive system of sewerage.

13

The corner of the first State House was laid July 4, 1837, on which occasion E. D. Baker — afterwards United States Senator, and the lamented colonel of Ball's Bluff memory — delivered one of his most thrilling and eloquent speeches. The building was of limestone, and, though then regarded with wonder and admiration as a model of architectural beauty, and of sufficient size to answer the purposes of the State for all time to come, now will make only a very moderate Court House for Sangamon County.

The corner-stone of the new State House was laid October 5, 1868, by the Grand Master of Masons for the State of Illinois. The oration was pronounced by Hon. John D. Caton, of Ottawa. The ground plan of the building is in the form of a great cross, and the superstructure is in the style called the classic order of architecture. It so blends the ancient and modern art of building as to secure the greatest strength and solidity, and yet preserve an exterior appearance so light and airy as to be very beautiful to the eye. The grand outlines are : total length from north to south, three hundred and fifty-nine feet, exclusive of the porticos, which add twenty feet to each end. From east to west it is two hundred and sixty-six feet, with twenty feet additional, in the grand portico at the east end, which is the principal front.

There is an excavation of ten feet depth underground throughout the entire area, for the heating apparatus and storage of fuel.

The next above this is the first story, nineteen feet high. It contains a few office-rooms, but the greater part of it is devoted to the storage of stationery, geological specimens, etc. The floor throughout is of marble.

Above this is the principal story of twenty-two and a half feet in height. On this floor are the main and grand corridors, running the entire length and breadth of the building, and crossing each other at right angles under the dome. The entire walls of the corridors, consisting of pilasters with their caps and bases, panels and their borders, and door finish, are all to be of variegated marble, and the ceiling to be frescoed. This story is occupied by the offices and rooms of the various officers of the State.

The next story is forty-five feet from floor to ceiling, and contains the two large and magnificent halls,— the Senate Chamber and the Hall of the House of Representatives, — with their accompanying and necessary rooms and offices. Each of these halls has a gallery extending on three sides.

The roof on all the wings is of the mansard style, covered with slate on the sides, and copper on the top. Above all this rises the stately dome, surmounted by a lantern with a ball on the pinnacle, three hundred and twenty feet from the earth, being forty-three feet higher than the Capitol at Washington. The lantern is sixteen feet wide, and twenty-four feet high. The frame-work is of iron, and the sides of glass.

The building is of cut stone, and the cost was nearly $3,000,000.

Springfield has one of the largest and best hotels in the west, the Leland House, of which she is justly proud. The State Arsenal also is located here, and contains many war trophies of great interest.

Springfield equally with Mount Vernon is the Mecca of America, for here is the grave of our Martyr President, Abraham Lincoln.

> "Now must the storied Potomac
>   Laurels forever divide;
> Now to the Sangamon fameless
>   Give of its century's pride, —
> Sangamon, stream of the prairies,
>   Placidly westward that flows,
> Far in whose city of silence
>   Calm he has sought his repose.

Over our Washington's river
　　Sunrise beams rosy and fair;
Sunset on Sangamon fairer,
　　Father and martyr lies there.

"Kings under pyramids slumber,
　　Sealed in the Libyan sands;
Princes in gorgeous cathedrals,
　　Decked with the spoil of the lands;
Kinglier, princelier sleeps he,
　　Couched mid the prairies serene,
Only the turf and the willow
　　Him and God's heaven between;
Temple nor column to cumber
　　Verdure and bloom of the sod, —
So in the vale by Beth-peor,
　　Moses was buried of God.

"Break into blossoms, O prairies!
　　Snowy and golden and red;
Peers of the Palestine lilies
　　Heap for your Glorious Dead, —
Roses as fair as of Sharon,
　　Branches as stately as palm,
Odors as rich as the spices, —
　　Cassia and aloes and balm, —
Mary the loved, and Salome,
　　All with gracious accord,
Ere the first glow of the morning,
　　Brought to the tomb of the Lord.

"Wind of the West! breathe around him
　　Soft as the saddened air's sigh
When to the summit of Pisgah,
　　Moses had journeyed to die;
Clear as its anthem that floated
　　Wide o'er the Moabite plain,
Low, with the wail of the people,
　　Blending its burdened refrain.
Rave, O wind! and diviner —
　　Sweet as the breeze that went by,
When over Olivet's mountain,
　　Jesus was lost in the sky.

> "Not for thy sheaves nor savannas
>   Crown we thee, proud Illinois!
> Here in his grave is his grandeur,
>   Born of his sorrow thy joy.
> Only the tomb by Mount Zion,
>   Hewn for the Lord, do we hold
> Dearer than his in thy prairies,
>   Girded with harvests of gold!
> Still for the world, through the ages,
>   Wreathing with glory his brow,
> He shall be liberty's savior, —
>   Freedom's Jerusalem thou!"
>
> Edna Dean Proctor.

The grave and monument of Lincoln are at Oak Ridge Cemetery. The monument is a granite obelisk one hundred feet high, adorned with four groups of statuary, representing the Infantry, Cavalry, Artillery, and Navy; and also a statue of President Lincoln and the coat of arms of the United States. This is surrounded by a terrace seventy-four feet square, and fifteen feet high. The obelisk is twelve feet square at the top of the terrace, and tapers to eight feet square at the apex. The shaft has a circular opening six feet in diameter, fitted with a stairway, which leads to a small square room at the top. At the northern side of the terrace, of the same height, there is a semicircular projection, the catacomb, which contains six crypts for the remains of Lincoln and his family. A similar oval projection at the south side, designed as a receptacle for articles associated with President Lincoln, is called Memorial Hall. The total cost of the monument will be nearly $200,000.

*Rockford.* — The city of Rockford is situated on both sides of Rock River, about midway between Lake Michigan and the Mississippi. But few towns in the northwest can claim such real beauty of location and surroundings. Through the midst of the town flow the clear waters of the river, from either side of which rise rounded bluffs, thus affording innumerable building sites of great beauty and desirability. Originally the river banks were crowned with groves of oak; the woodman's axe has been used but sparingly, other trees have been added and cared for, until now Rockford is called, by general consent, and most truthfully, the "Forest City." The attention which its citizens have devoted to horticulture and floriculture, the many beautiful and tastefully adorned grounds by which its homes are surrounded, have led to the suggestion that "Floral City" is a title equally appropriate.

The business portions of the town extend on both sides of the river, and are connected by the City Bridge, a substantial iron structure nearly four hundred and forty feet in length.

The river is also crossed by a railroad bridge, and the piers are built for still another. Rockford possesses one of the most extensive water-powers in the west, and is thus made of much importance as a manufacturing centre. Her great reapers and mowers are now famous throughout the land, and give to her still another *sobriquet*, — the "Reaper City." The Reaper Works are situated on the water-power on the west side of the river. There hundreds of men are employed, and a large number of reapers are turned out daily.

Rockford Female Seminary is one of the widely known and popular institutions of the kind in the west. It is situated in extensive and beautiful grounds on the eastern bank of the river. It was founded in 1852, and its prosperity has grown with its years. The building is commodious and substantial, and accommodates two hundred and fifty pupils.

## CHAPTER XXIII.

THE DELLS OF THE WISCONSIN, AND DEVIL'S LAKE; MILWAUKEE, SITUATION AND SURROUNDINGS.

WITHIN a few miles of Kilbourn City, Adams County, Wisconsin, are the Dells of the Wisconsin, and Devil's Lake, which in beauty, grandeur, and picturesqueness of scenery stand unrivalled in the entire northwest. Nature here, in one of her most frantic moods, has wrought most curious mass of conglomeration, tumbling and jumbling together, until

"All things are strange,
Rocks scarred like rough-hewn wood,"

and the whole presenting a most wild and romantic scenery, which to the tourist or pleasure-seeker must be "a thing of beauty and a joy forever." Here, in a delightful locality, upon the banks of a beautiful river, and upon the shores of a "silvery lake," are objects that captivate and amuse the beholder. Does inclination prompt to fishing, boating, hunting, or viewing, these localities are highly favored, and weeks can be passed in entire oblivion of time and its perplexing cares.

The Dells of the Wisconsin are formed by a channel carved by the Wisconsin River through sandstone rocks. The water has left so many curious and beautiful traces of its wonderful workmanship, so well displayed in the stereoscopic views, that one knows hardly what sights to mention, and is loath to pass any by.

The first object which met our eyes after pushing out into the stream is Eagle Cliff,— two towering rocks, separate at the base, and uniting in one at the top, with a small cave between.

A short distance up the ravine we find one of the greatest wonders of Wisconsin scenery,— Stand Rock. Back from the stream about two hundred feet, ascending an angle of forty-five degrees, stands this strange structure, evidently washed from the rocks by the current of some river of past geologic periods. Between the stones of this rock is the card-case of the Dells, where we left our cards to swell the number of those already left by others.

Just around the curve below Bailey's Eddy, the raftmen's peril, we visited Black Hawk's Cave, where he is said to have hid from his enemies during the Black Hawk War. It was well adapted for the purpose, as it is unapproachable by land, and it reaches back from the river into the rock in such a natural way that one would take it for the shadow of the overhanging cliff. The river at this point is at its narrowest; and as the legend has it, used to be jumped by the Indian chiefs in winning their dusky brides.

The sandstone islands in the river, christened Sugar-bowl and Inkstand, are the most beautiful specimens of this phase of scenery to be met with anywhere. The cliffs, fringed and crowned with trees and vines all along the river, defy description by reason of their varied and curious beauty, and many are the caves and grottos in their sides, wrought most wonderfully. Masses of rugged and broken rocks and bowlders, we visited, stretching for a long distance, almost impassable, — one of those strange and unaccountable freaks of nature.

*Devil's Lake.* — It was on a glorious day of Indian summer, when, after a hard and rough ride, with many a knock and jolt over the rocky way, we first caught a glimpse, and then, almost before we knew it, were on the shore of Devil's Lake. As we gazed upon the quiet bosom of the lake, unmoved save by a passing zephyr, and saw our image reflected in its silver waters, we found ourselves unconsciously murmuring: —

> "Thou wert calm,
> Even as an infant calm, that gentle evening:
> And one could hardly dream thou 'dst ever met
> And wrestled with the storm. A breath of air,
> Felt only in its coolness, from the west
> Stole over thee, and stirred thy golden mirror
> Into long waves, that only showed themselves
> In ripples on thy shore; far distant ripples,
> Breaking the silence with their quiet kisses,
> And softly murmuring peace."

The lake is no more than a mile and a half in length and half that in width, environed almost completely by precipitous cliffs six hundred feet in height, — these cliffs seared, rugged, and broken by nature's hidden forces, piled on each other in all kinds of fantastic positions, gray with their coverings of mosses, fringed with hardy evergreens, dark and forbidding in their appearance, amid the gathering of dusky twilight, stretching their shadows far over the dark waters, which seemed then fitly to be called *Devil's Lake.*

But when in the morning the golden sunlight penetrated the dark recesses, and we scaled the cliffs, gazed with wonder and admiration at the scenery, felt the cool breeze fanning our wayward locks, we would fain have called it the home of the nymphs, and by its new name, Spirit Lake; and we exclaimed, forgetful of the shadowy evening before:

> "On thy fair bosom, silver lake,
> O! I could ever sweep the oar,
> When early birds at morning wake,
> And evening tells us toil is o'er."

'Of the many weird and picturesque places at Devil's Lake, Wonder Notch is one of the most attractive.

To the student of geology this region furnishes ample scope for study, thought, and contemplation. The geological phenomena are curious and instructive. The rocks are primary in their character, unstratified, and of an igneous origin. They are hypozoic and procrystalline, with the greenstone variety of granite, and with veins of quartz crystals, feldspar, and hornblende in great variety. He who with nature sweet communion would hold, can truly find intellectual enjoyment and profit by delving and geologizing in the different kinds of minerals here scattered in profusion.

*Milwaukee.* — "Beautiful for situation," this fair city of the west is seated on the brow of a hill, whose base is lapped by the restless surf of Lake Michigan. Her harbor is one of the best on the whole chain of great lakes. Broad rivers pass among her thoroughfares, so that the largest boats can be brought to her very centre. The chief city of Wisconsin, a rival even of Chicago, she is perhaps most widely known throughout the country as having given name to that popular building material, the beautiful cream-colored brick, called Milwaukee brick. Her private residences, public buildings, and business blocks are built of it, its delicate color contrasting finely with the deep green of the shade-trees, and giving to the city a peculiarly airy and tasteful appearance. From its tint comes also her name, for she is termed "The Cream City."

The centre, near the Milwaukee and Menomonee Rivers, is the business quarter. The city has many and important railroad connections, and is itself a great railroad centre. The amount of shipping carried on here is immense, and great quantities of brick are exported to all parts of the Union. But commercially, Milwaukee is most noted for its vast and yearly increasing grain trade. It is the greatest primary wheat-market in the world. It contains many of the best flouring-mills in the west, and the reputation of several of its prominent brands of flour is unexcelled in eastern and continental markets. The provision trade of Milwaukee, also, promises to become second only to that of grain. The Iron Works and Rolling Mills of the city are among the largest of the United States.

The high bluffs overlooking the lake are the places most desirable for residences. Here are many streets of elegant dwellings with tastefully adorned surroundings.

There are many public buildings worthy of mention, but finest of all is the splendid new Court House, a building costing a million and a half; from the dome of which can be obtained an extended and magnificent view of the city, the adjacent country, and the lake. The Soldiers' Home is a beautiful structure. It is located three miles from the city. It is one of the four government asylums for disabled soldiers.

## CHAPTER XXIV.

### CINCINNATI, AND THE CINCINNATI FOUNTAIN.

CINCINNATI is the chief city of the State of Ohio, and the eighth in the Union in respect to population, ranking next to Boston. It lies on a natural plateau, through which the Ohio River passes. This plain is nearly twelve miles in circumference, and is divided by the river into two nearly equal parts. On the northern half is Cincinnati, and on the south are Covington and Newport. This great plain is entirely surrounded by hills three hundred feet in height, forming a most beautiful natural amphitheatre, from whose hill-tops may be seen the splendid panorama of cities below, with the winding Ohio gleaming in the sunlight. No other large city of the Union affords such a variety of position and scenery. "Its site is one a painter would have chosen for its beauty, and a shrewd mechanic for the utmost facilities of building, of water, and of drainage. Here is built one of the most prosperous and populous cities of America, concentrating in itself the productions of a great extent of country, and manufacturing the raw materials of mines and forests to be again distributed through the interior."

Well may Cincinnati be termed the "Queen City of the West." Her commercial growth has been rapid and immense; her manufactories are various and extensive; by river and by rail she has speedy and easy access to the regions that supply cotton, lumber, iron, wool, and coal; while in the vicinity are many and extensive vineyards, and the culture of the grape has become an interest of great profit and magnitude. Cincinnati, also, has long been known as the greatest pork-market in the Union.

But, above all, Cincinnati is distinguished for its benevolent and literary institutions. It has one Law School, three Theological Seminaries, six Medical Schools, four Commercial Seminaries, five Colleges, eight Female Seminaries, and many seminaries for boys, while the public schools are the pride of the city. Under the control and support of the city are an Infirmary, a Dispensary, a House of Refuge, and a Lunatic Asylum, the last, one of the largest buildings of the kind in the country.

The Cincinnati Observatory is situated in the eastern limits of the city, and is far famed for possessing one of the largest telescopes in the Union. This institution is inseparably associated with the memory of the astronomer and patriot, General O. M. Mitchel.

We have not space even to mention the many prominent public buildings of the city, some of which are of fine architectural style and imposing dimensions.

The suburbs of Cincinnati are of almost unrivalled loveliness, and have long been famous. The hill-tops are crowned with elegant and costly villas; spacious avenues extend for miles in every direction, only to meet equally beautiful rural villages where wealth and culture are lavish in their adornments.

*The Cincinnati Fountain.* — This beautiful and elaborate fountain of bronze, which was a gift to the city by two of her liberal citizens, the Queen City of the West counts among her rarest attractions. It is a public fountain, at once an ornament, and a practical benefit to the people.

" The structure is surmounted by a beautiful figure representing the genius of water, through whose outspread hands, extended to bless, falls an exquisitely fine shower, like gentle rain. Underneath, about the massive pedestal, stand four colossal groups, representing the most obvious benefits of water, — a mechanic on a burning roof imploring heaven for rain; a farmer beside his plough, whose labor will have no fruit without the kindly showers; a young girl leading her sick father to the healing fountain; a mother taking her child to the bath.

"Underneath these groups are four elegant basins, from which thirty-six streams of water play into a circular moat at the base of the structure. The pediment, to which these basins are attached, is richly adorned with compositions in relief, representing the uses of water in the most varied forms of human industry, — as in navigation, fishing, as a motive power directly applied in various kinds of mills, and indirectly as steam. These compositions are exquisitely finished, and the meaning of every design may be discerned at a glance."

An inscription upon the capital sets forth that the fountain is a gift to the people of Cincinnati, from Mr. Henry Probasco and Mr. Tyler Davidson.

The fountain was designed and cast in Munich, Germany; the artist and designer being Kreling, and the casting being done by Herr Miller, a celebrated founder.

## CHAPTER XXV.

#### MAMMOTH CAVE, KENTUCKY.

THE locality of the Mammoth Cave is in latitude 37° north, and longitude 9° west from Washington. Its only known entrance is in the eastern part of Edmondson County, Kentucky, on the south side of Green River, one hundred and ninety-four feet above the level of that stream, and ninety-four miles nearly due south from Louisville. It is equidistant from the cities of Louisville and Nashville, and immediately upon the nearest road between those two places.

*The Cave Hotel* is rather a primitive edifice, constructed in the form of the letter L. It is, in the aggregate, over six hundred feet long, and has a wide, covered porch along the sides facing the enclosed angle. Fronting this promenade is a beautiful lawn, thickly shaded by natural forest-trees and ornamental evergreens.

*Entrance to the Cave.* — A few minutes' walk, out through the garden, over the stile, and down a flight of wooden steps, brings us into a rocky ravine deeply shaded by tall forest-trees. Here the air is cool and bracing. The sensation is delightful, and we catch new inspiration from each long, deep draught of the vitalizing element. Proceeding on our way, we presently reach a dilapidated old log-building, in front of which there is a yawning chasm fifty feet deep, with irregular and precipitous sides. This is the dreary portal to the subterranean world. Green ferns and climbing vines cling everywhere to the projecting rocks, as if striving to cast some adorning drapery about their nakedness.

*The Cascade.* — A little spring of water pours a ceaseless

stream of silvery beads from a shelving rock above the entrance, and dashes it to spray in the chasm below. One fancies that the monotonous hum of the falling water, and the gloom of the thick, overhanging foliage, render the place a fit habitation for gnomes. The first emotions awakened at sight of the entrance and its weird surroundings, are less agreeable than we could have wished.

*The Old Entrance.* — Formerly, ingress was effected farther down the hill, near the Green River, where the cave may still be entered, and explored as far as the breach forming the present entrance. At the old entrance we walk into the cave on a horizontal line, as into a coal-mine or railroad tunnel. That part of the cave between the old and the new entrance is about half a mile long, and is known as Dickson's Cave. It contains nothing of special interest and is rarely visited.

*The New Entrance.* — At the new entrance we descend into a deep pit or shaft till we reach the floor of the cavern, about on a level with the old entrance. The present entrance was occasioned probably by the action of a little stream of water, causing the rocky roof, which was not very firm at this place, to break through. A knowledge of this fact may excite apprehensions of danger, but having once entered the cave, a sense of security steals over us, and we dismiss fear.

*Temperature.* — In these rocky chambers the temperature is uniformly about 59° F. The cave exhales or inhales, as the temperature outside is above or below the standard. In summer, a strong current of cool air rushes outward with such violence as to endanger our lights. In the cold weather of winter, the current sets inward. In the spring and fall, when the temperature outside is about equal to the temperature inside of the cave, there is no action whatever. This natural phenomenon is called the breathing of the cave. Change of season is unknown within it. Mornings and evenings have no existence in this nether world. Time itself produces no change in many parts of the cave; for where there is no variation of temperature, no water, and no light, the rocks may defy the three great forces of geological transformation.

*The Rotunda.*— This is a large cavern at the beginning of the main cave, and is said to be directly under the hotel. It is over seventy-five feet high, and one hundred and sixty feet across the floor. Several avenues put off in different directions from this, as from most other of the large rooms. In some parts the wall is abrupt, in others the ceiling slopes down gradually to the floor.

*The Main Cave.*— The main cave begins at the Rotunda, under the hotel, and extends to the distance of five or six miles. It varies in width from fifty to three hundred feet, and in some places it is one hundred feet high. For the distance of a mile it is straight, then turning to the left it forms with itself an acute angle; after which its course is irregular. Some of the small passages putting off from the main cave, after prolonged and tortuous windings, communicate with other caverns and domes, surpassing in grandeur and magnificence even the most renowned part of the main cave.

*The Church.* — About a quarter of a mile beyond the Rotunda is a second dome or enlargement in the main cave. This has a gothic roof or ceiling spanning the vast arch, forty feet above the floor. The hall is somewhat irregular, and has an area of many thousand square feet. At the left-hand corner of this hall there is a solid stone projection or platform about three feet higher than the main floor, and wide enough to hold a stand and several chairs. This is called the pulpit, and from it the gospel was formerly preached to the large and attentive audiences that were probably attracted thither by the novelty of the occasion. These old pump logs arranged into rows of seats may still bear testimony that the story of Christ crucified has been told even in the sunless caverns that underlie the "dark and bloody ground." A rude gallery extends around a part of this hall, perhaps twenty feet above the main floor.

*The Giant's Coffin.* — Just one mile from the entrance, on the right side of our path, there is a large rock, fifty-seven feet long, detached from the rest, and standing up a little from the floor. This bears so perfect a resemblance to a huge coffin, that any one can see the fitness of the name of " Giant's Coffin," by which it is known.

*The Maelstrom.* — This is a pit thirty feet in diameter and of unknown and unexplored depth. The openings of avenues are visible at considerable distance down the pit, but these have never been and probably never will be explored. In the summer of 1859, William Courtland Prentice attempted to explore this region by descending into the Maelstrom. He was let down in a basket attached to a rope arranged with pulleys. The working of the apparatus was then intrusted to the management of some young friends of the bold adventurer.

Several accounts of this perilous descent have been published. It has been made the thread of a spirited narrative poem, by George Lansing Taylor, from which we take the following extract. The poem is entitled —

### IN THE MAELSTROM.

"Down! down! down!
Into the darkness dismal;
Alone — alone — alone —
Into the gulf abysmal,

> On a single strand of rope,
> Strong in purpose and in hope,
> Lighted by one glimmering lamp,
> Half extinguished by the damp,
> Swinging o'er the pit of gloom,
>   Into the awful stillness,
> And the sepulchral chillness,
> Lower him into the Maelstrom's deeps,
> Where Nature her locked-up
>   Mysteries keeps;
> Lower him carefully,
> Lower him prayerfully,
> Lower and lower and lower,
> Where mortal never hath been before,
> Till he shall tell us, till he shall show
> The truth of the tales of long ago,
> And find, by the light that the lamp shall throw,
> If this be the entrance to hell or no."

In descending, the adventurer encounters a waterfall, or cascade, which is thus beautifully described:—

> "But behold from rocky wall,
> Circling round the shaft below,
> Spouts a crystal waterfall;
> All its coarseness,
> And its hoarseness,
> When he sees how fair their source is,
> Vanish, till by aid of vision,
> Sounds infernal grow elysian.
>   Now he swings anear the side
> Of this weird and wondrous tide,
> Where its limpid billows slide
> And its sheets descending glide,
> Veiled in whiteness like a bride;
> Glistening where his lamp is beaming,
> Sparkling, flashing, glittering, gleaming,
> Like a shower of diamonds streaming
> From the lap of Nature dreaming;
> Streaming downward, passing quickly,
> Sprinkling now upon him thickly,
> From the fissure far above him,
> As if all the naiads love him

With so rich a love and tender
That they shower baptismal splendor;
Floods of jewels for his visit, —
Is 't a flood of gems? or is it
That their kisses almost drown him?"

Enchanted by the beauty of these fearful depths, the young hero still demands to be lowered —

"Into the dark profound,
A deep that ne'er did plummet sound;
Still he descends,
And anxiously bends,
Gazing down in darkness that never ends —
Whose dimness,
And grimness,
And darkness,
And starkness,
And deepness,
And steepness,
And deadness,
And dreadness
More frightful are made by his lamp's sickly redness;
Till checked by sudden shock,
He stands on solid rock,
Ninety and a hundred feet
From the friends who hold that cable;
Will they lift it, are they able
Face to face once more to greet?
. . . . .
He enters a hall,
A huge niche in the wall,
Where echoes unnumbered respond to his call
From a roof that impends
Where a gallery extends,
Till, bounded by distance, in darkness it ends.
. . . . .
Now along its spacious flooring,
Eager, pleased, he roams exploring;
O'er obstructions, through wide chambers,
Onward still he wends and clambers,
Stalagmitic cones and masses
Glitter everywhere he passes,
Glitter through the gloom-like glasses;

> Shapes of beauty forming slowly,
> Arches, shrines, and altars holy;
> Groups of columns polyhedral,
> Like some rich antique cathedral;
> Nature's grand and gloomy glory,
> Fairer than the fanes of story.
>   Thus he wanders,
>   Roams and ponders,
> Through this gallery of wonders,
> Till a rocky barrier rising
> To an altitude surprising,
> All across the chamber closes,
> And effectually opposes
> All his efforts to get o'er it,
> And he stands repulsed before it;
> Yet he sees the cave extending
> Onward till in distance blending
> With the darkness, as if nature
> Were resolved to hold some feature
> Hidden still from mortal creature."

These beautiful verses are thus vigorously closed, with, as might be expected, a promise of future greatness and glory for the hero of this daring adventure:—

> "Down in that depth, where no other had trod,
> Where writing was none save the writing of God,
>   Was graven a name
>   By that glittering flame
> That shall live on the record of daring and fame."

William Courtland Prentice, the hero of these verses, espoused the Southern cause, and was killed in an attack on the town of Augusta, Kentucky, in 1862.

*End of the Cave.* — This is called the end of the cave. Though it is nine miles from the entrance, it is no more the end of the cave than is the last production of the sculptor or painter the end of art.

Some mathematical troglodyte has estimated the whole series of caves, grottos, halls, and rivers, at one hundred miles in extent. Whether it is more or less, we are unable to determine.

*Ownership.* — The cave, with seventeen hundred acres of land, is owned by the Croghan heirs. At the death of the original owner, Judge Underwood, of Bowling Green, became their trustee. The judge, being well advanced in years, is about taking the necessary steps to obtain a decree of court to enable him to sell the property. Should it fall into the hands of enterprising capitalists, it will probably become one of the most desirable, convenient, and interesting summer resorts on the continent. — *The Mammoth Cave and its Denizens.*

## CHAPTER XXVI.

### CALIFORNIA.

UNTIL a comparatively recent period, the whole country, from the boundaries of South America to the late Russian Possessions on the north, and from the Ocean to the Rocky Mountains, was included in California. The State of California lies between 32° 45′ and 42° N. Lat. It extends along the Pacific coast from southeast to northwest about seven hundred miles, and has an average breadth of nearly two hundred miles. It contains 158,687 square miles. Dr. E. D. G. Prime, in his "Around the World," in speaking of this State, says: California is a great State. I have been informed of that fact repeatedly, and by those who have lived in it long enough to know whereof they affirm; but it is, in truth, a great State. In territory, it is equal to all New England, New York, New Jersey, Pennsylvania, Maryland, and a part of Delaware. It is not only large enough, north and south, to constitute several climes, but it has a remarkable variety of climate within a narrow compass. If variety is the spice of life, California is the spiciest country to live in that I have found in all my wanderings. I have never before been where chills and fever were so prevalent. I do not mean the terrible disease bearing that name, of which I have a greater dread than of the yellow fever, but the alternate shakings and warmings which one gets in passing from one part of the State to another. The morning that I came into it (August 15th, at 5 o'clock), the thermometer stood in the car window on the Pacific Railroad at 34°, only two degrees above freezing. At 2 o'clock the same day, farther west, the same thermometer stood at 88°. This, it is true, was on different planes; but one may shiver and shake day after day at San Francisco, and an hour's sail will take him into the blandest atmosphere. In going up to Stockton, we left San Francisco, August 23d, at 3 o'clock, P. M., wrapped up in our warmest winter cloaks and overcoats, and stopping at Benicia, only thirty miles distant and on the same plane, we cast off our wraps and stepped into the most delightful summer weather, and saw the sun go down in a sea of gold, — a sensation and a sight which we had not enjoyed since our arrival. During the same journey the weather would be intensely warm during the day, and in the same locality, by midnight, we would find ourselves searching, half awake, for all the stray clothes within reach, and in the morning the thermometer would indicate frost. The same diversity and variations of temperature prevail in almost every portion of the State, and in some places that I have visited, I have been informed that the thermometer rises frequently as high as 110°, and even 120° in the shade.

One of the wonders of this great State is that everything does not die out utterly in the summer, and leave the valleys ever after as barren as the granite rocks of the walls of the Yosemite. Not a drop of rain falls in the summer in the great valleys which are the agricultural regions of the State.

In passing through these valleys in the month of August, they do not give the slightest signs of vegetation, excepting the trees, which are sparse. The ground is apparently as dry as an ash-heap fresh from the burning. You may travel all day long and never see a blade of grass, nor even a green weed; but, as soon as the fall rains commence, the hills and valleys are clothed with the richest verdure, another year's crop of grass and grain comes on, and the once arid slopes and plains are burdened with the harvest. Vegetation must have some strange power of lying dormant and then springing into life, or there must be latent moisture in the soil which preserves it from perishing; for while the surface of the earth is without the least evidence of vegetable life, the fruit and ornamental trees, whose roots strike deeper into the soil, are as luxuriant in their growth and in their foliage as if rain had fallen every day in the year. It is no uncommon thing to see a vineyard or plantation of fruit-trees in full and green leaf, and loaded with the richest fruit, standing in the midst of a perfectly arid tract of country, and this, too, without irrigation. My partial examination of California has satisfied me that agriculture in all its branches is to be the great interest of the State, and, indeed, it is so now.

The fruits of California have not equalled my expectations. It is true, the rage for mammoth productions, mammoth vegetables and fruits, of which we heard so much in the early settlement of the State, has given place to a more sensible attention to quality; but, even with this improvement, the fruits generally are not equal in flavor to those of the eastern States. They grow in a profusion that is without any parallel within the range of my observation, and with so little cultivation that they seem almost to be spontaneous; they have a smoothness and perfection of form which gives them the beauty of flowers; I have seen trees loaded with fruits of the largest size, on which an imperfect specimen could scarcely be found, and yet, when they come to be eaten, they do not fulfil their bright promise. The first, and, as it was said, the finest of the peaches had disappeared before we arrived; but those which we have eaten, although magnificent in appearance and rich in color, have been without the flavor that the peaches at the east preserve throughout the season. It is, perhaps, too early to form a judgment of the apples; but I have tried many varieties, and, while they are fair to look upon, — exceeding in size and smoothness all the productions of the eastern States, so that, to judge merely from their external appearance, one might suppose that this fruit, as well as many others, had taken a new lease of life for the Pacific coast, and had entered upon an entirely new career, — I have not tasted a good apple in California. This fruit, even more than others, is without flavor and without juice. Such quinces as I have seen growing in various parts of the State, among the mountains as well as in the valleys and on the plains, I never even imagined before. They grow to an enormous size, and are as smooth as an orange, — quite different, taking a whole tree together, from anything with which I have been familiar, and there can be little fear that this fruit is not sufficiently highly flavored.

But the glory of California fruit is its pears and grapes. The former grow with a luxuriance and rapidity, and with such abundance of large and luscious-looking fruit bending the trees to the earth, that, on entering any of the fruit-orchards, a stranger is compelled to break out continually in astonishment. All varieties of pears, if not actually indigenous to the soil, have found in California their true home, and many of them, at least, are as delicious as they are finely developed. Some specimens of this fruit, in years past, have been a wonder at the east; but there are a few more left. Pears have become so abundant, even the choicest varieties, that they have actually become a drug in the market; and

Bartletts which will weigh a pound, and which blush when you simply look at them, will scarcely pay for sending them to market. I was at a ranch not an hour's distance from San Francisco, containing all kinds of fruit and pears of every variety, hundreds of bushels of such fruit as was never seen in any other country, the owner of which said he should leave it all to rot upon the trees, as it would not pay for the picking.

Grapes grow everywhere in the State with the greatest luxuriance, and spontaneously. They require no sort of training; they are trimmed annually almost to the level of the soil, leaving a small stump, and before the season is over, such a burden of the finest fruit is seen, and in clusters like the grapes of Eshcol, as can now scarcely be found anywhere else on earth. The choicest of foreign grapes, which at the east are matured only in graperies by artificial heat, here revel in the open air. I believe all visitors in California, if not the citizens, unite in pronouncing the grapes the finest of its fruit, and they grow in such profusion that all classes may have them at this season as an article of daily diet. Figs and pomegranates grow with the same luxuriance; the former, as in Oriental countries, producing three crops in a season. The fig-tree grows with astonishing rapidity. I have seen, even among the mountains, and still more in the broad valleys, fig-trees twenty or twenty-five feet in height, that could not be more than ten or twelve years old, and covered with the second crop of the largest and finest figs. It is surprising to see so little account made of this fruit, which, in other countries, is an important article of food, and which is more nourishing than any of our native fruits. But the taste for it must be acquired, and it is evident that it has not been extensively acquired in California.

*The City of San Francisco.* — "The city and county of San Francisco embrace one municipality, the act of consolidation having taken effect July 1, 1856. The county comprises the northern end of a peninsula, about twenty-five miles long, formed by the bay of San Francisco on the east and the Pacific Ocean on the west, its entire area covering a space of 26,861 acres, including the Presidio reservation, of 1,500 acres, belonging to the general government. The city occupies the extreme northern point of this peninsula, which is here about four miles wide."

Prior to 1835 the present site of the city was wholly uninhabited, what few people there were in the neighborhood residing at the Presidio and the Mission Dolores.

"It is unfortunate that the city was originally projected with so little regard to regularity, to the natural irregularities of surface and its future wants, as relates to width of streets, reservation of grounds for parks, public buildings, etc.; owing to which, the inhabitants have already been subject to great inconvenience and expense in attempting to partially supply these omissions and remedy these defects.

"The city is already the owner of sixteen squares, ranging in size from one acre, or a little more, to seventeen acres, — the area of Yerba Buena, the largest of the number. The most of these squares contain four acres each, the area of the whole being 117.45 acres. Although nearly all of them are enclosed, only Portsmouth, the smallest of the number, and often called by way of distinction the 'Plaza,' has been improved."

*Improvement of Water Front.* — "Originally the water along the city front was so shallow, except at a few bluff points, that large vessels could not approach within a quarter of a mile of the shore, necessitating the use of boats and lighters for receiving and landing freight and passengers. Soon, however, wharves resting on piles were built, extending sufficiently far into the bay to admit every class of craft lying alongside them. Meantime the space between the outer end of these structures and high water line began to be filled in with earth, sand, and rubbish, carted in from the city, which, besides offending the senses and imperilling the public health, threatened, by gradually settling outward, to fill up and destroy the harbor. With a view to obviate these evils and arrest this danger, the plan of building a sea-wall having been determined upon, the construction of this work was commenced in 1867, and is now in progress; the intention being to prosecute it as rapidly as the revenues derived from the wharves will admit, these having been set aside for the purpose. This sea-wall, which is eventually to extend along the entire city front, a distance of 8,446 feet, is to be formed by a rocky embankment at the bottom, with a superstructure of solid granite, and will cost, when completed, according to estimate, about two and a half million dollars."

*Fear of Earthquakes, and its effects.* — " Owing to a fear of earthquakes, the houses in San Francisco are not built as high as in most other large cities, the greater part of them, including the leading public edifices, not exceeding three or four stories in height. There is not a brick building of any magnitude in the city having more than five stories, and, perhaps, not a dozen having more than four, exclusive of basement. Experience does not, to be sure, warrant the apprehension of grave danger or damage as likely to arise from this cause; no loss of life or serious injury to limb or property ever having happened in consequence thereof since the founding of the city. Earthquakes are, indeed, of frequent occurrence, one or more shocks being felt nearly every year. But with two or three exceptions they have been so slight as to cause no alarm, — scarcely to attract more than passing attention, — the majority of them not even being observed by most people.

" At the beginning of 1848, the city, composed of about

one hundred small buildings, contained a population of 480 souls, which three years thereafter had been swollen to about 20,000. In 1860, the city contained 56,831 inhabitants, of whom 53,073 were whites, 1,142 colored, and 2,616 Chinese. According to the census of 1870, it had a population of 149,473.

"The novelties of the city never cease. One is constantly reminded that, twenty years ago, here were only sand-hills, with the crumbling cathedral and rude adobe dwellings of a little Spanish post. Every morning he looks out in fresh surprise upon the teeming life of a great metropolis, with stately blocks of brick and stone, railroads, street-cars, gas, markets, exchanges, elegant residences, costly school-houses, imposing churches, and generous charities. San Francisco is far more cosmopolitan than any other American city except New York. It has four hotels which would be creditable to any metropolis in the world. At these, and along Montgomery Street, one sees that curious mingling of faces from every quarter of the globe, which is characteristic of Broadway."

*Seal Rocks.* — "Between the city and the ocean there is a neck of land, a high promontory of sand six or seven miles wide. The great drive of the town is across this promontory to the shore, where the waves come rolling in to rest after their long journey from Japan and China. About three hundred yards from the land two rugged rocks rise abruptly out of the water to the height of seventy-five feet, covering an area of perhaps an acre each. These rocks are the property and the habitations of an immense colony of sea-lions, as they are called, or seals, who hold undisturbed possession, and who are protected in their right of property and from all injury by statute law. Some of these sea-lions are of enormous size; and it is an amusing sight, which never loses its interest, to watch them in their clumsy efforts to climb to the very pinnacles of the rocks by means of their fins and tails. They often come in conflict, struggling for the high places, and then we are sure to hear the loud disputation, unlike any controversy which I have ever heard before, their fierce growls and barks being heard above the noise of old Ocean, whose waves are constantly breaking on the shore. There are seals of all sizes, from the tiny cubs to the strong old settlers, who look as if they might have been masters of the rock for a hundred years. I doubt if there is another such scene to be witnessed anywhere upon the earth or sea; and the great curiosity is, that these undomesticated denizens of two elements are living in a community of their own, almost within stone's-throw of a frequented shore, in as wild a state as when the continent was discovered, constantly within the sound of human voices, and yet as apparently unconscious of the vicinity of man as if they were a thousand miles from land."

*San Francisco Harbor.* — This, the safest, best, and most capacious harbor on the western coast of North America, is a securely land-locked bay, nearly fifty miles in length, by an average of about nine miles in width, with deep water, good anchorage, and well sheltered by the surrounding hills from the violence of the winds, from every point of the compass. The entrance to this bay, which none of the early navigators were able to discover, is in latitude 37° 48′ north, longitude 122° 30′ west from Greenwich, and is through a strait about five miles in length and a mile wide, which was most appropriately named Chrysopalae — the Golden Gate — by Frémont, in his "Geographical Memoir of California," written in 1847, before the source of the golden streams which have since flowed through it, was discovered.

*Farallone Islands.* — The Farallones consist of two clusters, comprising seven islands, the nearest of which is about twenty miles west from the Golden Gate. They are all utterly destitute of soil and vegetation, consisting of bare, rugged rocks, which are the resort of immense numbers of sea-lions, and of myriads of birds, the eggs of which at one time were a source of great profit to those who collected them. As many as 25,000 dozen were collected in some seasons lasting from the middle of May until the middle of June, which sold at from thirty to fifty cents per dozen. The southernmost of the group is the largest, containing about two acres, and is also the nearest to the coast. On this there is a first-class lighthouse, to warn the mariner of the dangers of the locality. No water fit for drinking, except such as was collected from rains and fogs, was obtainable on any of these islands until 1867, when some of the egg-gatherers discovered a spring on the main island, within a half mile of the light house. The water from this spring, which is of a pale amber color, and pleasant to the taste, possesses important medical qualities: by analysis, it is found to contain chlorides of sodium, lime, and magnesia, with traces of sulphate of ammonium and free hydrochloric acid.

*Baron Munchausen in California.*—The following is a fair representation, somewhat enlarged, of the "big talk" about the agricultural productions of the Pacific coast which one hears in those parts:—

Two weeks ago I started on a visit to the Yosemite Valley. I arrived at the wharf a moment too late to get on board; and, instead of waiting until the next day, I determined to go to Stockton on horseback. I accordingly crossed the bay to Oakland, or, as it is better known, "Little Pedlington," procured a horse, and rode over to the Livermore Valley, where I stayed all night with a rancher, who was known in the valley as "Clamps." They call him that because he got rich by holding on to his money with a degree of fortitude not universal in the country. As supper-time approached, "Clamps" asked me if I would like some egg, and how I preferred it — hard or soft, boiled or fried. I told him I would like some eggs, and that it would suit me best to have them soft-boiled.

In a few moments there came Clamps and his wife, rolling an egg the size of a flour-barrel, which they boiled in a short time in a large caldron, and then set it on end by madam's chair at the table. A hole was made in the top of the shell, and the egg was dipped out with a long-handled ladle. I was astonished at the size of the egg, and observed that his hens must be enormously large. "By no means," he replied. "You will not be so much surprised when I tell you that one hen did not lay this egg alone; it took seven or eight hens almost a week to lay it. It was a joint-stock production of the chickens; but still it is better than the individual responsibility plan."

At breakfast the next morning we had more egg, and then I went on the road to Stockton. I reached San Joaquin River at noon, and was ferried over in a unique-looking craft. While the ferryman was tugging silently at his big oars, I inquired whether his ferry was profitable.

"Does n't scarcely pay for raisin' the boat," he replied.

"Raising the boat?" I repeated. "What do you mean by raising the boat?"

"Mister," said he, resting for a while on his oars, "you be a stranger in these parts, bean't you?"

I replied that I had not been long in the country.

"Then," said he, pointing to the shore, "this 'ere boat growed in that pumpkin-patch over yonder."

"Growed in that pumpkin-patch!" I exclaimed.

"Growed in that pumpkin-patch, on a pumpkin-vine. Mister, this boat is a pumpkin-shell, cut in two. That patch is where it growed."

"Where, over by that barn?" I inquired.

"That ain't no barn," he answered, "unless you choose to call it so. That's a pumpkin too. But I made a hole in the end on't, and let the stock inside; and when the wet season sets in, why, you see, I plug up the hole and let 'em winter there. They come out awful fat in the spring. That big green-looking squash over yonder I'm hollerin' out to live in."

"Are these the growth of the season?" I asked.

"We don't have no such difference here on the San Joaquin as growin' seasons and them others. Things keep on growin' all the time till we pull 'em or they die."

As I was taking leave of the ferryman, he gave me a pumpkin-seed, with the remark that I might astonish the folks in the east with it; but before twenty-four hours had elapsed I came near having a calamity by reason of it myself.

It was in this wise: After riding several hours in the sun, I was so overcome by drowsiness as to find it impossible to keep in the saddle, and, dismounting, lay down on the ground, intending to take a short nap. I had the pumpkin-seed in my vest-pocket. During my slumbers it fell on the ground, and I rolled over on it. My great fatigue caused me to oversleep myself, and I awoke in the morning by being roughly hurried over the ground in my prostrate position, with what seemed to be a rope around my body. I howled lustily for help, and my cries attracted the attention of two men, who were on their way to the harvest-field.

On being relieved from my perilous position, the mystery became clear. The warmth of my body caused the pumpkin-seed to sprout and begin growing, and one of the tendrils of the new vine had coiled itself around my body, dragging me along in its rapid growth a distance of more than half a mile before I was awakened. My deliverers had a hard run to keep pace with me in the clutches of the pumpkin-vine, and finally arrested my progress by cutting it with their scythe-blades. I gave them the vine for their reward, and we counted on it no less than three hundred young pumpkins, ranging from the size of a hen's egg to a flour barrel.

There is but one more thing I will notice. Six years ago a gentleman residing near Stockton planted a grape-vine by his house. In two years the building was completely enfolded in the branches of the vine, and the gentleman was surprised at seeing his dwelling starting from its foundation. The vine grew with wonderful vigor, and carried the house unharmed up to the height of sixty feet in the air, where it remained. The gentleman now reaches his front door by means of a winding staircase around the trunk of the grapevine, and anybody who will take the trouble to go and see, will find it as I have said.

*The Yosemite Valley.* — The wonderful Yosemite Valley is nearly in the centre of California, north and south, and just midway between the east and west base of the Sierra, here a little over seventy miles wide. The Valley is nearly level, about six miles in length, and from half a mile to a mile in width, sunk almost a mile in depth below the general level of the neighboring region. It may be roughly likened to a gigantic trough hollowed in the mountains. This trough is quite irregular, until we arrive near its upper end, when it turns sharply at right angles almost, and soon divides into three branches, through either of which we may, going up a series of gigantic steps, as it were, ascend to the general level of the Sierra. Down each of these branches descend streams, forks of the Merced River, coming down the steps in a series of stupendous waterfalls. The principal features of the Yosemite, and those by which it is distinguished from all other known valleys, are: first, the steepness of its walls; second, their great height; and finally, the very small amount of fragments at the base of these gigantic cliffs. Besides these, there are many striking peculiarities, and features both of sublimity and beauty, which can be hardly surpassed, if equalled, by those of any mountain valleys in the world. Some of these may be briefly mentioned.

Among its grand mountain domes is El Capitan, an immense block of granite, projecting squarely out into the Valley, and presenting an almost upright sharp edge, 3,300 feet high. The sides or walls of the mass are bare, smooth, and entirely without vegetation. It is almost impossible for the observer to comprehend the enormous size of this rock, which in clear weather can be distinctly seen at a distance of fifty or sixty miles. Nothing, however, so helps one to realize the greatness of these masses about the Yosemite as climbing around and among them. El Capitan imposes on us by its stupendous bulk, which seems as if hewn from the mountains on purpose to stand as the type of eternal massiveness. It is doubtful if anywhere in the world there is presented so squarely cut, so lofty, and so imposing a face of rock.

At the angle where the Yosemite branches, we have the dome-shaped mass called the *North Dome*. This rounded mass of granite rises to an elevation of 3,568 feet above the Valley. Such dome-shaped masses are somewhat peculiar to granitic regions, but are nowhere developed on so grand a scale as in the Sierras. On the left-hand or north side of the river is a massive rock, solitary and nearly perpendicular on all sides, rising perhaps 2,000 feet above its base, and little inferior in grandeur to the North Dome. This has borne, at different times, a great variety of names; but is best known, at present, as the "Cap of Liberty." It has been climbed, and has on its summit, according to Mr. Hutchings' statement, a juniper-tree of great diameter.

The Half Dome (South Dome) is the loftiest and most imposing mass of those considered as part of the Yosemite. It is a crest of granite rising to the height of 4,737 feet above the Valley, perfectly inaccessible, being probably the only one of all the prominent points about the Yosemite which never has been, and never will be, trodden by human foot. On one side it is absolutely upright for 2,000 feet or more from the summit, and then falls off with a very steep slope to the bottom of the gorge. On the opposite face the Half Dome is not absolutely vertical; it has a rounded top and grows more and more steep at the bottom. This mountain has not the massiveness of El Capitan, but is more astonishing, and probably there are few visitors to the Valley who would not give it the first place among all the wonders of a region which is rapidly becoming famous, and drawing crowds of visitors from all parts of the world.

A very prominent object, in going up the Yosemite Valley, is the triple group of rocks known as the Three Brothers. These rise in steps one behind the other, the highest being 3,830 feet above the Valley. From its summit there is a superb view of the Valley and its surroundings. The peculiar outline of these rocks, as seen from below, resembling three frogs sitting with their heads turned in one direction, is supposed to have suggested the Indian name Pompompasus, which means, we are informed, "Leaping Frog Rocks."

Nearly opposite the Three Brothers is a point of rocks projecting into the Valley, the termination of which is a slender mass of granite, having something the shape of an obelisk, and called, from its peculiar position, or from its resemblance to a gigantic watch-tower, the "Sentinel Rock." The obelisk form of the Sentinel continues down for a thousand feet or more from its summit; below that, it is united with the wall of the Valley. Its entire height above the river at its base is 3,043 feet. Farther up the cañon of the Tenaya is a beautiful little lake, called "Mirror Lake," an expansion of the Tenaya Fork. It is frequently visited for the purpose of getting the reflection from its unruffled surface of a noble overhanging mass of rock, to which the name of Mount Watkins has been given as a compliment to the photographer who has done so much to attract attention to this region. Still farther up the Tenaya Fork, on the right-hand side, is "Clouds' Rest," the somewhat fanciful designation of a long, bare, steep, and elevated granite ridge, which connects the Valley with the high Sierra. This point is perhaps a thousand feet higher than the Half Dome, or nearly 10,000 feet above the sea level.

This whole general region abounds in strange and curious forms of rock, mountain-side, and valley. Among them is a natural curiosity which has been discovered on the line of the Union Pacific Railroad. It is a cut or cleft in the earth, with sides as perpendicular as if fashioned by man, and a smooth bottom running at an equal grade from the top of a lofty hill to the Weber River at its foot. The country round is desolate and uninhabited, and there is positively nothing to indicate the presence of a human agency. This is one of the strangest works of nature in the Western States, and is appropriately termed the "Devil's Slide."

*The Waterfalls in the Yosemite Valley.* — Among the beauties of this strange and lovely valley, not the least are its wonderful waterfalls. Their height, slenderness, and the sublime scenes around, conspire to invest them with peculiar interest. One of the finest is Bridal Veil Fall, which is formed by the creek of the same name, which rises a few miles east of Empire Camp, runs through the meadows, and finally falls over the cliff, on the west side of Cathedral

Rock, into the Yosemite, in one leap of 630 feet. The water strikes here on a sloping pile of loose rocks, down which it rushes in a series of cascades for a perpendicular distance of nearly 300 feet more, the total height of the edge of the fall above the meadow at its base being 900 feet. The effect of the Fall, as everywhere seen from the Valley, is as if it were 900 feet in vertical height, its base being concealed by the trees which surround it. The quantity of water in the Bridal Veil Fall varies greatly with the season. In May and June the amount is generally the greatest, and it gradually decreases as the season advances. The effect, however, is finest when the body of water is not too heavy, since then the swaying from side to side, and the waving under the pressure of the wind as it strikes the column of water, is more marked. As seen from a distance at such times, it seems to flutter like a white veil, producing an indescribably beautiful effect. The name Bridal Veil is poetical, but fairly appropriate.

The Yosemite Fall is formed by a creek of the same name, which heads on the west side of Mount Hoffman Group, about ten miles northeast of the valley. The vertical height of the lip of the fall above the Valley is, in round numbers, 2,600 feet. The lip or the edge of the fall is a great, rounded mass of granite, perfectly smooth, on which it is found to be a very hazardous matter to move. A difference of a hundred feet on a fall of this height would be entirely unperceived by most eyes. The fall is not in one perpendicular sheet. There is first a downright descent of 1,500 feet, when the water strikes on what seems to be a projecting ledge, but which, in reality, is a shelf or recess almost a third of a mile back from the front of the lower portion of the cliff. From here the water finds its way, in a series ef cascades, down a descent of 626 feet, and then gives one final plunge to the rocks at the base of the cliff.

One of the most striking features of the Yosemite Fall, as in the Bridal Veil, is the swaying of the upper portion from one side to the other, under the influence of the wind, which acts with immense force on so long a column. The descending mass of water is too great to allow of its being broken up into spray, but it widens out very much at the bottom, probably as much as 300 feet at high water, the space through which it moves being fully three times as wide.

The river descends, in two miles, over 2,600 feet, making, besides innumerable cascades, two grand falls, which are among the greater attractions of Yosemite, not only on account of their height and the large body of water in the river during most of the season, but also on account of the stupendous scenery in the midst of which they are placed. The first fall reached in ascending, is the Vernal, a perpendicular sheet of water, with a descent varying greatly with the season. The path up the side of the valley, near the Vernal Fall, winds around and along a steeply sloping mountain-side, always wet with spray, and, consequently, rather slippery in places. A remarkable parapet of granite runs along the edge of the Vernal Fall for some distance, just breast high, and looking as if made on purpose to secure the visitor a safe position from which to enjoy the scene.

The Nevada Fall, the last one of the Merced River, is, in every respect, one of the grandest waterfalls in the world, whether we consider its height, the purity and volume of the river which forms it, or the stupendous scenery by which it is surrounded. The fall is not quite perpendicular, as there is near the summit a ledge of rock, which receives a portion of the water, and throws it off with a peculiar twist, adding much to the general picturesque effect.

There are numbers of other falls, each surpassing in loftiness and beauty anything else known on the globe, but the above are some of the most noted, and will illustrate the superiority of some of our American scenery to much that has become famous in other lands. — *Whitney.*

## CHAPTER XXVII.

### NATIONAL PARK NEAR THE HEAD-WATERS OF THE YELLOWSTONE, MONTANA.

*Act of Congress, approved March 1, 1872.*

CHAPTER XXIV. An act to set apart a certain tract of land, lying near the Head-waters of the Yellowstone River, as a Public Park.

SECTION 1. Be it enacted by the Senate and House of Representatives of the United States of America, in Congress assembled, That the tract of land in the Territories of Montana and Wyoming, lying near the head-waters of the Yellowstone River, and described as follows, to wit : commencing at the junction of Gardiner's River with the Yellowstone River, and running east to the meridian passing ten miles to the eastward of the most eastern point of Yellowstone Lake ; thence south along said meridian to the parallel of latitude passing ten miles south of the most southern point of Yellowstone Lake ; thence west along said parallel to the meridian passing fifteen miles west of the most western point of Madison Lake ; thence north along said meridian to the latitude of the junction of the Yellowstone and Gardiner's Rivers ; thence east to the place of beginning, is hereby reserved and withdrawn from settlement, occupancy, or sale, under the laws of the United States, and dedicated and set apart as a public park, or pleasuring-ground for the benefit and enjoyment of the people ; and all persons, who shall locate or settle upon, or occupy the same, or any part thereof, except as hereinafter provided, shall be considered trespassers, and removed therefrom.

Sec. 2. That said public park shall be under the exclusive control of the Secretary of the Interior, whose duty it shall be, as soon as practicable, to make and publish such rules and regulations as he may deem necessary or proper for the care and management of the same. Such regulations shall provide for the preservation, from injury or spoliation, of all timber, mineral deposits, natural curiosities, or wonders within said park, and their retention in their natural condition. The secretary may in his discretion grant leases for building purposes for terms not exceeding ten years, of small parcels of ground, at such places in said park as shall require the erection of buildings for the accommodation of visitors; all of the proceeds of said leases, and all other revenues that may be derived from any source connected with said park, to be expended under his direction in the management of the same, and the construction of roads and bridle-paths therein. He shall provide against the wanton destruction of the fish and game found within said park, and against their capture or destruction for the purposes of merchandise or profit. He shall also cause all persons trespassing upon the same after the passage of this act to be removed therefrom, and generally shall be authorized to take all such measures as shall be necessary or proper to fully carry out the objects and purposes of this act.

Approved, March 1, 1872.

*Montana.* — Montana formed a part of Idaho until May, 1864, at which time it was organized into a distinct territory. It is bounded on the north by the British Possessions, on the east by Dakota, and on the south by Dakota and Idaho, and on the west by Idaho. Its length is about 560 miles, and its breadth about 275 miles, having an area of about 153,300 square miles.

The surface of the country is generally mountainous. The great Rocky Mountain range crosses the territory.

Gold and silver have been found in great abundance, and mining is now the most important industry of the territory. Montana is believed by many who have visited and "prospected" it, to be the richest placer-mining region in the United States.

The principal rivers are the Missouri, the Yellowstone, and their tributaries; the Big Horn, Powder Horn, Milk, and Manas Rivers.

*The Scenery of the Yellowstone.* — The Yellowstone is without exception the most extraordinary river on the continent. It had not been fully explored until the year 1870, and its wonders are as yet comparatively unknown. The Northern Pacific Railway, which will traverse the Territory, will in all probability be completed within the next three years, when the trip from the Atlantic seaboard to this wonderful region may be made within four days, and the rush of tourists to Montana will then scarcely be less than to California at the present time. With its tributaries, Big Horn, Powder Horn, etc., this great river drains the southern and eastern portions of the territory, in which nearly the whole of its course is included. Mr. N. P. Langford, the explorer of the Yellowstone, has furnished a series of well-written articles on the subject to "Scribner's Monthly," from which we make the following extracts : —

"The Yellowstone and Columbia, the first flowing into the Missouri and the last into the Pacific, divided from each other by the Rocky Mountains, have their sources within a few miles of each other. Both rise in the mountains which separate Idaho from the new territory of Wyoming, but the head-waters of the Yellowstone are only accessible from Montana. The mountains surrounding the basin from which they flow are very lofty, covered with pines, and on the southeastern side present to the traveller a precipitous wall of rock several thousand feet in height. This barrier prevented Captain Reynolds from visiting the head-waters of the Yellowstone while prosecuting an expedition planned by the government and placed under his command, for the purpose of exploring that river in 1859."

"*The Source of the Yellowstone* is in a magnificent lake, nearly 9,000 feet above the level of the ocean. In its course of 1,300 miles to the Missouri, it falls about 7,200 feet. Its upper waters flow through deep cañons and gorges, and are broken by immense cataracts and fearful rapids, presenting at various points some of the grandest scenery on the continent. This country is entirely volcanic, and abounds in boiling springs, mud-volcanoes, huge mountains of sulphur, and geysers more extensive and numerous than those of Iceland."

"*The Lower Cañon* of the Yellowstone, as a simple isolated piece of scenery, is very beautiful. It is less than a mile in length, and perhaps does not exceed 1,000 feet in depth. Its walls are vertical, and, seen from the summit of the precipice, the river seems forced through a narrow gorge, and is surging and boiling at a fearful rate, — the water breaking into millions of prismatic drops against every projecting rock."

*The Devil's Slide.* — "After travelling six miles over the mountains above the cañon, we again descended into a broad and open valley, skirted by a level upland for several miles. Here an object met our attention which deserves more than a casual notice. It was two parallel vertical walls of rock, projecting from the side of a mountain to the height of 125 feet, traversing the mountain from base to summit, a distance of 1,500 feet. These walls were not to exceed thirty feet in width, and their tops for the whole length were crowned with a growth of pines. The sides were as even as if they had been worked by line and plumb, the whole space between, and on either side of them, having been completely eroded and washed away. We had seen many of the capricious works wrought by erosion upon the friable rocks of Montana, but never before upon so majestic a scale. Here an entire mountain-side, by wind and water, had been removed, leaving as the evidences of their protracted toil, these vertical projections, which, but for their immensity, might as readily be mistaken for works of art as of nature, their smooth sides, uniform width and height, and great length, considered in connection with the causes which had wrought their insulation, excited our wonder and admiration. They were all the more curious because of their dissimilarity to any other striking objects in natural scenery that we had ever seen or heard of. In future years, when the wonders of the Yellowstone are incorporated into the family of fashionable resorts, there will be few of its attractions surpassing in interest this marvellous freak of the elements."

*The Great Cañon.* — "The Great Falls are at the head of one of the most remarkable cañons in the world, — a gorge through volcanic rocks fifty miles long, and varying from one thousand to nearly five thousand feet in depth. In this chasm the river falls almost 3,000 feet. At one point where the passage has been worn through a mountain range, our hunters assured us it was more than a vertical mile in depth, and the river, broken into rapids and cascades, appeared no wider than a ribbon. . . . All access to its margin is denied; even the voice of the waters cannot be heard."

*The Mud-Volcano.* — "While returning by a new route to our camp, dull, thundering sounds, which General Washburn likened to frequent discharges of a distant mortar, broke upon our ears. We followed their direction, and found them to proceed from a mud-volcano, which occupied the slope of a small hill, embowered in a grove of pines. Dense volumes of steam shot into the air with each report, through a crater thirty feet in diameter. The reports, though irregular, occurred as often as every five seconds, and could be distinctly heard half a mile. Each alternate report shook the ground a distance of two hundred yards or more, and the massive jets of vapor which accompanied them, burst forth like the smoke of burning gunpowder."

*The Giant Geyser.* — "'The Giant' has a rugged crater, ten feet in diameter on the outside, with an irregular orifice five or six feet in diameter. It discharges a vast quantity of water, and the only time we saw it in eruption the flow of water in a column five feet in diameter, one hundred and forty feet in vertical height, continued uninterruptedly for nearly three hours. The crater resembles a miniature model of the Coliseum."

*The Giantess Geyser.* — "Our search for new wonders leading us across Fire Hole River, we ascended a gentle incrusted slope, and came suddenly upon a large oval aperture with scalloped edges, the diameters of which were eighteen and twenty-five feet, the sides corrugated, and covered with a grayish-white silicious deposit, which was distinctly visible at the depth of one hundred feet below the surface. No water could be discovered, but we could distinctly hear it gurgling and boiling at a great distance below. Suddenly it began to rise, boiling and spluttering, and sending out huge masses of steam, causing a general stampede of our company, driving us some distance from our point of observation. When within about forty feet of the surface it became stationary, and we returned to look down upon it. It was surging and foaming at a terrible rate, occasionally emitting small jets of hot water nearly to the mouth of the orifice. All at once it seemed seized with a fearful spasm, and rose with incredible rapidity, hardly affording us time to flee to a safe distance, when it burst from the orifice with terrific momentum, rising in a column the full size of this immense aperture to the height of sixty feet; and, through and out of the apex of this vast aqueous mass, five or six lesser jets or round columns of water, varying in size from six to fifteen inches in diameter, were projected to the marvellous height of two hundred and fifty feet. These lesser jets, so much higher than the main column, and shooting through it, doubtless proceed from auxiliary pipes, leading into the principal orifice near the bottom, where the explosive force is greater. If the theory that water by constant boiling becomes explosive when freed from air be true, this theory rationally accounts for all irregularities in the eruptions of the geysers.

"This grand eruption continued twenty minutes, and was the most magnificent sight we ever witnessed. We were standing on the side of the geyser nearest the sun, the gleams of which filled the sparkling cloud of water and spray with myriads of rainbows, whose arches were constantly changing, dipping and fluttering hither and thither, and disappearing only to be succeeded by others, again and again, amid the aqueous column, while the minute globules into which the spent jets were diffused when falling, sparkled like a shower of diamonds; and around every shadow which the denser clouds of vapor, interrupting the sun's rays, cast upon the column, could be seen a luminous circle, radiant with all the colors of the prism, and resembling the halo of glory represented in paintings as encircling the head of Divinity. All that we had previously witnessed seemed tame in comparison with the perfect grandeur and beauty of this display. Two of these wonderful eruptions occurred during the twenty-two hours we remained in the valley. This geyser we named 'The Giantess.'"

*The Missouri River.* — The restless, turbid waters of the Missouri River flow fretfully 3,000 miles from their sources in the remote west, to their union with the Mississippi. The entire length of the river, including its course to the Gulf of Mexico by the Mississippi (1,272 miles more), is 4,272 miles. The head-waters of the Missouri are very near the springs which find their way to the Pacific through the channels of the Columbia River. Their course is northward for six hundred miles until they reach the remarkable cataracts known as the Great Falls.

*The Great Falls of the Missouri* are situated 2,548 miles from its mouth, and forty miles above Fort Benton. The descent of the swift river, at this point, is three hundred and fifty-seven feet in thirteen and a half miles. The falls embrace four cascades, the first of which is twenty-six feet, the next twenty-seven feet, a third of nineteen feet, and a fourth, and lowest, of eighty-seven feet. Between and below these cataracts there are stretches of angry rapids. This passage is one of extreme beauty and grandeur, and at some day, not very distant, perhaps, when these western wilds shall be covered with cities and towns and peaceful hamlets, this spot will be one of no less eager pilgrimage than many far less imposing scenes are now. The falls of the Missouri are esteemed, by the few tourists whose good fortune it has been to look upon these wonders, as holding rank scarcely below the cataracts of Niagara. The best, and, indeed, the only travelled approach is by boat from St. Louis, or Omaha, during the "spring rise" in the Missouri, to Fort Benton, 2,508 miles, and thence twenty-five miles by land. Fort Union, four hundred miles below Fort Benton, is the head of steamboat navigation during the summer months.

The upper waters of the Missouri flow through a wild, sterile country, and below pass vast prairie stretches. Above the River Platte the open and prairie character of the country begins to develop, extending quite to the banks of the river, and stretching from it indefinitely in naked grass plains, where the traveller may wander for days without seeing either wood or water. Beyond Council Bluffs commences a country of great interest and grandeur, denominated the upper Missouri. It is composed of vast and almost boundless grass plains, through which run the Platte, the Yellowstone, and the other rivers of this ocean of grass. Buffalo, elk, antelope, and mountain-sheep abound. Lewis and Clark, and other travellers, relate having seen here large and singular petrifactions, both animal and vegetable. On the top of a hill they found a petrified skeleton of a huge fish, forty-five feet in length.— *Appleton's Hand-Book of American Travel.*

*A Colorado Wonder.* — Twenty-one miles southeast of Denver lies the remains of a palm-tree preserved in stone. It is upon the hill-side, looking down upon Cherry Creek, and a hundred feet or more above the level of the valley of that stream. The soil is similar to that of most of the upland plain in Colorado, and covered at present with a thick crop of grass and weeds. Bunches of currant-bushes, laden with fruit, cluster about the *wooden* rocks, and above, to the top of the ridge and along its crest, are scrubby young pines and a few large trees. At the foot of the hill, three hundred yards to the westward, passes the old stage road from Denver to Sante Fe. The traveller, looking up, could see a ledge or mass of rough-looking rocks rising ten or twelve feet above the surface of the ground, and about forty feet in length. Camp-fires have been built against it, and campers have doubtless sought shelter from storm or sun under its projecting front, little dreaming that they reclined in the shadow of a palm-tree. The pupils of a school-house near by have played about it many a day. Last winter a hunter for curious specimens stumbled upon it and guessed its true character. Specimens were brought to Denver and pronouced by the best authorities petrified palm-wood. But the mass was reported so large that the story seemed incredible.

A careful examination reveals the following facts: The monster tree evidently grew where it lies, and there has been very little change in the surface of the ground at that point since its fall. Its fall was towards the north, and across a tongue or spur of the hill near the crest, on the south side of which it stood. The unevenness of the ground caused the part of the trunk now visible to break in two pieces. The first, or butt section, is thirty-nine feet long, and it has apparently rolled about half over, down the hill. In the heart was either a hollow or a mass of decayed wood, from four to six feet in diameter. The upper side of the log has been broken up by the action of the elements and frost, destroying between one third and one half its circumference, and the fragments lie scattered about in huge blocks. The more than half that remains intact is a huge trough; the surface of the earth even with its brim on the up-hill side and ten feet below it on the down-hill side. As before stated, this section is thirty-nine feet long. As near as can be determined without excavating the adjacent earth, the diameter of the tree at the base is twenty-two feet. Midway of its length, or twenty feet from the base, it is fifteen feet.

The second section is twenty-one feet long, and evidently lies where it fell. Striking square across the crest of the ridge, the immense weight almost buried it in the earth. Its outlines are hard to determine without digging. At mid-length, or fifty feet from the stump, it is certainly nine feet in diameter. The two sections, as described, measure just sixty feet in length. Above that point, the body of the tree fell into a gulch, which has been since nearly filled up by the wash from the hills above. Digging would doubtless reveal much more of the trunk.

And all this immense mass of wood has turned to stone, hard and flinty as porphyry. Some of it looks like agate, finely veined and delicately tinted; other with opaline lustre; some white as driven snow, or with the polished surface of chalcedony. Portions of the trunk must have been rotten, for its stony remains are honey-combed and the cavities filled with delicate crystals that sparkle in the sunlight like real diamonds. Breaking into the knots with heavy blows of sledge-hammer reveals miniature caves and grottos, glittering with stalactites and stalagmites of real crystal. Specimens of the bark can be chipped off, looking as natural, doubtless, as when its own green leaves waved in the breeze, and Darwin's inchoate man gambolled among the giant stems.

It is useless to speculate upon the time when that giant of the forest flourished; of the hundreds or thousands of years during which a torrid sun daily kissed its shining leaves; of its fall and long immersion in the silicious bath that changed its every fibre to flint. It is history in stone, telling of changes in the condition of climate of this part of the world that may well make one shiver if he expects to stop here fifty or a hundred thousand years longer. Meantime, it can supply materials for the walls of a court-house, window-sills and caps for all of Denver, or centre-table tops for the western States. It is the very biggest thing — in stone, and among trees it takes the *palm*. — *Denver News*.

## CHAPTER XXVIII.

#### SALT LAKE CITY.

THE name Utah signifies "those who dwell on the mountains." The Mormons, almost a mile above the sea, in view of some of the finest scenery in the world, are indeed dwellers among the mountain-tops.

Although thus elevated, Salt Lake City is situated in a great basin, in which blue lakes are set like gems, and across which shining streams stretch like ribbons of light. Beyond and around rise, range on range, the snow-tipped mountains.

The capital of Utah and of Mormondom is a city of neat houses, quaint public buildings, deep shade-trees, broad streets, and flashing rivulets. It contains a population of nearly twenty thousand, of which three fourths are Mormon. The houses are built of adobe, or sun-dried bricks. The streets are broad and without pavement. Between the carriage-way and the sidewalk is a shallow ditch filled with running water, which surrounds every block in the city, and serves to irrigate the gardens and lawns which are the charm of the town.

In 1847 the city was founded by a handful of fugitive wanderers, Mormon pioneers, — one hundred and thirty-nine men and four women. "Their prophet killed, themselves exiles from Missouri and Illinois, after a weary journey of many months they reached this basin to struggle for existence with the unkindly soil, with Indians, and with Mexicans. They claim that they left Missouri with no definite point of settlement; that on the route Brigham Young saw in a vision a beautiful mountain-guarded valley, which heaven assured him was their future home; that on coming in view of Ensign Peak, the Jordan, and Great Salt Lake, he instantly exclaimed, 'Here is the spot!'

"Snowy winters, rainless summers, hostile Indians, and all-devouring grasshoppers did not dishearten the Mormons. With religious enthusiasm they combined great wisdom in practical affairs. They learned a new agriculture, — with irrigation the soil is very productive. Now, settlements of Mormons extend hundreds of miles in every direction. Almost every valley in Utah is dotted with dwellings, herds of cattle, flocks of sheep, great stacks of hay and barley, and thriving young orchards."

The principal buildings of note within the city are the New Tabernacle, the Temple, the residence of Brigham Young, the City Hall, and the Theatre.

In regard to the Tabernacle, we have the following from a recent publication: —

"It is a monster in size, and a monstrosity of architecture. Elliptical in shape, it will seat from fifteen to twenty thousand people, and on a series of low brick walls, broken by so many doors that they are rather a succession of piers, sits an immense oval dome, like an old-fashioned 'cover' over a large Thanksgiving turkey."

The organ within the building is the largest in the country, with the exception of the one in Music Hall, Boston.

The Temple, that is to be, is the wonder of the city. The foundations are laid adjacent to the Tabernacle. The walls are now about six feet above the surface; when completed the building is to cost $10,000,000! It covers a much less space than the Tabernacle, but it is to contain, among other things, a throne for the Messiah, "when he shall descend and reign upon the earth." Furthermore, His descent, according to their creed, is to occur at the moment when the last finishing touch is given to the Temple. But in this connection it is worthy of remark, and suggestive to notice, that the work progresses very *slowly*. It is at present mainly carried on by Mormons who are in debt to the church, and are thus working out their tithes.

The enclosure of ten acres in which Brigham Young resides is in the very heart of the city, and is surrounded by a wall eleven feet high, of bowlders laid in mortar. Within are three houses, — his residence, a museum, and the "Fitting Office." In the rear of the latter are extensive sheds for the accommodation of the teams which come from the surrounding country with a "tenth of all the increase." Within the enclosure also are extensive gardens of flowers and fruit.

The Saints' Theatre was built while yet the town was a thousand miles from railway or steamboat, and cost a quarter of a million of dollars. It will seat eighteen hundred persons. Dramatic entertainments have ever been a leading feature of the Mormon faith, and but few city theatres possess finer stage scenery than this in the heart of the American desert.

In describing Great Salt Lake we take the words of Richardson. "Twenty miles from the city is the Lake, containing seven islands, all of rugged mountains. Though four fresh rivers flow in, it has no visible outlet, and is bitterly salt. At lowest stage, three gallons of its fluid produce one of clear fine salt. The Dead Sea is thirteen hundred feet below the sea; Salt Lake is forty-two hundred feet above. Both receive fresh-water Jordans. Both are so buoyant that one finds it difficult to wade in them, floats with ease, and could hardly drown save by strangulation. Neither has any known outlet. The Dead Sea is said to contain one species of fish. Salt Lake is believed to hold no animal life. The Dead Sea is forty miles by ten; Salt Lake, forty by one hundred and twenty."

## CHAPTER XXIX.

#### THE GREAT LAKES.

'FROM the western extremity of Lake Superior (92° west long.), one of whose tributaries interlocks its source with a branch of the Mississippi, we have a series of fresh-water Lakes, — Superior, Michigan, Huron, Erie, and Ontario, — collectively covering a surface of 80,000 square miles. These lakes have the outer margin of the basin at no very great distance from their shores, as may be inferred from the inconsiderable courses of the streams which they receive. Lake Superior is the highest of these inland seas, being six hundred and forty-one feet above the level of the Atlantic. Lakes Huron and Michigan, connected with Lake Superior by St. Mary's River, form a separate and somewhat lower basin; Erie, a third; and three hundred and thirty-three feet below Erie lies Lake Ontario, doubtless once at a much higher level than at present. The great Falls of Niagara, in the narrow channel that connects Erie and Ontario, show at once the great difference in the level of these lakes. The course of the St. Lawrence from the lakes has a singular conformity to that of the opposite Atlantic coast, having a general northeast direction. After its exit from Lake Ontario it receives the Ottawa near Montreal, and the Saguenay from the northeast, and, increased by numerous smaller streams, enters the Atlantic by a wide bay or gulf."

*Lake Superior.* — At the head of this great chain of lakes lies Lake Superior, the largest body of fresh water in the world, stretching four hundred and sixty miles in length, with an average width of eighty-five miles, and an area of 32,000 miles. Its waters, eight hundred feet in depth, are clear and cold, and abound in fish. Its tributaries, two hundred in number, drain a vast extent of fertile country, and the mineral wealth of the surrounding regions is incalculable. With the exception of the mouths of the rivers, which are generally sand-bars, the coast of Lake Superior is rock-bound, containing specimens of numerous geological formations.

*Duluth.* — At the foot of the lake on the north side of the great bay that extends to Superior City, a distance of ten miles, lies the town of Duluth. It is situated at the mouth of the St. Louis River, and is the terminus of the Superior and Mississippi Railroad, which connects the Mississippi with the Great Lakes, and of the Northern Pacific Railroad, which will soon establish communication with the Pacific coast. The rapid growth of this town is almost without a parallel even in the West. In 1869 the site of the town was an unbroken forest. Two years later we find a flourishing little city with a population of 4,000, with nine miles of graded streets, with churches, schools, and newspapers, and driving an active trade both by lake and rail.

*Apostle Islands.* — At the west end of the lake, but a short distance from the Wisconsin shore, are the Apostle Islands, twenty-seven in number. The largest is Madeline Island, which contains the fishing village of La Pointe. These Islands cover an area of about four hundred miles, of which one half is water. The soil seems hardly worth cultivating, although there are some fine sugar-tree lands and natural meadows. They are covered with fine forest-trees, and are a favorite resort for invalids who desire the bracing air of Lake Superior.

*Keweenan Point.* — East of the Apostle Islands, Keweenan Point extends into the lake for a distance of sixty miles. Its width is from ten to twenty-five miles. Here are the great copper-mines, and in this region is found most of the silver around Lake Superior. Keweenan Point is supposed to have been formerly an island separated from the main land by a strait which now forms Portage Lake. A canal has been cut across the foot of the Point, by which the difficult and dangerous circuit is avoided.

*Marquette.* — A short distance east of Portage Entry is the town of Marquette, remarkable for its trade in iron. Four immense piers run out into the lake, from which the ore is transferred to the boats in the same manner that grain is shipped. The mines lie back of the town about a dozen miles, in an elevated ridge known as Iron Mountain, having a height of eight hundred feet. South of Marquette, on the railroad, is the town of Negaunee. The grade between the two places is so steep that locomotives cannot run in winter. Negaunee is in the midst of a region so rich in iron that the embankments of the roads are filled with ore. The mines might better be called quarries, as the ore is dug from the surface of the ground in the same manner that building-stone is quarried. As these mines are worked in the same way, a visit to one suffices for all.

*Pictured Rocks.* — Still farther to the east lies the greatest wonder of the Superior regions, the Pictured Rocks. They rise abruptly from the water's edge to the height of from fifty to two hundred feet, worn by the action of the water into a thousand fantastic forms, and stained with the different minerals which enter into their composition. Miner's Castle, at the west end, rises to the height of one hundred and forty feet. It presents a marvellous resemblance to an ancient turreted castle, the Gothic gateway being plainly discernible. East of the Castle, the rocks pile themselves into huge masses gorgeously colored, and taking the most weird and fanciful shapes. Beyond this range of bright cliffs rises Sail Rock, which resembles the jib and mainsail of a sloop when spread. When the light falls upon the cliffs, the illusion is complete. Its height is forty feet. But the grandest group of the series is Grand Portal, an immense mass jutting out into the lake six hundred feet, having a frontage of from three hundred to four hundred feet, and a height of two hundred feet. The interior consists of vaulted passages, which connect with each other and with the great dome. The Portal itself, which opens into the lake, is one hundred feet high and over one hundred and sixty feet broad. Beyond the Grand Portal is the Chapel, a vaulted apartment, seemingly hewn from the solid rock, with an arching roof of sandstone resting on four columns. The room is about forty feet in diameter, and the same in height, and is furnished by Nature with a pulpit and altar, cut from the flinty rock. East of the Chapel, Chapel River throws itself over a high ledge into the lake. Lying between, and connecting Lakes Huron and Michigan, is Mackinaw Strait, a narrow channel forty miles long, and from five to twenty miles wide. On the Huron side is the Island of Mackinaw, an old military post. Upon the cliffs two hundred feet above the lake, stands Fort Mackinaw, which is garrisoned by United States troops. One hundred feet higher are the ruins of old Fort Holmes; and near by, three hundred and twenty feet above the lake, is a signal station. The island is covered with a heavy growth of hard wood, and the drives, walks, and surrounding objects of interest offer great inducements to the tourist.

*Lake Huron.* — Lake Huron extends from Mackinaw Straits to St. Clair River, a distance of two hundred and fifty miles. It is one hundred miles in width, and varies in depth from one hundred to seven hundred and fifty feet. Its two largest inlets are Saginaw Bay on the Michigan shore, and Georgian Bay on the Canadian side. The stormiest part of the lake lies between these two bays, where the wind sweeps with tremendous force. There are few islands in the lake, and the immense expanse of water, stretching as far as the eye can see, conveys to the traveller who has never been at sea some idea of the ocean. Connecting Lake Huron with Lake Erie is the narrow strait known as St. Clair River. It is forty-eight miles long, with a descent of fifteen feet, giving it a current of about four miles an hour. Its course lies through a fertile country, with well wooded and cultivated banks on each side. At the head of Lake St. Clair, into which the river widens, are large deposits of sand. These shallows, known as the St. Clair Flats, for a long time impeded navigation, but the difficulty has been obviated by the construction of a canal. This is a channel cut through the shifting sand, having a depth of fifteen feet. The excavated earth is deposited on each side, forming dikes about five feet in height. The lake, after a course of twenty-five miles, flows into Lake Erie.

*Lake Erie* is the shallowest and most dangerous of all the Great Lakes. It is two hundred and fifty miles long, sixty miles broad, and about one hundred feet in depth. It is five hundred feet above the level of the sea, and, together with Lakes Ontario, Huron, Michigan, and Superior, may be regarded as a sea rather than a lake.

## CHAPTER XXX.

#### ENGLAND.

SO well known as hardly to need even a single word of introduction. Its size is generally greatly over-estimated by those accustomed to the distance of a nation that occupies a large part of a continent. England is in fact, taken with Scotland, but twice the size of New York State, and it may be well to bear in mind that the area of Scotland is about the same as that of the State of Maine. On the other hand, England has not the wild, uncultivated tracts that meet the eye in this country. Her soil is so thoroughly cultivated as to seem one great garden; field after field of waving grain for miles. The population of England is 17,000,000. Its climate is temperate, and not subject to great extremes of heat and cold, by reason of its insular position. To this advantage it owes its rank as the first country in the world in the amount of its commercial interests.

*General View of London.* — London, the metropolis of Great Britain, is the most populous, wealthy, and commercial city in the world. It is difficult to obtain an adequate idea of its immense size. The area presenting a solid mass of houses is in length nine miles, and in breadth six. To walk over such an extent of ground, amidst the everlasting jostlings and interruptions which one has to encounter in the crowded thoroughfares, is no easy task. Its population is more than three millions. This vast multitude consumes in one year 12,800,000 bushels of wheat, 1,700,000 sheep, and over 4,000,000 head of game. To light the metropolis every night 360,000 gas-lights fringe the streets. 5,000,000 tons of coal are required to warm its people and supply its factories. The supply of bread and other food is undertaken by 2,500 bakers, 1,700 butchers, 2,600 tea-dealers and grocers. To look after the digestion of this enormous amount of food, upwards of 2,400 duly licensed practitioners are daily running to and fro, whose patients, in due course of time and physic, are handed over to the tender mercies of five hundred undertakers!

Till within the last forty years London displayed little architectural elegance. More recently, however, the erection of magnificent ranges of buildings in every direction has made the British metropolis as superior to most capitals in appearance as it has long been in wealth, cleanliness, and comfort. It is adorned with many large parks beautifully laid out, and with fine public squares in which are fountains and statues.

The river Thames, dividing the city, is about 1,000 feet in width, and is spanned by thirteen arched bridges. The view we give of the city is from the vicinity of the Parliament Houses, and looks towards the northeast.

*Houses of Parliament from Poets' Corner.* — Also called the New Palace of Westminster. This is probably the largest Gothic edifice in the world. It was built about 1840, and covers an area of eight acres. It has one hundred staircases, 1,100 apartments, and more than two miles of corridors!

The cost has exceeded two millions of pounds, or ten millions of dollars. The stone employed for the external masonry is a magnesian limestone, selected from all the building stones of England by scientific commissioners appointed for that purpose. There is very little wood about the building; all the front beams and joists are of iron. Within the building is Westminster Hall, the largest room in the world unsupported by pillars; the House of Peers, a magnificent room, in which is the Throne; and the Hall of the House of Commons.

*Buckingham Palace.*— At the west end of St. James Park. Its cost has been three and a half millions of dollars, but it is not a satisfactory place of residence for the Queen and her retinue even now: indeed one can hardly wonder, — for this costly palace, with all its grandeur, was so badly planned, that in a number of the passages lamps are required even during the day. From this palace the Queen proceeds in person to Parliament when it is to be opened or dissolved. The state procession includes six carriages, containing various persons of Her Majesty's retinue, and finally a state coach drawn by eight cream-colored horses, conveying the Queen, the mistress of the robes, and the master of the horse.

*Trafalgar Square.* — With Nelson's statue seen on the right, and at its base two of Landseer's four noble lions couchant. There are also in this square, statues to George IV, Sir Charles James Napier, and Sir Henry Havelock. A statue of George III is near here. Of the two wells which supply the fountains in this square, one is no less than four hundred feet deep.

*The Tower of London.* — This famous structure, or rather group of structures, is a cluster of houses, towers, barracks, armories, warehouses, and prison-like edifices, situated a little towards the suburbs of the city proper. Its area within the walls is about twelve acres. The Tower was founded by William the Conqueror to secure his authority over the inhabitants of London; but the original fort has been greatly extended by subsequent monarchs, and the whole was surrounded by a moat, now dry and used as a garden, but which was formerly filled with water from the Thames, which flows at the base of the Tower on the southern side. The tower is intimately connected with history. Here were confined Lady Jane Grey, Anne Boleyn, Queen Katherine Howard, all of whom were executed upon a scaffold erected within the walls; also several kings, Sir Walter Raleigh, Sir Thomas More, Archbishop Cranmer, and a host of other distinguished persons. Henry VI was murdered here. The Duke of Clarence was here drowned in a butt of malmsey, and the two young princes, Edward V and Richard, were here killed at the instance of Richard III that he might place the crown upon his own head. The buildings now contain a fine armory, a museum in which are complete sets of ancient armor, a beheading axe, thumb-screws, etc., and a jewel-room. In this, among other articles, is the crown of Queen Victoria, valued at $500,000.

*Shillingford Bridge.* — It crosses the Thames above London, and gives a very truthful idea of the appearance of the Thames, and its banks above the metropolis.

*The Crystal Palace.* — One special object of interest in the southern vicinity of London is the far-famed Crystal Palace. This structure, in many respects one of the most remarkable in the world, owed its existence to the great exhibition of 1851, in Hyde Park. The materials of that building being sold to a new company, towards the close of that year, were transferred to an elevated spot about seven miles from London. The intention was to found a palace and park for the exhibition of objects in art and science, and to make it self-paying. The original estimate was two and a half millions of dollars, but the expenditure reached nearly seven and a half millions, — too great to render a profitable return likely. The palace and grounds were opened in 1854; the water-towers and great fountains some time afterwards. The expenses have been $300,000 a year. The marvels of this unparalleled structure cannot adequately be described, at least not within our limited space. The building is about 1,600 feet long, three hundred and eighty wide, and, at the centre transept, nearly two hundred high. It consists of a nave and three transepts, all with arched roofs, and all made chiefly of iron and glass. Within, the building consists of a central nave, having marble fountains near the two ends, and it is lined with statues and plants throughout its whole length. On each side of the nave are compartments to illustrate the sculpture and architecture of different ages and countries, such as Roman, Greek, Assyrian, Egyptian, Pompeian, Saracenic, and others. Other compartments illustrate certain industrial products, such as cutlery, porcelain, paper, etc. On the first gallery are large collections of pictures, photographs, and casts from medallions and small works of art. Near the centre transept are all the necessary arrangements for two concert-rooms, — one on a stupendous scale, in which 5,000 singers and instrumentalists can sometimes be heard at once. An orchestra of unparalleled dimensions is constructed here for great festival commemorations. The botanical collection within the building is very fine; and to preserve the exotic plants, one end of the building is kept at a high temperature all the year round. Some portions of the galleries are let out as stalls or bazaars to shopkeepers; and there are very extensive arrangements for supplying refreshments to the thousands that visit the palace on the occasion of the many festivals held in it. In an upper gallery is a museum of raw produce. In long galleries in the basement are exhibited agricultural implements, and cotton and other machinery in motion.

The park and gardens are extensive, occupying nearly two hundred acres; they are beautifully arranged and contain an extremely fine collection of flowers and other plants, occupying parterres separated by broad gravel-walks. The terraces, stone balustrades, wide steps, and sculptures are all on a very grand scale. The fountains are perhaps the finest in the world, some of them sending up magnificent streams of water to a great height, and some displaying thousands of minute glittering jets interlacing in the most graceful manner. A portion of the water is made to imitate cascades and waterfalls. The jet from the central basin rises to one hundred and fifty feet; and those from the two great basins to two hundred and fifty feet. There are two cascades, each four hundred and fifty feet long, one hundred wide, and having a fall of twelve feet. When the whole of the water-works are playing, there are 12,000 jets in all; and when this continues for the length of time customary on some of the "grand days," the water consumed is said to amount to 6,000,000 gallons. Two water-towers of enormous height (nearly three hundred feet from the foundations), to which water is pumped up by steam-engines, supply the water-pressure by which the fountains are fed. The illustrations of extinct animals and of geology, in the lower part of the grounds, are curious and instructive.

*Windsor Castle.* — The town of Windsor, situated up the Thames, twenty-two miles from London, can only claim interest from its castle, which stands on a summit in its centre. This castle has been the principal seat of British royalty for nearly eight centuries. It was founded by William the Conqueror; the castle-gates are close upon the main street of the town, and lead to enclosures containing a number of quadrangles, towers, gates, mansions, barracks, and other structures. The terrace upon the summit of the round tower is supposed to be the noblest walk of its kind in Europe. From it twelve counties can be seen. In the exterior of the castle there is much to admire. A fine flight of steps leads from the east terrace to the new garden, a beautiful spot, adorned with many statues both of bronze and marble. The little park is four miles in circumference, and in the great park is the beautiful avenue of trees, three miles long. On another side are the new royal stables, the finest in England, having cost nearly $350,000. Of the castle's interior we can only say it is palatial. The corridor, five hundred and twenty feet in length, is adorned with bronzes, marbles, pictures, etc. The state-rooms are fitted up in a very superb style, and the different apartments are adorned with a great number of paintings by the most eminent masters. The Queen resides here a portion of the year.

*Peterborough Cathedral.* — A noble structure, measuring on the outside four hundred and seventy-one feet in length, and one hundred and eighty in breadth, chiefly in the Norman style, and erected at various periods. Here were buried Queen Katherine of Arragon and Mary Queen of Scots; but the remains of the latter were afterwards removed to Westminster Abbey. The cathedral is in the city of Peterborough, the birthplace of Dr. Paley.

*Stonehenge.* — At the distance of eight miles from Salisbury, situated in the plain near Amesbury, is this monument of antiquity. It consists of a number of very large stones arranged in a circular form, and still partly connected with each other at the top by flat pieces placed in a transverse direction. Antiquarians are not agreed as to the object of this rude structure, or by whom it was made. By some it has been attributed to the Druids; by others, to the Danes; and by a third party, to the Romans.

*Brendon-Hill Incline.* — The reader is referred to the photograph itself, on which is a sufficient account. There is a similar incline on the Glasgow and Edinburgh railway near the former city, which is operated in nearly the same manner.

*Ashburton.* — A neat town with a handsome church, situated in a valley, in the midst of scenery characterized by a grandeur and variety not surpassed in Devonshire. Near it is the Dart, a wild, tumultuous stream, whose "cry," in the stillness of night, may be heard far from its banks. It is said that a year never passes without one person being drowned in the river, and hence the people have this local rhyme, —

"River of Dart, O, river of Dart,
Every year thou claimest a heart!"

*Lynton.* — A village not large in numbers but great in enterprise. It is superior in the surroundings of its scenery to any of the places in the other southern counties of England, and its inhabitants are, if we believe visitors to it, equally ambitious and enterprising. Telescopes are in vogue at the rival hotels for the prompt discovery of the approaching traveller!

*Ilfracombe.* — A little watering-place, but chiefly known for the picturesque forms of the surrounding hills. In 1685 it contributed six ships to the English fleet, while one only was sent from the Mersey; a fact which is curious as showing the change which time has effected in the relative importance of the two harbors. At the northern point of Morte Bay is the Morte Stone, the Rock of Death, on which five vessels were lost in the winter of 1852. There is a whimsical saying, that no power on earth can remove it but that of a number of wives who have dominion over their husbands! In this village, too, is buried, it is said, William de Tracey, one of the four murderers of Thomas à Becket. According to tradition, the Traceys never prospered after the commission of this crime. Their descendants are supposed to languish under the curse of heaven, and hence, —

"All the Traceys
Have the wind in their faces."

*Conway Suspension Bridge and Castle.* — The bridge was erected in 1826. The entrances on either side are between two towers, built to harmonize with the general style of the castle, the distance of the roadway between them being three hundred and twenty-seven feet. This consists of layers of planks fixed by vertical bars to suspending chains, which are secured at each end respectively into the cliff below the castle, and a rock which formerly was insulated, but is now connected with the main-land by an embankment 2,000 feet long. The bridge crosses the waters of "Old Conway's foaming flood," as Gray, with a poet's license, has described the muddy tidal waters which here empty themselves into the sea. These muddy waters have long, however, been celebrated for their pearls. Spenser speaks of Conway, —

> "Which from out his stream doth send
> Plenty of pearls to deck his dames withal."

They are still found, but are of small value.

The castle was built in 1284 by Edward I, to secure his newly-obtained possession of Wales. The creative fancy of a painter could scarcely conceive a more picturesque object of its class. The graceful forms of its towers and turrets, their varied groupings, the partial and softening progress of decay, the draping ivy filling up the breaches and breaks in the walls, and the noble situation, are charms that make Conway equal to most of the castles on the Rhine, Moselle, or Danube. This castle now belongs to the Dowager Lady Erskine, who holds it from the Crown at the rent of six shillings and eight pence, — one dollar and sixty-nine cents, — and a dish of fish to the Queen whenever she passes this way.

*Blenheim Palace and Park*, the residence of the Duke of Marlborough, has been contrasted with Mount Vernon. The following is an extract from Edward Everett's Oration on the Character of Washington.

There is a splendid monumental pile in England, the

most magnificent perhaps of her hundred palaces, founded in the time of Queen Anne, at the public cost, to perpetuate the fame of Marlborough. The grand building, with its vast wings and spacious courts, covers seven acres and a half of land. It is approached on its various sides by twelve gates or bridges, some of them triumphal gates, in a circumference of thirteen miles, enclosing the noble park of twenty-seven hundred acres, in which the castle stands, surrounded by the choicest beauties of forest and garden and fountain and lawn and stream. All that gold could buy, or the bounty of his own or foreign princes could bestow, or taste devise, or art execute, or ostentation could lavish, to perfect and adorn the all but regal structure, without and within, is there.

Its saloons and its galleries, its library and its museum, among the most spacious in England for a private mansion, are filled with the rarities and wonders of ancient and modern art. Eloquent inscriptions from the most gifted pens of the age set forth on triumphal arches and columns the exploits of him to whom the whole edifice and the domains which surround it are one gorgeous monument. Lest human adulation should prove unequal to the task, Nature herself has been called in to record his achievements. They have been planted, rooted in the soil. Groves and coppices, curiously disposed, represent the position, the numbers, the martial array of the hostile squadrons at Blenheim. Thus, with each returning year, spring hangs out his triumphal banners. May's Æolian lyre sings of his victories through her gorgeous foliage; and the shrill trump of November sounds "Malbrook" through her leafless branches.

Twice in my life I have visited the magnificent residence, — not as a guest; once, when its stately porticos afforded a grateful shelter from the noonday sun, and again, after thirty years' interval, when the light of a full harvest-moon slept sweetly on the banks once shaded by fair Rosamond's bower, — so says tradition, — and poured its streaming bars of silver through the branches of oaks which were growing before Columbus discovered America. But to me, at noontide or in the evening, the gorgeous pile was as dreary as death, its luxurious grounds as melancholy as a church-yard.

It seemed to me, not a splendid palace, but a dismal mausoleum, in which a great and blighted name lies embalmed like some old Egyptian tyrant, black and ghastly in the asphaltic contempt of ages, serving but to rescue from an enviable oblivion the career and character of the magnificent peculator and miser and traitor to whom it is dedicated; needy in the midst of his ill-gotten millions; mean at the head of his victorious armies; despicable under the shadow of his thick-woven laurels; and poor and miserable and blind and naked amidst the lying shams of his tinsel greatness. The eloquent inscriptions in Latin and English as I strove to read them seemed to fade from arch and column, and three dreadful words of palimpsestic infamy came out in their stead like those which caused the knees of the Chaldean tyrant to smite together, as he beheld them traced by no mortal fingers on the vaulted canopy which spread like a sky over his accursed revels; and those dreadful words were, avarice, plunder, eternal shame!

. There is a modest private mansion on the banks of the Potomac, the abode of George Washington and Martha, his beloved, his loving, faithful wife. It boasts no spacious portal, nor gorgeous colonnade, nor massy elevation, nor storied tower. The porter's lodge at Blenheim Castle, nay, the marble dog-kennels were not built for the entire cost of Mount Vernon. No arch nor column, in courtly English or courtlier Latin, sets forth the deeds and the worth of the Father of his Country; he needs them not; the unwritten benedictions of millions cover all the walls. No gilded dome swells from the lowly roof to catch the morning or evening beam; but the love and gratitude of united America settle upon it in one eternal sunshine.

From beneath that humble roof went forth the intrepid and unselfish warrior, — the magistrate who knew no glory but his country's good; to that he returned happiest when his work was done. There he lived in noble simplicity; there he died in glory and peace. While it stands, the latest generations of the grateful children of America will make their pilgrimage to it as to a shrine; and when it shall fall, if fall it must, the memory and the name of Washington shall shed an eternal glory on the spot.

## CHAPTER XXXI.

### SCOTLAND,

FOR a person loving natural scenery, is, next to Switzerland, the most desirable country that could be visited in Europe; indeed, it excels Switzerland in the mild beauty of its mountain scenery, as much as Switzerland excels, in return, in the noble grandeur and power of her mountains. The lakes of both countries are beautiful beyond comparison; and yet on the Scottish lakes, as you drink in their beauty, you are talking and commenting on the new views that constantly open before you; on the Swiss lakes, the vastness of the silent heights about you quite tends to hush one into harmony with that impressive stillness all around. Scotland is far richer than Switzerland in historic associations. Many of its lakes, its rivers, castles, abbeys, and cities are associated with the writings or history of such names as Scott and Burns, and have received from them added interest.

The country itself is varied in surface, generally rugged

and mountainous; its soil is not very fertile; the climate, owing to its insular situation, is not so cold in winter or so warm in summer as in similar latitudes on the continent. Scotland's established church is Presbyterian; but from one half to two thirds of the people are dissenters, among whom may be found almost as great a variety of sects as among ourselves.

*Abbotsford*, well known as the home of Sir Walter Scott, is situated on a bank overhanging the Tweed. Farther up the river, on the opposite bank, venerable trees indicate the site of the old village of Boldside, of which a fisherman's cottage is now the only representative. Below the Selkirk road on the river may be seen the haunted church-yard extending along its bank. Immediately opposite, Sir Walter had a bower overhanging the Tweed, where he frequently sat musing, during the heat of the day. Abbotsford is now the property of the husband of Sir Walter's granddaughter. The principal rooms are the hall, panelled with oak, the drawing-room, the armory, the dining-hall, in which is a fine collection of paintings, the library, and the study. This room, of carved oak, contains 20,000 volumes. The study is most interesting, hallowed by associations with most of the writings of the great author. It contains a small table, a plain arm-chair covered with leather, and a single chair. Without the mansion, through the whole extent of the surrounding plantations, there are winding walks; and benches or bowers are erected on every position commanding a picturesque view. Melrose Abbey is but three miles from Sir Walter's home.

*Taymouth Castle from the Fort.* — This princely mansion was built in 1580. The possessions of the family who occupy it reach to the ocean, a space upwards of one hundred miles. The interior is splendidly fitted up. The pleasure-grounds are laid out with great taste, and present a striking combination of beauty and grandeur. The view from the hill in front of the castle is thus described in an impromptu of Burns :—

> " The meeting cliffs each deep sunk glen divides,
> The woods, wild scattered, clothe their ample sides,
> The outstretching lake, embosom'd 'mong the hills,
> The eye with wonder and amazement fills;
> The Tay, meandering sweet in infant pride;
> The palace rising by his verdant side;
> The lawns, wood-fringed, in nature's native taste,
> The hillocks dropt in nature's careless haste:
> The arches striding o'er the new-born stream,
> The village glittering in the noon tide beam."

*Ben Nevis from above Banavie.* — The little village of Banavie on the Caledonian canal, between Loch or Lake Eil and Loch Lochy, commands an excellent view of the mountain. Ben, or Mount, Nevis is the highest summit in Scotland, rising 4,460 feet above the sea's level, yet not quite one third the height of Mont Blanc! The distance from Banavie to the summit of Ben Nevis is some eight miles. There are eleven locks in the canal near Banavie, which rejoice under the name of Neptune's Steps!

*Balmoral Castle from the River.* — The Scottish summer residence of Her Majesty the Queen. The vale or dell in which it stands is formed by a circumvallation of " the everlasting hills," being really,

> " With rock-wall encircled, with precipice crown'd."

His Royal Highness, Prince Albert, purchased the estate in 1852, at a cost of £32,000, or $160,000; he pulled down the old and " built greater," erecting the present commodious building at his own expense. The new castle stands near the margin of the Dee, where, in a semicircle, it sweeps the base of a mountain range and forms a large peninsula, the plateau of which affords the most perfect privacy for the retirement of the royal family. The building is of the Scotch baronial style of architecture. The design consists of two separate blocks of buildings connected by wings, at the east angle of which the massive tower, thirty-five feet square, rises to the height of eighty feet, and is surmounted by a turret with circular staircase, rising to the height of one hundred feet from the level of the ground. From the summit of this tower the mountain scenery can be viewed to great advantage. The property contains upwards of 10,000 acres, a thousand of which are of wood. To this have been added extensive tracts from adjoining estates, which have been converted into a deer forest of 30,000 acres. The population in the neighborhood is feeling the benefit of this nearness of the royal family. Every tenant has his lease, every family the privilege of a school, and new and comfortable tenements are taking the place of the log huts of the poor. The schools were visited by their able patrons during the life of Prince Albert, and habits of economy and forethought were encouraged among the people.

*Birnam, from Birnam Hill.* — Birnam Hill, near which is Birnam Wood, so famous for its connection with the fate of Macbeth, is some 1,500 feet high. From its summit a magnificent prospect is commanded of the vale of the Tay, and of the extensive woods which environ Dunkeld.

*Drummond Castle from the Garden. Garden of Drummond Castle.* — About twenty miles west from Perth, near the east coast of Scotland. It is the ancient residence of the noble family of Perth. This castle was visited by Her Majesty on her tour through the Highlands, on which occasion a pavilion was erected for the dining-hall, the accommodation within the building being but limited. Immediately in front of the principal face of the castle, lie the flower-gardens of Drummond, known to most florists in the kingdom, a sight of which would make a pleasant and valuable lesson to any interested in the art of landscape gardening. The whole place has rather a foreign appearance, or at least the fashion of a day very different to that of our own. The terraced garden, the clipped yews, the trim box-trees are conspicuous. In the middle of summer, the view from the terrace is remarkably brilliant, yet produced simply by planting different beds with different kinds of ordinary flowers: one with marigolds, a second with heliotrope, a third with calceolaria, and so on.

*Suburbs of Stirling, Scotland.* — Stirling is built on the side of a slope, on whose summit is Stirling Castle, the view from which, on a clear day, is one of the loveliest in the kingdom. The distant hills bounding the view, the windings of the Forth, seen for miles below, as it flows through a wide expanse of fertile land, make a rare combination of natural beauty. Well in view is the Abbey Craig, some five hundred and sixty feet high, and close below " the Heading Hill," — the place of public executions.

> " The sad and fatal mound
> That oft has heard the death-axe sound,
> As on the nobles of the land
> Fell the stern headsman's bloody hand."
> *Lady of the Lake.*

A prominent object on the Abbey Craig is the yet unfinished monument of Wallace. In front of it he demolished the English under the Earl of Surrey. Indeed, from this point, eleven battle-fields are in view, including that of Bannockburn.

*Castleton of Braemar, from Craig-Coynach.* — This simple rustic village stands at the junction of four glens, where the turbulent stream of the Cluny clatters down to join the

Dee. It is at a height of some 1,100 feet above the sea, and is celebrated consequently for the extreme purity and bracing character of its air. From its nearness to the finest mountain scenery in Scotland, Braemar is a great centre of attraction. It is situated in the centre of a region of deer forests which cover some of the wildest and most unfrequented districts of the higher Grampians, and being strictly preserved from the intrusion of sheep or any other animals, exhibits a solitary and impressive grandeur rarely witnessed in any other part of the country.

*The Entrance to the Pass of Ballater.* — A precipitous, wooded ravine, near the village of the same name, some forty-two miles west of Aberdeen, on the river Dee. In its vicinity are Castleton of Braemar and Balmoral Castle.

*Ben Lomond from Luss.* — The mountain is the property of the Duke of Montrose. It rises 3,192 feet in height. On a very clear day the view from the summit is magnificent, embracing a panorama of nearly all the scenery in the south of Scotland. The most fascinating object, however, is Loch Lomond, clear below, in all its reaches and indentations, with its bright waters studded with islands. It is said by connoisseurs, that this lake is only equalled in beauty, in all Europe, by Lago Maggiore, and Lake Machlar in Sweden. Luss is a small village on the banks of Loch Lomond.

*Loch Katrine, from the Goblin's Cave.* — Nine miles long and two broad, at its widest part. Its chief renown comes from its being the scene of Sir Walter Scott's celebrated poem, "The Lady of the Lake." He thus speaks of it : —

> "Where gleaming 'neath the setting sun
> One burnished sheet of living gold,
> Loch Katrine lay, beneath him rolled;
> In all her length far winding lay,
> In promontory, creek and bay,

> And islands that, empurpled bright,
> Floated amid the larches light;
> And mountains that like giants stand
> To sentinel enchanted land."

The lake is in some parts five hundred feet deep. It gives its contribution to the useful as well as to the ornamental, supplying Glasgow — though thirty-four miles distant — with 70,000,000 gallons of pure bright water every day. It may thus boast of forming the finest reservoir in the world; but it is at a cost of $7,500,000. The Goblin's Cave or Coir-nan-Uriskin is the place where Douglas, as Scott tells us, hid his daughter, when he had taken her from Roderick Dhu's island.

*Loch Achray and Ben Venue.* —

> "High on the South, huge Ben Venue
> Down to the lake in masses threw
> Crags, knolls, and mounds, confus'dly hurl'd,
> The fragments of an earlier world,
> A wildering forest feather'd o'er
> His ruined sides and summit hoar."

Loch Achray is a very beautiful piece of water, thirteen miles long, by three fourths of a mile broad.

*The Clamshell Cave; Basaltic Colonnade and Fingal's Cave,* — on the island of Staffa, about a half day's journey by steamer from the west coast of Scotland. Staffa — Island of Staves — is only about a mile in circumference. It is the result of volcanic action. Persons visiting it land at Clamshell Cave, and walk over the Basaltic Colonnade to Fingal's Cave; this is two hundred and twenty-seven feet long, and from the water which fills it, to the roof, the distance is about sixty-six feet. From a long and glowing description by Walter Scott, we have but space for a few lines : —

> . . . "As to shame the temple decked
> By skill of earthly architect,
> Nature herself, it seemed, would raise
> A Minster to her Maker's praise!
> Not for a meaner use ascend
> Her columns, or her arches bend;
> Nor of a theme less solemn tells
> That mighty surge that ebbs and swells
> And still between each awful pause
> From the high vault an answer draws.
> In varied tone prolonged and high,
> That mocks the organ's melody."

*Pass of Killiecrankie from Railway Cutting.* — Celebrated for the battle fought here in 1689, between the generals of James VII and William III, in which the army of the former were victorious. The battle is graphically described by Macaulay. The scenery of the pass, which is about one and a half miles in length, is exceedingly beautiful, the river Garry foaming at the bottom in its rocky channel, while the wooded hills, rising on each side, shut it completely in.

*Faskally House.* — In the Pass of Killiecrankie. It is in a beautifully sheltered site on the bank of the river.

*Views of Glasgow.* — This city, the metropolis of Scotland, as far as commerce goes, has a population of 400,000. Like London and Paris, it is divided by a river,— the Clyde, — which is narrow in the city, but deep, and crowded with shipping, as it is also almost lined with iron ships in process of building. It is a smoky, cloudy, and on the whole not an interesting city to those who are used to the clear sunshine of America; but it must have credit for being full of business activity.

*Glasgow Bridge,* — over the Clyde. It has seven arches,

and is the lowest of the five bridges that cross the river. It looks west, — to the right in the view, — over the

*Broomielaw*, — as it is called, — the most remarkable work in Glasgow. It is almost entirely artificial, the river having been a broad, shallow stream, which continual dredging has made a handsome and roomy basin, capable of holding the largest vessels, while in 1851 no vessel of any burden could come nearer the town than fourteen miles. Campbell did not like the change, he thus writes: —

> "And call they this improvement? to have changed
> My native Clyde, thy once romantic shore,
> Where nature's face is banished and estranged,
> And Heaven reflected in thy wave no more;
> Whose banks, that sweeten'd May-day's breath before,
> Lie seer and leafless now in summer's beam,
> With sooty exhalations cover'd o'er;
> And for the daisied greensward, down thy stream,
> Unsightly brick lanes smoke, and clanking engines gleam."

*George Square.* — One of the most central places, and largest squares in the city. Of the several monuments that adorn the centre, the principal is Sir Walter Scott's, a Grecian Doric column about eighty feet in height, with a colossal statue of the great minstrel on the top. The figure is half enveloped in a shepherd's plaid. Here, too, is a pedestrian statue, in bronze, of the lamented Sir John Moore, who was a native of Glasgow.

*The Necropolis.* — The City of the Dead, as its name signifies. The bold and rocky eminence shoots suddenly up to the height of from two hundred to three hundred feet. The fine column erected to the memory of that Great Reformer, John Knox, stands conspicuous on the very summit of this hill of tombs.

*The Trongate.* — With Argyll Street and the Gallowgate

it forms the main thoroughfare; is nearly three miles long, and generally is densely crowded.

*Views of Edinburgh.* — Edinburgh has about 168,000 inhabitants. It is, therefore, not half so large as Glasgow, but it is a city of romantic beauty. It is often called the modern Athens, and from several points of view the resemblance is said to be complete. In Edinburgh centres the educational, in Glasgow the business interests of the kingdom. The city is built all of stone, upon a group of parallel hills separated by deep ravines.

*Holyrood Palace.* — The Old Town stands on the highest hill, which descends gradually to the palace. Holyrood is chiefly known in connection with the history of Queen Mary. In her apartments here, she was reproved by John Knox. Her bedroom and bed, with its musty, moth-eaten hangings, are shown. Here, too, is the back staircase up which came the murderers of Rizzio to the Queen's boudoir, where Mary and a small company were at supper. Over this very threshold Darnley and his conspirators dragged Rizzio, crouching behind Mary, to the top of the stairs, despatched, and left him there.

*Nelson's Monument.* — On the top of Calton Hill. Its position relative to the city can be seen by reference to one of the views of Scott's Monument. "Modelled exactly after a Dutch skipper's spy-glass or a butter-churn."

*Edinburgh Castle.* — The date of its foundation is unknown. Although before the days of gunpowder it was about impregnable, it is now a place of more apparent than real strength. It can be approached from but one side, the rest being very precipitous, and not less than three hundred and eighty feet high. The architectural effect of the castle has been much hurt by the erection of a clumsy pile of barracks, which Sir Walter Scott said would be honored by a comparison with the most vulgar cotton mill. The queen of Malcolm Canmore died in the castle in 1093.

Scott thus describes the retaking of the castle by the Scotch from the English in 1313.

"The attempt was undertaken by thirty men, commanded by Randolph, Earl of Moray, and guided by Francis, one of his own soldiers, who had been in the habit of descending and ascending the cliffs surreptitiously to pay court to his mistress. The darkness of the night, the steepness of the precipice, the danger of the discovery by the watchmen, and the slender support which they had to trust to, in ascending from crag to crag, rendered the enterprise such as might have appalled the bravest spirit. When they had ascended halfway, they found a flat spot, large enough to halt upon, and there sat down to recover their breath, and prepare for the further part of their perilous expedition. While they were thus seated, they heard the rounds or 'check watches,' as Barbour calls them, pass along the walls above them ; and it so chanced that one of the English soldiers, in mere wantonness and gayety, hurled down a stone and cried out at the same time, 'I see you well,' although without any idea that there was any one beneath. The stone rolled down the precipice, and passed over the heads of Moray and his adventurous companions as they sat cowering under the rock from which it bounded. They had the presence of mind to remain perfectly silent; and presently after, the sentinels continued their rounds. The assailants then continued their ascent, and arrived in safety at the foot of the wall, which they scaled by means of the ladder which they brought with them. Francis, their guide, ascended first, Sir Andrew Gray was second, and Randolph himself was third. Ere they had all mounted, however, the sentinels caught the alarm, raised the cry of 'treason,' and the constable and others rushing to the spot made a valiant though ineffectual resistance. The Earl of Moray was for some time in great personal danger, until, the gallant constable being slain, his followers fled or fell, and this strong castle remained in the hands of the assailants."

In one of the rooms of the castle James VI, Queen Mary's only son, was born. On the wall is the following inscription: —

> "Lord Jesu Christ, that crown'st was with Thornse,
> Preserve the Birth, quhais Badgie heir is borne,
> And send Hir sonne successione, to Reigne still,
> Lang in this Realme, if that it be Thy will.
> Als grant, O Lord, quhat ever of Hir proceed,
> Be to Thy Honor, and Prais, sobied."

The two public buildings in the view are the Royal Institution at the left, and the National Gallery. The former is in the Grecian Doric style. "The porticos cover entrance, and the flank colonnades are stepped against blocks, which give them character and meaning, and the whole is well proportioned." [*Fergusson's Modern Architecture.*] This building contains a museum; the National Gallery has a collection of paintings.

*Sir Walter Scott's Monument.* — Perhaps the most beautiful work of art in Edinburgh. It was made from designs by George Kemp, an architect previously unknown to fame, and who did not live to see his plans completed. He was an intense admirer of Melrose Abbey, and has endeavored in this monument to combine all the characteristics of that building. Four grand arches support the superstructure which serves as a canopy to the statue. An interior staircase leads to the top, which is two hundred feet from the ground. About the structure are fifty-six niches intended to be filled with statues representing the most prominent characters in Sir Walter's novels. Four have already been placed in the principal niches: Prince Charles (from *Waverley*), drawing his sword; Meg Merrilies (from *Guy Mannering*), breaking the sapling over the head of Lucy Bertram; the Lady of the Lake, stepping from a boat to the shore; and the Last Minstrel, playing on his harp. Beneath the main arches is placed a statue of Sir Walter Scott and dog, a first-rate work of art by Steele; a cast of this has recently been placed in the Central Park in New York.

*Melrose Abbey.* — About forty miles southeast of Edinburgh, and but three or four from Abbotsford. It is one of the finest specimens of Gothic architecture in Scotland. It was built before the sixteenth century, and is now a noble ruin. The stone of which it is built has resisted the weather for ages, and still retains perfect sharpness, so that the ornaments are as though newly wrought. The student of architecture here finds rare delight. Over the principal doorway is a magnificent window twenty-four feet in height and sixteen in breadth, divided by four bars which branch out or interlace each other at the top in a variety of beautiful curves. Over this window are nine niches; and two on each buttress formerly contained statues of our Saviour and his Apostles. Beneath the window is a statue of John the Baptist, with his eye directed upward as if looking upon the image of Christ above. All about the building are carved a variety of quaint figures, such as sculptured forms of plants and animals, musicians, etc., and in many of the niches there still remain statues. The eastern window in the chancel is uncommonly elegant and beautiful, and seems as if—

> "Some fairy's hand
> 'Twixt poplars straight the osier wand
> In many a freakish knot had twined;
> Then framed a spell when the work was done,
> And changed the willow wreaths to stone."
>
> *Lay of the Last Minstrel.*

*View at Quiraing, Isle of Skye.* — This island is situated just off the west coast of Scotland. It is about forty-four miles long, and its greatest width is twenty miles; but the coasts are so much indented by the sea, that no point of land is more than five miles from the water. It is said that there are usually three hundred and sixty wet days a year in Skye, but the soil is so shallow that a month's dry weather — and such a thing has been known there — constitutes a perfect drought. The country may be described as a wide tract of high moor-land; but little is produced on the island, owing to the incessant moisture of the climate. The Quiraing is a flat surface, of an elliptical shape, one hundred yards long and fifty broad, and at the north end is connected with the rest of the mountain. It is 1,000 feet above the sea, and covered with a smooth, soft turf; upon the east and south sides is a line of single and detached rock of various shapes, perpendicular and inaccessible, springing up like the outer turrets of a fortress. Through the intervals of these, charming views may be had of the sea and main-land. "Although the columns are not so accurately formed or so distinctly formed as at Staffa, their effect at the proper point of sight is equally regular, while from the frequent recurrence of groups, recesses, and projecting masses, and from the absence of any superincumbent load, they are far superior in lightness of appearance, as well as in elegance and variety of outline." — *McCulloch.*

## CHAPTER XXXII.

### IRELAND.

THIS famous island contains 31,874 square miles, or 14,000 square miles less than the State of New York. The longest straight line that can be drawn upon the island measures three hundred and two miles, but its greatest length, measured due north and south, is two hundred and thirty-seven miles. Carran-Tual, the highest land in Ireland, has an elevation of 3,414 feet. "The population of Ireland in 1861 was 5,764,543; in 1870, 5,525,210. The bulk of the population depend for subsistence upon the soil. About nine tenths of the land was forfeited under Cromwell and William III; and this vast amount of property was mostly either gratuitously bestowed upon, or was acquired at a very small sacrifice by, noblemen and gentlemen of fortune and influence in England. There was no sympathy between landlords and tenants. . . . Landlords lay out little or nothing on buildings. Such a thing as a barn is hardly known among the smaller occupiers; and the corn is not unfrequently thrashed on the public roads, which serve as barn-floors." — *McCulloch.*

The geology of Ireland differs from that of England, and, in a general point of view, rather resembles that of France. Limestone is a very prevalent formation, and it abounds in fossil remains. Coal is found in the south and east, the principal field being that of Kilkenny.

The Reformation never made any considerable progress in Ireland.

The climate of Ireland, owing to the proximity of the Atlantic Ocean, is more moist and less liable to severe cold than that of the neighboring countries. The mean annual temperature of Dublin is a little over 50° Fahrenheit.

*Kilkenny Castle, from John's Bridge. Kilkenny Castle, from the Terrace.* — The remarkable old city of Kilkenny, in interesting remains, associations, and situation, is surpassed by very few cities in the kingdom. The castle occupies an elevated site overlooking the Nore. It was originally built by Strongbow; it was added to by Le Mareschal, and has since then been so repeatedly altered and added to, that only two or three of the original towers are left. The latest improvements by the present Marquis have in effect amounted to a new building, forming two sides of a quadrangle. The grounds are well laid out, but are limited in space. .The interior contains some splendid suites of rooms, a picture-gallery full of family portraits of the Butlers, the original picture of the family of Charles I, by Vandyke, and some interesting tapestry, the manufacture of which was introduced into Kilkenny in the sixteenth century. For this purpose several workmen were brought from Flanders; but further than supplying the wants of the country, nothing of any permanence was done. There is a pleasant walk along the banks of the castle.

*The Giant's Causeway. The Great Causeway, and Roveran Valley Head.* — This remarkable columnar basaltic formation is on the northern coast of the county of Antrim, situated about midway between the towns of Ballycastle and Coleraine. The trap district, with which this formation is connected, occupies almost the whole of the county of Antrim, and a considerable portion of the eastern part of Londonderry, comprehending about eight hundred square miles, on both sides of the valley of the Bann. The surface rises gradually from the channel of this river, till it attains a considerable elevation on each side, when it breaks down in precipitous escarpments, sloping abruptly to the primitive district of Londonderry on the west, and overhanging the coast on the east and north, in a series of striking elevations, commencing near Belfast, and terminating west of the embouchure of the Bann. Throughout this area the basalt is found capping all the eminences, and constituting the general superstratum, in beds of an average thickness of about five hundred feet. Beneath the basalt occurs a series of secondary formations peculiar to this area, which has led to the supposition that they may have been elsewhere removed by some denuding force, "to which, in this quarter alone, an effectual resistance was opposed by the firm and massive superstratum of basalt which covered and protected them."

The mass of basalt is considerably thicker towards the northern extremity of the area, and it is here chiefly that the series of columnar formations occur. There are three distinct beds of such formations, the uppermost of which is perhaps traceable in the cliffs of the Cave-hill over Belfast, and is distinctly observable at Fairhead, on the northeastern extremity of the coast, where the mural precipice of greenstone is articulated into columns of enormous dimensions but rude structure, some of them measuring two hundred and fifty feet in length, by six feet on the side. The same formation appears again to recur along the verge of the precipice which trends westward from hence to Dunseverick, at a short distance from which the two lower beds emerge from the sea, and, rising along the escarpment of the rock, form colonnades of a most striking appearance for a distance of nearly three miles, when the upper one is lost in the surrounding masses of basalt, while the surrounding stratum sinks again under water, its denuded extremity forming that particular group of columns known as the Giant's Causeway.

It is observable that the dimensions of the columns diminish, and the perfection of their structure increases, as the strata descend. Thus the most perfect arrangement is found in the lowest stratum, of which arrangement the Causeway affords the most perfect specimen. The upper part of the stratum, being here denuded for a distance of about three hundred yards, exhibits an irregular pavement, formed of the tops of polygonal columns so closely arranged that the blade of a knife can with difficulty be inserted in the interstices. The columns are chiefly hexagonal, but polygons of five, seven, and eight sides are of frequent occurrence; and there is one instance of a triangular prism. These columns are divided into joints of unequal length; each joint is formed by the adjacent extremities being relatively convex and concave, an arrangement which is further secured by the overlapping of the external angles. These convexities and concavities are sections of spheres; the base of each of which occupies a circle inscribed in the polygon of the pillar; the intervals intercepted between the peripheries of these circles and the sides of the polygon are all in the plane perpendicular to the axis of the column. The stone is the most compact and homogeneous variety of basalt, and is more or less sonorous when struck with a hard substance. The entire mass of these columns, of which about thirty feet are exposed above the surrounding shingle, at the highest point of their denudation, bears a strong resemblance to an artificial mole, projecting from the base of the cliff into the sea.

It is probable that the columnar beds, of which the exposed edges present these remarkable appearances along the coast, underlie the capping of tabular basalt to a considerable distance inland, as columnar façades break out on the seaward slope of the entire line of elevations extending from Ballycastle to Bushmills, and indications of a columnar tendency have been observed in beds of tabular basalt as far inland as Glen Rovel, near Cushindall, and at the Cave-hill, near Belfast. Along the coast at Ushet-Haven, Roanscarave, and Thivigh, are several smaller causeways, nearly as perfect as the one described. The columnar strata of the islands of Rathlin and Staffa indicate the extent of the same formation, northward and eastward.

The vicinity of the Giant's Causeway affords numerous appearances confirmatory of the opinion that the basalt, when superinduced over the secondary strata, was in a state of fusion from heat; such are the conversion of old red sandstone into hornstone, the conversion of clay slate into flinty slate, the conversion of coal into cinders, and in numerous instances the conversion of chalk into granular marble, all arising from the contact of trap dikes with the altered strata.

*The Honey-Comb. Same,— near view of west side. Same, —from the Great Causeway.* — The Giant's Causeway is distinguishable into three platforms, generally known as the Little, Middle or Honeycomb, and Great Causeways, as they are approached from the west.

*The Wishing Chair.* — In the Middle, or Honey-comb Causeway, the principal curiosity is the Lady's Chair, or the Wishing Chair, a single hexagon pillar surrounded by several others of taller proportions, so as to form a comfortable seat. Thence the Great Causeway is entered through the Giant's Gateway, a gap bounded by columns on each side.

*Pleaskin Head.* — The coast presents various salient points, among which the finest occurs at Pleaskin. From Pleaskin Head, which is three hundred and fifty-four feet in height, the tourist has a magnificent view eastward, over Bengore and Fairhead. "The summit is covered with a thin, grassy sod, under which lies the basaltic rock, having generally a hard surface somewhat cracked and shivered. At the depth of ten to twelve feet from the summit, this rock begins to assume a columnar tendency, and forms a range of massive pillars standing perpendicularly to the horizon, and presenting the appearance of a magnificent gallery or colonnade, sixty feet in length." — *Hamilton's Antrim.*

## CHAPTER XXXIII.

FRANCE, A REPUBLIC OF EUROPE; PRESIDENT, ADOLPHE THIERS.

THE national assembly consists of seven hundred and thirty-eight members. Population, 36,594,845 : its increase is comparatively less than that of any other country in western Europe; during the first five months of the late war, the loss was upwards of 500,000. Ninety-six per cent of the people are Catholics. The country is richly fertile, and most fortunate in its climate.

*Paris*, the metropolis of France, is situated on the river Seine, has an area of about thirty square miles, and a population of 1,825,274. The river divides the city; on the northern side is the fashionable quarter where are the Boulevards, the hotels, and the Champs Elysées. Here all is bright and gay even now, since the city's sad experience: splendid modern houses, brilliant shops, crowded streets, with double rows of beautiful trees, countless carriages, and a bright atmosphere over all, afford a scene unequalled by any city in the world. On the opposite side of the river are the residences of the nobility, and most of the government offices. In the southern part is a large student population, and on the outskirts of the city are to be found its poor. Paris owes its beauty as a city mainly to the work of Napoleon III, since 1851. Like most continental towns, it formerly consisted of a dense mass of old lofty houses, only accessible by narrow and crooked streets, impervious to light and air. These have been mostly pulled down, and wide streets and open spaces substituted.

*General View of Paris taken from the Pantheon.* — The

dome of the Pantheon from which we are looking is considerably higher than any other building in Paris, and commands a magnificent view. It is on the southerly side of the river, and hence in the denser part of the city. The Cathedral of Notre Dame is in sight from here on an island in the Seine, whose spacious quays can be seen to the right.

*Rue de Rivoli.* — Perhaps the finest street in the world, though the style of architecture is tame. On it are very many of Paris' most celebrated edifices; the Palais des Tuileries stood on one side, the Louvre and Palais Royal are also on it. It is very nearly two miles in length, runs through the heart of the city, and forms a noble line of communication for military or civil purposes, from one end of the city to the other. The conflict between the Versailles troops and the Communists of Paris, in 1871, was on this avenue and in its vicinity.

*Revue du 14 Aout.* — In the Place de la Concorde, the largest and most strikingly beautiful square in Paris, where one hundred years ago was little more than waste ground. It is bounded by the Seine, the Champs Elysées, Rue de Rivoli, and the garden of the Tuileries. Its history is full of interest. The guillotine here first commenced its bloody work, in 1793, with the execution of Louis XVI, and from that time till May, 1795, more than 2,800 persons perished here in the same way, — among them the ill-fated queen Marie Antoinette; Robespierre, and many whose names are joined with his in history. In 1830, it was resolved to adorn the square with a monument that should be no reminder of political events. An opportunity was soon afforded by the offer of the Pacha of Egypt to give to the French government, in return for services rendered, one of the two beautiful ancient Egyptian obelisks that once stood in front of the great temple of ancient Thebes. A vessel accordingly was sent for it in 1831, and its erection in its present position finally effected in 1836, at a cost of two millions of francs. As the monolith weighs 500,000 pounds, the sarcasm-loving Parisians observe that the stone of which it consists has cost four francs (eighty cents) a pound. The obelisk, one of the most beautiful in the world, is seventy-two feet in height, inscribed with well-defined hieroglyphics on each side, laudatory of Rameses III of Egypt, who reigned 1,500 years before the Christian era. It is therefore upwards of 3,300 years old.

There are two magnificent fountains in the square, and eight marble statues around it; the carriage causeways are bordered with forty ornamental lamp-posts. Altogether the place is probably without a parallel in the world. The bridge, which is the principal subject of the next view, can be seen at a distance to the right.

*Pont et Place de la Concorde.* — Looking north in exactly the opposite direction to the last view: this is a handsome stone bridge of five arches, erected in 1790, partly with stone from the Bastile.

*Pont Neuf.* — The longest and most important of Paris' twenty-six bridges across the Seine. It was finished in 1604, by Henry IV; the original statue to him was melted in 1792 to make cannon; under Louis XVIII, three statues of Napoleon were melted to form the present one of Henry IV. It may be seen on the left of the bridge.

*Boulevard de Sébastopol.* — A magnificent street of great width, most of which has been cut through the thickest mass of the houses of old Paris, including the Cour des Miracles, described by Victor Hugo as a focus of villany, which has been altered and modernized.

*Boulevard de Strasbourg.* — Perhaps one of the most characteristic of these peculiarly French avenues. Like them all, it is thronged with carriages and pedestrians, especially in the evening, when the hosts of people sitting in cafés, the throng of loungers along the pavement, the lofty houses, the splendid shops, the brilliantly-lighted cafés, and the numerous theatres, form a scene nowhere else to be found.

*Avenue de l'Imperatrice.* — One of some twelve in number, starting from the Arc de Triomphe, and extending broad and roomy towards the suburbs of the city.

*Champ de Mars.* — A large open space surrounded by rows of trees, and used as an exercising ground, for reviews, etc. Here was a great festival of rejoicing in 1790, in the belief that the troubles of the revolution were at an end. In preparation for it, no less than 60,000 Parisians of both sexes assisted in closing the whole space by embankments: these were then furnished with seats, so that hundreds of thousands of the people could see the King and National Assembly swear fidelity to the new constitution. A similar festival was celebrated here with the utmost pomp by Napoleon, in 1815.

*Tour Saint Jacques.* — A handsome Gothic square tower, one hundred and sixty-four feet in height, erected early in the sixteenth century, and now the sole remnant of a church taken down in 1789, and sold as national property. The view from the summit is one of the finest in Paris. The purchase and restoration of the tower have cost the city nearly a million of francs [$200,000].

*Notre Dame.* — Situated on one of the two islands in the river, finished in the fourteenth century. It has its history of alterations that were not improvements, of desecrations, and of restorations. In 1793 it was designated the "Temple of Reason," and on the tenth of November was celebrated in it the feast of the Goddess, who, impersonated by the wife of one Momoro, and seated on the high altar, returned the devotion of her worshippers with a kiss! In the recent war it was entered by Communists, all the furniture thrown about, and the place sadly sacrileged, and its Archbishop killed. In the south tower of the Cathedral hangs a bell called the Bourdon, weighing sixteen tons. The elegant, tall, and slender spire was raised in 1860, to replace one which was pulled down in 1792. The interior has finally been restored in its simple, ancient grandeur, and now presents one of the most magnificent specimens of the early Gothic in any country. A few of its dimensions may not be uninteresting. Its length is three hundred and ninety feet, its width at the transept one hundred and forty-four feet. The towers are two hundred and four feet, and the spire two hundred and eighty feet high.

*Champs Elysées and Arc de Triomphe.* — The Elysian Fields — and the name is most expressive of what they are to the Parisians — are a continuation of the beautiful Place de la Concorde. It is in fact a pleasure-ground of about a half mile in length, intersected by regular walks and avenues. The principal avenue which traverses it is one of the most fashionable promenades in Paris, and is usually crowded with vehicles of all descriptions. It is a favorite resort for the lower as well as for the upper classes, and abounds with attractions calculated for the taste of the former, — such as danc-ing-dogs, show-booths, cake-stall, etc. These sources of entertainment become most popular towards evening, especially by gas-light, and form one of the characteristic phases of Parisian life.

The Arc de Triomphe or Triumphal Arch, closes the broad avenue which traverses the Champs Elysées from the Place de la Concorde. It is conspicuous from almost every part of the environs of Paris, is one hundred and fifty-two feet in height, and till recently was, beyond a doubt, the most magnificent structure of the kind in the world. It was begun in

1806 by Napoleon I, in commemoration of his victories, but was not finished till 1836. It consists of a vast arch ninety-five feet in height. On each face of the structure are scenes taken from the campaigns of Napoleon, executed in relief, and in the classic style. We have said this was, till recently, superior to any structure of the kind in the world. During the civil conflict in the city, the arch was struck repeatedly by shot, and the stone nicked and broken away. The figures of the reliefs are broken and mutilated, and sadly belie the name of the structure, and refuse to subserve the purpose for which it was built.

*The Louvre*, is the most important of all the public edifices by reason of its vast and valuable collections. It was begun on the site of an old fortress in 1541, and from that time till 1805 was used as a residence of the French monarchs, or for governmental offices. Its history up to that time, is, as may be supposed, associated with births, marriages, assassinations, and deaths of its royal occupants. It has been made what it now is, within the past seventy years. Here are now placed collections of nearly every conceivable nature. Especially is there a large and valuable collection of paintings. The Tuileries and the end of the Louvre next adjoining that palace, were destroyed in the fury of the Commune, but by far the greater part of the Louvre was uninjured.

A walk through the different apartments of the Louvre, on its three floors, without stopping, would, it is said, occupy three hours.

*Les Tuileries, Place de Carrousel, avec l'Arc de Triomphe.* — The Palais des Tuileries was founded in 1564, and takes its name from its occupying the site of a former brick or tile yard. It was 1,000 feet in length, and one hundred and five in width: it had been the official residence of the reigning monarch since 1600. It was rich in historical associations:

three times did its capture seal the fate of kingdoms; on the last occasion in 1848, the capture was succeeded by the most frightful scenes of devastation. The royal carriages and furniture were at that time burned in the palace yard. Within the past twenty years, the apartments of the palace were fitted up in a state of almost unparalleled magnificence, not perhaps with numerous works of high art, but with hangings, carpets, mirrors, and decorations of the most gorgeous description. All was ruthlessly destroyed in 1871, by the fury of the Commune.

The Place de Carrousel is an open space between the Tuileries and the Louvre Palace. It is of modern creation, having been occupied by houses, churches, a theatre, etc., till the present century. There was a square where the arch now stands, of this name, and so-called from a tournament held here in 1662. The final clearing away of the buildings was effected in 1858, and with the extension of the Louvre galleries, so far as to the Tuileries, cost $8,000,000!

*Arc de Triomphe.* — This structure, more particularly described above, was erected by Napoleon I, in 1806, in imitation of the triumphal arch of Severus at Rome. Handsome as it undoubtedly is, its proportions do not harmonize with the vast dimensions of the surrounding palaces.

*Salle des Gardes, and Salon de la Paix,* in the palace of the Tuileries. The palace was fitted up regardless of expense only within twenty years; it was utterly demolished in 1871.

*Luxembourg.* — This palace, the most extensive in Paris after the Louvre, the Tuileries, — while it existed, — and the Palais Royal, was erected and sumptuously decorated in 1615. Until the revolution it was a princely residence, then temporarily a prison. Napoleon I afterwards held Consulate sessions here, and the magnificent Senate-Hall was fitted up in gorgeous style in 1859. The museum contains a collection of about one hundred and seventy paintings of living artists; many of the pictures here are scarcely inferior in interest to those in the Louvre, in which, however, they are not exhibited until ten years after the death of the artists.

*The Luxembourg Park, Paris.* — These grounds are extensive, covering eighty-five acres. They form the favorite promenade of the inhabitants of this quarter of the city, and are the resort of the student population. A military band plays here on summer evenings. The garden on the right of the long alley of trees is celebrated for its collection of varieties of vines, said to exceed five hundred, and of roses; at the back of the garden is the statue where Marshal Ney was shot for carrying over a part of the army to Napoleon, after promising the Bourbons to bring him in a cage dead or alive.

*Palais Royal on Rue de Rivoli*, opposite the Louvre. It was rebuilt in 1781 as it now is, having been burnt in 1765. In the rear of the palace is the garden, and around it Philippe Egalité erected the present range of shops. This at first irritated the Parisians, as the gardens had always been public; but the splendor of the buildings and shops soon reconciled them to it. In this interior space are trees, a fountain, etc. A band usually plays, too, in fine evenings, in the middle of the garden. The history of the place is like that of all the French public buildings, rich in associations. In the garden the mob-orators of the revolution used to make their inflammatory speeches, and here was given the signal which resulted in the capture of the Bastile. Immense sums were lost in the palace by Marshal Blucher and others, when the allied armies occupied Paris. The interior has lately been splendidly fitted up, and the staircase and balustrades are magnificent.

*Place Saint Pierre.* — Another of the almost innumerable parks or open places in Paris.

*Salon des Fêtes, dans le Salon de Reception, and Le Pouff Salon de Reception;* interior views of the once magnificent Hotel de Ville. The building was begun in 1533, and was much enlarged in 1837, altogether at a cost of more than $3,000,000. Here Louis XIV and the daughter of Louis XV were married. From one of the windows Louis XVI was forced to show himself with a tricolored cockade. Here Robespierre took refuge, and was found bleeding from an unsuccessful attempt to blow out his brains.

Of late years the building has only been distinguished by the magnificent balls given here in the winter. The building was, for elegance, beyond all description. It formed a quadrangle with three courts, and in and upon it there were not less than five hundred statues. There were two suites of state apartments, and generally the rooms had been decorated so as to make them perhaps the most gorgeous apartments in gorgeous Paris, towards which painting, gilding, carving, glass, and velvet, had done their utmost. The Salon des Fêtes, in particular, was a vast ball-room magnificently furnished, surrounded by gilt Corinthian columns and lighted by chandeliers which contain one thousand wax-lights; it was lighted and thrown open to some 7,000 guests at the balls.

*Exposition Universelle de Paris,* 1867. These exhibitions have been growing in importance ever since the first one in Paris, in 1798. At an exposition in 1834, in La Place de la Concorde, there were nearly 2,500 exhibitors; in the Crystal Palace in 1851 were 18,000; and at the Exposition in 1867 there were more than 42,000 exhibitors. It was held in the Champ de Mars, which has an area of about two hundred acres; the building occupied one third; but the whole area was used for the purposes of the exhibition. Seen from the neighboring heights, it presented the appearance of a great camp. Here were gathered every conceivable product of nature and of art from all nations; Egyptian temples, statues, sphinxes, pillars, etc., occupied the park without, while within the building each nation had its special space, so that the visitor could easily compare the progress of one with that of another in agriculture, arts, and sciences. Nearly two hundred awards were made to American exhibitors: they were for pianos, sewing-machines, clocks, and many peculiarly American productions, — such as apple-parers, potato-diggers, and agricultural machines generally.

*Mabille.* — Our last views are of this, — one of the most beautiful of Parisian parks. This garden is on the south side of the Champs Elysées, and very near its main avenue. It is brilliantly lighted and handsomely decorated. As in some other of the gardens, balls are often held here at an admission fee of about fifty cents. The company at this Garden is one of the most respectable at any of these public balls, but even here it is not always of the most select description.

*Versailles.* — [Pronounced Ver-sy-yuh.] The town itself is a dull modern one, of 44,000 inhabitants. The palace with which these gardens are connected was built by Louis XIV. It is said he selected an uncommonly uncompromising spot, simply to show what could be done by art against nature! The supply of water proving insufficient, he undertook to build an aqueduct; but after untold expense, employing an army of 30,000 men on it at one time, the idea was abandoned! Here have lived Louis XV, Louis XVI and Marie Antoinette, Napoleon I, and Louis Philippe. The latter made the palace and gardens what they now are, at an expense of $4,500,000! The gardens were laid out by Le Notre, with all the regularity of an architectural work, and must be regarded as the stately adjuncts of a splendid palace. It should be recollected that the original site was a sandy waste, and that the trees were all cut down and the gardens replanted in 1775. Here are the usual catalogue of basins, statues, fountains, and gardens, almost unlimited in number, and obtained absolutely without regard to expense.

In the recent Franco-Prussian war, after the capture of Paris by the Germans, King William made this palace at Versailles his head-quarters. The distance to Paris is but nine miles. From here, too, still later, the Versailles troops marched to Paris when they drove out the Commune from that city, and in this same place the National Administration tried the Communist prisoners, confined near by, and here now they are holding their sessions.

*Le Petit Trianon* [the little Trianon], was a small cottage built by Louis XV in 1766. It was given by Louis XVI to Marie Antoinette, who had the gardens laid out as what the French call Jardin Anglais [English Garden], with rock-work, Swiss cottages, lakes, etc. Here Marie Antoinette and her court used to play at shepherds and shepherdesses.

*St. Cloud.* — [Sän Clew.] A small town of about 3,000 inhabitants, but utterly ruined in the recent war, being shelled by the French themselves after its occupation by the Prussians, in the vain effort to drive them from it. The streets were impassable, and one might almost say, that "scarce one stone was left upon another."

*The Pont de Pierre*, a view of which we give looking *from* St. Cloud, was cut in the centre in the recent war, by the French, in their retreat towards Paris. On an eminence above the town stood the Palace of St. Cloud. In the *Salle d'Orangerie*, Napoleon I, with his grenadiers, dispersed the assembly, and caused himself to be nominated first consul.

It is remarked that he ever after had a great preference for St. Cloud. The palace was also the summer residence of the recent Emperor. The park of the palace was laid out by Le Notre, and is considered his masterpiece. The Grand Cascade rises to the height of one hundred and forty feet. We find it hard to speak of these beautiful places, so rich, too, in associations with great men and important events in history, as *having been;* but it is even so. We visited the spot in the summer of 1871. The grounds, though still beautiful, had been injured not a little; and in parts were to be seen long rows of hospital tents occupied by the convalescent soldiers of the French army : but the palace itself! We walked upon the top of the foundation walls. The cellar was filled with the debris of stone and brick, always left by flames. At a few parts of the wall, enough of it remained to see where were the spaces filled with windows, — but this is all. Look at this view of the interior, the Salon d'Apollon, then recall to mind the ruins of the last large fire you have visited, and you have the contrast so often presented by war.

*Le Couvent de la Grand Chartreuse.* — This celebrated monastery, called the "Grande Chartreuse," is situated in an Alpine wilderness, known as the "Desert," on the borders of Savoy. It is 4,268 feet above the sea. The traveller from Lyons to Marseilles passes within six hours' journey of it. Bayard Taylor, in his "By-Ways of Europe," gives the following graphic description of the monastery, its monks, and its surroundings : —

Our way upward was through the shadows of immense walnut-trees, beside the rushing of crystal brooks, and in the perfume of blooming grass, and millions of meadow flowers. It seemed incredible that we should be approaching a "Desert," through such scenery.

In an hour or more we had reached the highest point of

the road, which ran along the base of tremendous mountains. On the topmost heights, above gray ramparts of rock, there were patches of rosy color, — forests of beech which the recent severe frosts had scorched. The streams from the heights dropped into gulfs, yawning at the base of the mountains, making cataracts of several hundred feet. Here the grain, already harvested in the valley of the Rhone, was still green, and the first crop of hay uncut. The road passes onward to a deep, narrow mountain gorge. In front, the mountains seem to close, and only a thin line of shadow reveals the split through which we must pass. The road is hewn out of the solid rock; the sides of the cliff are so near together, that the masonry supporting the road is held firm by timbers crossing the abyss, and mortised into the opposite rock. This closed throat of the mountain is short, it soon expands a little, and we come into the "Desert" whither San Bruno was directed to fly from the temptations of the world. But the word conveys no idea of the character of the scenery. For the whole distance it is a deep cleft in the heart of lofty mountains, overhung with precipices a thousand feet high, yet clothed, wherever a root can take hold, by splendid forests. Ferns and wild flowers hang from every ledge, and the trees are full of singing birds.

Finally the slope of the mountains becomes less abrupt, the shattered summits lean back, and the glen grows brighter under a broader field of sky. The buildings of the monastery presently come into view, a mass of quadrangular piles of masonry, towers, and pyramidal roofs enclosed by a high wall, more than a mile in circuit. The place, in fact, resembles a fortified city.

The monks of the Chartreuse now belong to the order of La Trappe. San Bruno first came hither in the year 1084. The Trappist, or silent system, arose in the sixteenth century. It is probably the severest and most unnatural of all forms of monastic discipline. Isolation is cruel enough in itself, without the obligation of silence.

At an appointed hour I was admitted with a whisper. Our attention was called to a notice which requested that all visitors should neither stand still, nor speak above their breath. We walked down the dim echoing vaults of solid masonry, and paused at a door, through which came the sound of a sepulchral chant. It was the church, wherein two ancient fathers were solemnly intoning a service which sounded like a *miserere*. The brother, our guide, conducted us to an upper gallery, dipped his fingers into the font, and presented the holy water to me with a friendly smile. I am afraid he was cut to the heart when I shook my head, saying: "Thank you, I don't need it." There was an expression of stupefaction in his large, innocent eyes, and thenceforward he kept near me, always turning to me with a tender, melancholy interest, as if hoping and praying that there might be for me some escape from the hell of heretics.

I was astonished at the extent of the buildings. There is a single corridor, Gothic, of solid stone, six hundred and sixty feet in length. Looking down it, the perspective dwindles almost to a point. Opening from it, and from the other intersecting corridors, are the cells of the monks, each with a biblical sentence in Latin painted on the doors. The furniture of these cells is very simple, but a human skull is always a part of it. In the rear of each is a small garden, enclosed by a wall, where the fathers and brothers attend to their own flowers and vegetables. They *must* have, it seems, some innocent solace; the silence, the fasting, the company of the skull, and the rigid ceremonials, would else, I imagine, drive the most of them mad. Those whom we met in the corridor walked with an excited, flying step, as if trying to outrun their own thoughts. Their faces were pale and stern; they rarely looked at us, and of course never spoke.

The gloom and silence, the hushed whispers of the guide, and the prohibition put upon my own tongue, oppressed me painfully. I longed to startle the dead repose of the corridors by a shout full of freedom and rejoicing.

It is always Lent in the Grande Chartreuse. Nevertheless, the dinner of eggs, fish, fruits, cheese, and wine, which was served to us, was of excellent quality. The bed was coarse, but clean, and after putting out my lamp to hide the reproachful eyes of the Virgin, I slept soundly.

Breakfast, however, was a little too lean for my taste. Instead of coffee, they gave me half-cooked cabbage soup, and a lump of black bread.

While I felt a positive respect for the industry, fortitude, and charity of the Monks of the Chartreuse, I drew a long breath of relief as I issued from its whispering corridors. I believe I talked to my guide in a much louder tone than usual, as we returned down the gorge. The visit was full of interest, yet I could not have guessed in advance how oppressive was the prohibition of speech. — *Bayard Taylor.*

One of the buildings within the enclosure of the convent was formerly an infirmary, but has now been devoted to the use of ladies, and is tenanted by the Sisters of Charity. The order of Carthusians at one time possessed nearly two hundred convents, — the Charterhouse in London was one of them.

*Panorama of Luz, pris de Solferino.* — Luz is a cleanly village situated on a Gave (*Gave* — water — is the generic name for *stream*, in the Pyrenees) of rapid flow. The church of Luz, enclosed within a castle furnished with battlements and loop-holed walls, is a great curiosity, bearing as it does the mixed character of the order of the Templars, — half monks, half soldiers, — by whom it was founded. They were planted here to guard the frontier in troublous times, forming an outpost of Christians against the Saracens at first, and Spaniards afterwards. The church is of the eleventh century. A good deal of the so-called crêpe de Barèges is made at Luz. In the middle of the village are the noted baths, supplied from springs of sulphurous water.

The summit of the *Pic de Bergons*, the hill behind Luz, 8,238 feet above the sea, is one of the best points of view among the Pyrenees.

## CHAPTER XXXIV.

### SWITZERLAND.

FROM Lake Geneva to Lake Constance, from Italy on the south to Germany on the north; such are the boundaries of that little land, small in area, yet world-renowned, and pre-eminent among all lands. Famed for its liberty-loving people, historical as the home of ancient heroes and reformers, but famous most of all as containing scenery which for grandeur and wonder is unsurpassed on the globe. Here we find lofty mountain ranges towering above the clouds, and beyond the limits of perpetual snow; enormous glaciers, descending from their sides and blocking up the higher valleys; magnificent lakes embosomed among mountains, which often rise from the water's edge for many thousand feet; and wild, romantic valleys, forming the channels of impetuous streams, fed by numerous torrents and cascades. "Nature seems here more than elsewhere vivified by the breath of God. The gigantic piles of riven rock, fixed in sublime ruggedness, proclaim with unwonted emphasis the awful hand that arrested their upheaving. The terrific fields of eternal ice, the nourishing mothers of great rivers, tempt the imagination towards the mysterious source of

Nature's processes. The common forms and elements of our globe are here exaggerated. Hills and valleys become mountains and gorges; winter dwells on peaks throughout summer, and summer lays her blooming cheek against the icy front of winter."

The loftiest mountain chains belong to the Alps. The immense mass of Mount St. Gothard forms the centre of a system of mountains crowned with perpetual snow and glaciers. The Alps cover all the central and southern portion of the country, and occupy more than half of its area.

### THE ALPS.

Proud monuments of God! sublime ye stand
Among the wonders of his mighty hand:
With summits soaring in the upper sky,
When the broad day looks down with burning eye;
Where gorgeous clouds in solemn pomp repose,
Flinging rich shadows on eternal snows,
Piles of triumphant dust, ye stand alone,
And hold in kingly state a peerless throne.

Where are the thronging hosts of other days,
Whose banners floated o'er the Alpine ways;
Who through their high defiles to battle wound,
While deadly ordnance stirred the heights around?
Gone like the dream that melts at early morn,
When the lark's anthem through the sky is borne:
Gone like the wrecks that sink in ocean's spray,
And chill Oblivion murmurs, Where are they?

Yet "Alps on Alps" still rise; the lofty home
Of storms and eagles, where their pinions roam;
Still round their peaks the magic colors lie,
Of morn and eve imprinted on the sky;
And still, while kings and thrones shall fade and fall,
And empty crowns lie dim upon the pall —
Still shall their glaciers flash, their torrents roar,
Till kingdoms fall, and nations rise no more.

W. G. Clark.

The Alps are famous in the records of military achievements, as having been crossed by the armies of Hannibal and Napoleon; and, pre-eminent for the picturesque grandeur of their scenery, are the most celebrated of all mountain elevations, and the highest in Europe. Mont Blanc, the loftiest peak, is an enormous mass of granite reaching the height of 15,750 feet, the ascent to which is rendered exceedingly difficult by the surrounding walls of ice, fearful precipices, and everlasting snows by which it is covered.

It is when man measures himself against the giant hills, that he most thoroughly realizes that he is a pigmy in stature, and an insect in power. When he sees peaks he cannot climb, and precipices down which he is afraid to look; when he listens to the roar of the merciless avalanche, or watches the fall of the granite particles which indicate the march of the stealthy but resistless glacier; when he is overtaken by one of those snow-storms which serve so often as the traveller's shroud, or hears the "live thunder" leap from crag to crag, whilst rock and sky are all ablaze with red lightning; then, if ever, the most unromantic wanderer will be likely to confess that there are more inspiring topics in the world than the rise and fall of stocks, or the result of the last election. And not only does Nature work upon a colossal scale in all her mountain transactions, but the changes and contrasts she presents are such as cannot fail to astonish dwellers on the plains. We set out, after breakfast, from a valley where we leave the heats of summer, and, crossing the frontier line of snow, find ourselves before dinner within the haunts of perpetual winter. Perspiring, we make the plunge from July to January; and, frozen, we return, in the course of a few hours, to the dog-days again. Through forests full of noble trees, and vineyards loaded with luscious grapes, we pursue our morning course; but before long we reach a region where not a shoot of grass is to be seen, and where no vegetable, however hardy in its habits, could be induced to grow. We proceed with the burning beams of the sun playing upon us as fiercely as if we were in India, and yet beneath our feet there may be a mass of ice as thick and solid as if it had been bred in Greenland; the very water in its pools producing such a deadly chill that it curdles the blood in our veins, and seems to drain out all the life from the part immersed. In fact, in the course of a single day, we pass through all climates, run through all seasons, and traverse all latitudes, from the smiling south to the frozen pole.

*Glaciers.* — Glaciers are met with in various arctic and Alpine regions, but those of the Alps have been most carefully investigated. It is calculated that in this range there are fields of ice covering an area of one thousand five hundred square miles, of one hundred feet in thickness.

Glaciers are masses of true ice, appendages of the snowfields, and as intimately related to them as a stream to a spring, or an icicle to a snow-covered roof. Their external aspect is that of a frozen torrent, depending upon the flanks of mountains, and extending from the higher summits into the lower valleys. They descend below the line of perpetual snow to the warm cultivated grounds, and though continually wasted, they are never destroyed, being constantly replenished from the icy world above.

The size of a glacier sometimes amounts to fifteen or twenty miles in length, and three miles in breadth, the thickness at the lower end varying from eighty to one hundred feet.

The contour of a glacier is the form of the valley into which it protrudes. The ice, when viewed in small pieces, is commonly white, but that of the entire mass exhibits every variety of blue tinge, from the faintest shade to the deepest hue, the blue frequently passing into green in the crevasses. No language can describe the beautiful effect of the different blue and green tints, contrasting with the pure white snow.

The lower extremities of glaciers are sometimes excavated by the melting of the ice into the form of immense grottos, adorned with the finest stalactic crystallizations, whose brilliant azure tints are reflected on the foaming streams and torrents which generally issue from these caverns, forming altogether so beautiful and imposing a picture as to defy the most faithful pencil to portray it accurately, and it is only through the *stereoscope*, with its wonderful reflect of perspective, that we can gain a sense of the beauty, the mystery, and the grandeur of these marvellous ice-caverns.

The descending march of glaciers, imperceptible to the eye, is yet evident; direct proofs of their progress have accumulated, and it is known that the Alpine glaciers move gradually and silently down the valleys at a rate of from two hundred and fifty to five hundred and fifty feet annually; though variations as to the rate depend upon the seasons. The movement is fastest in summer and by day, diminishing in winter and at night.

Philosophers and naturalists have attributed the downward motion to various causes, — Saussure maintained that it was nothing more than the slipping of the glacier upon itself, occasioned by its own weight; M. Agassiz ascribes this motion to the expansion of the ice, resulting from the congelation of the water which has filtered into it, and penetrated its cavities; while M. R. Mallet attributes it to the hydrostatic pressure of the water, which flows at the bottom and makes rents in the mass; and Professor Forbes maintains, that however stiff and rigid the mass of a glacier may appear, it is in reality an imperfect fluid, or viscous body, which is urged down the slopes by the mutual pressure of its parts.

Although theories may be conflicting in regard to the motion of the glaciers, the fact is undeniable; and while they creep down from the hills with a slow and impassionate movement, which seems to make no advance in the valley beneath, yet they travel onward with such prodigious force, that huge stones are carried like straws on their surface, and rocks are scored and ground to powder beneath them. The masses of rock and debris accumulated at the sides and termination of glaciers, are called *moraines*. Glaciers push themselves down into the warm cultivated valleys far below their source, and these immense piles of ice often lie directly in the lap of green grass and flowers.

Truly there is at all times something startling, nay, unearthly, in the presence of one of these ice monsters.

Like a huge serpent, it steals down from its mountain solitudes as if wearied of the wilderness of snow in which it had been reared. Far away in the verdant depths beneath, it espies the bright meadows and glowing corn-plots which checker the valley, as if it were some magnificent mosaic of green and gold. Why should not the nursling of the hills descend, and join the merry-making world below? Why not uncoil its snowy folds, and stretch its vast length along those pleasant plains which lie basking in the sweet sunshine, instead of lurking forever amidst tempest-torn crags, where the eagle never plies its wing, and the chamois never plants its foot? Down, therefore, it crawls. Slowly, warily, doubtfully it proceeds. With many a fearful wrench, and many a muffled cry of agony, it drags its ponderous frame, all agape with wounds, across the sharp rocks, and along the jagged ravines. On it creeps until, reaching the valley, it pauses with head upreared, as if preparing to strike its prey. But why does it seem to shrink and recoil? There is no barrier of solid rock to intercept its stealthy march, no fence of forest-trees to impede its sinuous advance, for a moment. That peaceful valley appears to lie wholly unprotected; yet it is not so. It is guarded by a rampart which no eye can see, no hand can touch, but which is stronger than oak, and more durable than granite. There is an invisible wall of temperature, a palisade of caloric, against which the snowy monster rears and plunges in vain. Pushing up the sward before him in big wrinkles, scattering the scales from his form in his useless writhings, that unseen boundary he cannot overleap. The Voice (unheard of men) which fixes limits to the play of the proud waves, has likewise laid its commands upon the frozen billows as they roll from their lofty springs; and thus, calmly and fearlessly, the husbandman sows his seed, and the herdsman tends his tinkling charge, beneath the very shadow of those wintry masses which seem to have been sent down to overwhelm them, from the regions of everlasting frost.

The crossing of a glacier is an exploit of interest and excitement. The following narration from the "British Quarterly" portrays the delights and dangers of such a journey.

"For some distance our route lies over one of these icy streams. Rougher travelling, in parts at least, can scarcely be well imagined; for where the frozen torrent has poured over some precipice or steep incline in its bed, it has cracked and shivered into big blocks, which assume the most fantastic forms, from the shapeless berg to the graceful pyramid or obelisk. Amongst these, in the very bowels of the glacier, we may have to thread our way for a while, the procession winding in and out like a captive snake, seeking some outlet from its dungeon. Then there are the crevasses, which render locomotion so toilsome, though certainly so picturesque, upon the surface. A turnpike road, perpetually intersected by ditches, trenches, rivulets, wells, and chasms (to say nothing of innumerable toll-gates), would afford commodious travelling compared with that which the back of a glacier affords. These fractures, which result from the unequal motion of the ice, may be a few inches in breadth, or several feet across. They may be clefts of no great depth, or they may penetrate into the very profundities of the mass. Between these fissures the ice frequently runs in a fine ridge, along which it may be necessary to creep with extreme caution, for a single erring footstep would send the wanderer shooting down the side until jammed in by the meeting walls, or plunged into depths from which return would be utterly impracticable. Frequently, too, a crevasse is concealed by a covering of snow. That a light impalpable material like this should ever suffice for the purposes of a bridge, vaulting a chasm of considerable span, may seem as improbable to an untravelled Englishman as the existence of solid water in winter did to that famous, perhaps fabulous, king of Siam, who has served to point so many a philosophical moral. But a little alternate melting and freezing will soon impart so cohesive a character to the fallen flakes, that when they unite to produce a roadway upward of a foot in thickness, they may easily sustain the weight of a man.

"To prevent accidents, however, as much as possible, it is customary to attach the adventurers to each other by means of a rope, which is either held in the hand or fastened to the waist. Every now and then one of the party may disappear, but the event often only excites hilarity, and his comrades proceed to draw the missing man to the bank. Let the precaution, however, be neglected, and the result may be very disastrous. In making the passage of the Col de Thiage, Mr. G. S. Fox found himself stopped by a chasm of unsearchable depth. He began to cut steps in the icy slope which adjoined, when one of his companions saw his feet suddenly shoot out as if struck from under him, and in a moment he vanished in the jaws of the crevasse. His comrade thus tells the story: "A thrill ran through me as I saw him go, but in another instant I was relieved, when craning down as well as I could, I caught sight of his hat and an arm, at the depth of not more than twelve or fifteen feet. Providentially, he had alighted astride of a projecting piece of ice, which brought him up, and by instantly striking the pick of his axe into the wall of a crevasse, steadied himself in that position. The guides cautiously approaching the edge, threw him a rope, and he was drawn up, none the worse for his slip. After this warning, however, we took further precautious. Bohren, round whose short person so many fathoms of rope were coiled that he looked like a walking capstan, was unwound, and we were put into harness, with Cachat as leader."

Mr. Packe tells us, that in ascending the Maladetta, in the Pyrenees, the party sat down to rest on the glacier where the snow appeared to be quite smooth. One of the guides released himself from the rope, in order to convey the wine bottle to each of the company.

"He was passing before us, and certainly not more than three yards from the spot where I was sitting, when he suddenly dropped through the snow and disappeared. There was no sound, neither cracking of the ice, nor cry from the man,—a slight convulsive shuddering as he fell, and the glacier quietly swallowed up its victim. It was horrible to witness, but of course there was only one thing to be done. We speedily disengaged the rope from our bodies, and carefully holding it in our hands, approached the hole, which was not large, my guide, Pierre Barrau, being the first. We let down the rope, and anxiously expected a reply to our shout. For some seconds, however, none came; and when it did come, it sounded fearfully indistinct and distant, stifled as it was by the snow and walls of ice. The man fell, according to the guide's estimate, eighteen metres (fifty-nine feet), but, from the length of the rope let down, I should say about thirty feet. Thanks to the bed of snow that fell with him, and in which he was partly buried, the man was not hurt, and he was able to fasten the rope round his body, so that in about five minutes we drew him up, and a right hearty squeeze of the hand he interchanged with each of us. He was not much the worse, but fearfully cold. He described his position as having been very perilous, having been caught on a ledge, below which sank a seemingly unfathomable abyss."

In many other cases adventurers have undergone a much longer imprisonment. A hapless hunter crossing the Trift glacier in 1803, went down into a crevasse of fearful depth, but was arrested by a projection of ice. There he was compelled to remain whilst his companions went off to the nearest village, a journey of four hours, to procure materials for his release. These obtained, they returned and lowered a rope, which the prisoner fastened round his waist, but the strands suddenly parted, and the poor man was flung back upon his ledge. What remained of the cord was now too short to reach him, and once more it became necessary for them to visit the distant houses. Sixteen hours were thus spent in a frozen cave, listening to the murmur of the glacier torrent beneath, and not knowing but that his life-heat might all be drained out of him, and his body consigned to those sunless waters before his comrades could reappear. Many a man, indeed, has been doomed to perish inch by inch in a gloomy crevasse, or hideous mountain gulf. A drummer belonging to the French army, under Macdonald, was precipitated into a fissure in the Cardinell pass, in the winter of 1800. His comrades could afford him no assistance, though for hours together the sound of his instrument rose up from the depths; the poor fellow being left, in fact, to drum himself to death.

Among the most remarkable phenomena connected with the Alps, are the whirlwinds. They arise with a great violence, often accompanied by thunder and lightning, tossing the snow in eddying clouds, which blind or perhaps overwhelm the traveller; and frequently setting in motion the still more formidable *avalanche.*

*Avalanches.* — These are enormous masses of snow, which, detached by various causes from their original position, roll with tremendous noise and force over rock and precipice, down to the plains below, overwhelming man and beast, forest and dwelling, in one common destruction. A touch of the foot or the slightest motion of the air, even that produced by the sound of a small bell, or other instrument, is often sufficient to set the avalanche in motion. The most destructive are those which are composed of hardened snow, and which, rolling or sliding down from the mountains, carry all before them. From the frequent occurrence of avalanches, some parts of the Alps are entirely uninhabited, and in others, large patches of the tallest and strongest trees are left standing, in order to arrest their progress; houses are built under the shelter of rocks, and all other available means are adopted to avoid the effects of these destructive visitants.

Some avalanches have been frightfully murderous. In 1719 the village of Leukerbad was overwhelmed, and fifty-five persons perished; the remainder of the inhabitants being extricated; and amongst others, a boy, who was heard singing psalms with a valiant voice, though he lay imprisoned in a cellar for a week. In 1720, eighty-four men and above four hundred head of cattle were put to death by an avalanche at Obergestelen in the Vallais; whilst another assassin of snow, in the same year, took the life out of sixty-one people at Fethau, in the Lower Engadine. Occasionally, these mountain freebooters exhibit a singular mixture of softness and ferocity. They have been known to bear away huts as quietly as a mother would carry her sleeping child to its cradle. One which descended upon the village of Rueras, in the Grisons, in the year 1749, and found the inhabitants buried in their slumbers, pushed some of the houses so gently forward, that the inmates were not aroused, and did not discover, until the long-continued darkness excited their surprise, that they were immersed in snow; upward of forty of their neighbors having fallen victims to this nocturnal attack.

Against these pitiless invaders the villagers have but scanty protection. The forest which overhangs the hamlet, if sufficiently near to the sources of the avalanche, may prop up the sheet of snow and prevent it starting from its bed. Should the wood, however, be distant, it is needless to say that it will be of no avail as a barrier when the loosened mass has once acquired the deadly momentum for which these destroyers are renowned; the helpless trunks will then be mown down like grass under the scythe. Every village, therefore, which lies exposed to such snowy raids, places itself, if possible, beneath the shelter of a plantation, which becomes as sacred to the inhabitants as a Druidical grove was to the ancient Britons, and infinitely more useful. The trees are tabooed. They must not be felled on any account. There may be scarcity of fuel, a perfect famine of fire-wood, and yet the natives will send to remote quarters for a supply, rather than burn a twig of the guardian forest.

*Avalanche of the Rossberg.* — No man can pass the Rossberg mountain without thinking of the dread catastrophe that here overwhelmed in so vast a burial three or four whole lovely villages at once,— one of the most terrible natural convulsions in all the history of Switzerland. Four hundred and fifty-seven persons are said to have perished beneath this mighty avalanche. The place out of which it broke in the mountain is a thousand feet in breadth by a hundred feet deep, and this falling mass extended bodily at least three miles in length. It shot across the valley with the swiftness of a cannon-ball, so that in five minutes the villages were all crushed as if they had been egg-shells, or the mimic toys of children.

The following is the simple and powerful narrative of Dr. Zay, of the neighboring village of Arth, an eye-witness of the tremendous spectacle.

"The summer of 1806 had been very rainy, and on the 1st and 2d of September it rained incessantly. New crevices were observed in the flank of the mountain, a sort of crackling noise was heard internally, stones started out of the ground, detached fragments of rocks rolled down the mountain; at two o'clock in the afternoon of the 2d of September a large rock became loose, and in falling raised a cloud of black dust. Towards the lower part of the mountain the ground seemed pressed down from above; and when a stick or a spade was driven in, it moved of itself. A man who had been digging in his garden, ran away from fright at these extraordinary appearances: soon a fissure, larger than all the others, was observed; insensibly it increased; springs of water ceased all at once to flow; the pine-trees of the forest absolutely reeled; birds flew away screaming. A few minutes before five o'clock the symptoms of some mighty catastrophe became still stronger; the whole surface of the mountain seemed to glide down, but so slowly as to afford time to the inhabitants to go away. An old man, who had often predicted some such disaster, was quietly smoking his pipe, when told by a young man running by that the mountain was in the act of falling, he rose and looked out, but went into his house again, saying he had time to fill another pipe. The young man, continuing to fly, was thrown down several times, and escaped with difficulty; looking back, he saw the house carried off all at once.

"Another inhabitant, being alarmed, took two of his children and ran away with them, calling to his wife to follow with the third; but she went in for another who still remained (Marianna, aged five); just then Francisca Ulrich, their servant, was crossing the room with this Marianna, whom she held by the hand, and saw her mistress; at that instant, as Francisca afterwards said, 'The house appeared to be torn from its foundation (it was of wood), and spun round and round like a teetotum; I was sometimes on my head, sometimes on my feet, in total darkness, and violently separated from the child.' When the motion stopped, she found herself jammed in on all sides, with her head downward, much bruised, and in extreme pain. She supposed she was buried alive at a great depth; with much difficulty she disengaged her right hand, and wiped the blood from her eyes. Presently she heard the faint moans of Marianna, and called to her by her name; the child answered that she was on her back among stones and bushes, which held her fast, but that her hands were free, and that she saw the light, and even something green. She asked whether people would not soon come to take them out. Francisca answered that it was the day of judgment, and that no one was left to help them, but that they would be released by death, and be happy in heaven. They prayed together. At last Francisca's ear was struck by the sound of a bell, which she knew to be that of Steinenberg; then seven o'clock struck in another village; then she began to hope there were still living beings, and endeavored to comfort the child. The poor little girl was at first clamorous for her supper, but her cries soon became fainter, and at last quite died away. Francisca, still with her head downward, and surrounded with damp earth, experienced a sense of cold in her feet, almost insupportable. After prodigious efforts she succeeded in disengaging her legs, and thinks this saved her life. Many hours had passed in this situation, when she again heard the voice of Marianna, who had been asleep and now renewed her lamentations. In the mean time, the unfortunate father, who, with much difficulty, had saved himself and two children, wandered about till daylight, when he came among the ruins to look for the rest of his family. He soon discovered his wife, by a foot which appeared above ground: she was dead, with a child in her arms. His cries, and the noise he made in digging, were heard by Marianna, who called out. She was extricated with a broken thigh, and, saying that Francisca was not far off, a farther search led to her release also, but in such a state that her life was despaired of: she was blind for some days, and remained subject to convulsive fits of terror. The house, or themselves at least, had been carried down about one thousand five hundred feet from where it stood before.

"In another place a child two years old was found unhurt, lying on its straw mattress upon the mud, without any vestige of the house from which he had been separated. Such a mass of earth and stones rushed at once into the Lake of Lowertz, although five miles distant, that one end of it was filled up; and a prodigious wave, passing completely over the island of Schwanau, seventy feet above the usual level of the water, overwhelmed the opposite shore, and, as it returned, swept away into the lake many houses, with their inhabitants. The village of Seewen, situated at the farther end, was inundated, and some houses washed away, and the flood carried live fish into the village of Steinen. The chapel of Olten, built of wood, was found half a league from the place it had previously occupied, and many large blocks of stone completely changed their position.

"The most considerable of the villages overwhelmed in the vale of Arth was Goldau, and its name is now affixed to the whole melancholy story and place. I shall relate only one more incident. A party of eleven travellers from Berne, belonging to the most distinguished families there, arrived at

Arth on the 2d of September, and set off on foot for the Rigi a few moments before the catastrophe. Seven of them had got about two hundred yards ahead; the other four saw them entering the village of Goldau, and one of the latter, Mr. R. Jenner, pointing out to the rest the summit of the Rossberg (full four miles off in a straight line), where some strange commotion seemed taking place, which they themselves, the four behind, were observing with a telescope, when all at once a flight of stones like cannon-balls traversed the air above their heads; a cloud of thick dust obscured the valley; a frightful noise was heard. They fled. As soon as the obscurity was so far dissipated as to make objects discernible, they sought their friends, but the village of Goldau had disappeared under a heap of stones and rubbish, one hundred feet in height, and the whole valley presented nothing but a perfect chaos!

"Of the unfortunate survivors, one lost a wife to whom he was just married, one a son, a third, two pupils under his care. Nothing is left of Goldau but the bell, which hung in its steeple, and which was found about a mile off. With the rocks, torrents of mud came down, acting as rollers; but they took a different direction when in the valley, the mud following the slope of the ground towards the Lake of Lowertz, while the rocks glanced across, toward the Rigi, high upon the sides of which trees were mowed down as they might have been by cannon."

## CHAPTER XXXV.

### SWITZERLAND, — GENEVA, MONT BLANC, ETC.

THIS is the largest city in Switzerland, and contains 33,000 inhabitants. It is beautifully situated at the foot of Lake Geneva, or Lake Leman, on both banks of the

River Rhone. Geneva as a town is not at all prepossessing in its appearance. It has no *sights*, and few fine buildings. Its situation, the beautiful scenery of its lake, and delightful climate, make it a desirable residence. "Mountains embrace it. Strength and beauty are its habitation."

The natives of Geneva are celebrated for their industry, which is chiefly devoted to the making of watches and ornamental jewelry. Nearly four thousand people are employed in the city in the manufacture of watches, over one hundred thousand being yearly made. A commission is appointed by the government to inspect the quantity of the gold and silver used in this manufacture, fearing, in case a base material were used, their productive branch of industry might suffer in consequence.

The natives of Geneva are very much like their French neighbors, in their manners and customs. Mr. Inglis says : "The stranger will find it difficult to discern any trace of the Puritanism and severity of manners for which the city was renowned in earlier times. I never was among a livelier or gayer population. Amusement seemed to be the reigning passion, and religion little less a matter of form than it is in France on Sunday. After listening to a favorite preacher, the Genevese flock to the theatre. The shops also open on a Sunday, and every man plies his trade as usual."

Geneva has produced many celebrated individuals, prominent among whom stands John Calvin, the great Reformer. The great Rousseau, Necker, Madame de Staël, Huber, and Dumont, were all natives of Geneva. Of Calvin and Rousseau a recent writer remarks : "These two give the flavor to Geneva. Of necessity far apart in time, for one would think the spirit of Calvin must have been wellnigh worn out or dormant ere the little Republic could have engendered a Rousseau. I figure Calvin as gaunt, fleshless; a man of gritty substance, on whom flesh could not grow. A nature tough as steel, unbending as granite, — as was needed for his task. With what a bold, biting lash he scourged the sensualities of his time! How he defied the principalities of the earth! How he scorned the tempests of papal and regal and popular wrath! They did but invigorate his will, sublimate his genius for the building up of a power that was to stretch over many nations, and endure for ages. Calvin, who was not born in Geneva, became there a ruler, and ruled with rigor for twenty-three years."

"Rousseau seems not to have been held in much account by his townsmen, until lately, when they have erected to him a statue, more out of pride, probably, than love. Rousseau was made of anything but granite; an unstable, tremulous nature, devoured by passions which yet had not life enough to energize him. Yet he too did a share of good; his sentimentality, insipid or sickening now, was savory and healing to his sophisticated generation."

The views of the mountains from Geneva are very fine. The Salève is a peculiar looking mountain, striped with different strata of rock, which have a singular effect in the hazy distance. The Mole is a dark mountain, whose blue-black outline looks blacker in clear weather, from being set against the snow mountains beyond. But most noteworthy are the views of the Alps and Mont Blanc, which, though fifty miles distant, can be seen upon a bright, clear day.

The following glowing description of a glimpse of Mont Blanc from Geneva, is from the pen of Rev. Charles Beecher: "In the afternoon we rode out across the Rhone, where it breaks from the lake, and around upon the ascending shore. It is seldom here that the Alps are visible. The least mist hides them completely, so that travellers are wont to record it in their diaries as a great event, — 'I saw Mont Blanc to-day.' Yesterday there was nothing but clouds and thick gloom; but now we had not ridden far before H. sprang suddenly as if she had lost her senses — her cheeks flushed, her eye flashing. I was frightened. 'There,' said she, pointing across the lake, 'there he is — there's Mont Blanc.' 'Pooh,' said I, 'no such thing.' And some trees for a moment intervened, and shut out the view. Presently the trees opened, and H. cried, 'There, that *white;* don't you see? there — there!' pointing with great energy, as if she were getting ready to fly. I looked and saw, sure enough, behind the dark mass of the Mole, the granite ranges rising gradually and grim as we rode; but farther still, behind those gray and ghastly barriers, all bathed and blazing in the sun's fresh splendors, undimmed by a cloud, unveiled even by a filmy fleece of vapor, and O, so white — so intensely, blindingly white! against the dark-blue sky, the needles, the spires, the solemn pyramid, the transfiguration cone of Mont Blanc. Higher, and still higher, those apocalyptic splendors seemed lifting their spectral, spiritual forms, seeming to rise as we rose, seeming to start like giants hidden from behind the black brow of intervening ranges, opening wider the amphitheatre of glory, until as we reached the highest point in our road, the whole unearthly vision stood revealed in sublime perspective. The language of the Revelation came rushing through my soul. Here is, as it were, a door opened in heaven. Here are some of those everlasting mountain ranges, whose light is not of the sun nor of the moon, but of the Lord God and of the Lamb. Here is, as it were, a great white throne, on which one might sit, before whose face heaven and earth might flee; and here a sea of glass mingled with fire. Nay, rather, here are some faint shadows, some dimmed and veiled resemblances, which bring our earth-imprisoned spirits to conceive remotely what the disencumbered eye of the ecstatic apostle gazed upon.

"With solemn thankfulness we gazed, — thankfulness

to God for having withdrawn his veil of clouds from this threshold of the heavenly vestibule, and brought us across the Atlantic to behold. And as our eyes, blinded by the dazzling vision, filled with tears, we were forced to turn them away, and fasten them on the dark range of the Jura, on the other side of us, until they were able to gaze again. Thus we rode onward, obtaining new points of view, new effects, and deeper emotions; nor can time efface the impressions we received in the depths of our soul."

*On the Route to Mont Blanc.* — Mont Blanc lies on the boundary line between France and Italy, and hence is not in Switzerland at all. But since it is so near the southern limit of this latter country, and is usually approached from it, and is so intimately connected with our thoughts of Switzerland, and Swiss Alpine scenery, it does not seem inappropriate to speak of it, and its surroundings, in connection with the general topic,— Switzerland.

The ride from Geneva to the Vale of Chamouni, which lies at the base of Mont Blanc, is usually taken in a diligence, and occupies a day. But to ride among the wonders of the Alps, inside of the diligence, is like contemplating infinity through the neck of a bottle. A seat on top, if somewhat airy, gives one the benefit of scenery unexcelled in the world. For many miles after leaving Geneva, the Mole is the principal object; this and its neighboring mountains look like old, sombre, haggard genii, half veiled in clouds, belted with pines, worn and furrowed with storms and avalanches, but not, like their loftier brethren, covered with snow.

*La Chute d'Arpenaz.* — The Cascade of Arpenaz is about midway on the tourists' road, from Geneva to Mont Blanc. The brook, not usually of great volume, falling several hundred feet, is converted into a fine spray, wafted away in a thin veil by the breeze. It is visible for a long distance, and, indeed, after rain, assumes more imposing dimensions.

*La Cascade de Chêde.* — The Cascade of Chêde is a very picturesque waterfall a few miles nearer Chamouni, and some thirty-five from Geneva.

*Salanches*, a town of Savoy, on the River Arve, is thirty-three miles from Geneva, and seventeen from the foot of Mont Blanc. It has been rebuilt since the fire of 1840, and contains nearly 2,000 inhabitants. A new high road, constructed in 1868, skirts the left bank of the river here. The environs are charming, and the sulphurous baths in the neighborhood are much frequented.

The River Arve here is a raving, brawling, turbulent stream of muddy water, and, like many other mountain streams, has many troublesome and inconvenient personal habits, such as rising up all of a sudden, some night, and whisking off houses, cattle, pine-trees; in short, getting up sailing parties in such a promiscuous manner that it is neither safe nor agreeable to live in its neighborhood.

*Servoz.*—This is a small place on the Arve, it lies but eight miles distant from Chamouni, on the Geneva road, being forty-two from Geneva itself. It lies in a valley of the same name, which was formerly a lake, and is separated from the valley of Chamouni by a steep, rocky ridge.

*The Village of Chamouni.* — This village lies in the valley of the same name, at the foot of Mont Blanc, and about fifty miles from Geneva. The village itself has nothing in particular to recommend it. The buildings and everything about it have a rough, coarse appearance. But it lies in a valley the most celebrated in the world for its picturesqueness, and the wild grandeur of its mountains and glaciers. And from this village, tourists start upon excursions to the various objects of interest in this famous region.

*The Valley of Chamouni.* — This valley, ever since public attention was drawn to its wonderful scenery, in 1741, by English travellers, has attracted thousands of visitors every season. Mont Blanc and his army of white-robed brethren rise around it, " glorious as the four and twenty elders around the great white throne." The valley itself lies everywhere flat, — valleys in the Alps seem to have this peculiarity, they are not hollows, bending downward in the middle, and imperceptibly sloping upward into the mountains, but they lie nearly level. The mountains rise around them like walls, almost perpendicularly. Five or six glaciers push their way down into this valley and lie, — gigantic piles of icy pillars, in the midst of cultivated fields, verdure, and flowers.

> " Ye ice falls! ye that from the mountain's brow
> Adown enormous ravines slope amain —
> Torrents, methinks, that heard a mighty voice,
> And stopped at once amid their maddest plunge;
> Motionless torrents! silent cataracts!
> Who made you glorious as the gates of heaven
> Beneath the keen full moon? Who bade the sun
> Clothe you with rainbows? Who with living flowers
> Of loveliest blue spread garlands at your feet?
> God! let the torrents, like a shout of nations,
> Answer! and let the ice plains echo God!
> God! sing ye meadow streams, with gladsome voice!
> Ye pine groves, with your soft and soul-like sounds;
> And they, too, have a voice, yon hills of snow,
> And in their perilous fall shall thunder God!"
> *Coleridge.*

*La Mer de Glace. The Sea of Ice.* — Of the glaciers that are born in the heights of perpetual snow, and in the sunshine look like rivers of light pouring down from the clouds, the largest, in the vicinity of Mont Blanc, is the Mer de Glace. It is fifteen miles long, from three to six miles wide, and from eighty to one hundred and twenty feet in thickness. It is broken by many crevices of fearful depth, through which may be seen the remarkable purity and deep blue color of the frozen mass. The upper portion of this stream is called the Mer de Glace, the lower the Glacier des Bois. A view of this icy sea is thus described by Mrs. Stowe: —

"Here a scene opened upon us never to be forgotten. From the distant gorge of the everlasting Alpine ranges issued forth an ocean tide, in wild and dashing commotion, just as we have seen the waves upon the broad Atlantic, but all motionless as chaos when smitten by the mace of Death; and yet, not motionless! This denser medium, this motionless mass, is never at rest. This flood moves as it seems to move; these waves are actually uplifting out of the abyss as they seem to lift; the only difference is the time of motion, the rate of change.

"These prodigious blocks of granite, thirty or forty feet long and twenty feet thick, which float on this grim sea of ice, *do float* and are *drifting*, drifting down to the valley below, where they must eventually arrive.

"We walked these valleys, ascended these hills, leaped across chasms, threw stones down *crevasses*, plunged our Alpen-stocks into pools of green water, philosophized and poetized.

"The ice was porous and spongy. I could see little drops of water percolating in a thousand tiny streams through it, and dropping down on every side. Putting my ear to it, I could hear a fine, musical trill and trickle, and that still small click and stir as of melting ice.

"Drop by drop the cold iceberg was changing into a stream, to flow down the sides of the valley, no longer an image of coldness and death, but bearing fertility and beauty on its tide. As I looked abroad over all the rifted field of ice, I could see the same change was gradually going on throughout. In every blue ravine you can hear the clink of dropping water, and those great defiant blocks of ice, which seem frozen with uplifted, warlike hands, are all softening in that beneficent light, and destined to pass away in that benignant change.

"I looked up the gorge, and saw this frozen river lying cradled, as it were, in the arms of needled, peaked giants of amethystine rock, their tops laced with flying silvery clouds. The whole air seemed to be surcharged with tints, ranging between the palest rose and the deepest violet, — tints never without blue and never without red, but varying in the degrees of the two. It is this prismatic hue diffused over every object, which gives one of the most noticeable characteristics of the Alpine landscape.

"This sea of ice lies on an inclined plane, and all the blocks have a general downward curve. The lower part of the glacier appears covered with dirt. Although it was a sultry day in July, yet around the glacier a continual high wind was blowing, whirling the dust and debris of the sides upon it. Some of the great masses of ice were so completely coated with sand as to appear at a distance like granite rocks. The effect of some of these immense brown masses was very peculiar. They seemed like an army of giants bending forward, driven, as by an invisible power, down the valley."

In crossing the Mer de Glace there is really no danger, though great care is necessary in passing along rather narrow ridges at times between deep fissures. Every day in summer, one or two men are to be met with, cutting steps in the more inaccessible places, relying, and not in vain, on the practical appreciation of the tourists passing either way. The warm summer's sun compels the daily renewal of the steps made.

*The Glacier des Bossons.* — This glacier is situated near a village of the same name, in the southern part of the valley of Chamouni. Imagine the sky flushed with a rosy light, a background of purple mountains, with darts of sunlight streaming among them, touching point and cliff with gold. Against this background rises the outline of the glacier like a mountain of clearest white crystals, tinged with blue; and against their snowy whiteness in the foreground, tall forms of pines.

*Caverne le Glacier des Bossons.* — There is a similar cavern, artificial, however, in the Upper Grindelwald Glacier, extending several rods into the solid ice, and terminating in a chamber beautifully cool but damp, with water constantly trickling from the sides and ceiling.

*Aiguille de Dru.* — One of the several peaks that surround the entire chain of Mont Blanc: it is separated from the chain itself by the valley which is occupied by the Mer de Glace.

### MONT BLANC.

Hast thou a charm to stay the morning star
In his steep course? So long he seems to pause
On thy bald, awful head, O sovereign Blanc!
The Arve and Arveiron at thy base
Rave ceaselessly: but thou, most awful form,
Risest from forth thy silent sea of pines,
How silently! Around thee and above,
Deep is the air and dark, substantial, black,
An ebon mass! methinks thou piercest it,
As with a wedge. But when I look again,
It is thine own calm home, thy crystal shrine,
Thy habitation from eternity.

O dread and silent Mount! I gazed upon thee
Till thou, still present to the bodily sense,
Didst vanish from my thought: entranced in prayer
I worshipped the Invisible alone.

Yet like some sweet beguiling melody,
So sweet we know not we are listening to it,
Thou, the meanwhile, wast blending with my thought,
Yea, with my life and life's own secret joy;

> Till the dilating soul, enrapt, transfused,
> Into the mighty vision passing — there
> As in her natural form, swelled vast to heaven.
>
> Awake my soul! not only passive praise
> Thou owest! not alone these swelling tears,
> Mute thanks, and secret ecstasy! Awake,
> Voice of sweet song! Awake, my heart! awake,
> Green vales and icy cliffs! all join my hymn.
>
> Thou first and chief, sole sovereign of the vale!
> O, struggling with the darkness all the night,
> And visited all night by troops of stars,
> Or when they climb the sky, or when they sink —
> Companion of the morning star at dawn
> Thyself earth's rosy star, and of the dawn
> Co-herald — wake, O wake, and utter praise!
>
> Coleridge.

*Mont Blanc*, "the monarch of all European mountains," is 15,780 feet above the level of the sea,—Monte Rosa being 15,364; and the third in height, more than a thousand feet below either. The name signifies "white mountain," so called from the snow which covers it. Its highest elevation is but a narrow pinnacle, and its summit, for a distance of seven thousand feet down either side, is clothed with perpetual snow.

It presents the most magnificent appearance when seen from the north, from the vale of Chamouni, whence it seems to arise into the sky like a dome, above all neighboring peaks. It is composed chiefly of Alpine granite. The sides, to the height of three to four thousand feet, are skirted with forests, the more elevated of which contain nothing less hardy than pines and larches. The surface of its higher parts are diversified and very irregular; there are numerous jutting rocks called *aiguilles* or needles; large fields of ice are often broken into fissures of unknown depth; and grottos excavated beneath masses of ice, by the warmer temperature below, and hanging with splendid stalactitic formations.

Thirty-four separate glaciers are found in the chain of Mont Blanc, occupying a surface estimated at ninety-five square miles.

The beauty of the mountain, as it appears in the evening, is the wonder of every traveller. The following is a description of it, as viewed from the valley of Chamouni. "On our right hand were black, jagged furrowed walls of mountain, and on our left Mont Blanc, with his fields of glaciers and worlds of snow; they seemed to hem us in, and almost press us down. But in a few moments commenced a scene of transfiguration. The cold, white dismal fields of ice gradually changed into hues of the most beautiful rose color. A bank of white clouds, which rested above the mountains, kindled and glowed, as if some spirit of light had entered into them. You did not lose your idea of the dazzling spiritual whiteness of the snow, yet you seemed to see it through a rosy veil. The sharp edges of the glaciers, and the hollows between the peaks, reflected wavering tints of lilac and purple. The effect was beyond expression solemn and spiritual. These words which had been often in my mind through the day, and which occurred to me more often than any others, while I was travelling through the Alps, came into my mind with a pomp and magnificence of meaning unknown before, — "For by Him were all things created in heaven and on earth, visible and invisible, whether they be thrones, or dominions, or principalities, or powers; all things are by Him and for Him; and He is before all things, and by Him all things subsist."

Mont Blanc was first ascended in 1786, by a guide. The fatigue and exposure brought on a serious illness, from which he recovered only to climb again with his doctor! Several parties ascend now every year; it is, however, productive of but little enjoyment, laborious and expensive, and the view from the summit is but a poor return; as all objects from the great distance appear indistinct. There is now but little risk, the mountain being well known, and the proper precautions well understood. From the valley and return occupies three days, the intervening nights being spent in a stone hut about half-way up to the summit. Sleeping there is said to be not so easy, on account of the noise of the avalanches and the bites of the fleas! But two women ever ascended to the top, — a peasant woman of Chamouni, and a lady of Geneva. As to the gentlemen, it is a serious consideration to attempt the ascent. In the first place, the affair costs about one hundred and fifty dollars apiece, takes three days of time, uses up a week's strength, all to get an experience of some very disagreeable sensations, which could not afflict a man in any other case. It is no wonder, then, that gentlemen look up to the mountain, lay their hands on their pockets, and say "No."

*Chamouni to Martigny, by the Tête Noire.* — The first portion of the route lies beside a broad, joyous mountain torrent, called the Eau Noire, or "black water," from the darkness of its waters. The road passes through one of the most charming of Alpine valleys, green meadows and flowery fields are on every side, and above are the silent white mountains, — "the everlasting hills." But soon the character of the route changes; after about two hours' ride from Chamouni, carriages are exchanged for mules; you ascend dizzy heights by narrow rocky paths, you look down into chasms so deep that the tallest pines look like twigs below, you look up the precipices above you, and the giant trees at the top seem like a fluttering fringe. Up and up you climb, until, passing around an angle, you enter a dark tunnel blasted through the solid rock; you emerge, and see before you the far-famed Tête Noire, or "black ledge," on whose face, so high is the opposite cliff, the sun never shines.

This road through the Pass of the Tête Noire used to be very dangerous; a very narrow bridle-path, undefended by any screen whatever. To have passed it in the old days would have been too much of the sublime to be agreeable. The road as it now is is wide enough for three mules to go abreast, and the tunnel is blasted through the most difficult and dangerous point. A little beyond the tunnel is the Hotel de la Couronne.

If any one desires to stop in the wildest and most lonesome place in the Alps, and wishes to become saturated with a sense of savageness and desolation, this hotel is recommended.

A traveller remarks: "When we were on our way to the Tête Noire, winding along the narrow path, bearing no more proportion to the dizzy heights above and below than the smallest insect creeping on the wall, I looked across the chasm and saw a row of shepherds' cottages perched midway on a narrow shelf, that seemed in the distance not an inch wide. By a very natural impulse I exclaimed, 'What does become of the little children there? I should think they would fall over the precipice!' My guide looked up benevolently at me, as if he felt it his duty to quiet my fears, and said in a soothing tone, 'O, no, no, no!'

"What can they think of, — these creatures, who are born in this strange place, half-way between heaven and earth, to whom the sound of avalanches is a cradle hymn, and who can never see the sun above the top of the cliff on either side, until he really gets into the zenith?"

From the Pass of Tête Noire, the road descends into the beautiful valley of the Rhone. This valley lies flat, like other Swiss valleys, green as a velvet carpet, studded with buildings and villages which look like dots in the distance, and embraced on all sides by magnificent mountains, of which those nearest in the prospect can be distinctly made out with their rocks, pine-trees, and foliage. The next in the receding distance are fainter, and of a purplish green; the next of a vivid purple; the next lilac; while far in the fading view the crystal summits and glaciers of the Oberland Alps rise like an exhalation. On one of the lower ranges the ruins of an old Roman tower stand picturesquely prominent.

*Martigny* stands on the southern bank of the River Rhone. It is beautifully situated at the foot of the passes of the Tête Noire and the Col de Balme, on the Simplon road to Italy; it is also at the foot of the Great St. Bernard, twenty-seven miles from the famous monastery. Here also is the splendid waterfall of the Salchenche, one of the grandest in Switzerland.

*The Monastery of St. Bernard.* — Close on the limits of perpetual snow, rise the solitary walls of the *hospice* or Monastery of St. Bernard, the highest dwelling on the Alps. Its monks are celebrated for their exertions, in which they are aided by their famous breed of dogs, in rescuing travellers from the dangers of this region. In their hospice, at times, as many as five or six hundred travellers have been accommodated at once. The snow around the monastery averages seven to eight feet in depth, and the drifts sometimes rest against it, and accumulate to the height of forty feet. The severest cold recorded was twenty-nine degrees below zero, and the greatest heat sixty-eight degrees above. The convent was founded in 962, by St. Bernard. It has remained unchanged in its rules, and unrivalled in its hospitalities to strangers, who, with their mules or horses, are gratuitously entertained for three days. Tourists ought to leave in the convent box at least as much money as they would pay at a hotel, as poor travellers are lodged and fed free, summer and winter. The route over the Great St.

Bernard was traversed, in 1800, by the French, under Napoleon. About forty miles east, and somewhat north of the Great St. Bernard, lies

*Zermath.* — One of the loveliest spots among the Alps, noted for its splendid glaciers and the glorious views of the adjacent mountains.

It is a secluded village, difficult of access, and contains less than four hundred inhabitants. It may be approached on the north from Visp, on the Simplon road, thirty miles distant. The journey will occupy ten hours on horseback; the road is good but narrow. From the south it may be reached through the famous Pass of St. Theodule, which is practicable on foot in summer, with good guides.

Notwithstanding it is thus shut in by mountain barriers, it is much frequented, for the very bulwarks by which it is surrounded form scenery which for grandeur and sublimity is unsurpassed. Above it tower the lofty peaks of the Matterhorn and Monte Rosa, the latter inferior only in elevation to Mont Blanc, from which it is fifty miles distant. The Matterhorn, called also Mont Cervin, is celebrated for its matchless picturesqueness and beauty. Prof. Forbes describes it as the most striking object he had seen, "an inaccessible obelisk of rock, not one thousand feet lower than Mont Blanc." And Byron, because of its imposing form, calls it "the ideal shape of a mountain."

Other noted peaks are in this vicinity, among which may be mentioned the Görner Gratt; this and also the Görner Glacier are much visited.

*The Gorge of the Trient.* — This singular and remarkable gorge is two miles from Martigny, on the road from that village to the head of Lake Geneva. A pathway has been constructed far into this wonderful defile.

You enter, — the walls of black rock seem ready to close

upon you, frowning precipices and overhanging cliffs darken your path; below is a deep gulf; you look over the parapet, — your pathway, jutting out from the perpendicular rock, has apparently no support; below is only white hissing water, and yawning chasms.

The seclusion, the gloom, the terrifying grandeur, all tend to make a visit to this gorge of intense interest.

*Bex.* — A small town near the head of Lake Geneva, famous for its salt mines and delightful walks, on the high road to Brieg. It is situated at the foot of the mountains, the Dents de Morcle and Midi.

*The Castle of Chillon.* — On the shore of Lake Geneva, a short distance from Montreux, at the eastern extremity of the lake, stands the Castle of Chillon. It has been immortalized by Byron in his "Prisoner of Chillon." His name may be seen with the names of Hunt, Schiller, and many other celebrities, inscribed on one of the dungeon pillars. Bonnivard, Prior of St. Victor, in his endeavors to free Geneva from the tyranny of Charles V, of Savoy, became very obnoxious to that monarch, who had him seized secretly, and conveyed to the Castle of Chillon, where for six long years he was confined in a dungeon. The castle walls ascend perpendicularly from the lake, where the water is said to be a thousand feet in depth.

Those visiting the castle are shown the pillar to which Bonnivard was secured by a chain, four feet long. He could take only three steps, and the stone floor is deeply worn, by the prints of those weary steps. "*Six years* is easily said, but to *live* them, alone, helpless, a man burning with all the fires of manhood, chained to that pillar of stone, and only those three unvarying steps! Seed-time and harvest, summer and winter, and the whole living world went on over his grave. For him no sun, no moon, no star, no business, no friendship, no plans, — nothing! The great millstone of life emptily grinding itself away!"

What a power of vitality there was in Bonnivard, that he did not sink into lethargy, or that his energies did not become petrified, like the stones by which he was surrounded. But they did not; it is said when the victorious Swiss army broke in to liberate him, they cried, —

"Bonnivard, you are free!"

"*Et Genève?*"

Geneva is free also!"

Near by are the relics of the cell of a companion of Bonnivard, who made an ineffectual attempt to liberate him. On the wall are seen sketches of saints, and inscriptions by his hand. This man one day overcame his jailer, locked him in his cell, ran into the hall above, and threw himself from a window into the lake, struck a rock, and was killed instantly.

The judgment hall is also shown to visitors, where prisoners were tried. From this it is but a short distance to the torture-chamber. Here are pulleys, by which limbs were broken; the beam, all scorched with the irons by which feet were burned; the oven where the irons were heated; and the stone on which victims were laid to be strangled after torture. In an adjacent tower is what is called the *oubliette*, — the place where the unfortunate prisoner was made to kneel before the image of the Virgin, while the treacherous floor, falling beneath him, precipitated him into a well forty feet deep, where he was left to die of broken limbs and starvation. Below this is still another pit, now walled up, filled with knives, into which, when the torturers were disposed to be merciful, the victims were dropped.

> "Chillon! thy prison is a holy place,
> And thy sad floor an altar,—for 't was trod
> Until his very steps have left a trace
> Worn, as if thy cold pavement were a sod,
> By Bonnivard! May none those marks efface,
> For they appeal from tyranny to God."

> "Lake Leman lies by Chillon's walls;
> A thousand feet in depth below
> Its massy waters meet and flow;
> Thus much the fathomed-line was sent
> From Chillon's snow-white battlement,
> Which round about the wave enthralls;
> A double dungeon wall and wave
> Have made — and like a living grave.
> Below the surface of the lake
> The dark vault lies wherein we lay,
> We heard it ripple night and day."

> "In Chillon's dungeons deep and old,
> There are seven columns massy and gray,
> Dim with a dull imprison'd ray,
> A sunbeam which hath lost its way,
> And through the crevice and the cleft
> Of the thick wall is fallen and left,
> Creeping o'er the floor so damp,
> Like a marsh's meteor lamp."
> *Byron.*

## CHAPTER XXXVI.

### SWITZERLAND, — THUN, INTERLAKEN, ETC.

THUN, the chief town of Oberland, situated upon the Aar, to the northwest of the Lake of Thun, is one of the most picturesque towns of Switzerland. Its beautiful suburbs make it one of the most agreeable residences in Switzerland; it forms the most frequented approach to the Bernese Oberland, the famous summer resort of tourists. The town itself contains nothing of particular interest within its walls, if we except the picturesque castle of Keyburg, and the old cathedral church.

*Interlaken.* — The situation of Interlaken is one of the best in Switzerland, being between the lakes Thun and Brienz, nearly at the base of the Jungfrau, the most magnificent mountain of the Alps, and having (all within a few miles) two of its most celebrated waterfalls, Giesbach on the Lake Brienz, and Staubbach in the most beautiful valley of Lauterbrunnen, the glorious views from Mürren and the Schienige Platte; the glaciers of Grindelwald, the mountain Faulhorn, and the Wengern Alp, a fine pass, with respect to near and distant views of the Alps.

*Lauterbrunnen.*— Lauterbrunnen, about three hours' walk from Interlaken, is in a valley of waterfalls, chief of which is Staubbach. This is the highest waterfall in Europe, the water descending nearly nine hundred feet. The body of water is not large, which gives it the appearance of spray or dust, long before it reaches the bottom; hence its name. Byron, in his Manfred, compares its appearance to the tail of the white horse on which Death was mounted.

*The Jungfrau.* — The name signifies "Maiden," or "Virgin." It is the eighth in height of European mountains, and considered by some to be the most picturesquely beautiful of all. It reaches an altitude of 13,718 feet, and derives its name either from the pure mantle of snow which covers its crest, or from the fact that until the present century it was deemed inaccessible. In 1811, however, the brothers Meyer, of Aarau, claimed to have climbed it. In 1828 the highest peak was reached by some peasants from Grindelwald, and in 1841, by Prof. Agassiz and Prof. Forbes. Although the thermometer fell to $6\frac{1}{2}°$ below zero, lichens were found on the most exposed heights. The highest peak rises in a sharp point, being not more than two feet broad. The following are the impressions of a well-known authoress, while viewing the Jungfrau. "But now we mount higher, the breezy dells, enamelled with flowers and grass, become fewer, the great black pines take their place. Right before us in the purest white, as a bride adorned for her husband, rises the beautiful Jungfrau, wearing on her forehead the Silver Horn and the Snow Horn. The Silver Horn is a peak, dazzlingly white, of snow, and its crest is now seen in relief against a sky of the deepest blue.

"There is something celestial in these mountains. You might think such a vision as that to be a bright footstool of heaven, from which the next step would be into an unknown world. Above us rise the stern, naked rocks, where only the chamois and the wild goat live. But still, fair as the moon, clear as the sun, looks forth the Jungfrau.

"We turn to look down. That Staubbach, which in the valley seemed to fall from an immense precipice, higher than we could gaze, is now a silver thread far below our feet. The valley of Lauterbrunnen seems as nothing. Only bleak purplish crags, rising all around us, and the silent silver mountains looking over them."

*The Eiger.* — One of the peaks of the Bernese Alps, not far distant from the Jungfrau. "A gigantic ploughshare of rock, set up against the sky, its thin, keen, purple blade edged with glittering frost; for so sharp is its point that only a dazzling line marks the eternal snow on its head."

*The Wetterhorn.* — The name signifies "Peak of Tempests." It is one of the mountains of the Bernese Alps, and lies between the valleys of Hasli and Grindelwald. It reaches an elevation of 12,162 feet, and was first ascended in the year 1845.

*Grindelwald.* — A village of about three thousand inhabitants, situated thirty-five miles southeast of Berne, at the foot of Schreckhorn, in the Bernese Alps. It is three thousand five hundred feet above the sea, and near it are the glaciers of the Upper (Supérieur) and Lower (Inférieur) Grindelwald.

The village is only distant about two hours' ride from

Lauterbrunnen. It is a most lovely, idyllic spot of great resort, not only for tourists, but for excursionists from Interlaken. It is noted for its glaciers and the beauty of its mountains. Avalanches are seen and heard from here with great distinctness. The glaciers of Grindelwald descend into the very midst of grass, flowers, and corn-fields. The lower glacier is the larger, an immense mass of blue ice, shattered into the wildest confusion of peaks and crevices. The upper glacier has the same wild and imposing appearance, the immense crystals and pillars of ice are piled together in every conceivable form. There are large vaults, or caverns, at the foot of both glaciers. Travellers can ascend into them by steps cut in the ice. The roof is arched, and sometimes a hundred feet above the floor of the ice-cave. The scene within is remarkably wild and beautiful. Above your head a roof of clear blue ice from which are pendent brilliantly-white stalactites; below your feet is a black chasm, in which may be seen the flashing foam of a cascade as it leaps away in the darkness. The scene brings to mind the words of Coleridge, which seem forcibly appropriate.

> "And you, ye five wild torrents fiercely glad!
> Who called you forth from night and utter death,
> *From dark and icy caverns called you forth,*
> Down those precipitous, black, jagged rocks,
> Forever shattered, and the same forever?
> Who gave you your invulnerable life,
> Your strength, your speed, your fury, and your joy,
> Unceasing thunder and eternal foam?"

*The Glacier of Rosenlani.* — From Grindelwald to Meyringen, over the Scheideck mountain. Following this route, you come to Rosenlaui, situated by the glacier, from which it takes its name. This is proverbially the bluest of all glaciers, and is noted for the purity of its surface. It is situated in a tremendous ravine, where the mountains seem rent asunder, and it lies between the dark towering cliffs, like a frozen waterfall arrested in its descent.

*The Glacier of the Aar.* — From Meyringen up the valley of the Aar to the Grimsel. This glacier is found at the Grimsel pass, but a few miles distant from the glacier of the Rhone. It is remarkably even in surface; in it chasms and *crevasses* rarely occur. It is eighteen miles long, and two miles broad. From it the river Aar rushes, and plunges down the gorge of Handeck like an avalanche of silver cauliflowers.

*The Glacier of the Rhone*, in which the Rhone river originates, is one of the grandest in Switzerland. It is situated at the Furca pass, about six thousand feet above the sea. It lies southeast from Grindelwald, and east of the Jungfrau, between it and St. Gothard, which latter mountain, although not the highest, is considered the culminating peak of the Alps.

The glacier is thus described: "Opposite gleamed the vast glacier of the Rhone, — the second in size among the five hundred in Switzerland, — its blue slopes and chasms smitten by the sun, and its broad glittering disk looking like a large breastplate on the shaggy, strong breast of the mountain, its icy bosses standing out like burning opals, and shining beautifully iridescent in the glancing morning light. There was the cradle-bed of the Rhone, the drippings from this great ice-field forming the little trickling streamlet which grows by degrees into the broad hurrying current of the Mississippi of Europe."

*The Pass of St. Gothard.* — Through this pass is constructed the only carriage road which is carried over the crest of the mountains; the others generally cross by the beds of torrents. The road is a wonderful piece of engineering, mounting apparently inaccessible heights by a series of terraces or *tourniquets* so that carriages are very easily driven up. The Reuss flows down, and the sound of the water is heard the whole distance, though the river is sometimes so deep below the road that one can scarcely see it. Then the rocky walls rise steep and bare on either side, seeming to rest on the deep foundations of the earth, and to support the sky on their summits.

A recent traveller describes the journey through the pass: " First through green fields and firs, then rugged wastes, and finally torrents, snow and bare rock, up, up, up we went, for three or four hours, the steep road making its way zigzag on terraces. The summit of the pass, a scene of cold, dreary sterility, is a great geographical centre; for within a circuit of ten miles are the sources of four of the great rivers of Europe, the Rhine, the Rhone, the Reuss, the Ticino.

"Now we set off on a race with the Reuss, which bounds five thousand feet down the mountain, to rush into the Lake of Four Cantons, at Fluellen. We crossed the Devil's Bridge, the northern extremity of St. Gothard Pass; and the *Pfaffensprung*, so called from the tradition of a monk having leapt from rock to rock, across the torrent, with a maiden in his arms. That is a fine tradition. One cannot but have a kind of respect for the bold, amorous monk. He deserved the maiden — better than any other monk. The beautiful maiden — for beautiful she could not but be, to inspire a feat so daring — must have been still and passive in the arms of her monastic Hercules, for had she struggled, whilst in mid-air, over that fearful chasm, I fancy the tradition would have been more tragical."

After a tour through this region of southern Switzerland, Bayard Taylor writes: " We had six days among the high Alps, without a cloud in the sky, — at most a gauzy scarf of vapor floating around the snowy cones, to sharpen the sharpness of their profiles on the deep blue of the air. We crept into the ice caverns of the glaciers, and from under their vaults of translucent sapphire looked on the rose-tinted foam of the cataracts; we saw the splendid Wetterhorn hanging over the dark-green fir forests; we listened to the roar of avalanches from the Jungfrau, and watched their snow-dust crumbling a thousand feet down the precipice; we held our heads under the Staubbach, which flung its waters upon us from a height of nine hundred feet; we leaned over the Aar where it plunges down the gorge of Handeck, and noted its wonderful resemblance to boiled cauliflower; and finally at Interlaken we bade adieu to the Bernese Alps."

*Altorf*, made celebrated in history by the brave William Tell. The village contains nothing of importance to the traveller. The spot where Tell shot the apple from off his son's head, is marked by a fountain, surmounted by a statue of father and son.

*Stanz.* — A town of about a thousand inhabitants, situated seven miles southeast of Lucerne, and but a short distance from the lake. It is beautifully located, and contains several buildings and monuments of interest. Its town-hall is of historic celebrity, and contains a series of historic portraits. In its market-place is a statue of Arnold von Winkelried, a native of Stanz; and near the village is a monument to the inhabitants of the town, massacred by the French, in 1798. The place also contains a beautiful and costly church, which well repays a visit.

*Lucerne*, is beautifully situated at the northwest extremity of Lake Lucerne. It contains a population of ten thousand inhabitants. The river Reuss, on which the town is located, is crossed by several curious bridges, some of them hung with paintings. The principal object of attraction at Lucerne, is the monument erected to the Swiss Guards, who fell defending Louis XVI, during the Revolution of 1792. It represents a lion of colossal proportions, eighteen feet high by twenty long, hewn out of sandstone; the lion holds the *fleur-de-lis* in his paws, which he endeavors to protect with his last breath, his life-blood oozing from a wound made by a spear, which still remains in his side. Below are inscribed in red letters, as if charactered in blood, the names of the brave officers of that devoted band. From many a crevice in the rock drip down trickling springs, forming a pellucid basin below, whose dark glossy surface, encircled with trees and shrubs, reflects the image. The design of the monument is by Thorwaldsen, and the whole effect of it has an inexpressible pathos.

*Rigi*, a well-known mountain range, between the lakes of Lucerne and Zug. The view from the summit, six thousand feet above the sea, is unrivalled for extent and grandeur. The horizon has a circumference of three hundred miles, and includes in the prospect thirteen lakes, the whole range of the mountains of the Black Forest of Germany, the peaks of the Jura from Geneva to Basle, and, on the south, the mighty chain of the Bernese Alps, while on the east are the snowy heights of Glarus and Appenzell.

The ascent is easily accomplished; chairs are ready for invalids, horses are also to be had. The new Rigi Railway, however, opened in 1871, affords a more expeditious way of gaining the summit. The railroad extends from Lake Lucerne up to Stafflehöhe, five thousand feet high, and runs, supported by iron pillars, on an incline seven miles long, watched by seven men, — one to each mile. It is a single track of three rails, the middle one fitted for cog-wheels. Only one carriage is provided, with an engine behind to push or retard. Usually tourists go up in the afternoon to see the sunset, and remain over night to see the sunrise.

The following, from the pen of George Calvert, is a graphic description of sunrise from Rigi: —

"The next morning before dawn, with cloaks about us, we were out. From the top of this isolated peak, a mile above the lakes at its base, we saw light breaking slowly over the earth, as yet without form in the darkness. We had almost a glimpse of the creative mystery. We were up in the heavens, and beheld the Spirit of God move upon the face of the earth. We witnessed with magnificent accompaniment the execution of the mandate, — Let there be Light. The peaks in the sun's path rose first out of darkness, to meet the coming dawn, their jagged outline fringed with gray, then with gold. Day had hardly broke about us when, off to the south fifty miles, a rosy tint shone on the snowy heads of the Bernese Alps, the first to answer the salutation of the sun. Soon the summits of all the mountains rose up in the growing day, a world of peaks, the giant offspring of the Earth awakened by the Morning. Below was still twilight. Gradually, light came down the mountains, and rolled away the veil of night from the plain. The sun grew strong enough to send his rays into the valleys, and opened the whole sublime spectacle, — a spectacle affluent in sublimities, that lifted the thoughts out of their habits, and swelled them to untried dimensions. The eye embraced a horizon of three hundred miles circuit; the mind could not embrace the wealth of grandeur and beauty disclosed.

Towards the west, the view ranged over what from such a height seemed an immense plain, bounded by the far, dim Jura: an indistinct landscape, with woods and rivers and lakes; or rather, a hundred landscapes melted into one, that took in several of the largest, most fertile cantons, covering thousands of square miles. Turning around we stood amazed before the stupendous piles of mountain. From five to fifty miles away, in a vast semicircle, rose in wondrous throng their wild bulks, — rugged granite, or glittering snow, towering in silent grandeur, an upper kingdom, their heads in the sky. They looked alive as with a spectral life, brought from the mysterious womb of the earth. You gaze, awed, baffled, in their majestic presence, overwhelmed by the very sublimity of size."

*The Valley of the Linth*, a beautiful and secluded valley of eastern Switzerland. The river Linth flows through it, in a northerly direction, and empties into the little lake, Wallenstadt. Lofty mountains encircle it, and from these snow-capped hills, the cradle of vast glaciers, innumerable torrents pour into the valley, and during the spring and summer often cause fearful devastation. Grain and fruit are cultivated to some extent. One of the most important manufactures is that of the well known *schabzieger*, or " green cheese," made of the milk of cows and goats mixed with churned milk, and flavored and colored with the blue pansy.

In this retired Alpine valley is situated the thriving manufacturing town of —

*Glarus*, — capital of the Canton of the same name. It is built at the foot of Mounts Glärnisch and Schilt, and on the river Linth. The streets are crooked and narrow, the houses are fantastically painted. In midwinter the town is almost continually in the shadow of the mountains, the sun being visible only four hours of the day.

*Appenzell*. — A Canton of Switzerland situated in the northeastern part, and near Lake Constance. Bayard Taylor says of it: "Appenzell is an Alpine island, wholly surrounded by the Canton of St. Gall. It lies all aloft; from whatever side you approach, you must climb to get into it. It is a nearly circular tract, falling from the south towards the north, but lifted at almost every point over the adjoining lands. *Appenzeller Ländli*, as it is called in the endearing diminutive of the Swiss-German tongue, — the Little Land of Appenzell. Its altitude and isolation is an histori-

cal as well as a physical peculiarity. When the abbots of
St. Gall, after having reduced the entire population of what
is now two cantons, to serfdom, became more oppressive as
their power increased, it was the mountain shepherds who,
in the year 1403, struck the first blow for liberty. Once
free, they kept their freedom, and established a rude democ-
racy on the heights. An echo from the meadow of Grütli
reached the wild valleys around the Sentis, and Appenzell,
by the middle of the fifteenth century, became one of the
original states out of which Switzerland has grown. Appenzell is not a table-land, but a region of mountain ridge
and summit, of valley and deep, dark gorge, green as emerald up to the line of snow, and so thickly studded with
dwellings grouped or isolated, that there seems to be one
scattered village as far as the eye can reach. To the south,
over forests of fir, the Sentis lifts his huge towers of rock,
crowned with white, wintry pyramids. The inhabitants of
some portions of Appenzell are employed in the manufacture
of fine muslins and embroideries; there are looms in almost
every house. The population is dense, and there are signs
of wealth on every hand. The dwellings are large, stately,
and even luxurious. In other portions of the Canton the
people are herdsmen, and there is no greener land upon the
earth than these sections. A smooth, even, velvety carpet
of grass is spread upon the landscape, covering every undu-
lation of the surface, except where the rocks have frayed
themselves through. The grass, from centuries of cultivation, has become so rich and nutritious that the inhabitants
can no longer spare even a little patch of ground for a vegetable garden, for the reason that the same produces more
profit in hay. The green comes up to their very doors, and
they grudge even the foot-paths which connect them with
their neighbors. Their vegetables are brought from the
lower valleys. The first mowing had commenced at the

time of my visit, and the farmers were employing irrigation and manure to bring on a second crop. By this means they are enabled to mow the same fields every five or six weeks. The process gives the whole region a smoothness, a mellow splendor of color, such as I never saw elsewhere.

"The people of Inner-Rhoden are the most picturesque of the Appenzellers. The men wear a round skull-cap of leather, sometimes brilliantly embroidered, a jacket of coarse drilling drawn on over the head, and occasionally knee-breeches. Early in May the herdsmen leave their winter homes in the valleys, and go with their cattle to the *Matten*, or lofty mountain pastures. The most intelligent cows, selected as leaders, march in advance, with enormous bells, sometimes a foot in diameter, suspended to their necks by bands of embroidered leather; then follow the others; and the bull, who singularly enough carries the milking-pail, garlanded with flowers, between his horns, brings up the rear. The Alpadores are in their finest Sunday costume, and the sound of yodel-songs — the very voice of Alpine landscapes — echoes from every hill. Such a picture as this under the cloudless blue of a fortunate May-day makes the heart of the Appenzeller light. He goes joyously up to his summer labor, and makes his herb cheese on the heights, while his wife weaves and embroiders muslin in the valley until his return."

*St. Gall*, — capital of the Canton of St. Gall, is situated in an elevated valley eighteen miles southwest of Lake Constance. "It is still surrounded by antique walls flanked with towers; but the ditches have been filled up, and converted into gardens. It is tolerably well built and paved, is well supplied with fountains, contains a cathedral, once an old abbey church, but completely modernized, and an old monastery well worthy of visit. St. Gall is said to owe its existence to a Scotch monk, who, in the early part of the seventh century, travelled over Europe, and finally settled on the banks of the Steinach, then covered with forests in which bears and wolves had their haunts, founded an abbey, and made it the nucleus of civilization to the surrounding districts."

*The Falls of Schaffhausen, or The Falls of the Rhine.* — In the extreme north of Switzerland, about two miles from Schaffhausen, — a town of frescoed and stuccoed houses, ancient castles, and antique halls, — are the famous Falls of the Rhine, considered by many to almost equal the great Falls of Niagara in sublimity, and without doubt the finest in Europe. The Rhine here is three hundred feet wide, and very deep. And although the falls are only eighty feet high, the volume of water is immense, and the sound of the thundering waves, and clouds of foam which are thrown into the air, make the Falls of the Rhine almost matchless. The tremendous roar of the waters can be heard at a distance of six miles. The points of view have been so admirably cut out of the rocks beneath, that the spectator is able to stand quite under the fall, within reach of the spray, without getting wet. The rock which is in the middle of the fall is reached easily in a small boat, and is in no way attended with danger.

*Ragatz.* — A romantic village in the grandest of mountain scenery. It contains about one thousand inhabitants, and is situated thirty miles southeast of St. Gall, at the mouth of a wild gorge, through which the Tamina River rushes in its course to join the Rhine.

*Pfaffers or Pfeffers-bad*, a famous watering-place in the Canton of St. Gall, and two miles and a half from Ragatz. The Baths are situated in one of the most remarkable spots in Switzerland, in a gorge the most savage of all in the whole chain of the Alps. Here the broad splendors and expanded grandeurs of Alpine mountain ranges and snowy pinnacles seem condensed into intenser sublimities. The beholder is astonished, amazed, awed, by the gigantic scenery around him. He is down deep in a fearful abyss; black, savage walls of rock overhang him; beetling precipices close around him; the sky is not visible; he seems buried in darkness; beside him is a foaming torrent leaping past like some wild creature; all is gloomy and terrific.

> "At noonday here
> 'T is twilight, and at sunset blackest night."

*The Via Mala.* — But a few hours' journey from Pfaffers is still another tremendous defile, the Via Mala. A carriage road extends through this awful chasm, and bridges are carried over depths through which the Upper Rhine thunders, without being seen, and where walls of rock tower sixteen hundred feet above the river. These mighty cliffs, grim and savage, rise often perpendicularly on both sides, and in many places are not more than ten yards apart.

Three bridges cross the chasm, — of these the Middle Bridge is the most striking; with a single arch it spans the deep, dark abyss below.

This pass was called by the peasants, Trou Perdu, or the "Lost Gulf," because for a long time it was deemed inaccessible.

It seems wrenched from the heart of the mountain — as if some Titanic battle-axe had cleft the rocks asunder, had first scarred by stern blows the mountain peaks, and then descending, with fiercer, deeper strokes, had riven black, jagged gashes into the very centre of the mountain fastnesses.

## CHAPTER XXXVII.

### ITALY,—THE CHANGE FROM SWISS TO ITALIAN SCENERY.

THE transition from Swiss to Italian scenery is rapid and complete. It is thus described: "Now we are over dark chasms, under beetling precipices, carried across the deafening rush of waters, with the wonders of a sublime pass all exhibited to us as freely as to the winged eagle's gaze. On we go, downward, downward. At last the descent slackens, the stream that had bounded and leapt beside us runs among the huge rocky fragments, the gorge expands to a valley, the fresh foliage of chestnut-trees shadows the road, the valley widens, the mountain is behind us, a broad, even landscape before us, the air is soft, the sun shines hotly on fields where swarthy men are at work,— we are in Italy. It was a passage from sublimity to beauty. We are soon among vines and strong vegetation. This, then, is Italy. How rich and warm it looks! These are the 'twice-glorified-fields of Italy.' This is beautiful, passionate Italy, the land of so much genius, and so much vice, and so much glory. This is the land, for centuries the centre of the world, that in boyhood and in manhood is so mixed in our thoughts, with its double column of shining names familiar to Christendom."

*Cormayeur*, lying at the foot of the south side of Mont Blanc, surrounded as it is by some of the most magnificent mountain scenery of the world, is interesting only as affording superb views of Col du Geant and Mont Blanc, and being a centre from which excursions are made, in the splendid scenery of the Graian Alps.

*Aosta.* — Aosta, on the direct route from the St. Bernard

Pass, is a well-built town, in one of the most beautiful valleys of northern Italy. The town contains a population of about seven thousand. The chief objects of interest are the cathedral, and the remains of a Roman amphitheatre and triumphal arch.

*Lake d'Orta.* — A few miles west of Lake Maggiore lies the beautiful miniature lake, called by the Italians, "Lago di Orta." The clear water, the bright Italian skies, the snow-white houses of the villagers, the handsome cassinos of the gentry, and the rich and varied vegetation of the shores, make the ride around this lake one of the most beautiful and enchanting imaginable. During the ascent of the Sacred Mont, the view of the lake and surrounding scenery forms a variety of pictures unequalled for diversity of mountain, wood, and water. The magnificent snow-clad Alps, clear and distinct, though distant; the chain of Monte de Rosa standing out in bold relief; and the quiet, peaceful lake below, form one of the grandest and at the same time most beautiful scenes of northern Italy.

Immediately opposite the little town of Orta, the Island of St. Jules rises from the bosom of the lake, three hundred and seventy yards in length, and two hundred yards in width. It contains two hundred inhabitants. This fairy isle was the habitation of St. Jules during the fourth century, and during the epoch of the Longobards was considered the most important place in the dukedom; and was once the refuge of king Berengario.

*Mont Cenis.* — Mont Cenis is the general name for the dividing ridge between the valley of the Arc, and the Dora Rinaria valley. This ridge, dividing France from Italy, is now crossed by two routes, the Pass road, built by Napoleon in 1810, the first road passable at all seasons over these Alps, and the Tunnel route, opened in 1871. The grand and beautiful scenery still draws many travellers over the Pass, but to others the Mont Cenis Tunnel is of more interest.

This tunnel, one of the greatest triumphs of man over nature, the work of two nations, was commenced in 1857, and finished September, 1871. It is seven and a half miles long, thirty-three feet wide, and nineteen and a half feet high; and contains a double track. The French mouth is thirty feet lower than the Italian. The work was begun at both ends at once, and when the workmen met, three miles and a half from the light of the sun, and with three thousand four hundred and eighty feet of mountain piled above them, one of the greatest and most difficult questions that has ever puzzled the world, was solved, and the Alps were pierced.

*Genoa.*— Genoa, a celebrated city of north Italy, formerly capital of an independent republic, and now of a province of the kingdom of Sardinia, stands at the head of the gulf of the same name. It is a city of great antiquity, and contains a population of one hundred and twenty thousand.

The land on which Genoa is built, rises to the height of five hundred feet, and gives it a grand and imposing appearance, especially from the sea. In the background rise the Apennines, which, during a portion of the year, are covered with snow. The city has been frequently increased in size, and its walls very much enlarged; some traces of the old Roman walls are yet visible. At the end of the seventeenth century, this magnificent city was bombarded, and almost reduced to ashes, by Louis XIV, whom she had offended by selling ammunition to the pirates, and by building ships for the Spanish navy. The Doge and principal senators were sent to Paris to deprecate the vengeance of Louis.

The old portion of the city is laid out in narrow, crooked streets, but in the newer portion they are wide and handsome. The style of architecture in Genoa is very magnificent; some of the gates of entrance to the palaces are forty feet high; there are not so many remains of ancient splendor as in Venice, but more actual wealth and comfort. The palaces are superior in style to those of Rome; the roofs are frequently flat, and adorned with shrubs, and such trees as orange, lemon, pomegranate, oleander, etc., refreshed by fountains which play constantly, during the heat of summer.

The renowned discoverer of America, Christopher Columbus, was born at Genoa, in 1442. A costly and appropriate monument has been erected to his memory.

*Milan.* — Milan is the principal city of northern Italy, nearly circular in its formation, and is surrounded by a wall which was mostly erected by the Spaniards in 1555. The space between the canal and wall is laid out in gardens and planted with fine trees; the city proper is about eight miles in circumference, and, although like most ancient cities, it is very irregularly laid out, yet it is one of the most interesting in Europe, full of activity and wealth, has some noble thoroughfares, and displays a number of fine buildings, kept in thorough repair.

*The Cathedral of Milan, or the Duomo.* — This magnificent cathedral astonishes and enchants the beholder. Fear not that you are expecting more grandeur and beauty than you will realize, for this is impossible. "Its forest of pinnacles, its wilderness of tracery, delicately marked against the gray sky, the impression sinks deeper and deeper into the mind, wonderful!. wonderful!" What a head was that which gave birth to this conception! How it must have glowed as the great temple sprang forth within it, holding up its pinnacles to heaven, and shedding this sense of grandeur upon earth. The style of architecture, although somewhat varied in consequence of being such a length of time in process of erection, and the different ideas of a large number of artists displayed upon it, is universally admitted to be of exquisite beauty. It is constructed entirely of white marble from the quarries of the Gandoglia, beyond Lake Maggiore.

The history of the erection of this cathedral is the history of centuries. One age made a cupola, another a central tower and a spire, another a façade, another a nave. One inserted a superb row of Gothic windows, and his successor took those away and introduced Roman designs. From 1100 until the present year, there has never been a time when a scaffolding has not been erected upon some part of the building, and the work of repairing or rebuilding going on.

At this day the work is continued with a good deal of spirit by the Austrian government, but it is impossible to believe it will ever be entirely completed. It is calculated, that, in order to be finished, the niches and pinnacles of the exterior will require four thousand five hundred statues, as many as make the entire population of some towns. Of these three thousand are now done: and as you walk slowly around the building, it seems as if you were in a village where the inhabitants had been suddenly changed into stone. Besides these statues, there are a vast number of basso-relievos, with an almost endless variety of story and legend. With our Saviour, the Virgin, saints, and martyrs, we see mixed up heathen mythology. The roof seems a perfect forest of pinnacles and buttresses, while the numberless statues look like the ghosts of men wandering around among them.

In order to appreciate fully the grandeur of the Duomo, every person who can do so should ascend the flight of one hundred and sixty steps to the roof. The most delightful time for enjoying this, the widest and loveliest prospect in Italy, is before sunrise or after sunset, particularly the latter, as an Italian sky at this hour of the day is surpassingly beautiful.

> "All its hues,
> From the rich sunset to the rising star,
> Their musical variety diffuse;
> And now they change; a paler shadow strews
> Its mantle o'er the mountains; parting day
> Dies like the dolphin, whom each pang imbues
> With a new color as it gasps away;
> The last still loveliest, till — 't is gone, and all is gray."

"The ground plan of the cathedral is a Latin cross. As you enter the front portal you are at once struck with the loftiness and the size. One broad nave with four aisles divides the body of the church, and the aisles are separated by four ranges of colossal, clustered pillars, with nine columns between. Fifty-two pillars, each formed by a cluster of eight shafts, support the arches upon which the roof rests. The pillars are eighty feet high, with a diameter for the shaft of eight feet; so, if one will take the trouble to look at something of similar height, he may obtain some idea of a building where fifty-two of such support the roof. The vaulting of the roof springs at once from the pillars, so there is no arch, gallery, or any other thing to bewilder the eye as it takes in the immense height above. As there are no chapels to break the surface, the whole impression is received at once; and in this respect it differs from any other cathedral in Europe. The beautiful capitals of the pillars of the nave and choir are formed by a wreath of foliage mixed with figures of children and animals; above is a circle of eight niches corresponding to the distance between the shafts of the clustering column, and each niche is adorned with a statue covered with a canopy. Each pillar, however, has a different design; and the only question the visitor has, which is the most beautiful. The roof itself is painted in very elaborate fret-work, the work done by modern artists, but the design one which was made soon after the first building of the Duomo."

Directly in front of the centre doorway are two large, solid, granite columns, made from a single stone. These were given by San Carlo, a saint to whom the cathedral, as well as Milan, owes much. These are the largest shafts in Italy, and were, until recently, the largest in Europe; now they have some larger at St. Petersburg, in the church of St. Ivan.

The pavement, composed of red, blue, and white mosaics, is arranged most tastefully in different figures. The three immense windows behind the high altar are very imposing, and the dark bronzes of the pulpit increase the brilliancy of the background.

Suspended from the vaulting over the altar, is a casket containing one of the nails of the cross, which is always exposed at the annual feast of the " Invention (finding) of the Holy Cross," at which time it is also carried through the streets with all due solemnity, and followed by a procession. Among the other relics belonging to the cathedral, is the towel with which Christ washed the feet of the disciples, part of the purple robe which he wore, and some of the thorns from his crown; a stone from the Holy Sepulchre; the rod of Moses; teeth which belonged to Daniel, Abraham, John, and Elisha, etc.,— though, we imagine, if all the pieces of the "true cross" were collected, enough for several crosses would result, and if the Saints and Prophets once possessed all the teeth, nails, fingers, etc., attributed to them, they were most liberally supplied.

This cathedral is certainly the finest Gothic edifice in Italy, and, as a church, ranks next to St. Peter's. No person can fail to be impressed with its sublimity; and the idea suggests itself to one beholding it, that, although Nature in her works was so perfectly faultless and impressive, man, in his efforts to compete with her, was brought into very close alliance.

*Venice.* — The city of Venice, formerly called the "Queen of the Adriatic," is unrivalled as to beauty and situation. It stands on some islands in a bay near the Gulf of Venice. These islands lie within a line of long, narrow islands, running north and south, seventy-two in number, and inclose the lagoon or shallow which surrounds the city and separates it from the main-land.

Dr. Prime, in his interesting work, "Around the World," gives his impression of Venice in the following words: —

There are only two cities in the world that I have found just what I expected. When I first caught sight of Jerusalem in crossing the hills of Judea, and when I looked down upon it from the Mount of Olives, it was the Jerusalem of my thoughts; I had been there often before. When I reached the railway terminus on the lagoon at Venice, and took a gondola instead of an omnibus, and was rowed by moonlight through one street after another, and at length landed at the door of the hotel, into which I stepped from the gondola; and when, on the following days, I floated through the liquid streets, into and along the Grand Canal, past the old and now deserted palaces, beneath the Rialto, and under the Bridge of Sighs; and as I stood on the grand square of San Marco, and entered the Doge's Palace, and walked through its great historic halls, and descended into its subterranean and subaqueous dungeons, I found myself just where I had been a hundred times. It was not the realization of a dream, — it was the dream prolonged; everything was as I had fancied it. Venice is a city so peculiar, so unlike all other cities we have ever known, that we do not base our conceptions of it upon what we have seen of other places, but upon actual descriptions.

In this singular city, travellers must needs become amphibious. They sleep in houses, not upon the land, but anchored in the sea. If they step into the street, they step upon the water. If they wish to make a call upon a friend, they order, not a carriage, but a gondola. There is not a carriage in all Venice, and only one horse, which is kept on an adjacent island as a curiosity. He would have been, in truth, *rara avis*, if he had not been a horse. Over the streets, which are water, a stillness reigns throughout the year, which to many becomes oppressive, absolutely painful; but to me it is a positive luxury. Here the noise and bustle of life are suspended, the days float along as still as the flight of a bird in the air, or as smoothly as one of the gondolas in which we glide over the surface of the water.

Thoroughly to enjoy Venice, one must come at the right season, and have plenty of time. In midwinter the air is too cool to enter into the spirit of the place. In midsummer, and all through the warm season, the canals are offensive, reminding one of the streets of Cologne; and if one has been to China, they will slightly remind him of the cities of the Celestial Empire. The month of May, when the air is balmy, and just warm enough to enjoy the open air without exercise (for exercise here is almost out of the question), is perhaps the best time of the year. And then to take a gondola in front of the Doge's Palace, and allow your gondolier to row you gently into the Grand Canal, and through its whole extent, and give you — as he will if you secure an intelligent gondolier — the name and the story of each one of the old marble palaces as you glide by it, or pause to read up its history; to enter these ancient halls of the Venetian princes, as you may by a suitable introduction; to bring up the days of the Old Republic, when these water streets were resplendent with naval displays, with gorgeous regattas, and with the magnificence of Oriental sights — all this bewilders and delights the imagination, until one can scarcely do anything but give way to the intoxicating influence of the scenes and associations by which he is surrounded. Even visiting and studying the works of art which abound in Venice seem almost too much like servile labor for the atmosphere of the place. Venice itself is a work of art, which each one will most delight to contemplate.

## CHAPTER XXXVIII.

### ITALY, — ROME.

> "Thou art in Rome! the city where the Gauls,
> Entering at sunrise through her open gates,
> And through her streets silent and desolate,
> Marching to slay, thought they saw gods, not men;
> The city that by temperance, fortitude,
> And love of glory, towered above the clouds,
> Then fell; but falling kept the highest seat,
> And in her loneliness, her pomp of wo,
> Where now she dwells, withdrawn into the wild,
> Still o'er the mind maintains from age to age
> Her empire undiminished.
>
>       There as though
> Grandeur attracted grandeur, are beheld
> All things that strike, ennoble — from the depths
> Of Egypt, from the classic fields of Greece,
> Her groves, her temples — all things that inspire
> Wonder, delight. Who would not say the forms
> Most perfect, most divine, had, by consent,
> Flocked thither to abide eternally
> Within those silent chambers where they dwell
> In happy intercourse?"

BY means of the stereoscope we are permitted to visit this great city, to stand face to face with its hoary ruins, to behold the spots once trod by emperors, to enter its temples reared to the true God, to stand beneath the crumbling walls of heathen shrines, to wander among the mouldering arches of the Coliseum, and to view from St. Peter's dome the world-renowned Campagna, extending from the Apennines to the sea.

*St. Peter's.* — At the head of the churches of Rome stands the Cathedral of St. Peter, which is not only the largest and most beautiful church that has ever been erected, but is without exception the noblest work of architecture ever produced by man. It stands on the right bank of the Tiber, between the Janiculum and the Vatican. Its approach is through a magnificent piazza, the buildings along which are concealed by a superb colonnade, forming two semicircular porticos, consisting of two hundred and eighty-four columns, with an entablature on which stand one hundred and ninety-two statues of saints, each eleven feet in height. The main body of the building consists of a Greek cross, with a dome of gigantic dimensions, rising from its centre and borne up by four colossal piers. The dome, projected by Michael Angelo, may be regarded as the boldest and most astonishing effort of human architecture. The extreme lengths within the walls are six hundred and seven feet in the central body, and four hundred and forty-five feet in the transepts; the height from the pavement to the cross, is four hundred and fifty-eight feet. St. Peter's covers the area of five acres, and its cost is estimated from sixty to eighty millions of dollars. The edifice was begun under Julius II, in 1506, and was completed at the close of the seventeenth century, having extended over the reigns of no less than forty-three popes. It was planned and commenced by Bramante, but altered and carried on by Michael Angelo, and many other artists.

*Interior of St. Peter's.* — Whatever preparation one may suppose themselves to have received, from the descriptions which they have read, and from the extensive and splendid architecture by which it is surrounded, the first feeling, as the curtain falls behind you and you stand within the church, is one of grandeur and awe, unlike that received from any other work of art. A recent traveller has said : " Recalling it months after, I could compare it with nothing but the emotion with which I first stood before Niagara Falls. Vastness, sublimity, a grandeur not of man, seemed breathed from its solemn walls, and we stood, not wishing to advance, not daring to speak, lest we should break the spell.

"This *is* St. Peter's !" said some one at last, and we slowly advanced, while we repeated to ourselves these lines,—

> " But thou of temples old or altars new,
> Standest alone — with nothing like to thee —
> Worthiest of God, the holy and the true.
> Since Zion's desolation, when that He
> Forsook his former city, what could be
> Of earthly structures in his honor piled,
> Of a sublimer aspect? Majesty,
> Power, glory, strength, and beauty, all are aisled
> In this eternal ark of worship undefiled.
>
> " Enter: its grandeur overwhelms thee not;
> And why? it is not lessened, but thy mind,
> Expanded by the genius of the spot,
> Has grown colossal, and can only find
> A fit abode wherein appear enshrined ·
> Thy hopes of immortality; and thou
> Shalt one day, if found worthy, so defined,
> See thy God face to face as thou dost now
> His Holy of Holies; nor be blasted by his brow."

" The measurements of the interior of St. Peter's are all accurately given in English feet; but the impression is so valueless conveyed by them, that we hesitate to give them. Size is by no means one of your first thoughts; the richness and perfect proportion of the whole directs you entirely from feet and inches. There is a broad, open space, running from the entrance to the Baldachino, or canopy over the high altar, which stands directly under the dome. Five massive piers, supporting four arches, separate this open space or nave from the side aisles. Each pier is faced by two Corinthian pillars of stucco, having in two niches, which are made between them, colossal statues of the saints, and the founders of different religious orders. Corresponding with these great arches, are side aisles, and from these aisles open a variety of chapels, almost all of which are worthy of special notice.

"We proceeded directly up the nave, looking before and behind us, now catching a view of a piece of statuary at our right, and now a large picture at our left, until we reached the spot towards which, we noticed, all on entering first bent their steps. Here we found a seated bronze figure, about the size of life, with the right foot extended, but the position otherwise that of one quite at his ease. The figure represented a man past middle life, with very little expression, excepting that which necessarily belongs to bronze; a high, bald forehead; unmarked features, which received no aid from plain drapery. A rude, coarse thing,— could it be the far-famed statue of St. Peter? We waited to see a party of those well-dressed Italians approach it, determined to watch the salutation. They first rubbed the handkerchief slightly over the toe, as if to remove the last breath left upon it, then kissed it, then pressed their foreheads against it, again kissed it, again pressed their foreheads, and passed on to one of the boxes designed for confessional. It is said that the toe has been once renewed, having been fairly *kissed off*. However this may be, it had now diminished in length an inch, if not more, and presented a worn, shiny appearance, very unlike that of any other part. We turned away from it with disgust; and only a few steps from us was the high altar, with numberless lamps in full blaze before it. This altar is immediately over the—

*Grave of St. Peter*, and under the dome. Of course it is a fitting spot to receive the costliest finish. The Baldachino is made of solid bronze, supported by four spiral columns of the composite order, and covered with the richest ornaments, many of which are of gilt. It is ninety-nine and a half feet high to the summit of the cross, and cost one hundred thousand dollars. This for the canopy alone. The altar itself exceeds it in magnificence, and is esteemed too sacred to be used only on solemn ceremonies.

" Above this sacred spot rises the dome, at once the pride and glory of the church. As you stand by the altar you look up, up, until the mosaics and ornaments are lost in the distance, and you can only discern that you have not, as yet, found the roof that covers you. Michael Angelo, in this dome, was able to do, what so few are in this world, make good his boast. He did, indeed, hang a dome in the air, which exceeded by two feet, in the measurement of its outer walls, the diameter of the Pantheon. It rises from four colossal piers, each one having two niches, one above the other, facing towards the high altar. In these lower niches are statues sixteen feet high. They are of four saints, — St. Veronica, St. Helena, St. Longinus, and St. Andrew."

*The Papal Benediction.* — The pronouncing the benediction from the balcony in front of St. Peter's, is another ceremony which hallows to the Catholics their great church.

Dressed in his gorgeous robes, the Pope comes slowly out upon the balcony, and the immense concourse in the square before sway to and fro, at first like the waves of the sea. But it is all perfect stillness; not a sound betokens that there is more life there than in the statues, which, like the Pope, look down still and cold upon them. At length he, in a slow, solemn voice, repeats the benediction.

At the last clause, the Pope rises and makes the sign of

the cross in front and on each side over the people, then he stretches his arms out to heaven, and then folds them over his breast. Then the cardinal deacon reads in Latin and Italian the bulls of plenary indulgence. After he has finished them he throws them among the people, the military bands strike up, the bells of St. Peter's and the artillery of St. Angelo join in the chorus; and amid these sounds the Pope retires.

*The Vatican.* — This palace is far superior to any in the world, in history being the most ancient and decidedly the most celebrated of all the papal palaces, composed of a mass of buildings erected by many different popes, covering a space 1,200 feet in length and 1,000 in breadth, with over four thousand apartments. It is the winter residence of the Pope, and is contiguous to St. Peter's. It is distinguished for its magnificent collection of ancient and modern art. The library of the Vatican comprises upward of 80,000 printed books and about 35,000 manuscripts. The collection of manuscripts exceeds any other in Europe; among them are the celebrated Codex Vaticanus, or Bible, of the end of the fourth century, in Greek, and Cicero *de Republicâ*, considered the oldest Latin MS. in existence.

*The Gardens of the Vatican.* — The gardens of the Vatican, carefully laid out and adorned with statuary and shrubbery, afford a fine view of the dome of St. Peter's, and are of themselves of considerable interest.

*The Church of St. Agnes.*— This church is so named from being erected on the spot where St. Agnes was publicly exposed, after her torture. It is one of the purest and most elegant specimens of the Greek cross.

*The Roman Forum.* — The piece of ground between the Capitoline and Palatine Hills, irregular in its outline, and comprising some seventy or eighty thousand square feet in extent, bore the proud name of "Forum Romanum," — the Forum of Rome. No spot on earth is more imposing, for it is overshadowed with the power and majesty of the Roman people. Here was laid the foundation of that wonderful political system, which lasted so long and worked so well; which was strong enough to hold the whole world in its grasp, and wise enough to exercise a controlling influence over the legislation and jurisprudence of the civilized world down to the present day. It is a place illustrated equally by the wisdom of great statesmen and the eloquence of great orators.

No one, unless forewarned by books and engravings, can have any conception of the change and desolation which have come over this illustrious spot. An unsightly piece of ground, disfeatured with filth and neglect, with a few ruins scattered over it, and two formal rows of trees running through it, is all that we see with the eye of the body. A few peasants wrapped in their mud-colored cloaks, a donkey or two, a yoke of the fine gray oxen of Italy, or perhaps a solitary, wild-eyed buffalo, are the only living forms in a scene once peopled with wisdom, valor, and eloquence. Nothing gives a stronger impression of the shattering blows which have fallen upon the Eternal City, than the present condition of the Forum.

In the Forum every foot of ground has been the field of antiquarian controversy. Each ruin has changed its names two or three times. The most prominent and important of the ruins are those of the Temples to Vespasian, Saturn, and Concord at the base of the Capitol, the Arch of Severus near them, and the Arch of Titus at the other extremity of the Forum, and also the Temple of Minerva, marked by those beautiful Corinthian columns, and a solitary column erected to the Emperor Phocas.

## The Coliseum. —

> "Arches on arches! as it were that Rome,
>   Collecting the chief trophies of her line,
>   Would build up all her triumphs in one dome,
>   Her Coliseum stands; the moonbeams shine,
>   As 't were its natural torches, for divine
>   Should be the light which streams here, to illume
>   This long-explored but still exhaustless mine
>   Of contemplation: and the azure gloom
> Of an Italian night, where the deep skies assume
>
> "Hues which have words, and speak to ye of heaven,
>   Floats o'er this vast and wondrous monument,
>   And shadows forth its glory. There is given
>   Unto the things of earth, which Time hath bent,
>   A spirit's feeling; and where he hath leant
>   His hand, but broke his scythe, there is a power
>   And magic in the ruin'd battlement,
>   For which the palace of the present hour
> Must yield its pomp, and wait till ages are its dower."
>
> *Byron.*

In the open space between the Esquiline and Palatine Hills are to be seen the ruins of the Coliseum, or Flavian Amphitheatre. This is the most familiar of all the ancient Roman monuments; it is by far the largest amphitheatre known in the world, and is unquestionably the most august ruin. This gigantic edifice, the boast of Rome and of the world, is in form an ellipse, and covers an area of about five and a half acres. The external elevation consisted of four stories, — each of the three lower stories having eighty arches supported by half columns, Doric in the first range, Ionic in the second, and Corinthian in the third. The wall of the fourth story was faced with Corinthian pilasters, and lighted by forty rectangular windows. The space surrounding the central arena within the walls, was occupied with sloping galleries, rising one above another, resting on a huge mass of arches, and ascending towards the summit of the external wall. One hundred and sixty staircases led to the galleries, and an immense movable awning covered the whole. It is said to have had seats for eighty-seven thousand spectators, and standing room for twenty thousand more.

The amphitheatre was begun by Vespasian, in A. D. 72, on the seat of the Stagnum Neronis, and dedicated by Titus in his eighth consulate, A. D. 80, ten years after the destruction of Jerusalem; but only completed by Domitian as high as the third division of the seats, and the portion above this by Titus and his successor. The church tradition tells us that it was designed by Gaudentius, a Christian architect and martyr, and that many thousand Jews were employed in its construction. It received successive additions from the later emperors, and was altered and repaired at various times until the beginning of the sixth century.

Within the area of the Coliseum, gladiators, martyrs, slaves, and wild beasts combated during the Roman festivals; and here the blood of both men and animals flowed in torrents to furnish amusement to the degenerate Romans. At the dedication of the building by Titus, five thousand wild beasts were slaughtered in the arena, and the games in honor of the event lasted nearly one hundred days. The gladiatorial combats were abolished by Honorius. A show of wild beasts which took place in the reign of Theodoric, and a bull-fight at the expense of the Roman nobles in 1332, are the last exhibitions of which history has left us any record. During the persecutions of the Christians, the amphitheatre was the scene of fearful barbarities. In the reign of Trajan, St. Ignatius was brought from Antioch purposely to be devoured by wild beasts in the Coliseum; and the traditions of the church are filled with the names of the martyrs who perished in its arena.

The building was originally called the Flavian Amphithe

atre, in honor of the family name of the empress by whom it was commenced, continued, and completed; and the first mention of the name "Coliseum"—from its colossal dimensions—occurs in fragments of the Venerable Bede, who records the famous prophecy of the Anglo-Saxon pilgrims:—

> "While stands the Coliseum, Rome shall stand;
> When falls the Coliseum, Rome shall fall;
> And when Rome falls, the world."

This prophecy is generally regarded as a proof that the amphitheatre was tolerably perfect in the eighth century. Nearly all authorities agree that two thirds of the original building have entirely disappeared. After the ruin had been converted into a fortress, in the Middle Ages, it supplied the Roman princes, for nearly two hundred years, with building materials for their palaces. The palaces of St. Mark, the Farnese, and the Barberini, were in great part built from its ruins. But Benedict XIV put a stop to its destruction, by consecrating the whole to the martyrs whose blood had been spilled there. In the middle of the once bloody arena stands a crucifix, and around this, at equal distances, fourteen altars consecrated to different saints are erected on the dens once occupied by wild beasts.

The material of which the Coliseum is built, is exactly fitted to the purposes of a great ruin. It is a travertine, of a rich, dark, warm color, deepened and mellowed by time. There is nothing glaring, harsh, or abrupt in the harmony of tints. The blue sky above, and the green earth beneath, are in unison with a tone of coloring not unlike the brown of one of our own early winter landscapes. The travertine is also of a coarse grain and porous texture, not splintering into points and edges, but gradually corroding by natural decay. Stone of such textures everywhere opens laps and nooks for the reception and formation of soil. Every grain of dust that is borne through the air by the lazy breeze of summer, instead of sliding from a glassy surface, is held where it falls. The rocks themselves crumble and decompose, and thus turn into a fertile mould. Thus, the Coliseum is throughout crowned and draped with a covering of earth, in many places of considerable depth. Trailing plants clasp the stones with arms of verdure; wild flowers bloom in their seasons, and long grass nods and waves on the airy battlements. Life has everywhere sprouted from the trunk of death. Insects hum and sport in the sunshine; the burnished lizard darts like a tongue of green flame along the walls, and birds make the hollow quarry overflow with their songs. There is something beautiful and impressive in the contrast between luxuriant life, and the rigid skeleton upon which it rests. Nature seems to have been busy in binding up with gentle hand the wounds and bruises of time. She has covered the rents and chasms of decay with that drapery which the touch of every spring renews. She has peopled the solitude with forms, and the silence with voices. She has clothed the nakedness of desolation, and crowned the majesty of ruin. She has softened the stern aspect of the scene with the hues of undying youth, and brightened the shadows of dead centuries with the living light of vines and flowers.

As a matter of course everybody goes to see the Coliseum by moonlight. The great charm of the ruin under this condition is, that the imagination is substituted for sight, and the mind for the eye. The essential character of moonlight is hard, rather than soft. The line between light and shadow is very sharply defined, and there is no gradation of color. Blocks and walls of silver are bordered by, and spring out of, chasms of blackness. But moonlight shrouds the Coliseum in mystery. It opens deep vaults of gloom, where the eye meets only an ebon wall, but upon which the fancy paints innumerable pictures in solemn, splendid, and tragic colors. Shadowy forms of emperor and lictor, and vestal virgin, and gladiator and martyr, come out of the darkness, and pass before us, in long and silent procession. The breezes which blow through the broken arches are changed into voices, and recall the shouts and cries of a vast audience. By day, the Coliseum is an impressive fact; by night, it is a stately vision. By day, it is a lifeless form; by night, a vital thought.

"I do remember me that in my youth,
When I was wandering, upon such a night
I stood within the Coliseum's walls
Midst the chief relics of almighty Rome;
The trees which grew along the broken arches
Waved dark in the blue midnight, and the stars
Shone through the rents of ruin. From afar
The watch-dog bay'd, beyond the Tiber; and
More near, from out the Cæsar's palace came
The owl's long cry, and, interruptedly,
Of distant sentinels the fitful song
Began and died upon the gentle wind.

"Some cypresses beyond the time-worn breach
Appear'd to skirt the horizon, yet they stood
Within a bowshot where the Cæsars dwelt,
And dwell the tuneless birds of night, amid
A grove which springs through levell'd battlements,
And twines its roots with the imperial hearths;
Ivy usurps the laurel's place of growth;
But the gladiator's bloody circus stands,
A noble wreck in ruinous perfection,
While Cæsar's chambers and the Augustan halls
Grovel in earth in indistinct decay.

"And thou didst shine, thou rolling moon, upon
All this, and cast a wide and tender light,
Which softened down the hoar austerity
Of rugged desolation, and fill'd up,
As 't were anew, the gaps of centuries;
Leaving that beautiful that still was so,
And making that which was not, till the place
Became religion, and the heart ran o'er
With silent worship of the great of old,—
The dead but sceptred sovereigns, who still rule
Our spirits from their urns." *Byron.*

*Naples.* —

> This region surely is not of the earth.
> Was it not dropped from heaven? Not a grove,
> Citron, or pine, or cedar; not a grot,
> Sea-worn and mantled with the gadding vine,
> But breathes enchantment. Not a cliff but flings
> On the clear wave some image of delight,
> Some cabin-roof glowing with crimson flowers,
> Some ruined temple or fallen monument,
> To muse on as the bark is gliding by.

The beauty of Naples and its environs can as little be described as exaggerated. The extreme points of the two projecting arms which enclose the bay on the northwest and southeast, are about twenty miles distant from each other in a right line. They are similar in their shape and character, but by no means identical. The southern promontory stretches farther out to sea; but the balance is restored by the Island of Ischia on the north, which is larger and more distant from the land than its southern sister, Capri. The curve of the gulf lying between them is not regular, but the line of the coast makes nearly a right angle at Naples and also at Castellamare: the intervening space being nearly straight. Vesuvius occupies a point about half-way between the projecting points. The whole space is crowded with human life, and comprises within itself nearly every form of beauty into which earth and water can be moulded. On one side, from a liquid plain of the most dazzling blue, a range of mountains, the peaks of which are for many months covered with snow, rise in the air. Forests of oak and chestnut encircle them midway. Between them and the sea there is hardly a terrace of level land, and the cliffs that line that tideless shore are often crowned and draped with luxuriant vegetation. In another direction the primitive features are less grand; but the action of volcanic agencies has given great variety of surface within a small compass. Numberless points are crowned with villas, monasteries, and houses, linked together by a glowing succession of orange groves, vineyards, orchards, and gardens. Over all the unrivalled scene, Vesuvius towers and reigns; forming the point of convergence in which all the lines of beauty and grandeur meet. One never sees a mountain that so impresses the mind as this. Although not quite four thousand feet high, it produces the effect of a much greater elevation, because its whole bulk, from the level of the sea to its summit, is seen at a glance. Besides the peculiar interest which belongs to it as a volcano, it is remarkable for its flowing and graceful outline, and the symmetrical regularity of its shape. A painter could nowhere find a better model from which to draw an ideal mountain. But when to this mere lineal beauty we add the mysterious and awful power of which its smoke and fire are symbols, and those fearful energies of destruction which the imagination magnifies at will, it becomes a feature in the landscape, which, considering its position and proximities, has no parallel on the globe. It would seem as if volcanic agency were necessary to crown the earth with its most impressive loveliness and grandeur, just as the human face never reveals all its beauty till passion burns in the eye and trembles on the lip. The action of fire alone heaves up those sheer walls and notched battlements of rock, and sets the mountain lake in those deep and wooded sockets by which the most impressive landscapes are formed, and through which great effects are produced without the aid of great space. Water shapes and smooths the earth into something like a Grecian regularity of outline, but fire sharpens and points it after Gothic types.

The whole coast from Pozzuoli to Sorrento repeats and renews the same curves and waves of beauty. The land is rounded, scooped, and hollowed; holding out jutting promontories and projections, like arms of invitation. No rigid lines of defence are thrown up; no castellated masses of granite stand along the coast like line-of-battle ships drawn up for an engagement; nowhere is an expression of defiance stamped upon the scene. Along the rocky and iron-bound shores of New England, the junction of the sea and land is like the meeting of enemies under a flag of truce; even the sunshine and calm speak of conflicts past and to come. Upon the practical and unromantic coast of England, their meeting is like that of men of business who have come together to talk over a bargain. But in the Bay of Naples, the meeting of the sea and the land is like the embrace of long-parted lovers. The earth is a beautiful and impassioned Hero, and the waves lie on her bosom like the dripping locks of Leander.

Naples itself is only the core and nucleus of this fertile and populous shore, which everywhere swarms with life, and glitters with human habitations. It is principally in respect to situation that this city surpasses most others. The streets are straight, and paved with square blocks of lava laid in mortar, and said to resemble the old Roman roads. Owing to the mildness of the climate, a great deal of business is carried on in the open streets, and while walking along, one is accosted by numerous different traders. There is but little real magnificence in architecture; and, though very many of the buildings are erected on a very grand scale, they are generally overloaded with ornament. The houses resemble those of Paris, except that they are on a larger scale. The whole of the ground-floor of these tenement buildings is occupied by store-keepers, while the upper portion is the dwelling of numerous families. The society of Naples is anything but moral. Goldsmith's picture of Italian manners is more applicable here than in any other portion of Italy : —

"But small the bliss that sense alone bestows,
And sensual bliss is all the nation knows.
In florid beauty groves and fields appear,
Man seems the only growth that dwindles here.
Contrasted faults through all his manners reign;
Though poor, luxurious; though submissive, vain;
Though grave, yet trifling; zealous, yet untrue;
And, even in penance, planning sins anew."

*Sicily.* — Sicily is the largest, finest, most fruitful, and most celebrated island in the Mediterranean. Its greatest length is about one hundred and eighty miles, by upward of one hundred in its widest limits. It is separated from the southern extremity of Italy by the narrow Strait of Messina, only two miles across. The shape of the island is triangular, and it gradually narrows from its eastern shores toward its westernmost limit. A range of mountains extends through the length of Sicily in the neighborhood of the northern coast. All the lower portion of these mountains, which average six thousand feet in height, is covered with dense and beautiful vegetation. Higher up, the woody region encircles the mountains, and the upper part is naked, and blackened by the fires of numerous eruptions. The valleys of Sicily are thickly inhabited, and covered with olives, vines, corn, fruit-trees, and aromatic herbs. Sicily is well watered by numerous small rivers, and its harbors are considerable and good. Near the eastern side of the island rises the gigantic cone of Ætna, called by the Sicilians, Mount Gibello. Its base is eighty miles in circumference, and it rises to the stupendous height of ten thousand eight hundred and seventy-two feet above the level of the Mediterranean. Its base is highly cultivated; higher up is the woody district, and above the forest there is a waste of black lava. The crater is about two miles in circumference; in addition to which, there are numerous small cones, where the fire contained within has burst through its shattered sides.

*Palermo.*— This city, which is regularly built, is situated on the southwest side of an extensive bay, in a wide plain, bounded by Alpine mountains, which, from its luxuriance, has been termed the "Golden Shell." Everywhere the eye can rest one sees orchards in bloom, fields of cactuses glistening in the sun, gardens of orange-trees, fields watered by small canals that fertilize the soil of Palermo.

Palermo has a great number of convents and churches. There are said to be about seventy-five of the former. The churches, especially those which line the Toledo, are almost all magnificent; immense amounts have been lavished in splendid marbles and costly alabasters. Many of them are absolutely covered with mosaics; the floors, chapels, and columns, of inlaid marble; and the altars and tabernacles of precious stones, lapis lazuli, verd-antique, malachite, and jasper.

This city, the ancient capital Panormus, contains a population of one hundred and seventy-five thousand.

## CHAPTER XXXIX.

### ITALY, — HERCULANEUM AND POMPEII.

"MANY a calamity has befallen the world ere now, yet none like this, replete with instruction and delight for remote generations."— *Goethe.*

*View of Naples and Mount Vesuvius.* — Near the modern city of Naples, at the foot of Mount Vesuvius, once stood the ancient cities of Pompeii and Herculaneum. While the former was considerably removed from the volcano, the latter was seated immediately at the base of the mountain, on a promontory projecting into the bay.

Vesuvius was not considered dangerous by the ancient

occupants of the soil, as no eruption had ever been known to take place. Strabo noticed the igneous character of its rocks, but the whole district being covered with vines and plantations, undisturbed since the memory of man, he thence assumed the fires to be extinct, for want of fuel. Even the sides of the mountain were overgrown with trees, and the summit alone continued barren and rough. The inhabitants of the neighborhood were probably less inclined to consider the possibility of danger to themselves, from the existence of two active volcanoes not far from them, which seemed to serve as a vent for all subterranean commotions, — the one, Mount Ætna; the other, Mount Epopeus, in the island now called Ischia. Ætna, the majestic, snowy mountain of Sicily, more than three times the height of Vesuvius, has been known, from the earliest times, as an active volcano.

The convulsions of nature have changed the outline of the mountain, but the varied charms of the beautiful coast remain in undiminished attraction. Deep shades and crystal streamlets, sunny banks and refreshing groves, display the natural loveliness of a locality favored with the most luxuriant vegetation and the finest climate in the world. These enable us fully to comprehend the pains and trouble bestowed by the ancient Romans in building villas and marine residences in so charming a situation. Thus, in the earliest times of the empire, the more wealthy and luxurious Romans established what we moderns should denominate watering-places, for fashionable resort, on the coast, — Baiæ, Dicæarchia, afterwards Puteoli, Cumæ, Neapolis, and Herculaneum; but the warm springs of the first two rendered them the most favorite resorts.

Pompeii was somewhat removed from these enchanting scenes, being on the other side of the bay of Naples, and the situation was not so pleasant as that of its fellow-sufferer, Herculaneum. This city stood on a promontory, open, as

Strabo says, to the south wind, which made it especially healthy. In fact, the art and style of everything found at Herculaneum show it to have been the resort of a superior class of people. Pompeii is supposed to have stood on the banks of the river Sarnus. The town itself was raised upon a considerable eminence, so as to be protected, in a great measure, from the floods that at certain times of the year devastated the surrounding plain.

The peace and tranquillity of these beautiful regions were first disturbed by natural convulsions, in the year 63, A. D. A violent earthquake on the 16th February threw down many parts of Pompeii, and seriously injured Herculaneum; six hundred sheep were swallowed up at once, statues were split, and many persons became insane. From this period the Pompeians were disturbed by frequent shocks of earthquake; between the first symptoms in 63, and the dreadful catastrophe which involved their destruction, evidences still exist of the persevering endeavors of the inhabitants at restoration and repair. Many mosaics have been found, which display traces of a very different order of workmanship, in the repair of damage caused by the earthquake, from that employed in their original construction.

In the reign of the emperor Titus, in the year 79, the celebrated eruption of Vesuvius broke out, suddenly ejecting dense clouds of ashes and pumice-stones, beneath which Herculaneum, Pompeii, and Stabiæ were completely buried. Awful as such a phenomenon must at all times appear, the event was still more appalling to the inhabitants, as they were unable, in the confusion of the moment, to comprehend the source whence these horrors proceeded. An eye-witness has fortunately left a detailed account of the event, in two letters which are still preserved. We insert the greater part of them, as best exhibiting the realities of the scene, and the excitement of the unfortunate sufferers.

*Pliny's Letter to Tacitus.*—" Your request that I would send you an account of my uncle's death, in order to transmit a more exact relation of it to posterity, deserves my acknowledgments. . . . He perished by a misfortune which involved at the same time a most beautiful country in ruin. . . ."

" He was at that time with the fleet under his command at Misenum. On the 24th of August, about one in the afternoon, my mother desired him to observe a cloud which appeared of a very unusual size and shape. He had just returned from taking the benefit of the sun, and after bathing himself in cold water, and taking a slight repast, was retired to his study. He immediately arose and went out on an eminence from whence he might more distinctly view this uncommon appearance. It was not at that distance discernible from what mountain this cloud issued, but it was found afterward to ascend from Mount Vesuvius. I cannot give you a more exact description of its figure, than by resembling it to that of a pine-tree, for it shot up a great height in the form of a trunk, which extended itself at the top into sort of branches, occasioned, I imagine, either by a sudden gust of air that impelled it, the force of which decreased as it advanced upwards, or the cloud itself being pressed back again with its own weight, expanded in this manner; it appeared sometimes bright and sometimes dark and spotted, as it was either more or less impregnated with earth and cinder. This extraordinary phenomenon excited my uncle's philosophical curiosity to get a nearer view of it. He ordered a light vessel to be got ready, and gave me the liberty, if I thought it proper, to attend him. I rather chose to continue my studies; for, as it happened, he had given me an employment of that kind. As he was coming out of the house he received a note from Rectina, the wife of Bassus, who was in the utmost alarm at the immediate danger which threatened her; for her villa being situated at the foot of Mount Vesuvius, there was no way to escape but by sea; she earnestly entreated him, therefore, to come to her assistance. He accordingly changed his first design, and what he began with a philosophical, he pursued with an heroical, turn of mind. He ordered the galleys to put to sea, and went himself on board, with an intention of assisting not only Rectina, but several others; for the villas stand extremely thick upon that beautiful coast. When hastening to the place from whence others fled with the utmost terror, he steered his direct course to the point of danger, and with so much calmness and presence of mind as to be able to make and dictate his observations upon the motion and figure of that dreadful scene. He was now so nigh the mountain, that the cinders, which grew thicker and hotter the nearer he approached, fell into the ships, together with pumice-stones, and black pieces of burning rock. They were likewise in danger not only of being aground by the sudden retreat of the sea, but also from the vast fragments which rolled down from the mountain, and obstructed all the shore. Here he stopped to consider whether he should turn back again; to which the pilot advising him, 'Fortune,' said he, 'befriends the brave; carry me to Pomponianus.' Pomponianus was then at Stabiæ, separated by a gulf which the sea, after several insensible windings, forms upon the shore. He had already sent his baggage on board; for though he was not at that time in actual danger, yet being within the view of it, and indeed extremely near, if it should the least increase, he was determined to put to sea as soon as the wind should change. It was favorable, however, for carrying my uncle to Pomponianus, whom he found in the greatest consternation. He embraced him with tenderness, encouraged and exhorted him to keep up his spirits, and the more to dissipate his fears, he ordered, with an air of unconcern, the bath to be got ready; when, after having bathed, he sat down to supper with great cheerfulness, or at least, what is equally heroic, with all the appearance of it. In the mean while, the eruption from Mount Vesuvius flamed out in several places with much violence, which the darkness of the night contributed to render still more visible and dreadful. But my uncle, in order to soothe the apprehensions of his friend, assured him it was only the burning of the villages, which the country people had abandoned to the flames. After this he retired to rest, and it is most certain he was so little discomposed as to fall into a deep sleep, for being pretty fat, and breathing hard, those who attended without actually heard him snore. The court which led to his apartment being now almost filled with stones and ashes, if he had continued there any time longer, it would have been impossible for him to have made his way out; it was thought proper, therefore, to awaken him. He got up and went to Pomponianus and the rest of his company who were unconcerned enough to think of going to bed. They consulted together whether it would be most prudent to remain in the houses, which now shook from side to side, with frequent and violent concussions, or to fly to the open fields, where the calcined stones and cinders, though light indeed, yet fell in large showers, and threatened destruction. In this distress they resolved for the fields, as the less dangerous situation of the two. A resolution which, while the rest of the company were hurried into by their fears, my uncle embraced upon cool and deliberate consideration. They went out, then, having pillows tied upon their heads with napkins, and this was their whole defence against the storm of stones that fell round them. It was now day everywhere else, but there a deeper darkness prevailed than in the most obscure night; which, however, was, in some degree dissipated by torches and other lights of various kinds. They thought proper to go down farther upon the shore, to observe if they might safely put out to sea, but they found the waves still run extremely high and boisterous. There my uncle having drank a draught or two of cold water, threw himself down upon a cloth which was spread for him, when immediately the flames, and a strong smell of sulphur, which was the forerunner of them, dispersed the rest of the company, and obliged him to arise. He raised himself up with the assistance of two of his servants, and instantly fell down dead, suffocated, as I conjecture, by some gross and noxious vapor, having always had weak lungs, and frequently subject to difficulty of breathing. As soon as it was light again, which was not until the third day after this melancholy accident, his body was found entire, and without any marks of violence upon it, exactly in the same posture that he fell, and looking more like a man asleep than dead.

"During all this time my mother and I, who were at Misenum —, but as this has no connection with your history, as your inquiry went no further than concerning my uncle's death; with that, therefore, I will put an end to my letter. Suffer me only to add, that I have faithfully related either what I was an eye-witness of myself, or received immediately after the accident happened, and before there was time to vary the truth. . . . Farewell."

*To Cornelius Tacitus.* — "The letter, which, in compliance with your request, I wrote concerning the death of my uncle, has raised, it seems, your curiosity to know what terrors and dangers attended me, while I continued at Misenum; for there, I think, the account in my former broke off. Though my shocked soul recoils, my tongue shall tell. My uncle having left us, I pursued the studies which prevented my going with him, till it was time to bathe. After which I went to supper, and from thence to bed, where my sleep was greatly broken and disturbed. There had been for many days before some shocks of an earthquake, which the less surprised us, as they are extremely frequent in Campania; but they were so particularly violent that night, that they not only shook everything about us, but seemed, indeed, to threaten total destruction. My mother flew to my chamber, where she found me rising in order to awaken her. We went out into a small court belonging to the house, which separated the sea from the buildings. As I was at that time but eighteen years of age, I know not whether I should call my behavior in this dangerous juncture courage or rashness; but I took up Livy, and amused myself with turning over that author, and even making extracts from him, as if all about me had been in full security. While we were in this posture, a friend of my uncle's, who was just come from Spain to pay a visit, joined us, and observing me sitting by my mother with a book in my hand, greatly condemned her calmness, at the same time that he reproved me for my careless security. Nevertheless, I still went on with my author. Though it was now morning, the light was exceedingly faint and languid; the buildings all around us tottered, and though we stood upon open ground, yet as the place was narrow and confined, there was no remaining there without certain and great danger; we therefore resolved to quit the town. The people followed us in the utmost consternation, and (as to the mind distracted with terror, every suggestion seems more prudent than its own) pressed in great crowds about us on our way out. Being got at a convenient distance from the houses, we stood still in the midst of a most dangerous and dreadful scene. The chariots which we had ordered to be drawn out, were so agitated backwards and forwards, though upon the most level ground, that we could not keep them steady, even by supporting them with large stones. The sea seemed to roll back upon itself, and to be driven from its banks by the convulsive motion of the earth; it is certain, at least, that the shore was considerably enlarged, and several sea animals were left upon it. On the other side a black and dreadful cloud, bursting with an igneous, serpentine vapor, darted out a long train of fire, resembling flashes of lightning, but much larger. Upon this our Spanish friend, whom I mentioned above, addressing himself to my mother and me with greater warmth and earnestness, 'If your brother and your uncle,' said he, 'is safe, he certainly wishes you to be so too; but if he perished, it was his desire, no doubt, that you might both survive him. Why, therefore, do you delay your escape a moment?'—'We could never think of our own safety,' we said, 'while we were uncertain of his.' Hereupon our friend left us, and withdrew from the danger with the utmost precipitation. Soon afterwards the cloud seemed to descend and cover the whole ocean; as indeed it entirely hid the island of Caprea, and the promontory of Misenum. My mother strongly conjured me to make my escape at any rate, which, as I was young, I might easily do; as for herself, she said, her age and corpulency rendered all attempts of that sort impossible; however, she should willingly meet death, if she could have the satisfaction of seeing that she was not the occasion of mine. But I absolutely refused to leave her, and taking her by the hand, I led her on; she complied with great reluctance, and not without many reproaches to herself for retarding my flight. The ashes now began to fall upon us, though in no great quantity. I turned my head, and observed behind us a thick smoke, which came rolling after us like a torrent. I proposed, while we had yet any light, to turn out of the high road, lest we should be pressed to death in the dark, by the crowd that followed us. We had scarce stepped out of the path when a darkness overspread us, not like that of a cloudy night, or when there is no moon, but of a room where it is shut up, and all the lights extinct. Nothing then was to be heard but the shrieks of women, the screams of children, and the cries of men; some calling for their children, others for their parents, others for their husbands, and only distinguishing each other by their voices; one lamenting his own fate, another that of his family; some wishing to die, from the very fear of dying; some lifting up their hands to the gods; but the greater part imagining that the last and eternal night was come, which was to destroy both the gods and the world together. Among these, there are some who augmented the real terrors by imaginary ones, and made the frighted multitude falsely believe that Misenum was in flames. At length a glimmering light appeared, which we imagined to be rather the forerunner of an approaching burst of flames (as in truth it was), than the return of day; however, the fire fell at a distance from us, then again we were immersed in thick darkness, and a heavy shower of ashes rained upon us, which we were obliged every now and then to shake off, otherwise we should have been crushed, and buried in the heap; I might boast that, during all this scene of horror, not a sigh or expression of fear escaped from me, had not my support been founded in that miserable, though strong consolation, that all mankind were involved in the same calamity, and that I imagined I was perishing with the world itself. At last this dreadful darkness was dissipated by degrees, like a cloud of smoke; the real day returned, and even the sun appeared, though very faintly, as when an eclipse is coming on. Every object that presented itself to our eyes (which were extremely weakened) seemed changed, being covered over with white ashes as with a deep snow. We returned to Misenum, where we refreshed ourselves as well as we could, and passed an anxious night between hope and fear, though, indeed, with a much larger share of the latter; for the earthquake still continued, while several enthusiastic people ran up and down heightening their own and their friends' calamities, by terrible predictions. However, my mother and I, notwithstanding the danger we had passed, and that which still threatened us, had no thoughts of leaving the place, until we should receive some account of my uncle.

"And now you will read this narrative without any view of inserting it in your history, of which it is by no means worthy; and indeed you must impute it to your own request, if it shall appear scarce to deserve even the trouble of a letter. Farewell."

Shortly after the catastrophe, all memorials of the devoted cities were lost; discussions on the places they had once occupied were excited only by some obscure passages in classical authors. Five successive eruptions contributed to bury them still deeper under the surface, and the sixth, which occurred in the year 1036, is the first instance of an emission of lava. Before that time the only agents of desolation were showers of sand, cinders, and scoriæ, together with loose fragments of rock. Volcanic ashes, poured out in a current, have been known to darken the air for hours, and even for days. Such must have been the nature of the phenomenon which the younger Pliny saw and compared to a lofty pine. Dion Cassius states that the ashes of this eruption were carried as far as Africa, and that the dust was so abundant as even to darken the air in the neighborhood of Rome. Steam poured out in vast quantities, and uniting with the ashes that fell upon Herculaneum, formed a torrent of mud, imbedding all in solid tufa, whilst the ashes of Pompeii were not impregnated, and all lay in this city loose and unconsolidated. Stones of eight pounds' weight fell on Pompeii, whilst Stabiæ was overwhelmed with fragments about an ounce in weight, which must have drifted in immense quantities. During a later eruption, fine ashes were borne by the wind as far as Constantinople. Whilst the ancient cities thus lay buried and forgotten, Neapolis, the residence and burial-place of Virgil, grew into the great modern city of Naples, extending its suburban villages along the shore, and connecting itself by a chain of houses to the very roots of Vesuvius. The next town to Naples is Portici. It contains 6,000 inhabitants. Immediately adjoining Portici is the still larger town of Resina, with a population of 11,000 souls. These bustling and much frequented places are built upon the lava which covers Herculaneum.

*Discovery of the Ancient Cities.* — In the year 1689, during some excavations in the plain at the foot of Vesuvius, where it was subsequently proved that Pompeii had flourished, a workman observed the regularity with which successive layers of earth and volcanic matter had been deposited. He compared them to pavements one upon the other; with remains of burnt vegetation, charcoal, and common earth beneath each volcanic deposit. Under one of these dense masses of scoria, dust, and pumice-stone, he found large quantities of carbonized timber, locks, and iron work, evidently the remains of habitations, which, together with some old keys, and inscriptions giving the name of the locality, satisfied the learned of the day that they belonged to the ancient city of Pompeii. The discovery created but little excitement at the time; the government was indisposed to prosecute the research, and no further excavation was carried on until the year 1749.

Meanwhile the accidental sinking of a well in another place brought to light such treasures of art as to induce a systematic exploration in a more profitable locality. This was in the neighborhood of Naples, where after seventeen centuries the city of Herculaneum was once more rescued from oblivion. The circumstances which led to the discovery are briefly these. The Prince d'Elbœuf, of the house of Lorraine, came to Naples in 1706, and ordered the construction of a marine villa for himself at Portici, in 1711. He had a Frenchman in his service who possessed the art of making a durable stucco from pulverized marble, and as many fragments of antique marbles as possible were collected for the manufacture of his composition. One day a countryman presented himself, asserting that in sinking a well at Resina, he had discovered a variety of precious marbles, some of which he had brought with him as specimens. These marbles were so beautiful and rare, that the prince was induced to purchase of the man the right of further excavation, and he immediately commenced a systematic course of exploration upon that spot. The stucco prepared by the Frenchman was not only an imitation of precious marbles, but also a cement similar to that employed by the ancients. Most of the antique buildings were so plastered internally, as it was harder and more durable than marble in its natural state. The excavators, therefore, were more delighted when they found large plain slabs and shafts of columns than elaborately carved foliage and statues, because the latter afforded them a smaller quantity of actual material. The works were carried on, branching sidewise from the well, just above the level of the water; at the expiration of two days they found a statue of Hercules, evidently from a Grecian chisel, and they remarked with astonishment that it had formerly been restored. Some days after this they came upon a female statue, which was at once pronounced to be a Cleopatra. They next extricated a large square mass of marble, and upon removing a crust of bituminous matter, it was found to be the architrave of a gateway, with letters of bronze inlaid into the surface. The inscription was

APPIVS PVLCHER CAII FILIVS.
*vir* epvlonvm.

Many columns of variegated alabaster were next discovered, and this led to the excavation of a circular temple, with twenty-four columns, and statues of marble between them. The pavement of this building was constructed of that rich yellow marble, called *giallo antico*, and many columns of the same material lay in the vicinity. Seven of the twelve figures belonging to the temple were female, executed in a superior Grecian style. Prince Elbœuf despatched them to Vienna as a present to Prince Eugene of Savoy. The best of these statues were afterward sold to the King of Poland for 60,000 scudi; they are now at Dresden. The prince evidently knew very little of the real value of his discoveries, and during the next five years continued disinterring pieces of mosaic alabaster slabs, and a few statues, some of which decorated his villa, and the rest were sent over to France. Upon the discovery of a beautiful statue of one of the daughters of Balbus, the State interfered, and the Neapolitan government prohibited any further excavations. For thirty years the site was almost forgotten. In 1736, the king Carlo III resolved to build a palace at Portici, and the ancient well was once more resorted to. The excavations were resumed, and very important results followed.

Animated discussions were still maintained respecting the name of the ancient city, — for a city the excavations had already proved it to be. The Marquis Venuti, superintendent of the excavations, has left minute records of his proceedings. He commenced 12th November, 1738, by carrying a kind of tunnel laterally from the old well. In a short time two bronze equestrian statues were found, and soon after three full-length marble figures, larger than life, of Roman dignitaries, dressed in the toga, with massive piers of brick between, plastered with stucco, and painted with arabesques in various colors. The excavators had now reached the interior of the theatre, which the numerous seats and steps clearly indicated. An inscription, moreover, on the architrave, contained part of the word theatro, the name of the person at whose cost the building was erected, and that of the architect. A second inscription on the corresponding architrave of the opposite side is almost a repetition.

These architraves covered the side entrances to the orchestra, and both of them supported a colossal group in bronze, of a chariot and two horses. The central group of the building was a quadriga, and probably represented the emperor in his chariot, with four horses. All these bronze statues had been gilt. Some fine columns of *rosso antico* were transported to the cathedral of Naples, and others to the Royal Palace; they appear to have adorned the proscenium. The theatre was one of the most perfect specimens of ancient architecture. It had, from the floor, upwards of eighteen rows of seats, and above these three other rows, which seem to have been intended for the female part of the audience, and were covered with a portico to screen them from the rays of the sun. Statues of Drusus and Antonia, and of the Nine Muses, were found in other parts of the building. A bronze colossal statue of Titus, filled with lead, was so heavy that twelve men were unable to move it. Many other bronze statues of municipal authorities and benefactors, were found with their respective inscriptions.

The theatre was capable of containing 8,000 persons. Nearly the whole of its surface, as well as the arched walks leading to the seats, was cased with marble. The area or pit was floored with thick squares of *giallo antico*, the beautiful marble of a yellowish hue. The pedestal, of white marble, which supported a chariot and four bronze horses, is still to be seen in its place; but the group itself had been crushed and broken to pieces by the immense weight of lava which fell on it. The fragments having been collected, might have been easily reunited, but they were carelessly thrown into a corner, like old iron, and part of them were stolen. The body of one horse and part of the charioteer, being deemed useless, were accordingly fused, to be converted into two large framed medallions of their Neapolitan majesties. The remaining fragments were cast into the vaults of the royal palace; and, at last, it was resolved to make the best use of what was left: which was, to convert the four horses into one, by taking a foreleg of one of them, a hinder leg of another, the head of a third, and when the breach was irremediable to cast a new piece. To this contrivance the famous bronze horse now in the Museum owes its existence; and, considering its patchwork origin, still conveys a high idea of the skill of the ancient artist. A pompous inscription upon its pedestal records the circumstances of its construction.

On the south side of the theatre stood a basilica, or public building, which contained the celebrated equestrian statues of the Balbi, of one block of marble. These fine statues possess the additional value of having finally set at rest the question respecting the proper name of the city. On the front of the pedestals is inscribed,—

M. NONIO, M. F.<br>
BALBO PR. PRO. COS.<br>
Herculanenses.

The certainty of this city having been the ancient Herculaneum, is said to have materially increased the energy of the excavators. In the same basilica were found the famous pictures of Hercules and Telephus, Theseus and the Minotaur, and many others, together with bronze statues of Nero and Germanicus, and a Vespasian, with two sitting figures of marble, nine feet high. The streets of the city were paved with blocks of lava, they were flanked with causeways, and lined with porticos. The private buildings, which resembled those of Pompeii, were very difficult of access, from the nature of the material that overwhelmed them, and could only be examined in small portions at a time. One large villa seems to have been a very important structure. It was surrounded by a garden, enclosed within a square wall and ditch. The floors were ornamented with beautiful mosaics, and the halls contained a rich variety of busts and statues. One of the chambers served the purpose of a bath; another, supposed to have been a sacrarium, was painted with serpents, and within it was found a brazen tripod, containing cinders and ashes; but the most curious discovery of all, was an apartment in this villa used as a library, and fitted up with wooden presses around the walls, about six feet in height; a double row of presses stood in the middle of the room, so as to admit of a free passage on every side. The wood of which the presses had been made, was burned to a cinder, and gave way at the first touch, but the volumes, composed of a much more perishable substance, the Egyptian or Syracusan papyrus, were, although completely carbonized, through the effect of the heat, still so far preserved as to admit of their removal. A number of these supposed pieces of charcoal were at first carried off, which by accidental fracture exposed the remains of letters, and proved to be so many ancient manuscripts. The Greek manuscripts consisted of rolls scarcely a foot in length, and but two or three inches in thickness. Some had a label in front, at one end of the roll, with the name of the work or the author, which was visible from its place in the library. The sixteen centuries during which the substances had been crushed together, rendered it almost hopeless to unroll, and still less to decipher them; but Camillo Paderni devoted twelve days to the occupation underground, and succeeded in carrying away three hundred and thirty-seven manuscripts. Almost all are in Greek, very few in Latin, and some of the rolls are forty or fifty feet in length. The lines are arranged in columns across the shortest surface, as in our newspapers, each line extending only two or three inches in length. The greater part of the works in this collection relate to Epicurean philosophy. Their decipherment has naturally occupied much of the attention of the learned, and many of the manuscripts have been published at Oxford (England).

The condition of Herculaneum was, at the period of its discovery, more interesting and much more worthy the notice of the traveller than it is at present. The object of its excavation having, unfortunately, been confined to the discovery of statues, paintings, and other curiosities, and not carried on with a view to lay open the city, and thus to ascertain the features of its buildings and streets, most of the latter were again filled up with rubbish, as soon as they were divested of everything movable. Even the marble was torn from the temples.

Herculaneum may therefore be said to have been overwhelmed a second time by its modern discoverers; and the appearance it previously presented can now only be ascertained from the accounts of those who beheld it in a more perfect state. The existence of the large towns of Portici and Resina overhead, render it impossible for many parts of the excavations to remain open to the sky; one portion, however, was allowed to be so until the sinking of the main road, subject to incessant traffic, compelled the government to have the under-cuttings filled in, and the apertures blocked up. A part of the city nearer to the mountain has been thrown open, and the sun is again permitted to shine upon gardens and habitations now desolate and mouldering.

From the hard nature of the rock at Herculaneum, the city was for a long time supposed to have been buried in lava, and the darkness and obscurity of the passages prevented the discovery of the truth. But now, since daylight has been admitted, the whole mass is found to be nothing more than hard tufa, rendered, at the lower parts, still more compact by the percolation of water, which in all cases leaves the finest possible sediment. Lava is stone which has been actually melted, and flows over the surface in the same way as molten iron issues from a furnace. The beds of real lava may be easily distinguished in the upper levels of the earth laid open in these excavations. All the timber of the houses has been completely reduced to charcoal, but every beam was found perfect as to shape, and in its proper position; many of the bronzes, however, were melted. These effects seem to be the result of an intense heat diffused through the entire mass at a subsequent period; for, at the time of the first eruption, great quantities of boiling water appear to have been mixed with the fine dust and scoria, the same materials that fell dry and loose upon Pompeii.

An entrance from the road at Resina to the excavations was formed in 1750. It is still the only means of access to the most important buildings, and consists of a narrow passage cut through the solid lava. The ancient city lies at a depth of seventy feet below the modern level.

The great difficulty of excavating Herculaneum, on account of the soil above being occupied by crowded habitations, induced the government to turn their attention more particularly to Pompeii.

"Nearly seventeen centuries had rolled away when the city of Pompeii was disinterred from its silent tomb, all vivid with undimmed hues; its walls fresh as if painted yesterday; not a hue faded on the rich mosaic of its floors; in its forum the half-finished columns as left by the workman's hands; in its gardens the sacrificial tripod; in its halls the chest of treasure; in its baths the strigil; in its theatres the counter of admission; in its saloons the furniture and the lamp; in its triclinia the fragments of the last feast; in its cubicula the perfumes and the rouge of faded beauty; an everywhere the bones and skeletons of those who once moved the springs of that minute, yet gorgeous machine of luxury and of life.

"In the house of Diomed, in the subterranean vaults, twenty skeletons (one of a babe) were discovered in one spot by the door, covered by a fine ashen dust, that had evidently been wafted slowly through the apertures, until it had filled the whole space. There were jewels and coins, candelabra for unavailing light, and wine hardened in the amphoræ for a prolongation of agonized life. The sand, consolidated by damps, had taken the forms of the skeletons as in a cast, and the traveller may yet see the impression of a female neck and bosom of young and round proportions.

"It seems to the inquirer as if the air had been gradually changed into a sulphurous vapor; the inmates of the vaults had rushed to the door to find it closed and blocked up by the scoria without, and, in their attempts to force it, had been suffocated with the atmosphere.

"In the garden was found a skeleton with a key by its bony hand, and near it a bag of coins. This is believed to have been the master of the house, who had probably sought to escape by the garden, and been destroyed either by the vapors or some fragment of stone. Beside some silver vases lay another skeleton, probably of a slave.

"The houses of Sallust and of Pansa, the temple of Isis, with the juggling concealments behind the statues, — the lurking-place of its holy oracles, — are now bared to the gaze of the curious. In one of the chambers of that temple was found a huge skeleton with an axe by the side of it: two walls had been pierced by the axe, — the victim could penetrate no farther. In the midst of the city was found another skeleton, by the side of which was a heap of coins, and many of the mystic ornaments of the fane of Isis." — *Bulwer's* "*Last Days of Pompeii.*"

Linen and fishing-nets; loaves of bread with the impress of the baker's name; even fruits, as walnuts, almonds, peach-stones, and chestnuts, were distinctly recognizable. Eggs have been found whole and empty, and a jar of oil had olives still floating in it; the oil burnt upon application of flame, but the fruit was flavorless. Very few jewels were discovered, which shows that the inhabitants had time to escape; a wooden comb was found with teeth on both sides, closer on one side than the other. Lace fabricated of pure gold, a folding parasol similar to those now in use, a case of surgeon's instruments, balances, sculptors' tools, chisels and compasses, writing materials, vessels of white cut and colored glass, coals collected for fuel, and wine still remaining in jars, may all be found in the curious catalogue of articles that had braved the lapse of time. Other circumstances there are which claim our better feelings. At the city gate, the sentinel, faithful to his trust, was found in his sentry-box, a skeleton, clothed in

"The very armor he had on,"

when his dreadful doom overtook him; in the barracks near the triangular forum, malefactors were found in the public stocks; the crumbling remains of prisoners were discovered in the dungeons near the Temple of Jupiter, no one in that hour of general horror and confusion having thought of them or of their wretchedness, in being thus immured alive. The bones of the ass that worked the baker's mill were found there; the skeletons of horses remained in the cribs in which they had stabled for the last time.

The discoveries which had been made long before the arrival of Prince Elbœuf, and which were communicated to the French Academy of Science, 1689, were remembered by the Neapolitan Government, and in the beginning of the year 1749, we have the first authentic reference to the ancient city of Pompeii. "On the 18th of January, at a place called Civita," so runs the official announcement, "not far from Torre dell' Annunciata, where the ancient Pompeii may have been, was found an apartment decorated with sixteen charming little dancing females brightly colored, two centaurs and figures, bands of arabesques forming panels with Cupids in the midst, and twelve fauns dancing on a rope, all upon a black ground." They are very small figures, and have since been removed to the Museo Borbonico. About the same time a laborer, whilst ploughing in the neighboring fields, found a statue of brass.

Among the earliest buildings excavated at Pompeii was the Amphitheatre; it was cleared in 1755, and seems to have been capable of holding ten thousand people. In the amphitheatre games were held, gladiators fought for their lives with wild beasts, or with one another, and these savage spectacles were under the particular superintendence of an edile. We are informed by Dion Cassius, that the eruption came on whilst the populace were assembled in the theatre, but which of the theatres is meant, as there were several, remains doubtful. Thus far is certain, that sufficient time was left for escape, as no skeletons were found in either of them. From the seats of this amphitheatre may certainly be obtained the grandest view of the mountain, and if, as Bulwer's romance "The Last Days of Pompeii" depicts it, the assembly was held on this spot, the first signs of the coming destruction would have been seen by all the multitude. An announcement connected with these performances has since been discovered upon the walls of the Basilica. A placard — the playbill of those times — announced that the troops of gladiators belonging to Ampliatus would contend in the amphitheatre on the 17th of May, and that another exhibition would take place on the 31st,— exactly three months before the destruction of the city.

The temple of Isis was accidentally discovered in 1765, by some workmen employed in making a subterraneous aqueduct to Torre dell' Annunciata. These discoveries induced Charles III to transfer his attention exclusively to Pompeii. The Triangular Forum, the Temple of Æsculapius, and the two great theatres were all laid open in the course of two or three successive years. These buildings are all in the sa e quarter of the town, but quite remote from the great forum and public buildings, which were not discovered until 1816.

It is a remarkable fact that Fontana, the great architect, carried a subterraneous canal, in 1592, directly under the court of the temple of Isis. He was employed to convey the waters of the river Sarus to the town of Torre dell' Annunciata; and it seems wonderful that the existence of this interesting city was not made known at the time.

The situation of Pompeii, as it originally stood, was upon an elevation surrounded by a fertile plain. Pompeii was never *buried* beneath the surface of the ground; on the contrary, many of its walls were always *conspicuous*, as, for instance, that at the back of the tragic theatre. The locality seems to have been known to the peasants of the vicinity by the name of civita (city). The rains of successive seasons may probably have carried away most of the stones and ashes that fell around the city, whilst the walls of the houses themselves would serve to retain all that had fallen upon them.

Other villas also were excavated at Gragnano, the ancient Stabiæ, and most of the decorations were removed to the Museo Borbónico.

When the French occupied Naples, the walls surrounding the city of Pompeii were entirely cleared; this was in October, 1812, and in the March following the street of tombs. Murat defrayed most of the expenses of excavation, and in a short time the Forum and Basilica with the adjacent buildings were laid open. At one time 3,000 men were employed in the work of exploration.

The Forum is the largest, and by far the grandest spot in Pompeii. It is surrounded by a Grecian Doric colonnade, the temple of Jupiter, two triumphal arches, forming the north end, and the Temple of Venus and Basilica on the west. Facing the temple of Jupiter were large buildings, profusely decorated with statues, called the Curiæ and Ærarium, and the remaining side of the Forum was occupied by various buildings, among them the Pantheon and the Chalcidicum of Eumachia; these were excavated between 1817 and 1821. The discovery of the public baths did not take place until 1824. These contributed materially to a better comprehension of many passages in ancient authors, being more perfect examples than the vast ranges for similar purposes still existing at Rome.

The general result of the Pompeian excavations up to the present time, may be thus summed up: three forums, nine temples, a basilica, a chalcidicum, three piazze, an amphitheatre, two theatres, a prison, double baths, nearly one hundred houses and shops, several villas, town walls, six gates, and twelve tombs. — *Scharf's Pompeian Court.*

## CHAPTER XL.

### GIBRALTAR.

*Bird's-eye View of the Town. — The Town and Castle, looking north.— Coast of Spain in distance.*

THE town and fortress of Gibraltar, in the south part of Spain, belong to Great Britain. They are situated at the narrowest part of the strait of the same name; distance from Madrid three hundred and twelve miles, south-southwest. The fortress stands on the west side of a mountainous promontory or rock, projecting into the sea about three miles, in a southerly direction, and from one half to three fourths of a mile in breadth. The southern extremity of the rock, eleven and a half miles north from Ceuta in Africa, is called Europa Point. Its north side, fronting the narrow and low isthmus which connects it with the main-land, is perpendicular and wholly inaccessible. The east and south sides are steep and rugged, so as to render an attack upon them next to impossible. The west side has a gradual slope towards the bay; this is the only place where a successful attack would be possible, and here the defences are of astonishing strength. The town contains about 16,000 inhabitants. It lies at the foot of the rock, on the northwest side. It has a principal street about a mile in length, intersected by many shorter streets. There is an excellent public library founded in 1843, and a small theatre. The Protestant church will contain 1,048 persons, the Governor's chapel three hundred more, and the Roman Catholic church 1,500. The Wesleyan Methodists and other denominations have places of worship, and there is a Jews' synagogue.

The bay of Gibraltar is spacious, protected from all dangerous winds, and has a depth of one hundred and ten fathoms. Although well adapted for shipping, and a free port, subject to no duties or restrictions, its commerce has fallen into decay, owing in part to the policy of the Spanish government.

Gibraltar, the *Calpe* of the Greeks, formed with Abyla, on the African coast, the pillars of Hercules. Its name was changed to Gibel-Tarif in the beginning of the 8th century, when Tarif Ebu Zarca landed, with a large army, to conquer Spain, and erected a strong fortress on the mountain side. It was taken from the Moors by Ferdinand, king of Castile, in the fourteenth century. It was soon recaptured, and held by the Moors until 1462, when it became a possession of Spain. In 1704, during the war of the Spanish succession, the English and Dutch fleets attacked the fortress, which surrendered, after some hours' resistance. Since that time the Spaniards have made several attempts to regain it; but it remains, and is likely so to remain for an indefinite length of time, in the hands of the English.

## CHAPTER XLI.

### TURKEY AND GREECE.

THE Turkish empire is in Europe, Asia, and Africa. Square miles, 1,920,944; population, 43,600,000. Railroads are making steady progress in Turkey, bearing civilization in their train. In 1871, there were but one hundred and eighty-five miles in operation in Turkey in Europe; but in 1872, several lines, embracing an aggregate of 1,487 miles, are being pushed forward with energy.

*Constantinople. View of the Seraskier Tower looking towards Pera.*— This city stands on the European shore of the sea of Marmora. Its position is fitted by nature for the site of a great commercial city. The walls on the side next the sea are in a very ruinous state; but on the land side there is a double line of strong and lofty walls. "Within gunshot," says Mr. Dickens, "beyond this great city, with its 600,000 inhabitants, there is not a road nor a bridge upon the most frequented ways; there is not a house, nor a garden, nor a thriving tree. . . . The Turks do nothing."

### GREECE.

Present ruler, George I, third son of the King of Denmark. Area, 19,353 square miles; population in 1870, 1,457,894.

*The City of Athens, Greece.*— This city is about five miles from the sea-coast. One of the principal mountains of the north frontier is now known as Mount St. George. The history of this city is exceedingly interesting and instructive, but we have not room even for an abstract.

---

## CHAPTER XLII.

### SYRIA AND PALESTINE.

TWO of the most celebrated regions of the Eastern Hemisphere,— the latter sometimes called the Holy Land, from its being the theatre of most of the great events recorded in sacred history. The entire length of the two countries may be about four hundred and fifty miles; breadth, from one hundred to three hundred miles. The population is not far from two millions. Of these, one million are estimated to be Moslems, 440,000 to be Christians; then there are 45,000 Jews, and several thousands attached to other religions. The country has long been a part of Asiatic Turkey, but is sadly misruled and oppressed. The coast portion of Syria is generally mountainous, while its interior is flat. Palestine consists principally of rugged hills and narrow valleys, though it has some fertile plains of considerable size. The Euphrates and Jordan are its chief rivers; 1,800, and one hundred and fifty miles long respectively. The most remarkable lake is that of the Dead Sea; the next in size is that of Gennesaret, the theatre of some most remarkable miracles (Luke v. and Matthew xiv. 34). It is about sixteen miles in length, and from five to six in breadth. Syria and Palestine may be said to have two climates,— the one very hot, on the coast and in the plains; and the other temperate in the mountains, at least to a certain height. The country is extolled by modern travellers for its beauty, fertility, and variety of products; but bad government has reduced it of late to a state of depression to which it had never previously sunk. Still, the condition of the peasantry is said to be as good as that of the laboring classes in England.

*Jerusalem.* — A famous city of Palestine, interesting from its high antiquity, but far more from its intimate connection with the history of the Jews, and the eventful life of the Great Founder of Christianity. Its population is rudely estimated at 16,000, of whom about two thirds are Mohammedans. The city stands on a hill between two valleys. The modern city, built about three hundred years ago, is entirely surrounded by walls, barely two and a half miles in circumference, and flanked here and there with square towers. The interior is divided by two valleys intersecting each other at right angles, and forming four hills on which history has stamped the imperishable names of Zion, Acra, Bezetha, and Moriah. The streets of the city are narrow; the houses, except those belonging to the Turks, are shabby; and the shops are poorly supplied. All around the site of Jerusalem are rounded irregular summits: the Mount of Olives; the so-called Hill of Evil Council; the Hill Scopus, a western projection of the ridge of Olivet. The words of the Psalmist are thus true, when he says, —

> "Jerusalem, mountains encompass her;
> Jehovah encompasseth his people from henceforth
> and forever."—Ps. cxxv. 2.

*Wall of Jerusalem, Turkish Tombs, and Arab Shepherds.* — Jerusalem is surrounded by walls, high and imposing in appearance, but far from strong. A single discharge of heavy artillery would lay them prostrate; yet they are sufficient to keep in check the roving Arab tribes and the turbulent peasantry. They were erected as they now stand, in 1542, and they appear to occupy the site of the walls of the Middle Ages, from whose ruins they are mainly constructed. There are five open gates, or entrances, through the walls to the city.

*Jerusalem from Mount Zion.* — At the farther side of the city is seen the Mosque of Omar, and beyond it is the Mount of Olives.

*The Garden of Gethsemane and the Mount of Olives.* — The greatest interest of the Kedron is connected with the closing scene of our Saviour's life in the Garden of Gethsemane. On the night of His betrayal, after a long conversation with His followers in that "upper room" in the city where the supper was instituted, He went forth with them over the brook Kedron, to a garden where he ofttimes resorted with his disciples. Just beyond the bridge which crosses the dry bed of the brook between the paths that lead up to the Mount of Olives, is a little square enclosure encompassed by a high white wall. This is the reputed Gethsemane. Within are eight venerable olives; their decayed trunks supported by stones, and their sparse branches still flourishing. The pilgrim to the garden is shown the rocky bank where the apostles fell asleep when our Lord left them to pray! Then he is led to the "Grotto of the Agony," — a cave of some depth, in which Jesus is said to have prayed. Next the place where Judas betrayed his master with a kiss, is pointed out. "That the tradition" — that this is the location of the Garden of Gethsemane — "reaches back to the age of Constantine, is certain. How far it agrees with the slight indications of its position in the gospel narrative will be judged by the impressions of each individual traveller. Some will think it too public; others will see an argument in its favor from the close proximity to the brook Kedron; none, probably, will be disposed to receive the traditional sites which surround it, the Grotto of the Agony, the rocky bank of the three apostles, the 'terra damnata' of the Betrayal. But in spite of all the doubts that can be raised against their antiquity or the genuineness of their site, the eight aged olive-trees, if only by their manifest difference from all others on the mountain, have always struck even the most indifferent observers. They are now indeed less striking in the modern garden enclosure built round them by the Franciscan monks, than when they stood free and unprotected on the rough hillside; but they will remain, so long as their already protracted life is spared, the most venerable of their race on the surface of the earth; their gnarled trunks and scanty foliage will always be regarded as the most affecting of the sacred memorials in or about Jerusalem; the most nearly approaching to the everlasting hills themselves in the force with which they carry us back to the events of the Gospel History." — *Stanley's Sinai and Palestine.*

The Mount of Olives is situated immediately beyond the Kedron, on the east of, or, as it is expressed in the Bible, "before" Jerusalem (1 Kings xi. 7). It is before one's eyes from almost every part of the city; and forms the most striking object in every view around it. It is more a ridge than a mount, graceful in outline, and delicate in color. In the centre is a rounded top, and from it the sides of the mount descend gently and uniformly, to two rounded summits of about equal altitude, and then break down more rapidly to the level of the adjoining ridges. The face of the hill is streaked with strips of green and gray, — the former the terraces of corn, the latter the supporting walls and ledges of rock; while the whole is dotted with rounded, trim-looking olive-trees.

*Bethany, Jerusalem, and the Mount of Olives.* — We cannot better introduce the history connected with these views than in the words of Stanley: "From Bethany we must begin. A wild, mountain hamlet, screened by an intervening ridge from the view of the top of Olivet, is perched on a broken plateau of rock, the last collection of human habitations before the desert-hills which reach to Jericho. High in the distance are the Peræan mountains; the foreground is the deep descent to the Jordan valley. On the further side of that dark abyss, Martha and Mary knew that Christ was abiding, when they sent their messenger. Up that long ascent they had often watched His approach,— up that long ascent He came, when outside the village, Martha and Mary met Him, and the Jews stood around weeping.

"Up that ascent He came, also, at the beginning of the week of his suffering. One night he halted in the village as of old; in the morning he set forth on his journey. . . .

"Two vast streams of people met on that day. The one poured out from the city, and as they came through the gardens (Mark xi. 8; John xii. 12), whose clusters of palm rose on the southern corner of Olivet, they cut down the long branches, as was their wont at the Feast of Tabernacles, and moved upwards towards Bethany, with loud shouts of welcome. From Bethany streamed forth the crowds who had assembled there on the previous night, and who came testifying (John xii. 17) to the great event at the festival of Lazarus. . . . Along the road the multitudes threw down the boughs severed from the olive-trees, through which they were forcing their way, or spread out a rude matting, formed of the palm-branches which they had already cut as they came out. The larger portion — those, perhaps, who escorted him from Bethany — unwrapped their loose cloaks from their shoulders, and stretched them along the rough path, to form a momentary carpet as he approached (Matt. xxi. 8). The two streams met midway. Half of the vast mass, turning round, preceded; the other half followed. Bethany is hardly left in the rear, before the long procession must have swept up and over the ridge, where first begins 'the Descent of the Mount of Olives' towards Jerusalem. At this point the first view is caught of the southeastern corner of the city. The Temple, and the more northern portions are hid by the slope of Olivet on the right; what is seen is only Mount Zion, now for the most part a rough field, crowned with the mosque of David, and the angle of the western walls, but then covered with houses to its base, surmounted by the Castle of Herod, on the supposed site of the palace of David, from which that portion of Jerusalem, emphatically 'The City of David,' derived its name. It was at this precise point (Luke xix. 37), 'as He drew near at the descent of the Mount of Olives,'— may it not have been from the sight thus opening upon them? — that the hymn of triumph, the earliest hymn of Christian devotion, burst forth from the multitude, 'Hosanna to the son of David! Blessed is He that cometh in the name of the Lord. Blessed is the kingdom that cometh of our father David. Hosanna . . . peace . . . glory in the highest.' There was a pause as the shout rang through the long defile; and, as the Pharisees who stood by in the crowd, complained, He pointed to the 'stones' which, strewn beneath their feet, would immediately 'cry out' if 'these were to hold their peace.'

"Again the procession advanced. The road descended a slight declivity, and the glimpse of the city is again withdrawn behind the intervening ridge of Olivet. A few moments, and the path mounts again; it climbs a rugged ascent, it reaches a ledge of smooth rock, and in an instant the whole city bursts into view. As now the dome of the Mosque El Aksa rises like a ghost from the earth before the traveller stands on the ledge, so then must have risen the Temple-tower; as now the vast enclosure of the Mussulman sanctuary, so then must have spread the Temple-courts; as now the gray town on its broken hills, so then the magnificent city, with its background — long since vanished away — of gardens, and suburbs on the western plateau behind. Immediately below was the Valley of the Kedron, here seen in its greatest depth, as it joins the Valley of Hinnom, and thus giving full effect to the great peculiarity of Jerusalem, seen only on its eastern side — its situation as of a city rising out of a deep abyss. It is hardly possible to doubt that this rise and turn of the road, this rocky ledge, was the exact point where the multitude paused again, and 'He, when He beheld the city, wept over it.' . . . This, almost the only spot which the gospel narrative fixes with exact certainty, is almost the only unmarked spot — undefiled or unhallowed by mosque or church, chapel or tower — left to speak for itself, that here the Lord stayed His onward march, and here His eyes beheld what is still the most impressive view which the neighborhood of Jerusalem furnishes, and the tears rushed forth at the sight."

*The Mosque of Omar.* — "The other buildings of Jerusalem which emerge from the mass of gray ruin and white stones are few, and for the most part unattractive. What, however, these fail to effect, is in one instant effected by a glance at the Mosque of Omar. From whatever point that graceful dome with its beautiful precinct emerges to view, it at once dignifies the whole city. A dome graceful as that of St. Peter's, though of course on a far smaller scale, rising from an elaborately finished circular edifice, — this edifice raised on a square marble platform rising on the highest ridge of a green slope, which descends from it north, south, and east to the walls surrounding the whole enclosure, — platform and enclosure diversified by lesser domes and fountains, by cypresses and olives and planes and palms, —

the whole as secluded and quiet as the interior of some cathedral garden, only enlivened by the white figures of veiled women stealing like ghosts up and down the green slope, or by the turbaned heads bowed low in the various niches for prayer — this is the Mosque of Omar: the Haram es-Sherif, 'the noble sanctuary,' the second most sacred spot in the Mohammedan world, — that is, the next after Mecca; the second most beautiful mosque, — that is, the next after Cordova." — *Stanley.*

There can be no doubt that the Mount Moriah on which this mosque now stands, was once crowned with the House of the Lord built by Solomon at a cost and with a magnificence of which we can form no adequate idea (1 Kings vi. and vii.). The Mosque of Omar was begun by the caliph Omar in six hundred and thirty-seven, is of an octagonal shape, surmounted by a lead-covered dome, above which is a glittering crescent. It has four entrances, one of which, seen at the left in our view, is adorned by a fine portico, supported by eight Corinthian pillars of marble. Its forty-eight windows are of stained glass, and the walls are faced below with blue and white marble, and above with glazed tiles of various colors. It is altogether a fine specimen of light and elegant Oriental architecture. The interior is not allowed to be entered except by followers of the prophet, and but few Christians have ever been admitted within its walls.

*Bethlehem.* — In sacred interest this village is second only to Jerusalem itself. Few can climb the terraced acclivities that lead up to it, without calling to mind that event which has given its name to our era. But independent of all associations its appearance is striking. It is situated on a narrow ridge, which breaks down in abrupt terraced slopes to deep valleys. The terraces — admirably kept, and covered with rows of olives, intermixed with the fig and vine —

sweep in graceful curves round the ridge, regular as stairs.

The town is about six miles south of Jerusalem; there are in it a little above 3,000 inhabitants, by far the greater part of whom are Christians. They are peasants, living by the cultivation of their fields and gardens; and a few of them spend their spare time in carving beads, crucifixes, etc., for the pilgrims and travellers. Their houses are mean in the extreme. The country around — though, as in other parts of this neglected land, sadly wanting cultivation — is extremely fruitful, yielding figs, grapes, and olives in great abundance.

*Baalbek*, — Anciently a large and splendid city, is situated about forty miles northwest of Damascus. Its population in 1751 was 5,000; but in 1835 it was not more than two hundred. The remains of ancient architectural grandeur are however more extensive in Baalbek than in any other city of Syria, save Palmyra. Finely grouped together on the west side of the town are three temples, the largest having a circuit of more than half a mile, and originally consisting of a portico, hexagonal court, and a quadrangle, besides the peristyles of the temple itself. Of this last, — seen in the general view of the temples, — six gigantic and highly polished pillars, seventy-one and one half feet in height, and twenty-three feet in circumference, with their cornices and entablature remain to attest the stupendous magnitude and the beauty of the structure of which they made a part. In one wall there are still three enormous stones, of which two are sixty, and the other sixty-three feet in length, their common breadth and thickness being twelve feet. These gigantic masses are more than twelve feet from the ground. The doorway is surmounted by a superb basso-relievo, representing an eagle hovering, as it were, over the worshipper when about to render homage to the presiding deity. Walls, ceilings, capitals, entablatures, every spot where the chisel could be introduced, is covered with the most exquisitely-finished carving and sculpture, and though little cement has been used, the joints are so admirably formed that a penknife cannot be introduced into them. As Robinson says, "In vastness of plan, combined with elaborateness and delicacy of execution, they seem to surpass all others in Western Asia, in Africa, and in Europe." The whole neighborhood looks like an immense stone quarry, the country being covered for ten or twelve miles around with Greek, Roman, and Saracenic ruins, all evidently connected with the former greatness and prosperity of the city.

*Damascus.* — The virtual metropolis of Syria, Damascus, has about 120,000 inhabitants, and is remarkable as being the only city of the east which has not dwindled from its former greatness, while Babylon, Nineveh, and Palmyra have wholly vanished, and Antioch and Aleppo are but the shadows of their ancient glory. Of the people, about 12,000 are Christians, and as many are Jews, the rest being Mohammedans. The private residences of the gentry are the most striking objects to a stranger, not for their exterior appearance, which presents nothing but a gloomy wall of mud, or sun-dried bricks, but for the combined convenience, magnificence, and taste which mark the interior arrangements, and realize all that can be imagined of eastern splendor. Twenty thousand dollars are sometimes expended on the fitting up of a single apartment.

Damascus is very ancient; it is mentioned in Gen. xiv. 15, as existing 1,913 years B. C.; it was subdued by David (2 Sam. viii. 6), but recovered its independence again (1 Kings xi. 24). Allusion is also made to it in 1 Kings xv. 18, and in 2 Kings xvi. 9; as a Roman city it figures conspicuously in the history of the Apostle Paul (Acts ix.).

*Shiloh.* — For its location see Judg. xxi. 19, about a day and a half journey north from Jerusalem. The contour of the region, as the traveller views it on the ground, indicates very closely where the ancient town must have stood. A moderate hill rises from an uneven plain, surrounded by other higher hills, except a narrow valley on the south, which hill would naturally be chosen as the principal site of the town. The ruins found there at present are very inconsiderable. They consist chiefly of the remains of a comparatively modern village, with which some large stones and fragments of columns are intermixed, evidently from much earlier times. Near a ruined mosque flourishes an immense oak, the branches of which the winds of centuries have swayed. At the distance of about fifteen minutes' walk from the main site, is a fountain which would be a very natural resort for a festal party, and very probably was the place where the "daughters of Shiloh" were dancing, when they were surprised and borne off by their captors (Judg. xxi. 19, 21, 23). It is certainly true, as some travellers remark, that the scenery of Shiloh is not specially attractive; it presents no feature of grandeur or beauty, adapted to impress the mind, and awaken thoughts in harmony with the memories of the place. At the same time it deserves to be mentioned that, for the objects to which Shiloh was devoted, it was not unwisely chosen. It was secluded, and therefore favorable to acts of worship and religious study, in which the youth of scholars and devotees, like Samuel, was to be spent. Yearly festivals were celebrated there, and brought together assemblages which would need the supplies of water and pasturage so easily obtained in such a place. Terraces are still visible on the sides of the rocky hills, which show that every foot and inch of the soil once teemed with verdure and fertility. The ceremonies of such occasions consisted largely of processions and dances, and the place afforded ample scope for such movements. The surrounding hills served as an amphitheatre, whence the spectators could look and have the entire scene under their eyes. The position, too, in times of sudden danger, admitted of an easy defence, as it was a hill itself, and the neighboring hills could be turned into bulwarks. To the other advantages, we should add that of its central position for the Hebrews on the west side of the Jordan. An air of oppressive stillness hangs now over all the scene, and adds force to the reflection that truly the "oracles" so long consulted there "are dumb"; they had fulfilled their purpose and given place to "a more sure word of prophecy." — *Smith.*

*Shechem.*— The present city of Nabulus, known in Bible times by the name of Shechem, has a population of about five thousand, among whom are five hundred Greek Christians, one hundred and fifty Samaritans, and a few Jews. The enmity between the Jews and the Samaritans is as inveterate still, as it was in the days of Christ; the Mohammedans of course make up the bulk of the population. The city lies near the Mediterranean, in a sheltered valley at the foot of Mounts Ebal and Gerizim. Its streets are narrow, and the houses are of stone, of the most ordinary style.

Travellers vie with each other in the language which they employ to describe the scene that bursts upon them on arriving, in spring or early summer, at this paradise of the Holy Land. "As the traveller descends towards it from the hills," says Dr. Clarke, "it appears luxuriantly embosomed in the most delightful and fragrant bowers, half concealed by rich gardens, and by stately trees collected into groves, all around the bold and beautiful valley in which it stands." "The whole valley," says Dr. Robinson, "was filled with gardens of vegetables, and orchards of all kinds of fruits, watered by fountains which burst forth in various parts, and flow westward in refreshing streams. It came upon us suddenly, like a scene of fairy enchantment. We saw nothing to compare with it in all Palestine." It need hardly be said that it is from the abundant supply of water that this beauty is derived; twenty-seven springs, each known by its peculiar name, besides a crowd of smaller sources, pour their treasures into the valley, and have thus secured the perennial glory of its green, grassy sward, its olive-groves, its orchards of fig and vine and pomegranate. It was these features, no doubt, so unlike to those of Jerusalem, that made Shechem the first spot on which Abraham halted when he had crossed the Jordan, on his way from Chaldæa to the land which God should give him. It was the "place of Shechem." Shechem itself, it would seem, was not yet built; all was still in its primeval state. Yet there was enough of those noble groves to attract the wanderer's steps. Upon the "plain of Moreh" (Gen. xii. 6), now covered by a growth of olive-trees, Abraham rested, and built the first altar the Holy Land had known. Jacob, too, advanced through this valley, and pitched his tent before the city; and the spot where he had at last found a home, after his long wanderings, became the first possession of himself and his race in Palestine.

"He bought 'the' parcel of 'the' field where he had spread his tent," "of the children of Hamor, Shechem's father, for an hundred pieces of money."

*Nazareth.* — Nazareth is a small town, with a population numbering about 3,000, situated some seventy miles northeast of the city of Jerusalem. A few of its people are Mohammedans, the rest, Latin and Greek Christians. The houses are of stone, with mud floors and roofs. As streams in the rainy season are liable to pour down with violence from the hills, every "wise man," instead of building upon the loose soil on the surface, digs deep and lays his foundation upon the rock which is found so generally in that country, at a certain depth in the earth. The streets and lanes are narrow and crooked, and after a rain are so muddy as to be almost impassable.

Nazareth derives its celebrity almost entirely from its connection with the history of Christ, and in that respect has a hold on the imagination and feelings of men which it shares only with Jerusalem and Bethlehem. Fifteen gently rounded hills "seem as if they had met to form an enclosure" for this peaceful basin; they rise around it like the edge of a shell to guard it from intrusion. In this basin or enclosure, along the lower edge of the hill-side, lies the quiet secluded village in which the Saviour of men spent the greater part of His earthly existence. The surrounding heights vary in altitude; some of them rise to four hundred or five hundred feet. They have rounded tops, are composed of the glittering limestone which is so common in that country, and, though on the whole sterile and unattractive in appearance, present not an unpleasing aspect, diversified as they are with the foliage of fig-trees and wild shrubs, and with the verdure of occasional fields of grain. Our familiar hollyhock is one of the gay flowers that grow wild there. The enclosed valley is peculiarly rich and well cultivated; it is filled with corn-fields, with gardens, hedges of cactus, and clusters of fruit-bearing trees. Being so sheltered by hills, Nazareth enjoys a mild atmosphere and climate. Hence all the fruits of the country, such as pomegranates, oranges, figs, and olives, ripen early, and attain a rare perfection. "These are the natural features," says Stanley, " which for nearly thirty years met the almost daily view of Him who "increased in wisdom and stature within this beautiful seclusion. It is the seclusion which constitutes its peculiarity and its fitness for these scenes of the gospel history. Unknown and unnamed in the Old Testament, Nazareth first appears as the retired abode of the humble carpenter. Its separation from the busy world may be the ground, as it certainly is an illustration, of the Evangelist's play on the word 'He shall be called a Nazarene.' Its wild character, high up in the Galilean hills, may account both for the roughness of its population, unable to appreciate their own prophet, and for the evil reputation which it had acquired even in the neighboring villages, one of whose inhabitants, Nathanael of Cana, said, 'Can any good thing come out of Nazareth?' There, secured within the natural barrier of the hills, was passed that youth, of which the most remarkable characteristic is its absolute obscurity; and thence came the name of Nazarene, used of old by the Jews, and used still by Mussulmans, as the appellation of that despised sect which has now embraced the civilized world."

*Mount Carmel.* — This mountain — "the well-wooded place," as its name signifies — is in the southern part of Palestine, and forms a wall, as it were, between the plains of Sharon on the south, and Esdraelon on the north. It consists of a soft white limestone rock, and, as is common in limestone formations, abounds in caves, — as many as 2,000 in number, often of great length. Its highest summit is 1,728 feet above the level of the sea. It is still clothed with "excellency of wood" (Is. xxxiii. 9; Mic. vii. 14). Modern travellers speak of its "thick shrubberies," its "rocky dells and deep jungles of copse," its "impenetrable brushwood of oaks and other evergreens," or its "hollyhocks, jasmine, and various flowering creepers." Carmel is rendered familiar to the modern world by its being the Mount on which Elijah brought back Israel to allegiance to Jehovah, and slew the prophets of the foreign and false god; here at his entreaty were consumed the successive "fifties" of the royal guard; but here, on the other hand, Elisha received the visit of the bereaved mother whose son he was soon to restore to her arms (2 K. iv. 25, etc.).

The first of these three events, it is now generally accepted, took place at the eastern end of the ridge of the mountain. "There may well have stood on its sacred 'high-place,' the altar of Jehovah which Jezebel had cast down. Close beneath, on a wide upland sweep under the shade of ancient olives and round a well of water, said to be perennial, and which may therefore have escaped the general drought, and have been able to furnish water for the trenches round the altar, must have been ranged on one side the king and people with the eight hundred prophets of Baal and Astarte, and on the other the solitary and commanding figure of the prophet of Jehovah. Full before them opened the whole plain of Esdraelon: the city of Jezreel with Ahab's palace, and Jezebel's temple distinctly visible: in the nearer foreground, immediately under the base of the mountain, was clearly seen the winding bed of the Kishon. From the slaughter by the river's side, the king went up to the glades of Carmel to join in the sacrificial feast. And Elijah too ascended to the 'top of the mountain,' and there with his face on the earth remained wrapt in prayer, while his servant mounted to the highest point of all, whence there is a wide view of the blue reach of the Mediterranean, over the western shoulder of the ridge. . . . Seven times the servant climbed and looked, and seven times there was nothing. . . . At last out of the far horizon there rose a little cloud, and it grew in the deepening shades of evening till the whole sky was overcast, and the forests of Carmel shook in the welcome sound of the mighty winds which in eastern regions precede a coming tempest."

*Travellers on Dromedaries.* — The dromedary is a species

of camel. These animals are both natives of Asia, where, from the earliest ages to the present day, they have been the chief means of communication between the different regions of the east. Their peculiar adaptation to the uses and needs of their native clime, is a wonderful instance of the goodness and wisdom of the Creator. Their home is the desert, and they were made to be the carriers of the desert. The coarse and prickly shrubs of the wastes are to them the most delicious food; and even of these they eat but little. So few are the wants of their nature, that their power of going without food as well as without water, is most wonderful. Equally so is the adaptation of their broad, cushioned foot to the arid sands and gravelly soil, which it is their lot chiefly to traverse. They are also very sure-footed; their sense of smell is very acute; when all around were dying from thirst, they have been known to break the halter and run in a direct line to a spring a great distance off. The dromedary is a swift riding camel, distinguished from the latter by higher breeding and finer qualities.

*Ezion Geber.* — Its position is described in the Bible as " beside Eloth, on the shore of the Red Sea, in the land of Edom "; it was the last station named for the encampment of the Israelites, before they came to " the wilderness of Zin, which is Kadesh"; and was, subsequent to this, the station of Solomon's navy. Its position is designated, but does not rest beyond controversy. (See Num. xxxiii. 35; Deut. ii. 8; 1 K. ix. 26; xxii. 48; 2 Chron. viii. 17.)

*Hebron*, situated among the mountains, about twenty miles south from Jerusalem, like Damascus, is one of the oldest cities still in existence. It was a well-known town when Abraham entered Canaan 3,780 years ago (Gen. xiii. 18). It now contains about 5,000 inhabitants. It is picturesquely situated in a narrow valley, surrounded by rocky hills. The houses are all of stone, solidly built, flat-roofed, each having one or two small cupolas.

The chief interest of the city arises from its connection with the lives of the patriarchs; after Sarah's death, here Abraham bought the field and cave of Machpelah to serve as a national tomb. "High above us on the eastern height of the town," says Stanley, "which lies nestled, Italian-like, on the slope of a ravine, rose the long, black walls, and two stately minarets of that illustrious mosque, one of the four sanctuaries of the Mahometan world, sacred in the eyes of all the world besides, which covers the cave of Machpelah, the last resting-place of Abraham, Isaac, and Jacob (Gen. xlix. 31). . . . We walked round the western hills of Hebron. What deep delight to tread the rocks and drink in the view, which had been trodden by the feet and met the eyes of the patriarchs and kings. I observed, too, for the first time, the enclosures of vineyards with stone-walls, and towers at the corners for guards. The hills, except where occupied by vineyards and olive-groves, are covered with disjointed rocks and grass. . . . And marvellous, too, to think that within the massive enclosure of that mosque, lies, possibly, not merely the last dust of Abraham and Isaac, but the very body, — the mummy, — the embalmed bones of Jacob, brought in solemn state from Egypt, to this (as it then was) lonely and beautiful spot."

*Mount of Transfiguration.* — It is argued by Professor Stanley, in his "Sinai and Palestine," that Hermon is the mountain on which Christ was transfigured before his three disciples; and we believe this is now the generally received opinion among Biblical scholars, though probably it can never be settled beyond question. The position of Hermon is defined in Scripture, as being on the northeastern border of Palestine (Deut. iii. 8; Josh. xii. 1), over against Lebanon (Josh. xi. 17); adjoining the plateau of Bashan (1 Chr. v. 23). It is at the southern end of the anti-Libanus range, and makes its culminating point; it towers high above the ancient border city of Dan, and the fountains of the Jordan, and is the most conspicuous, as well as the most beautiful, mountain in Palestine or Syria. "From the moment that the traveller reaches the plain of Shechem in the interior, nay, even from the depths of the Jordan-valley by the Dead Sea, the snowy heights of Hermon are visible. The ancient names are all significant of this position. It is 'Sion,' 'the upraised' (Deut. iv. 48); or 'Hermon,' 'the lofty peak'; or 'Shenir,' and 'Sirion,' the glittering 'breast-plate' of ice (Deut. iii. 9; Cant. iv. 8; Ezekiel xxvii. 5)." So, now it is called "the chief mountain," and the "snowy mountain,"—which is certainly a name peculiarly appropriate. When the whole country is parched with the summer sun, white lines of snow streak the head of Hermon. "It was associated with their northern border, almost as immediately as the sun was with the western (Deut. iii. 8; iv. 48; Josh. xi. 17; xiii. 5; 1 Chr. v. 23). In one passage Hermon would almost seem to be used to signify "north," as the word "sea" is for "west"—"The north and the south Thou hast created them; Tabor and Hermon shall rejoice in Thy name" (Ps. lxxxix. 12). The reason is, that from every quarter and from great distances, that pale-blue, snow-capped cone forms the one feature on the northern horizon. In Psalms cxxxiii. 3, Zion is probably used for Sion, which, as we have seen, was a former name for Hermon. "As the dew of Hermon, the dew that descended upon the mountains of Zion." It appears that the snow on the summit of Hermon condenses the vapors floating in summer, in the higher regions of the atmosphere, causing light clouds to hover around it, and abundant dew to descend on it, while their whole country elsewhere is parched, and the whole heaven elsewhere cloudless. A knowledge of the fact that Hermon has three summits, will be of value in understanding Psalms xlii. 6, and perhaps also 1 Chron. v. 23. The snow never entirely leaves the summits, and in spring and early summer the top is entirely covered.

*Sinai, the Wilderness of Paran.* — Sinai, the Plain of the Assemblage. Nearly in the centre of the peninsula which stretches between the horns of the Red Sea, lies a wedge of granite, grünstein, and porphyry rocks, rising to between 8,000 and 9,000 feet above the sea. This nucleus of rocks in its general configuration runs into neither ranges nor peaks, but is that of a plateau cut across with intersecting water-courses, — dry save in the rainy season, — whence spring the cliffs and mountain peaks. This whole mountain section is known as Sinai.

Enclosed within this section is the Wilderness of Paran, a stretch of chalky formation, the chalk being covered with coarse gravel, mixed with black flint and drifting sand. The surface of this extensive tract is a slope ascending towards the north, and in it appear to rise three chalky ridges, as it were, terraces of mountainous formation. Whether or not this is the Paran of Scripture is not settled beyond controversy; but there are many strong evidences that it is, drawn from the correspondence between the natural formation of the region and the descriptions in the Old Testament.

It is again matter of doubt which of the main summits of the mountainous section known by the general name of Sinai is the Mount Sinai of the Bible. Sinai is clearly a summit distinctly marked. Thus in Neh. ix. 13, we read, "Thou camest down upon Mount Sinai." It would be impossible for us from want of space, besides being without the purpose of these sketches, to follow the arguments of scholars on this difficult historical problem; it must be sufficient for us to say the strongest authorities adopt the spot of which our views are taken, as the site of the assembling of the Israelites to receive the law.

The scene is thus described by Stanley : " Here is a basin surrounded by lofty peaks. That which commands the widest view is covered with giant blocks, as if the mountain had there been shattered and split by an earthquake. A vast cleft divides the peak into two summits. But whether or not this high mountain be the Mountain of the Law, the plain below will still remain the essential feature of the view of the Israelite camp. That such a plain should exist at all in front of such a cliff is so remarkable a coincidence with the sacred narrative, as to furnish a strong internal argument, not merely of its identity with the scene, but of the scene itself having been described by an eye-witness. The awful and lengthened approach, as to some natural sanctuary, would have been the fittest preparation for the coming scene. The low line of alluvial mounds at the foot of the cliff, exactly answers to the ' bounds' which were to keep the people off from 'touching the mount.' The plain itself is not broken and uneven, and narrowly shut in, like almost all others in the range, but presents a long retiring sweep, against which the people could ' remove and stand afar off.' The cliff, rising like a huge altar in front of the whole congregation, and visible against the sky in lonely grandeur from end to end of the whole plain, is the very image of ' the mount that might be touched,' and from which the ' voice' might be heard far and wide over the stillness of the plain below, widened at that point to its utmost extent by the confluence of all the contiguous valleys."

Our view of the Plain is from the Convent of Mount Sinai, which we cannot well pass without a somewhat lengthened description. It has been well spoken of as an " oasis to the desert pilgrim." After the fatigue and anxiety of a journey amid the native wastes of that country, and with no better company than that of the wild Bedouin, a sweet feeling of rest and security comes over the traveller on entering it, only to be fully realized with such an experience. There is something soothing, too, in the moaning of the mountain breeze as it sweeps through the long and silent corridors; in the grave costume and solemn step of the holy fathers; in the quiet grandeur of the hills around, and more than all in the plaintive murmur of the chanted prayers breaking forth from the old church amid the death-like stillness of the night. Here, too, there is all the wild magnificence of nature, combined with historic interest and sacred associations, to attract and inspire the pilgrim.

The labyrinth of buildings that constitute the convent, forms a quadrangular area measuring two hundred and forty feet by two hundred feet, encompassed by thick and lofty walls of granite, with little towers at intervals, on some of which are mounted a few small and antiquated cannon. The space enclosed is cut up into many little courts, some of them with beds of flowers and vegetables, and others with cypresses and trees of other kinds; vines are trained along the walls or over the trellis-work. A garden, also surrounded by a wall, adjoins the convent. It is gained by a subterranean passage, secured by a heavy iron door. The olive, almond, and apricot trees are of great age, and look like patriarchs amid the more numerous groups of figs, pears, apples, mulberries, and quinces. Here and there are beds of vegetables, and though the holy fathers are neither industrious nor skilful, yet the garden is a gem in the desert.

In the very centre of this bright and joyous spot, is a low building, partly subterranean, which has for centuries been the last resting-place of the monks. Entombed here are the remains of two hermits, brothers of exalted rank, as tradition has it. Bound to each other through life by a massive chain, they wore away their weary years in some rock-hewn cave; and thus linked, encountered death together.

In the church, the most important building of the convent, is a representation in mosaic, on the vaulted roof, of the Transfiguration,— Christ in the centre, Moses on the right, and Elias on the left; and the three apostles are beneath, Peter being prostrate. There is also a portrait of Moses on his knees before the burning bush, and on the opposite side of the window he is represented receiving the tablets of the Law.

The discipline of the convent is extremely severe. Not simply do these men banish themselves from society, but they also submit to other privations, such as few men would endure. Flesh and wine are entirely prohibited; and during the great fast, the monks are forced to abstain from butter, milk, and every species of animal product, and even from olive-oil. Their only food is bread, boiled vegetables, and fruit. Add to this that the service of the Greek ritual is performed in the church *eight* times, in the twenty-four hours; and every brother must be present at least four times, twice during the day, and twice during the night.

*Defile near the Red Sea. The Wâdy El Aim.* — "Of the Spring," a tortuous valley (Wâdy signifies valley), having a rill of clear, fresh water descending into it, and from which it takes its name. "Its course," says Stanley, "is marked by rushes, the large-leaved plant called 'Esher,' tamarisks, and wild palms. The rocks rise, red granite or black basalt, occasionally tipped as if with castles of sandstone, to the height of about 1,000 feet. They are absolutely bare, except where the green 'lasaf,' or caper plant, springs from the clefts. Occasionally they overlap and narrow the valley greatly. Finally they open on the sea, the high Arabian mountains rising beyond. At the mouth of the pass are many traces of flood, — trees torn down, and strewed along the sand."

These springs, whose sources are for the most part high up in the mountain clefts, occasionally send down into the wâdys rills of water, which, however scanty, however little deserving of the name even of brooks, yet become immediately the nucleus of whatever vegetation the desert produces. Wherever these springs are to be found, there, we cannot doubt, must always have been the resort of wanderers of the Desert.

*The Cedars of Lebanon.* — " The visit of Sennacherib is a direct reflection of his scornful speech as reported by the prophet Isaiah (xxxvii. 24, 25), and opens to us a striking historical scene in this portion of Syria. 'By the multitude of my chariots am I come to the height of the mountains, and to the sides of Lebanon; and I will cut down the height of his cedars and the beauty of his cypresses; and I entered into the height of his border, and the forest of his park. I have digged, and drunk waters; I have made a bridge.' ' The multitude of his chariots,' such as they are seen on the Assyrian monuments of the farther East, must have wound their difficult way through those romantic gorges, up to the very 'height of the mountain ranges,' and along ' the extreme edges of Lebanon,' along the valleys of the streams which he drained off by his armies, or over which he threw bridges for them to pass.

" But there was one spot more sacred than all to which the conqueror boasts that he had penetrated. He had gone into ' the extremest height of Lebanon, the forest of its park'; and there he had cut down with relentless insolence ' the height of its cedars, the beauty of its fir trees.' "

In these words it is hardly possible not to recognize the sacred recess of the present cedars of Lebanon.

It is from the village of Ehden, with its many churches and its beautiful viaducts surrounding the castle of its daring chief, Sheyeh Joseph, that the ascent is made to the cedars. A wide view opens of the long terraces of the *moraines* (as they are technically called) of ancient glaciers descending into the valley. Here a slip of cultivated land reaches up into the verge of their desolate fields. Behind this is a semicircle of the snowy range of the summit of Lebanon. Just in the centre of the view, in the dip between the moraines and the snow-clad hills behind, is a single dark massive clump, — the sole spot of vegetation that marks the mountain wilderness. This is the Cedar Grove. It disappears as we ascend the intervening range, and does not again present itself till we are close upon it. Then the exactness of Sennacherib's description comes out. It is literally on the very "edge" of the height of Lebanon. The outskirts of the eminence are clothed with the younger trees, whose light feathery branches veil the more venerable patriarchs in the interior of the grove. This younger growth, which has entirely sprung up within the last two centuries, amounts now to more than three hundred. The older trees, which are so different in appearance as to seem to belong to a different race, are now about twelve in number. They stand at the apex, so to say, of the vegetable world.

In ancient days the grove must have been very extensive. Now the great trees are huddled together in two or three of the central vales.

We know not who first attacked the forests of Lebanon. But the great destroyer, long remembered, was Sennacherib. The great trees have, since his time, become rarer and rarer. By the time of Justinian, the supply of cedar-wood was about exhausted, and by the time of Edward IV entirely so, for all purposes of building. And now, for at least two centuries, they have become invested, by the veneration of pilgrims, and by the increased admiration of nature, with a sanctity almost approaching to that with which they were revered as special miracles of Divine power by the Hebrew Psalmist. — *Stanley's Sinai and Palestine.*

## CHAPTER XLIII.

### EGYPT, OR THE LAND OF HAM.

EGYPT is called in the Bible "the land of Ham," not because pork was so plentiful there, but because Ham, the son of Noah, went towards Egypt, and some of his descendants settled in that country.

Egypt is often spoken of in the Bible, and its history is very interesting. But we are not going to tell you now about Joseph being in prison there, nor of the Israelites in slavery, nor of the holy child Jesus being carried into that land to escape the anger of Herod: you can read about all these things in the Scriptures.

*The Pyramids.* — There are about forty of them in what is called "Middle Egypt." They extend up and down the valley for eight or ten miles. Most of them are comparatively small; but a few of them are large enough to cause them to be reckoned among "the wonders of the world." Cheops is the name of the largest. It is built of great stones, and covers an area of nearly thirteen acres. What a mountain of stone that must be for human hands to rear! Many a man with thirteen acres of land would think he had quite a farm. And then how high it is! — more than twice the height of Bunker-Hill Monument, which is called two hundred and twenty-one feet. Imagine a tree eighty feet high (and that is a very tall tree); and yet it would take five or six of these, one above another, to be as high as the Great Pyramid. These Pyramids have stood for thousands of years. They seem to have been designed for tombs of kings, though they may have served other purposes.

But see the *Sphinx!* It looks like a man's head and shoulders coming up out of the ground. It is facing the east, and looks small because it is so near the Pyramid; and yet it is more than fifty-five feet high; and the head measures round the forehead about eighty-eight feet. It is a monolith; that is, it is of one piece, cut from the naked rock of the limestone ledge of which it forms a part.

We have not time nor space to tell you about the palm-trees and camels and pillars: but if what we have said leads you to read some good books about this ancient kingdom of Egypt, you will there find them described; and it will do you much more good than reading a multitude of trashy novels. The Bible says God has "done great things in Egypt, wondrous works in the land of Ham, and terrible things by the Red Sea" (Ps. cvi. 21,22); and an acquaintance with these Bible wonders will be better for you than a knowledge of a great many other things. — *Youth's Visitor.*

*Pompey's Pillar.* — "This monument stands on an eminence about 1,800 feet to the south of the present walls. It consists of a capital, shaft, base, and pedestal, which last reposes on substructions of smaller blocks, once belonging to older monuments, and probably brought to Alexandria for the purpose. On one I observed the name of the First Psammetichus. . . . Its substructions were evidently once under the level of the ground, and formed part of a paved area, the stones of which have been removed (probably to serve as materials for more recent buildings), leaving only those beneath the column itself, to the great risk of the monument.

"The name given to this column has led to much criticism. . . . To me it appears probable that this column silently records the capture of Alexandria by the arms of Diocletian in A. D. 296." A Greek inscription on the column contains the name of Diocletian.

"The total height of the column is ninety-eight feet nine inches, the shaft is seventy-three feet, the circumference twenty-nine feet eight inches, and the diameter at the top of the capital, sixteen feet six inches." — *Wilkinson*. A statue was, doubtless, at one time standing on the summit. Some English sailors who had ascended it a few years ago, observed remaining there the foot of a statue; and in an old picture or plan of Alexandria, where some of the ancient monuments are represented, is the figure of a man standing on the column.

*Cleopatra's Needle.* — "The obelisks known as Cleopatra's Needles, Pliny mentions as standing before the Temple of Cæsar. He supposes them to have been cut and sculptured by Mesphes. In this, indeed, he is not far from the truth, since the Pharaoh whose ovals they bear was the third Thothmes; and it is remarkable that the names of two kings who lived about that period, the first and second Thothmes, are written in Manetho's list, as Mesphra-Thothmosis. In the lateral lines are the ovals of Rameses the Great, the supposed Sesostris, and additional columns of hieroglyphics at the angles of the lower part, present that of a later king, apparently Sethei or Osirei II, the third successor of the great Rameses.

"They stood originally at Heliopolis, and were brought to Alexandria by one of the Cæsars; though fame has attached to them the title of Cleopatra's Needles, with the same disregard to truth that ascribes to her the honor of erecting the Hepastadium and the Pharos. They are of red granite of

Syene, like most of the obelisks in Egypt, and about fifty-seven paces apart. The standing obelisk is about seventy feet high, with a diameter at its base of seven feet seven inches. Pliny gives them forty-two cubits, or sixty-three feet. One is still standing, the other has been thrown down, and lies close to its pedestal, which stood on two steps of white limestone; the pedestals of Egyptian obelisks being usually a square dado or die, without any moulding, scarcely exceeding the diameter of the obelisk, and placed upon two plinths, the one projecting beyond the other in the form of steps.

"The height of the fallen obelisk, in its mutilated state, is about sixty-six feet, and of the same diameter as the other. It was given by Mohammed Ali to the English, who were desirous of removing it to England, as a record of their successes in Egypt, and of the glorious termination of the campaign of 1801. But, from its mutilated state, and the obliteration of many of the hieroglyphics, by exposure to the sea air, it was considered unworthy the expense of removal, and the project was wisely abandoned."— *Wilkinson.*

*Cairo. From the citadel, with Mosque of Sultan Hassan.*
— "Musr el Kaherah, corrupted by the Italians into Cairo, was founded by Góher, a general of El Moez, or Aboo Tummim, the first of the Fowatem, or Fatemite dynasty who ruled in Egypt. He was sent in the year 358 of the Hegira, A. D. 969, with a powerful army from Kayrawan (in the modern regency of Tunis), the capital of the Fowatem, to invade Egypt; and having succeeded in conquering that country, he founded a new city near the citadel of Kuttaëea under the name of Musr el Kaherah. This in 362 (A. D. 973) became the capital, instead of Fostat; which then, by way of distinction, received the name of Musr el Ateekeh, or old Musr, . . . which has been transformed by Europeans into old Cairo.

"The epithet Kaherah, is derived from Kaher, and signifies victorious."

"The walls of Cairo were built of brick, and continued in the same state till the reign of Yoosef Sala-e-deen, who substituted a circuit of stone, and united to the original town the whole of that part lying between the Bab Zooayeh and the citadel." — *Wilkinson.*

Yoosef Sala-e-deen is well known in the history of the crusades, under the name of Saladin. Shortly before his arrival, and during the troubles that obscured the latter end of the reign of the Fowatem, whom he had expelled, Cairo had been attacked by the Franks, and partly burnt upon their approach. Their designs against the city were unsuccessful; but in order to place it effectually beyond the reach of similar attempts, Saladin raised around it a stronger wall of masonry, and observing that the elevated rock to the south of the city offered a convenient position for the construction of a fortress, to command and protect it, he cleared and walled in that spot; and discovering a large well near the centre, that had been cut by the ancients, and was then filled with sand, he excavated it, and brought another welcome supply of water to the citadel by an aqueduct, which conveyed a continuous stream from the Nile, at Fostat, to the new citadel. This last was merely a conduit, supported on wooden pillars. In 1518, the stone aqueduct, still used for the same purpose, was substituted by order of Sultan el Ghóree.

"It is probable that the well above mentioned, which now bears the name Beer Yoosef, 'Joseph's well,' from the Calif Yoosef, was hewn in the rock by the ancient Egyptians. . . . It seems, indeed, to be generally allowed by the Cairenes, that Yoosef was not the real author of this great work; and some have claimed it with little show of probability for Amer, the first Moslem conqueror of Egypt. It consists of two parts, the upper and lower well; and a winding staircase leads to the bottom, a depth of about two hundred and sixty feet. The water is raised by oxen, by means of wheels and buckets. The exact part of Cairo occupied by the Egyptian town is uncertain; but we learn from Arab writers that two villages existed there before the time of Góher, one called El Maks, where the Copt quarter now stands, and the other El Kuttaëea."

All travellers agree in stating the view from the ramparts of the citadel to be incomparably magnificent. The whole city, with its gardens, fountains, squares, palaces, mosques, and minarets, lies stretched out at your feet; the port of Bulak, the populous town of Fostat, the broad, majestic stream of the Nile, interspersed with islands, with its rich valley from Sakkara on the south, to the apex of the Delta on the north, the village of Ghiza, on the opposite bank, and those eternal monuments of human skill and folly, — the pyramids,—are under your eye. Though at least twelve miles off, the courses of stones of which the pyramids are composed, with the head of the Sphinx rising out of the sand, are perfectly distinguishable by the naked eye, so enormously great are those masses. From the city to the port of Bulak on the north, the intervening ground is clothed with fields of corn, groves of lime and orange trees; and the road is raised some feet, to preserve it from the inundation of the river. On the west side, the rich alluvial plain is checkered with long avenues of trees, luxuriant fields, rich gardens, and spacious villas. On the opposite or east side, there are no suburbs; all here is desolate, — a sea of sand, dry and lifeless. The road to old Cairo on the south passes through a highly cultivated district.

*Tombs of the Mamelukes, showing the Citadel.* — " Besides the well described above, the citadel contains many interesting objects; among which may be mentioned the palace, the new mosque built by Mohammed Ali, and the arsenal. Part only of the old citadel walls now remain, the others having been replaced by bastions and curtains of European construction; and what strikes a stranger, the portion most strongly and regularly fortified, is that least open to foreign aggression, the town side.

"The spot is shown a little to the north of the Roomáylee gate, where Emin Bey escaped, during the well-known massacre of the Memlooks, by leaping his horse over a gap in the then dilapidated wall. But, independent of that opening, a large mound of rubbish had accumulated below, from the fallen materials, and it is to this that his safety must principally be attributed." — *Wilkinson.*

In reference to the Tombs, see *post.*

*Egypt. — Cairo. Mosque of Mohammed Ali.* — This mosque stands on the site of Joseph's Hall. It consists of an open square, surrounded by a single row of columns, ten on the north and south, thirteen on the west, and twelve on the east, where a row leads to the inner part, or house of prayer; as in the Tayloon and other mosques of a similar plan. The columns have a fancy capital supporting round arches, and the whole, with the exception of the outer walls, is of Oriental alabaster. But it has not the pure Oriental character of other works in Cairo; and it excites admiration for the materials, rather than for the style of its architecture.

*Egypt. — Cairo. Tombs of the Mamelukes.* — The number of tombs in the neighborhood of Cairo is enormous. All the different races of men have distinct burying-grounds. The English are buried with the Greeks. The tombs of the Memlook (or Mameluke) sultans, immense cemeteries, crowned with domes, minarets, and gilt pavilions, are much more magnificent than the abodes of the living. This necropolis, or city of the dead, hardly less in extent than one third of the city itself, is a little to the east of Cairo, on the dreary and sandy skirts of the desert.

The name "Mameluke" is derived from an Arabic word signifying a *slave*. The corps of Mamelukes was instituted in the early part of the thirteenth century. Malek Salech, grandson of Safadeen, brother of the famous Saladin, conceived the idea of purchasing a large number of slaves, and training them to arms, as a means of protecting his dominions, and making head against his enemies. It was easier to raise such a force than to control it. The markets of Asia were at that time glutted with slaves, in consequence of the devastating wars of Genghis Khan. Malek Salech bought 12,000, chiefly young natives of the Caucasian regions. These were trained in military exercises and embodied into a corps which became formidable to its masters; in 1254 they revolted and killed Tooran Shah, the successor of Malek, and placed Ibegh, one of their own number, on the throne. Their dominion in Egypt continued two hundred and sixty-three years. The command was usually held by the bravest of their number. During this time they made some important conquests, and in 1291 drove the Franks entirely out of the East. In 1517 they were defeated by Selim I, sultan of the Ottomans; but he was obliged to maintain them as a sort of military aristocracy. The Beys of the Memlooks, twenty-four in number, continued to be the governors of as many districts. With but little dependence on the Porte, this aristocracy continued until July, 1798, when, in the battle of the Pyramids, the Memlook cavalry was nearly destroyed by dashing itself upon the French squares, which were supported by artillery. The remains of this once splendid body with their beys retreated into Upper Egypt. In 1801, the captain Pacha treacherously murdered several of the beys whom he had invited to a conference. And on the 1st of March, 1811, the famous Mehemet Ali invited the remaining beys to a banquet in the citadel of Cairo; and as they were leaving the feast, they were fallen upon and slain, with the exception of a few who escaped into Dongola. They are now extinct as a body. "The Memlooks were recruited from Caucasian slaves. The office of bey was not hereditary, but was elective among them. Their morals were very depraved; they were rapacious and merciless, and their extinction has been rather an advantage than a loss to humanity." — *Penny Cyc.*

*Egypt. — Cairo. Tombs of the Caliphs.* — "These tombs, called by Europeans 'Tombs of the Caliphs,' are really the tombs of the Mameluke kings. They are outside of the walls to the east of the town. The true 'Tombs of the Caliphs' occupied the site of what is now the Bazaar of Khan-Khaléel, but they are all destroyed with the exception of that of the seventh and last caliph of the Eiyoobite dynasty." — *Wilkinson.*

*The Great Pyramid and Sphinx, erected before Abraham went down into Egypt.* — The *pyramids* have been frequently mentioned by ancient and modern writers; but the statements of the former respecting their founders are far from satisfactory, and no conjecture seems to explain the object for which they were erected. The Great Pyramid, according to Herodotus, was founded by King Cheops. The ascent of this pyramid is by no means difficult. On the summit is a space about thirty-two feet square (larger than in the time of Pliny), having been increased when the casing and the outer tiers were removed by the caliphs, to serve for the construction of buildings in Cairo.

The Great Pyramid covered an area of 571,536 square feet. Present area, 535,824 square feet.

The length of each face, when entire, was seven hundred

and fifty-six feet, by measurement. Present base, seven hundred and thirty-two feet. Perpendicular height when entire, four hundred eighty feet nine inches, by calculation. Present height by calculation, four hundred and sixty feet.

The interior of the Great Pyramid contains several chambers, passages, and galleries. The principal apartment is thirty-four feet long, seventeen feet seven inches broad, and nineteen feet two inches high. The roof is flat, and formed of simple blocks of granite resting on the side walls, which are of the same materials. Towards the upper end is a sarcophagus of the same kind of red granite, three feet one inch high, seven feet four inches long, by three feet broad. The sarcophagus is destitute of hieroglyphics and of every kind of sculpture. The names of *Suphis* and *Nou-Shofo* are found in the great pyramid, in several places, having been painted on the stones before they were built into the walls. The pyramids stand exactly due north and south, and while the direction of the faces east and west might serve to fix the return of a certain period of the year, the shadow cast by the sun at the time of coinciding with their slope, might be observed for a similar purpose. Suphis probably lived 2400 B. C.

The colossal sphinx, near the group of pyramids, has recently been uncovered by Caviglia. It is about one hundred and fifty feet long, and sixty-three feet high; the body is monolithic, but the paws which are thrown out fifty feet in front, are composed of masonry. Between the paws was found an altar, where no doubt sacrifices were offered, and near the body in front three tablets, on one of which King Thothmes IV is represented offering on one side incense, on the other, a libation to the figure of a sphinx.

*Pyramid of Sakkara.*—About nine miles south of the Great pyramid are the Pyramids of Sakkara. The largest has its degrees or stories stripped of their triangular exterior. It measures, according to Col. Vyse, three hundred and fifty-one feet and two inches, on the north and south faces, and three hundred and ninety-three feet eleven inches, on the east and west, and is surrounded by what may be considered a sacred enclosure, about 1,750 feet by nine hundred and fifty feet. Within, it resembles a hollow dome supported here and there by wooden rafters. At the end of the passage opposite to the entrance of this dome is a small chamber, on whose doorway are hieroglyphics, containing the square title or banner of a very old king.

*Egypt. — Thebes. The Temple of Luksar, the Propylons, Obelisk, etc.* — "Luxor, with several adjacent villages, stands on the site of the ancient city of Thebes. It is on the right bank of the Nile. Near the shore are the stupendous remains of an ancient temple. The rear of this temple rests upon the river. The front looks east, towards the village of Karnak and its ruins, with which this temple was formerly connected by an avenue of sculptured sphinxes, one and a half miles in length. The propylon or gateway of the temple is about 1,000 feet from the Nile. It may be described as two towers or oblong masses of masonry, rising on either side of the entrance into the temple. The length of both, including the space or door between them, is about two hundred feet. These towers, or parts of the propylon contract regularly to the summit. They are fifty-seven feet in height, above the present surface. Two staircases — one impassable, the other nearly so — lead to their summits, where a good view is gained of the plan of the temple itself, which it is not so easy to obtain from below, and of the site and plain of Thebes. A few yards in front of the propylon, and south of the entrance, stands a beautiful obelisk of red granite, ten feet square at the base, and more than eighty feet high. It is covered with hieroglyphics, the most perfect and beautiful I have seen. They are nearly two inches deep, and appear as fresh and entire as a recent inscription. There was another obelisk similar to this in front of the north half of the propylon. It is now standing in the Place de la Concorde, in Paris, close to the spot where Louis XVI, Robespierre, etc., were beheaded. Between the obelisks and the propylon, on the right and left of the entrance, are two colossal statues, said by Wilkinson to be those of Rameses II, which, though buried in rubbish to the breast, still measure twenty-two feet in height. The front of this massive pile, through which we enter the temple, is covered with sculpture, representing a battle-scene. The most ancient portion of this edifice is ascribed to Amunoph III, who ascended the throne B. C. 1430."

## CHAPTER XLIV.

### THE BIG TREES OF CALIFORNIA.

THESE wonders of the forest, we are told by Dr. Prime, were discovered in 1852, by a hunter, whose story met with no credence, until others had penetrated the same wilds, and had seen for themselves. They have now a name and celebrity throughout the wide world, and although they are not indigenous in any other country, or in any other part of this country, they are now growing in almost every land, propagated from seeds taken in the cone from California.

The generic name of the tree — *Sequoia* — perpetuates the memory of George Guess, the ingenious Cherokee half-breed, who invented an alphabet that was for a long time in use among that nation. His Indian name — Sequoyah — was given to the newly-discovered Redwood of California, by the learned botanist, Eudilcher, who first defined the genus, calling the tree *Sequoia sempervirens*. The leaf of the Redwood is flat, like that of the *Arbor Vitæ*. The particular species abundant throughout the vicinity of the Yosemite Valley, is called *Sequoia gigantea*. They are in patches or groves, of which there are eight principal ones.

The Calaveras Grove was the first one discovered, and contains the tallest trees, though not the largest. It is composed of about one hundred trees, one of which, twenty-seven feet in diameter, was felled some years since, by boring at its base, and the stump, smoothed off about six feet from the ground, has been made the scene of festivities, in which a large company has taken part. It was carefully examined to ascertain its age, and 1,255 concentric circles, indicating as many years, were counted. Another tree, of seventy-six feet circumference, was carefully sawed, and the rings counted to the number of 1,935. The average height of the trees in this grove is three hundred to three hundred and twenty-five feet. The highest one is named the "Keystone State."

The Mariposa Grove is situated about fifteen miles south of the Yosemite Valley, and was ceded, in connection with the Valley, by act of Congress, to the State of California, for preservation. It has one hundred and twenty-five trees which are more than forty feet in circumference. The largest ones are ninety-two, ninety-one, eighty-seven, and eighty-two feet. One tree in this grove, now partially burned at the base, was originally more than one hundred feet in circumference. The Sequoia is peculiarly exposed to the ravages of fire. The bark is some eighteen inches thick, is as fibrous in its texture as a bale of cotton, and being perfectly dry, invites the raging element to a contest of strength.

There are tall trees in Australia, where the *Eucalyptus* has been known to reach the height of four hundred and eighty feet, but, taking them all in all, there are no vegetable wonders elsewhere that equal the Big Trees of California.

# INDEX.

## A.

Abbey, Craig, 261.
Abbot, Francis, "The Hermit of Niagara," 47, 58.
Abbotsford, Scotland, 258.
ADIRONDACK WILDERNESS, 144.
   Au Sable Chasm in, 148.
   Great Indian Pass in, 148.
   Location of, 145.
   Night Scene in, 146.
   Saranac Lakes, 148.
   Scenery of, 146.
   Upper Saranac, St. Regis, and Tupper's Lakes, 148.
Aiguille de Dru, 315.
Altorf, 330.
Alps, The, 292.
Aosta, 338.
Apostle Islands, 242.
APPENZELL, 333.
   Employment of the People, 334.
   Dress of the People, 335.
Arve River, 311.
Ashburton, England, 252.
Athens, Greece, 380.
AVALANCHES, 301.
   Destruction by, 301.
   of the Rossburg, 302.

## B.

Baalbek, 397.
Ballater Pass, 262.
Balmoral Castle, 259.
BALTIMORE, 116.
   Cathedral of, 118.
   Druid Hill Park, 118.
   Monuments in, 117.
   Paintings in, 118.
Banavie, Scotland, 259.
Ben Lomond, 262.
Ben Nevis, 259.
Bethany, 392.
Bethlehem, 396.
Bex, 322.
Birnam Hill, 260.
Blenheim Palace, 254.
BOSTON, MASS., 77.
   Churches of, 85.
   City Hall, 82.
   Common, 86.
   Custom-House, 82.
   Events in, during the Revolutionary War, 79.
   Exchange, 82.
   Faneuil Hall, 80.
   First Meeting-house, 79.
   First Newspaper, 79.
   First Settlement of, 77.

BOSTON, General Court of, 78.
   Hotels of, 86.
   Institutions of, 85.
   Museum, 84.
   Music Hall, 83.
   Old Granary Burying-Ground, 87.
   Post-Office, 83.
   Public Library, 84.
   Public Gardens, 87.
   State House, 81.
   Theatre, 84.
   Whence the Name of, 78.
Braemar Village, Scotland, 261.
Brendon Hill Incline, 252.
BROOKLYN, N. Y., 133.
   Greenwood Cemetery in, 133.
   Prospect Park, 133.
BUFFALO, N. Y., 139.
   Streets of, 140.
   Public Buildings in, 140.
Bunker-Hill Monument, 88.

## C.

CAIRO, EGYPT, 417.
   Joseph's Well, 418.
   Mosque of Mohammed Ali, 420.
   Tombs of the Caliphs, 422.
   Tombs of the Mamelukes, 419, 420, 422.
   View from Citadel, 419.
   Walls of, 418.
CALIFORNIA, 209.
   Apples of, 212.
   Area of, 209.
   Baron Munchausen Stories of, 218.
   Big Trees of, 425.
   Calaveras Grove, 426.
   Fig Trees of, 213.
   Fruits of, 211.
   Mariposa Grove, 426.
   Pears and Grapes, 212.
   Scarcity of Rain in, 210.
   Variety of Temperature, 210.
Calvin, John, 307.
Cambridge, Mass., 91.
Cape Cod, 75.
Cascade of Arpenaz, 310.
Cascade of Chède, 311.
Castle of Chillon, 322.
CATSKILL MOUNTAINS, 137.
   Clove of the Catterskill, 137.
   View from the Village of Catskill, 137.
Cedars of Lebanon, 412.
Chamouni, Valley of, 312.
   " Village of, 311.
CHICAGO, in 1870, 165.
   Bridges in, 168.
   Buildings of, 168.
   Court House, 172.
   Course of the fire, 170.

## 428                                    INDEX.

CHICAGO, Crib, The, 167.
   Description of the Great Fire, 174.
   First Settlement of, 167.
   Great Fire of Oct. 8th and 9th, 1871, 169.
   Happy Occasion in, 182.
   Horrors of the Fire, 183.
   Lincoln Park, 173.
   Mistake, a heart-rending, 181.
   Origin of the Fire, 170.
   Pacific Hotel, 171.
   Parks of, 168.
   Poem, by Carleton, "The burning of Chicago," 186.
   River of, 168.
   Relief for the Sufferers by the Fire, 184.
   Strange Error, 182.
   Sufferings of Women, 180.
CINCINNATI, 199.
   Commerce of, 200.
   Fountain of, 201.
   Inscription upon Fountain, 201.
   Literary Institutions, 200.
   Observatory in, 200.
   Position of, 199.
   Suburbs, beauty of the, 200.
Constantinople, 388.
Convent of Mount Sinai, 409.
Conway Castle, Eng., 253.
   " Suspension Bridge, Eng., 253.
Convent de la Graud Chartreuse, 287.
Cormayeur, 338.

### D.

Damascus, Syria, 398.
Dart River, 253.
DELLS OF THE WISCONSIN RIVER, 195.
   Black Hawk's Cave, 196.
   Eagle Cliff, 195.
   Stand Rock, 196.
   Sugar Bowl and Inkstand Islands, 196.
DEVIL'S LAKE, 196.
   Wonder Notch, near, 197.
Discovery of Ancient Cities, 374.
District of Columbia, 119.
Dromedaries, 404.
Drummond Castle, 260.
   " Garden, 260.
Duluth, Minn., 242.

### E.

Eddystone Lighthouse, 93.
EDINBURGH, 266.
   Castle of, 266.
   Holyrood Palace, 266.
   National Gallery, 268.
   Nelson's Monument, 266.
   Royal Institution, 268.
   Scott's Monument, 268.
Eiger, The, 326.
England, 246.
EGYPT, 414.
   Cleopatra's Needle, 416.
   Great Pyramid, 422.
   Luxor, or Thebes, 424.
   Obelisk of Luxor, 424.
   Pompey's Pillar, 415.
   Pyramids of, 414.
   Pyramid of Sakkara, 423.
   Statues, 425.
   Sphinx, 423.
   Temple of Luksar, 424.
Ezion Geber, 405.

### F.

FALLS OF MONTMORENCI, 63.
   Ice cone of, 64.
   " " ascent and descent of the, 65.
Falls of the Rhine, 336.
   " " Schaffhausen, 336.
Farallone Islands, 217.
Fenians, 51.
FINGAL'S CAVE, 263.
   Clamshell Cave, 263.
   Basaltic Colonnade, 263.
Fort Mackinaw and Fort Holmes, 244.
France, 276.

### G.

GENEVA, SWITZERLAND, 306.
   People of, 307.
Genoa, Italy, 340.
GIANTS' CAUSEWAY, 272.
   Honey Comb, 275.
   Lady's Chair, or Wishing-Chair, 275.
GIBRALTAR, the town of, 386.
   Bay of, 387.
   Fortress of, 387.
   Rock of, 387.
   Whence the name of, 387.
Giesbach Falls, 325.
GLACIER of the Aar, 328.
   Des Bossons, 314.
   " " Cavern of, 315.
   of Grindelwald, 327.
   Mer de Glace, 312.
   of the Rhone, 328.
   of Roseniaui, 327.
GLACIERS, 274.
   Accidents in ascending, 298.
   Causes of the Motion of, 295.
   Crossing of, 297.
   Motions of, 295.
Glarus, 333.
GLASGOW, 264.
   Bridge, 264.
   Broomielaw, 265.
   George Square, 265.
   Necropolis, 265.
   Scott's Monument, 265.
   The Trongate, 265.
Gorge of the Trient, 321.
Greece, 388.
Grindelwald, 326.

### H.

Harvard College, 91.
Hebron, 405.
HERCULANEUM, 363, 365.
   Ancient Manuscripts found in, 379.
   Bronze Statues in, 378.
   Difficulty of Excavating, 381.
   Equestrian Statues found in, 376, 378.
   Excavations near, 374.
   Private Dwellings of, 378.
   Theatre in, 377.
Hotel de la Couronne, 319.
Housatonic River, 104.

### I.

Ice Caverns, 295, 315, 327.
Ilfracombe, England, 253.
Interlaken, 324.

# INDEX. 429

Isle of Skye, 270.
Italy, 338.
Italian Scenery, 338.
ITHACA, N. Y., 138.
   Cornell University, 138.
   Enfield Falls, 139.
   Numerous Falls, 138.
   Taghanic Falls, 139.
IRELAND, area of, 270.
   Climate of. 271.
   Geology of, 271.
   Great Causeway, 272.
   Landlords of, 271.
   Pleaskin Head, 275.
   Population of, 271.
Island of St. Jules, 339.

## J.

JERUSALEM, 390.
   Gates of, 391.
   Gethsemane, 391.
   How situated, 390.
   Journey of Christ, 393.
JERUSALEM, Mountains about, 390.
   Mount of Olives, 392.
   Mosque of Omar, 395.
   Turkish Tombs and Arab Shepherds, 390.
   Walls of, 390.
Jungfrau, 325.

## K.

KILLIECRANKIE PASS, 264.
   Faskally House, 264.
Kilkenny Castle, 271.

## L.

Lake Erie, 245.
LAKE GEORGE, 134.
   Anecdote of Maj. Rogers, 135.
   Rogers' Rock, 134.
Lake Huron, 244.
   " d'Orta, 339.
LAKE MEMPHREMAGOG, 40.
   Balance Rock and Skinner's Cave, 42.
   Origin of the name of, 40.
   Scenery and Atmosphere of, 41.
Lakes of North America, 241.
LAKE SUPERIOR, 241.
   Keweenan Point, 242.
   Pictured Rocks, 243.
Lake Winnipiseogee, 16.
Lauterbrunnen, 325.
Le Petit Trianon, 286.
Loch Achray and Ben Venue, 263.
   " Katrine, 262.
   " Lomond, 262.
LONDON, ENG., area of, 246.
   Architecture of, 247.
   Buckingham Palace in, 248.
   Crystal Palace in, 249.
   Food required for, 246.
   Parliament, Houses of, 247.
   River Thames in, 247.
   Shillingford Bridge, 249.
   Tower of, 248.
   Trafalgar Square, 248.
   Westminster Hall, 247.
LOWELL, MASS., 96.
   Cotton Mills and amount manufactured in, 97.

Other manufacturing establishments, 97.
   Sixth Mass. Regiment, 97.
LUCERNE, SWITZERLAND, 330.
   Monument to the Swiss Guards, 330.
Lundy's Lane Battle-Ground, 58.
Luss, 262.
Luz, France, 290.
Lynton, England, 253.

## M.

MAMMOTH CAVE, KY., 202.
   Cascade in, 202.
   Cave Hotel, 202.
   Church in, 204.
   Dickson's Cave, 203.
   End of Cave, 208.
   Entrance to, 202, 203.
   Giant's Coffin, 205.
   Length of the, 208.
   Maelstrom in, 205.
   Main Cave, 204.
   Narrative Poem, "The Maelstrom," 205.
   Ownership of the Cave, 209.
   Rotunda, The, 204.
   Temperature of, 203.
Marquette, Mich., 243.
Martigny, Switzerland, 320.
Matterhorn and Monte Rosa, 321.
Melrose Abbey, 258, 269.
MILAN, 341.
   Cathedral of, or the Duomo, 341.
MILWAUKEE, WIS., 198.
   Brick of, 198.
   Commerce of, 198.
   Mills and Public Buildings, 199.
MINOT'S LEDGE LIGHTHOUSE, 93.
   Destruction of, 94.
   Difficulties attending the erection of, 94.
   Poem, "Minot's Ledge," 95.
   Rebuilding of, 94.
MISSOURI RIVER, 234.
   Great Falls of, 234.
Monastery of St. Bernard, 320.
Montana, 228.
MONT CENIS, 339.
   Tunnel of, 340.
MONTREAL, CANADA, 62.
   Victoria Bridge in, 62.
Mount Auburn, 92.
   " Blanc, 308, 309, 310, 312, 315.
   " Carmel, 403.
   " of Transfiguration, 406.
   " Sinai, 408.
   " Vernon, 256.

## N.

Naples, 359.
NATIONAL PARK, 227.
   Acts of Congress relating to, 227.
NATURAL BRIDGE, VIRGINIA, 151.
   Great height of, 153.
   Thrilling story of Miss Randolph, 153.
Nazareth, 401.
Negaunee, 243.
NEW HAVEN, location of, 98.
   a City of Refuge, 99.
   "Blue Laws," 98.
   Cemetery, 104.
   East and West Rocks, 100.
   Elms, 100.
   Hillhouse Avenue, 104.
   Monument to the Regicides, 99.

Old Buildings, 102.
New Buildings, 103.
Yale College, 101.
NEW ORLEANS, LA., 161.
 Custom House in, 162.
 Jackson Square, 161.
NEW YORK, 125.
 Battery, 126.
 Central Park, 127.
 "   "  Bridal Road, 130.
 "   "  Cave, 133.
 "   "  Central Lake, 131.
 "   "  Drive, 130.
 "   "  Flower Garden, 132.
 "   "  Fine Carriages, 129.
 "   "  Mall, 132.
 "   "  Ramble, 130.
 "   "  Tower Hill, 133.
 Harbor of, 126.
 Manhattan Island, 125.
NIAGARA FALLS. 43.
 Location and Dimensions of, 45.
 Biddle's Stairs, 52.
 Burning Spring, 54.
 Cave of the Winds, 54.
 Ferry House, 47.
 Falls receding, 57.
 Goat Island, 46, 47, 51.
 General description of, 45.
 Hotels, 46.
 Iris Island, 51.
 Narrow escapes from, 53.
 New Suspension Bridge, 56.
 Niagara in Winter, 54.
 Rapids, 45.
 Suspension Bridge, 55.
NIAGARA FALLS, Table Rock, 48.
 Terrapin Tower, 51.
 The Maid of the Mist, 48, 58.
 Three Sisters, 52.
 Under the Horse-Shoe Fall, 50.
 View from Prospect Point, 47.
 View from Suspension Bridge, 46.
 Whirlpool, 58.
NORTH CAROLINA, 154.
 Black Mountains in, 155.
 Chimney Rocks in, 156.
 French Broad in, 155.
 Gingercake Rocks in, 156.
 Mount Mitchell, 155.
NORTH CONWAY, N. H., 27.
 Artists' Brook in, 28.
 Nancy's Brook in, 28.
 Nancy's Tragedy in, 29.

O.

OWL'S HEAD MOUNTAIN, 42.
 Views from the top of, 43.

P.

Palermo, 363.
Palestine, 389.
PARIS, how situated, 276.
 Avenue de l'Imperatrice, 279.
 Boulevard de Sebastopol, 278.
 Boulevard de Strasbourg, 278.
 Champ de Mars, 279.
 Dome of the Pantheon, 277.
 Elysian Fields, 280.
 Hotel de Ville, 284.
 Houses of, 276.
 Luxembourg, 282.
 Park, 283.
 Mabille, 285.

Notre Dame, 277, 279.
Palais Royal, 283.
Place de Carrousel, 282.
Place de la Concorde, 277.
Place Saint Pierre, 284.
Pont Neuf, 278.
Pont et Place de la Concorde, 278.
Revue du 14 Aout, 277.
Rue de Rivoli, 277.
Salle des Gardes, and Salon de la Paix, 282.
The Louvre, 281.
The Tuileries, 281.
Tour Saint Jacques, 279.
Triumphant Arch, 282.
Universal Exposition in, 284.
Pass of St. Gothard, 328.
Peterborough Cathedral, 252.
Pfaffers, 336.
PHILADELPHIA, its name and early settlement, 105.
 Area of, 105.
 Am. S. S. Union Building, 113.
 Broad street, 114.
 Carpenters Hall, 107.
 Chestnut street, 112.
 Comfortable Homes for the Poor, 106.
 Custom House, 112.
 First Church, 108.
 Fairmount Park, 115.
 Franklin's Epitaph, 110.
 Girard College, 111.
 Graveyard of Christ Church, 110.
 Independence Hall, 106.
 Laurel Hill Cemetery, 114.
 Library, 113.
 Old Swedes Church, 108.
 Penn's Cottage, 108.
 The Mint, 113.
 The Vista Drive, 116.
 Treaty Monument, 111.
 United States Navy Yard, 114.
 View from the steeple of Christ Church, 109.
 Washington square, 107.
PLYMOUTH, MASS., 69.
 Autographs of the Pilgrims, 70.
 Burial Hill, 69.
 Cole's Hill, 69.
 Elms in, 69.
 First Church, 69.
 "  House, 69.
 Pilgrim Hall, 71.
 "  Rock, 68, 70.
Plymouth, N. H., 19.
POMPEII, 363, 364, 365, 373, 374.
 Amphitheatre in, 384.
 Excavations in, 381.
 Forum, 386.
 Pliny's letters to Tacitus, 366, 369.
 Skeletons found in, 382.
 Temple of Isis, 385.
 Undiscovered so long, why, 385.
Pont de Pierre, 286.
 Pompey's Pillar, 415.
PROVINCETOWN, MASS., 76.
 Compact signed in the Harbor of, 75.
 Improvements in, since 1836, 77.
 Salt Works, 76.

Q.

Quebec, Canada, 63.
QUEENSTON, 60.
 Brock's Monument in, 60.
Quiraing, 270.

## R.

Ragatz, 336.
Red Sea, defile near the, 411.
RIGI, 306, 331.
   Sunrise from, 331.
ROCKFORD, ILL., 193.
   Beauty of, 193.
   Rockford Female Sem. in, 194.
   Water Power in, 194.
Rock of Death, 253.
Rocks of Wisconsin, 197.
ROME, ITALY, 347.
   Church of St. Agnes, 352.
   Coliseum, 354.
      " by moonlight, 357.
   Dome of St. Peter's, 351.
   Forum, 352.
   Gardens of the Vatican, 352.
   Grave of St. Peter, 351.
   Interior of St. Peter's Church, 348.
   Library of the Vatican, 352
   Papal Benediction, 351.
   Statue of St. Peter, 350.
   St. Peter's Church, 348.
   Vatican, The, 352.
Rousseau, 307.

## S.

Saguenay River, 67.
Salt Lake, 240.
SALT LAKE CITY, 238.
   Brigham Young's residence, 240.
   Early settlement of, 238.
   Tabernacle of, 239.
   Temple in, 239.
   Theatre in, 240.
Salanches, 311.
Sam Patch, famous leaps of, 52.
SAN FRANCISCO, CAL., 213.
   Earthquakes in, 215.
SAN FRANCISCO, CAL., Growth of, 216.
   Harbor of, 217.
   Houses of, how built, 215.
   Seal Rocks of, 216.
   Variety of people in, 216.
   Water Front in, 214.
Saratoga Springs, N. Y., 135.
Scotland, scenery of, 257.
Servoz, 311.
Shechem, 400.
Shiloh, 399.
Sicily, 362.
Sinai, 409.
SPRINGFIELD, Ill., 189.
   Early Residents of, 189.
   First State House in, 190.
   Grave of Lincoln, 191.
   Internal Improvement, 189.
   Lincoln's Monument, 193.
   New State House in, 190.
Staffa Island, 263.
St. Augustine, Fla., 159.
Stanz, 330.
Staubbach Falls, 325.
St. Cloud, 286.
St. Gall, 335.
Stirling Castle, Scotland, 261.
ST. LAWRENCE RIVER, 61.
   Rapids of, 61.
   Dangers of, 62.
ST. LOUIS, MISSOURI, 162.
   Benton's Statue in, 163.
   Bitter feeling in, during the Rebellion, 163.
   Bridge of, 164.
   Educational Institutions, 163.
   Public Buildings, 162.
Stonehenge, 252.
Switzerland, 291.
SYRIA, 389.
   Location of, 389.
   Climate of, 389.

## T.

TALLULAH FALLS, GEORGIA, 157
   Indian Legend, 159.
Taymouth Castle, Scotland, 258.
Tête Noire, 318.
Thun, 324.
Thousand Isles, 61.
TICONDEROGA, 134.
   Fort of, 134.
Trou Perdu, 337.
Turkish Empire, 388.

## V.

Valley of the Linth, 333.
Valley of the Rhone, 319.
Venice, 345.
Versailles, 285.
Vesuvius, Mt., 359, 360, 363, 365.
Via Mala, 337.
Views from Geneva, 308.
View of Mont Blanc, 308.

## W.

Wâdy El Aim, 411.
WASHINGTON, D. C., 119.
   Capitol, The, 120.
   Dome, The new, 122.
   Hall of Representatives, 122.
   Monument of Washington, 124.
   Navy Yard, 123.
   Observatory, 123.
   Paintings in Rotunda of Capitol,
   Patent Office, 124.
   Sculpture, 121.
   Senate Chamber, The new, 122.
   Smithsonian Institute, 124.
   White House, 122.
WATKINS' GLEN, 140, 144.
   Glen Alpha, 141.
   Glen Cathedral, 142.
   Glen of Difficulty, 143.
   Havana Glen, 144.
   Mountain House, 142.
   Rainbow Fall, 143.
WEBSTER, DANIEL, First Plea of, 19.
   Extract from Speech of, 72.
   Speech of, 30.
      " " at Bunker Hill, 88.
      " " Washington, 121.
West Point, 136.
Wetterhorn, The, 326.
WHITE MOUNTAINS, 13-16.
   Berlin Falls, 36.
   Chocorua Peak and Lake, 24.
   Eagle Cliff, 20.
   Echo Lake, 22.
   Flume, 23.
   Franconia, 23.
   Glen Ellis Fall, 37.
   Great Stone Face, 20.
   Mount Washington Railroad, 37.
   Night Scene from Mount Washin

Silver Cascade, 37.
Story of Chocorua's Curse, 24.
Summit of Mount Washington 38.
Suspended Bowlder, 23.
The Notch, 30.
The Willey House, 31.
Wilderness of Paran, 408.
Windsor Castle, 251.
Wonders of Colorado, 235.

### Y.

YOSEMITE VALLEY, CALIFORNIA, 221.
Bridal Veil Fall, 224.
Clouds, Rest, 224.
Devil's Slide, 224, 230.
El Capitan, 222.
Features of the, 221.
Half Dome, 223.
Location of, 221.
Mirror Lake, 224.
Nevada Fall, 226.
North Dome, 222.
Sentinel Rock, 223.
Three Brothers, 223.
Vernal Fall, 226.
Yosemite Fall, 225.
YELLOWSTONE RIVER, 229.
Giant Geyser, 232.
Giantess Geyser, 232.
Great Cañon, 231.
Lower Cañon, 230.
Mud Volcano, 231.
Source of the, 230.

### Z.

Zermath, 321.

www.ingramcontent.com/pod-product-compliance
Lightning Source LLC
Chambersburg PA
CBHW020541300426
44111CB00008B/756